Over the course of several decades, rational choice theory has gained considerable influence among scholars engaged in social and political inquiry. Increasingly, its methods are being employed and debated across the breadth of political science and other social sciences. And, almost needless to say, it has also generated equally broad controversy. The present volume is a collection of outstanding essays applying rational choice theory in three of the central disciplines of political science: comparative politics, international relations, and political philosophy. In each of these subfield groupings, the editors have selected essays that represent the diversity of these substantive applications as well as the capacity of rational choice theory, and the debates about it, to cast radically new light on areas of vital importance to social scientists.

Politics and rationality

Politics and rationality

Edited by

William James Booth
Patrick James
Hudson Meadwell

CAMBRIDGE
UNIVERSITY PRESS

Published by the Press Syndicate of the University of Cambridge
The Pitt Building, Trumpington Street, Cambridge CB2 1RP
40 West 20th Street, New York, NY 10011-4211, USA
10 Stamford Road, Oakleigh, Melbourne 3166, Australia

First published 1993

Printed in the United States of America

Library of Congress Cataloging-in-Publication Data

Politics and rationality / edited by William James Booth, Patrick James, Hudson Meadwell.

p.   cm.

Includes index.

ISBN 0-521-43409-2. – ISBN 0-521-43568-4 (pbk.)

1. Political sociology.   2. Social choice.   3. Political science – Economic aspects.   I. Booth, William James.   II. James, Patrick, 1957–   .
III. Meadwell, Hudson.
JA76.P622   1993
306.2–dc20   93-10911
                                                                    CIP

A catalog record for this book is available from the British Library.

ISBN 0-521-43409-2 hardback
ISBN 0-521-43568-4 paperback

Contents

Part III. International politics

Contributors

William James Booth is an associate professor of political science at McGill University. His most recent book is *Households: On the Moral Architecture of the Economy* (Cornell University Press, 1993).

Mark A. Boyer is an associate professor of political science at the University of Connecticut (Storrs). He is the author of *International Cooperation and Public Goods: Opportunities for the Western Alliance* (Johns Hopkins University Press, 1992).

Barbara Geddes is an assistant professor of political science at UCLA. Her book, *Politician's Dilemma: Reforming the State in Latin America*, is forthcoming from the University of California Press.

Jean Hampton is professor of philosophy at the University of Arizona. She is the author of *Hobbes and the Social Contract Tradition* (Cambridge University Press, 1986).

Patrick James is professor of political science at Florida State University (Tallahassee). He is the author of *Crisis and War* (McGill-Queen's University Press, 1988).

Peter Lange is professor of political science at Duke University. He is the co-author, with Michael Alvarez and Geoffrey Garrett, of "Government Partisanship, Labor Organization and Macroeconomic Performance," *American Political Science Review* 85 (1991).

Hudson Meadwell is an associate professor of political science at McGill University. His most recent publication is "The Politics of Nationalism in Quebec," *World Politics* 45 (January 1993).

T. Clifton Morgan is an associate professor of political science at Rice University. His publications include articles in the *American Journal of Political Science* and *Journal of Conflict Resolution*.

Mancur Olson is professor of economics at the University of Maryland. He is the author of *The Rise and Decline of Nations* (Yale University Press, 1982) and *The Logic of Collective Action* (Harvard University Press, 1965).

Amartya Sen is Lamont University Professor of economics and philosophy at Harvard University. He is the author of *Choice, Welfare and Measurement* (Blackwell, 1982) and *Poverty and Famines* (Oxford University Press, 1981).

Michael Taylor is professor of political science at the University of Washington. He is the author of *The Possibility of Cooperation* (Cambridge University Press, 1987).

George Tsebelis is an associate professor of political science at UCLA. He is the author of *Nested Games: Rational Choice in Comparative Politics* (University of California Press, 1990).

Acknowledgments

The preparation of this volume was an equal and collaborative effort among its three editors and thus their names are ordered alphabetically.

The editors wish to thank the FCAR (Fonds pour la Formation de Chercheurs et l'Aide à la Recherche) and the Social Sciences and Humanities Research Council for grants, which facilitated the editing of the final version of the manuscript.

The following chapters have been published previously:

Chapter 1: Amartya Sen, "Liberty and social choice." Reprinted by permission from *The Journal of Philosophy* 80 (1983), 5–28.

Chapter 2: Jean Hampton, "The contractarian explanation of the state." Reprinted by permission from French, Uehling, and Wettstein (Eds.), *Midwest Studies in Philosophy,* vol. 15. *The Philosophy of the Human Sciences.* © 1990, University of Notre Dame.

Chapter 4: Michael Taylor, "Structure, culture, and action in the explanation of social change." Reprinted by permission from *Politics and Society* 17 (1989), 115–162; © Sage Publications, Inc.

Chapter 6: Barbara Geddes, "A game-theoretic model of reform in Latin American democracies." Reprinted by permission from *American Political Science Review* 85 (1991), 371–392.

Chapter 8: Mancur Olson, "Economic nationalism and economic progress." Reprinted from *The World Economy* by permission of the author.

Chapter 9: Mark A. Boyer, "Comparative advantage and public security perceptions in Western alliance security policies." Reprinted by permission from Mark A. Boyer, *International Cooperation and Public Goods,* Johns Hopkins University Press (1992).

Introduction

*William James Booth, Patrick James,
and Hudson Meadwell*

The quest for microfoundations is "a pervasive and omnipresent feature of science" (Elster, 1983: 23). Among students of politics, the pursuit of microlevel explanations for aggregate patterns of behavior, and debates about related conceptual and normative issues – structure versus agency in explanation; individuality and community – have attracted attention for a very long time. Of the available research strategies, models, and methods, theories of rational choice stand out as a coherent and rigorous potential solution to the problem of the linkage of the micro- and macrolevels of analysis. Rational choice theory can also serve as a framework for conceptual and normative analysis. The basic purpose of this volume is to demonstrate how theories based on rational choice can make important contributions to the study of politics. In selecting essays, we have emphasized work that shows how theories of rational choice are used to address issues in political theory and to explain a range of empirical phenomena in comparative and international politics.

Theories of rational choice have been the subject of considerable controversy. The critics are many: feminist, Marxist, communitarian, institutionalist; and their arguments have appeared in virtually all subfields of political science. The debates in which they and their opponents appear are part of the intellectual flourishing to which rational choice contributes. The essays making up this book represent an effort to follow in the tradition of rational choice as an interdisciplinary program of research.

Rational choice theory is actually a family of approaches and arguments. Together these approaches depend on methodological individualism. This amounts to the position that explanation must at some point go through the individual. On strictly conceptual grounds, it is argued that explanations which do not include attributes located at the level of individual intention – usually the conjunction of beliefs and desires – are unsatisfactory. This position distinguishes theories of rational choice from all forms of holism and determinism. Rational choice explanations, further, are nonfunctionalist (although both rational choice and functionalist accounts are teleological). Finally, rational choice theories are not constructed, in the first instance, in terms of efficient causes, since their explanations of action are intentional.

Although rational choice theories are not deterministic, neither are they dependent on a full-blown voluntarism. The interest in individualism is methodological; rational choice theorists do not conceive of persons as atomized, self-sufficient monads. Rather, persons are thought of as embedded in networks, contexts, and institutions, and choice is considered to take place within constraints (or, as sometimes described in neoinstitutional approaches, "opportunity structures"). Theories of rational choice could not get off the ground if their subject matter was a "decontextualized" actor. Moreover, persons are thought to be neither essentially selfish nor myopic. They can make, and act on, plans that stretch into the future and that are organized around self-interests which do not imply distributive advantages over others. The range of application of this approach, further, is not limited to the modern West. Research in comparative politics by Bates (1981), Levi (1988), and Popkin (1979) supports this argument.

While these theories draw on the philosophy of action, they also are a particular form of intentional explanation. Rational choice theorists do not assume that outcomes of interdependent action can be read off from the intentions of actors. Instead, the theoretical expectation is that unintended consequences of action can arise when actors are in interdependent relationships. Interdependent choice under constraints yields a form of strategic understanding, which is a distinctive feature of rational choice theory.

These theories therefore are not a form of instrumentalism, although rational choice theorists are sometimes able to demonstrate that structuralist and institutionalist arguments draw some of their explanatory power from implicit assumptions about the instrumental choices of actors. This is true, for example, of structuralist interpretations of social revolutions (e.g., Taylor, 1988). In international politics, a similar argument has been advanced about the microfoundations of structural realism (e.g., Bueno de Mesquita, 1981; Morrow, 1988). In political theory, "analytical Marxism" (e.g., Elster, 1985; Cohen, 1988; Roemer, 1982) has reworked the intellectual legacy of Marxism along choice-theoretic lines.

These theories are not appropriate for all action, but just for those instances in which their analysis of the relationships among beliefs, desires, action, and outcomes in historical and institutional settings provide explanations. The justification for rational choice theory need not be that individuals act "as if" they are rational, but that they are rational. Nor are rational choice theorists compelled to argue that application is justified only by predictive results, that is, by the requirement that actions and outcomes in particular cases are consistent with predictions. Instead, the explanatory power of rational choice theory can be emphasized.

Rational choice theory is also not simply an extension of neoclassical economics. As Rogowski (1977: 247, n.6) has noted, not all rationalist work is economic, even if almost all economics is rationalist. Some of the most central formal work in the rationalist tradition is more an elaboration of applied mathematics than a type of economic analysis. For example, the literature on preference aggregation from Condorcet (1785) through Arrow (1963 [1951]), Murakami (1968), Sen (1970), and McKelvey (1976) depends more on formal logic than economic theory. Game theory also developed as a branch of applied mathematics (Von Neumann and Morgenstern, 1953 [1947]). And one of the first extensions of work on gaming was to the problem of belief in God – Pascal's Wager (Hacking, 1972).

Summary of the chapters

In his chapter, Amartya Sen develops the arguments that he first broached in his seminal article, "The Impossibility of a Paretian Liberal." There Sen sought to demonstrate that even in its weak version ("Everyone strictly preferring x to y must make x socially better than y," Sen 1970: 156) the Pareto principle comes into conflict with basic liberal values, specifically the idea of the individual's "protected sphere." The importance of this finding is that it shows that what Sen has called the "sense of ethical invulnerability" of the Pareto principle, a sense based on its unanimity requirement, is in fact ill-founded. As a result, welfare economics more generally may be said to rest uneasily with certain (weak) liberal demands. In the present essay, Sen sets out to show the relevance of this social choice impossibility finding for ethics and political philosophy, and especially its implications for judging outcomes and decision-making procedures. In the course of his contribution, Sen recapitulates the impossibility argument and shows that a variety of attempts to resolve it by modifying its main conditions end in failure. He then goes on to examine different understandings of social preference and liberty, explores and criticizes the idea of liberty as control and analyzes the notion of a market in rights as a way around the impossibility claim.

Jean Hampton's contribution shows how the rational choice approach can be used to cast new light on a core and long-standing area of political philosophical inquiry, here the foundations of the state and social contract theory. Hampton's essay aims to do three things: to illuminate the common problem underlying the work of two of the major figures in the contractarian tradition, Hobbes and Locke; to defend the contractarian method as a way of explaining the state and, last, to redefine the central issues raised by that tradition. Hampton shows that both Hobbes and Locke are in fact engaged in solving (what we can read as) the same game-theoretic problem, not as a Prisoners' Dilemma game but rather a conflict-ridden coordination game over governance. The solution to this game is to be found, Hampton argues, less in strict and explicit contracts than in the parties converging on a salient equilibrium, that being the development of a (leadership) convention. This allows us to understand more precisely what are commonly called "tacit" or "as if" contracts, and to provide an answer to those critics of contract theory who argue that the social contract has no historical foundation and that contracts construed as "as if" agreements are strictly meaningless. In her conclusion, Hampton points to the limits of the coordination game, its conventional solution, and the agency model of governance that it yields for explaining the nature of political power, a power in which the domina- tion moment is (it seems) always present.

William James Booth explores a body of thought, Marxism, that might on its face appear among the most hostile to microlevel, rational choice types of expla- nation. Booth argues that this reading does not capture a more sophisticated side of Marx's work. In the first section of his essay, Booth maps out the functionalist dimension of Marx's thought and analyzes its core explanatory and normative/ critical aspects. On this (first) logic of capitalism, individual behavior, competi- tion, and so forth are derivative phenomena, the explanation of which is to be found in the deep structure of capitalism, which is a lawlike process working behind the backs of persons. Booth then shows how that logic plays out in Marx's theory of class and autonomy. In the second part of his essay, Booth ventures a different reconstruction of Marx's logic of capitalism, one that focuses on uncoordinated individual actions, on optimizing under constraints and, in more general terms, on a microlevel analysis of the "laws of motion" of capital developed without an actorless deep structure of capital. Booth concludes that while this second logic of capital offers a more coherent and defensible analytical structure than the outmoded metaphysics of the first, it nevertheless brings to light still more basic problems in Marx's account of capitalism, namely those involved in Marx's attempt to give explanatory/causal primacy to a "purely economic" sphere.

In his chapter, Michael Taylor develops a conceptual analysis of rational choice theory and illustrates his discussion with historical examples. His central point is that causal relations between structures and cultures, on the one hand, and structural and cultural outcomes, on the other, are mediated by actions. These actions must be explained intentionally by actors' desires and beliefs. The form of intentional explanation that he uses conforms to a "thin" theory of rational choice, which he defines in the chapter. Taylor demonstrates that the scope of application of rational choice theory is broader than many of its critics have argued. He illustrates his conceptual arguments in diverse historical settings by discussing peasant community in parts of early modern Europe, the moral economy of peasant rebellion in Southeast Asia, the evolution of kinship norms in Europe and Africa, and political mobilization in Nigeria.

Peter Lange and George Tsebelis address a central feature of the political economy of capitalist democracies. The goal of their chapter is to provide an explanation for the combination of powerful labor movements and very low strike rates that is characteristic of neocorporatism. Their conclusions are derived from a model of collective bargaining that is based on two important assump- tions. The first is that employers and unions are fully strategic actors. The second is that their bargaining relationship is characterized by incomplete information: Capital does not know the strength of Labor. This model provides the microfoun- dations for a reworking and extension of explanations of strikes, and neocorporatism, drawn from other research traditions in political economy and sociology. Lange and Tsebelis argue that, when the strength of labor is anticipated by the offers of employers in collective bargaining, strikes are unnecessary. The absence of strikes reflects the fact that unions are getting as much from employers as they can rationally expect.

In her chapter, Barbara Geddes offers a general explanation for administrative reform, specifically merit-based hiring, in democratic systems in which political competition precedes the establishment of a rational-legal state apparatus. She develops a game-theoretic model of the incentives that legislators and party activists face. Geddes argues that two conditions must be met if reforms are to be passed in legislatures. The first is an even distribution of patronage among the larger parties. When patronage is unevenly distributed, the party with advantages in patronage will not support reform and the disadvantaged party will not have the votes to pass legislation. When patronage is evenly distributed, reform will not change the competitive position of parties. This condition is conducive to reform, because it removes an incentive for resistance, but it is not sufficient. As a second condition for the abolition of patronage, there must be incentives to vote for reform. These can include a shared interest in public goods (the stabilization of democracy, better quality economic policy), or the interest of party activists in reform and their ability to influence the behavior of legislators. Geddes tests this model against the experience of Latin American democracies.

The chapter by Hudson Meadwell develops an approach to ethnic nationalist mobilization. He argues that there is a distinctive feature of ethnic nationalist politics: the problem of transitions to political independence and the economic viability of the ethnic group, if independence is achieved. The consequences of these problems of transition and viability are examined in two contexts: the developing world and the developed West. For this first class of cases, Meadwell examines the logical structure of, and evidence for, the argument that ethnic groups fight for secession, despite the economic costs, because to do otherwise would violate their identity. For the developed West, he presents a model of mobilization that takes into account the problems of transition and viability and that specifies how they affect both levels of support for independence and factional politics in nationalist organizations.

Olson's chapter reveals how rational choice theory can be used to uncover hidden political determinants of national economic performance. His central insight is that the geographic expansiveness of barriers to trade is more important than their magnitude. The creation of larger zones of free trade, or "jurisdictional integration," is crucial in stimulating commercial activity. Economies of sufficient size, such as that of the United States, are not affected as much by protection, because so much exchange can take place inside the state's borders. For smaller states, however, the development of organizations that act collectively to lobby government or to collude and cartelize markets to fix wages or prices is a very serious problem. This process is detrimental to trade and economic life in general, because these "distributive coalitions" lack the incentive to pursue policies that are efficient for society as a whole. When the jurisdiction expands, it becomes more difficult for these groups to succeed in redistributive political activity. Olson provides evidence that, among smaller states, the level of exports is linked inversely to protectionism. This result is a logical consequence of the impact of economic nationalism on relative efficiency. When economic activity is protected by government, international competitiveness is reduced. The evidence suggests that political activism of self-interested, distributive coalitions is harmful to economic progress.

Boyer's chapter on security as pursued by the United States, Japan, and Western Europe features a novel application of the concept of comparative advantage. Rather than a narrow focus on relative contributions in the military domain, Boyer advocates a more comprehensive analysis of burden-sharing among these states. Specifically, comparative advantage of a *political* nature creates the opportunity to enhance overall security without destructive conflict over appropriate levels of military spending. Respective members of "Western" alliances may be capable of contributing more in some areas than others, so specialization should be encouraged. For example, states with colonial histories may be more efficient – and willing – providers of foreign aid. Since elites are assumed to pay heed to political constraints on security-oriented spending, specialization also makes sense in the domestic context. Boyer's opinion data reveals that public attitudes do vary with respect to favored types of security-related activity. These results suggest that standard treatments of burden sharing within NATO and other alliances have neglected an important political aspect of how efficiency may be enhanced within security regimes.

Morgan's chapter on third parties in international crises combines utility-based bargaining theory with the spatial theory of voting. His model reveals that the effects of intermediaries are not straightforward, because both role and motivation determine impact. These complications are illustrated by allusions to Agadir in 1911 and the more recent series of crises over Cyprus. Propositions about the probability of war are derived from a formal treatment of third parties in crises. Anticipated effects for intermediaries depend on whether the role is that of mediator or ally, along with the degree of separation among the issues raised by the crisis. Morgan's analysis concludes with the provocative notion that an effective mediator need not be impartial, demonstrating the ability of his approach to generate counterintuitive arguments, which certainly merit systematic evaluation.

James's chapter uses a game-theoretic model to assess patterns of response to provocation in superpower crisis. Based on Chicken, a game on the unit square identifies the minimum acceptable level for response, given the intensity of the threat attributed to the rival superpower. According to the model, it is appropriate to react more strongly to minor threats, in order to discourage the adversary, while it is best to underreact to a major threat, to dampen the tendency toward escalation but still show disapproval. Focusing on superpower crises from the Berlin Blockade onward, James finds support for propositions derived from the model of superpower response. Retaliation usually reached the minimum required level. Furthermore, both goal achievement and overall satisfaction are linked to meeting that threshold. These results suggest that the model should be elaborated and subjected to further, possibly case-oriented, testing.

This collection illustrates the range of application of rational choice theory. In each subfield – political theory, comparative politics, and international politics – the authors address central conceptual and empirical issues. Their chapters demonstrate that rational choice theory is a rigorous and fertile approach to the study of politics.

References

Arrow, Kenneth J. (1963 [1951]). *Social Choice and Individual Values,* 2d ed. New York: John Wiley.

Bates, Robert H. (1981). *Markets and States in Tropical Africa.* Berkeley and Los Angeles: University of California Press.

Bueno de Mesquita, Bruce. (1981). *The War Trap.* New Haven, Conn.: Yale University Press.

Cohen, G. A. (1988). *History, Labour and Freedom.* Oxford: Clarendon Press.

Condorcet, Marquis de. (1785). *Essai sur l'application de l'analyse à la probabilité des décisions rendues à la pluralité de voix.* Paris: Imprimerie Royale.

Elster, Jon. (1985). *Making Sense of Marx.* Cambridge: Cambridge University Press.
  (1983). *Explaining Technical Change: A Case Study in the Philosophy of Science.* Cambridge: Cambridge University Press.

Hacking, Ian. (1972). "The Logic of Pascal's Wager." *American Philosophical Quarterly* 9: 186–92.

Levi, Margaret. (1988). *Of Rule and Revenue.* Berkeley and Los Angeles: University of California Press.

McKelvey, Richard. (1976). "Intransitivities in Multi-dimensional Voting Models and Some Implications for Agenda Control." *Journal of Economic Theory* 16: 472–82.

Morrow, James D. (1988). "Social Choice and System Structure in World Politics." *World Politics* 41: 75–97.

Murakami, Y. (1968). *Logic and Social Choice.* London: Routledge and Kegan Paul.

Popkin, Samuel. (1979). *The Rational Peasant.* Berkeley and Los Angeles: University of California Press.

Roemer, John E. (1982). *A General Theory of Exploitation and Class.* Cambridge, Mass.: Harvard University Press.

Rogowski, Ronald (1977). "Rationalist Theories of Politics: A Mid-Term Report." *World Politics* 30: 296–323.

Sen, Amartya. (1979). "Personal Utilities and Public Judgements." *The Economic Journal* 89: 537–58.
  (1970). "The Impossibility of a Paretian Liberal." *Journal of Political Economy* 78: 152–7.

Taylor, Michael. (1988). "Rationality and Revolutionary Collective Action." In Michael Taylor (Ed.), *Rationality and Revolution.* Cambridge: Cambridge University Press.

Von Neumann, John, and Oscar Morgenstern. (1953 [1947]). *Theory of Games and Economic Behavior.* Princeton, N.J.: Princeton University Press.

PART I

Political theory

1.   Liberty and social choice

Amartya Sen

Does individual liberty conflict with the Pareto principle – that cornerstone of welfare economics which insists that unanimous individual preference rankings must be reflected in social decisions? A result in social choice theory, the so-called impossibility of the Paretian liberal, has indicated that there can indeed be such a conflict (Sen, 1970a, b), and this result has been followed by a great many other results – some extending the conflict and others proposing ways of avoiding it (see section IV of this chapter). However, the rather special format of social choice theory makes it a little difficult to be sure of the *relevance* of this class of results to ethics, welfare economics, or social and political philosophy. This essay is concerned with discussing that issue.

There are two further objectives. First, the formal conditions used in social choice theory can be given more than one interpretation, and the practical import of the results clearly does depend on the interpretations chosen. This applies not merely to the impossibility of the Paretian liberal, but also to other results in the field, including the deeper impossibility result presented by Kenneth Arrow (1963; Sen, 1979a, 1977). One particular source of variation is the content of "social preference," and in this essay three different interpretations are distinguished and discussed.

Second, the formulation of liberty (more accurately, that of some minimal implications of respecting liberty) in social choice theory has been deeply questioned (Barry, 1986; Bernholz, 1974; Buchanan, 1976; Chapman, 1981; Gärdenfors, 1981; Nozick, 1974, 1973; Roberts, 1976; Rowley and Peacock, 1975; Sugden, 1981), and indeed that formulation is at variance with at least some of the more traditional characterizations of liberty, seeing liberty in terms of procedures rather than outcomes. An attempt is made in this essay to go into this broader question of how liberty should be seen, and in this context a critique of purely procedural formulations of liberty is offered.

For helpful comments, I am grateful to Peter Hammond, Susan Hurley, Isaac Levi, Jim Mirrlees, Robert Sugden, John Vickers, and Bernard Williams.

I. Social preference

The typical social-choice-theoretic format is that of transforming a set (in fact, an n-tuple) of individual preference orderings into a social preference relation or a social choice function. Arrow required the social preference relation to be a complete weak ordering (reflexive, complete, and transitive) and the social choice function to specify the best elements (the choice set) with respect to that social preference relation for each nonempty set of social states (the feasible set, or "menu"). Others have demanded less exacting properties of the social preference relation (permitting intransitivity or incompleteness), or less limiting types of social choice function (permitting nonbinary choice), and various possibility and impossibility results have been presented.

Though various interpretations of social preference are possible, here I shall confine myself to only three interpretations of "x is socially preferred to y":

1. *outcome evaluation:* "x is judged to be a better state of affairs for society than y";
2. *normative choice:* "decision making in the society should be so organized that y must not be chosen when x is available";
3. *descriptive choice:* "social decision systems are so organized that y will not be chosen when x is available."

I should emphasize that although the latter two interpretations link preference to choice, neither of them requires that the choice function – normative or descriptive – be "binary" in character, in the sense of being representable by a binary relation (Fishburn, 1973; Hansson, 1968; Herzberger, 1973; Plott, 1976; Schwartz, 1976; Sen, 1971). Each just imposes a condition that the choice functions, respectively, should *or* will satisfy; whether or not the totality of social choices can be captured by a binary relation is left open.

Within these three broad interpretations, there are, of course, further distinctions, based on the context of the statements. For example, the outcome-evaluation statement can reflect a *particular person's* moral judgment, or the result of the application of some *evaluation procedure* (e.g., yielded by a particular "objective function" used in planning or policy making).

II. The impossibility of the Paretian liberal

The Pareto principle, in its weak form, demands that, if every individual prefers a social state x to a social state y, then x must be socially preferred to y. Individual liberty can be seen to require, among other things, that each individual should have a *recognized personal sphere* in which his preference and his alone would count in determining the social preference. For example, consider a person who would like to read a particular novel, other things given, and assume that for some given configuration of other things that choice is in his recognized personal sphere; then the social preference must put his reading the novel above not reading it, given the other things. The condition of *minimal liberty* (ML, for short), is, in fact, a weaker requirement than this, demanding that there be such a nonempty personal sphere for *at least two* persons (not necessarily for all – which would do, but isn't required).[1]

A *social decision function* determines a complete and consistent (free from cycles) social preference defined over the set of alternative social states for any set (in fact, *n*-tuple) of individual preference orderings (one ordering per person). A social decision function has an *unrestricted* domain if it works for any logically possible *n*-tuple of individual preference orderings. The impossibility of the Paretian liberal is the theorem establishing that there cannot exist a social decision function satisfying the unrestricted domain, the Pareto principle (even in its weak form) and minimal liberty ML.

The traditional interpretation of preference has been in terms of desires,[2] and I shall stick to that usage. An alternative approach, developed under the influence of the theory of "revealed preference," defines preference as the binary relation underlying choice. This rather unnatural usage of preference empties the term of much of its normal meaning, and – more importantly – the implied identification of two distinct notions leaves us short of one important concept. Further, not all choice functions have binary representation.

Though it is not sensible to identify preference and choice definitionally, it is traditional in social choice theory to make the empirical assumption that individual choices will, in fact, be entirely based on individual preference. Arrow (1963: 9–21) has outlined the characteristics of such a model of individual behavior, and I shall call this the assumption of *universal preference-based choice*. A much weaker version of this assumption is adequate for the social-choice characterization of liberty, to wit, that, in choices over an individual's *recognized personal sphere*, the individual will be guided entirely by his preference. If (x, y) is a pair of states such that it belongs to i's recognized personal sphere and he strictly prefers x to y, then he will not choose y when x is available for him to choose.[3] I shall call this the assumption of *minimal preference-based choice*, of which *universal* preference-based choice is a special case.

---

[1] This condition was originally christened "minimal liberalism," with a warning about possible misunderstanding: "The term 'liberalism' is elusive and open to alternative interpretations. Some uses of the term may not embrace the condition defined here. What is relevant is that Condition L represents a value involving individual liberty that many people would subscribe to" (Sen, 1970a: 153). In a later paper the condition was called "minimal libertarianism." Neither term is very satisfactory, and the term used here – minimal liberty – has the advantage of concentrating on the concept of liberty itself rather than on its advocacy through one approach or another.

[2] This is true in traditional economic theory as well (Hicks, 1939), and also in moral discussions. See, for example, Hare (1952).

[3] The issue here concerns what the person would choose *if* x and y are both, in fact, *available* to him for choosing (possibly along with other alternatives). This question of preference-choice correspondence should not be confused with the different – but important – issue discussed by Allan Gibbard (1974) of what an individual should choose if his preferred alternative (x, in this case) is *not actually available* because of the exercise of other people's rights or the application of the Pareto principle. It is, of course, an *implication* of the theorem of the impossibility of the Paretian liberal that both the alternatives in a pair in each individual's personal sphere cannot actually be made available to him for choosing in the way specified by ML, if the Pareto-inferior alternatives must also be rejected.

Consider now any configuration of recognized personal spheres over which the respective individuals are acknowledged – under rules satisfying ML – to have a special authority; the exact content of that authority is specified by the chosen interpretation of social preference. Let (x, y) belong to i's recognized personal sphere, and let him strictly prefer x to y. Not only does he desire to have x rather than y, but also – under the assumption of limited preference-based choice (and, a fortiori, under universal preference-based choice) – he will choose x if he has to choose one of the two alternatives. He will, in fact, never choose y if he is actually given a choice over a set that contains x. Under the outcome-evaluation interpretation of social preference, the condition of liberty incorporating ML requires that, given the circumstances specified, x be judged to be a better state of affairs for the society than y [see (1) in the last section].

Under the normative-choice interpretation, it is required that decision making in the society should be so organized that, in the circumstances specified, y must not be chosen when x is available [see (2)]. This is, it should be noticed, a less demanding requirement than the condition that the choice between x and y (with or without the presence of other alternatives) be left to individual i himself, so that he can dislodge an about-to-be-chosen y and get his preferred x selected instead. If it were left to him, he would of course not choose y. Such an assumption of "individual control" is adequate for ML, but not necessary, since ML needs only that, no matter how social decisions are made, y does not end up being chosen. As the theorem under discussion is an *impossibility* result, a weaker requirement cannot be objected to, since the impossibility must remain unaffected by any strengthening of the condition – by requiring that i be given "individual control" in the choice or nonchoice of y when x is also available.

Under the descriptive-choice interpretation, it is postulated that the social decision systems are so organized that y is not chosen when x is a feasible choice [see (3)].

Similar interpretational variations are applied to the weak Pareto principle, using the different interpretations of social preference given by (1), (2), and (3), respectively.

It is now straightforward to see the contents of the impossibility of the Paretian liberal under three different interpretations, respectively:

I.   *Outcome-evaluation impossibility:* For some configuration of individual preferences, there can be no consistent and complete evaluation of social states satisfying the weak Pareto principle and minimal liberty, interpreted as in (1).

II. *Normative-choice impossibility:* There is no good way of organizing decision-making in the society so that – no matter what the individual preferences happen to be – some state gets chosen from any nonempty set of states, when the goodness of the decision making requires satisfying the weak Pareto principle and minimal liberty, interpreted as in (2).

III. *Descriptive-choice impossibility:* Any actual social decision system that is able to choose – no matter what the individual preferences are – some state from any nonempty set of states, will be unable to satisfy the weak Pareto principle and minimal liberty, interpreted as in (3).

III. An illustration

Various illustrations of the Pareto-liberty conflict have been presented in the literature (Barnes, 1980; Fountain, 1980; Gibbard, 1974; Green, 1980; Sen, 1970b: ch. 6). The example involving the reading or not of *Lady Chatterley's Lover* (Sen, 1970b: 80) has probably had more attention than it deserves, and I shall use here a less tired example, namely the so-called work-choice case (Sen, 1976: 222–3).

Persons 1 and 2 both prefer having a full-time job (1) to a half-time job ($\frac{1}{2}$) and a half-time job to being unemployed (0), given the job situation of the other. But, spoiled as they are by the competitive society in which they live, each prefers that the other be jobless (i.e., 0 to $\frac{1}{2}$ to 1, for the other). Indeed, each is green-eyed enough to get more fulfillment out of the joblessness of the other than from his own job. Given the nature of the jobs involved, there happen to be four possible alternative states for these two persons, represented here by four pairs, with the first number of each pair describing person 1's job situation and the second number person 2's. The two persons' preferences are displayed in Table 1.1, in descending order. Let persons 1 and 2 each have a recognized personal sphere with the properties specified by minimal liberty ML. Individual 1's personal sphere covers the choice over the pair $(1, \frac{1}{2})$ and $(0, \frac{1}{2})$; he should be free to work if he so prefers, given the job situation ($\frac{1}{2}$) of the other. Similarly individual 2's personal sphere covers the choice over $(\frac{1}{2}, 1)$ and $(\frac{1}{2}, 0)$ and person 2 also should be free to work if he so prefers, given the job situation ($\frac{1}{2}$) of person 1.

Now consider the three different interpretations of social preference. With the outcome-evaluation interpretation, the exercise is one of ranking the four alternative states in terms of how good they are for the society of these two people. One particular context may be that of a person's "social welfare judgment," discussed earlier. The judge could be an outsider *or* indeed either of these two persons themselves making a *moral* judgment. On grounds of minimal liberty, the judge puts $(1, \frac{1}{2})$ over $(0, \frac{1}{2})$, since person 1 actually prefers $(1, \frac{1}{2})$, person 2 isn't directly involved in this decision about 1's job, and in fact the pair is in person 1's personal sphere. On similar grounds, $(\frac{1}{2}, 1)$ is put above $(\frac{1}{2}, 0)$ in line with 2's preference, noting that 1 is not directly involved in this particular choice and that in fact the pair is in 2's personal sphere. But if the judge also adheres to the Pareto principle, then he must put $(\frac{1}{2}, 0)$ over $(1, \frac{1}{2})$, since both prefer the former, and on exactly similar grounds place $(0, \frac{1}{2})$ over $(\frac{1}{2}, 1)$. And this combination involves a cycle of social preference: $(1, \frac{1}{2})$ is better than $(0, \frac{1}{2})$, which is better than $(\frac{1}{2}, 1)$, which is better than $(\frac{1}{2}, 0)$, which is better than $(1, \frac{1}{2})$. Every state is worse than some other state.

Consider next the *descriptive*-choice interpretation. Perhaps the simplest case is that of direct control over one's personal sphere. If $(0, \frac{1}{2})$ is about to be chosen,

Table 1.1. *The work-choice case*

Person 1	Person 2
$(\frac{1}{2}, 0)$	$(0, \frac{1}{2})$
$(1, \frac{1}{2})$	$(\frac{1}{2}, 1)$
$(0, \frac{1}{2})$	$(\frac{1}{2}, 0)$
$(\frac{1}{2}, 1)$	$(1, \frac{1}{2})$

person 1 is given the power to get $(1, \frac{1}{2})$ chosen instead. Similarly, if $(\frac{1}{2}, 0)$ is about to be chosen, then person 2 has the power to make $(\frac{1}{2}, 1)$ be chosen instead. So the actual choice will be confined to $(1, \frac{1}{2})$ and $(\frac{1}{2}, 1)$. But *both* happen to be Pareto inefficient.

Under the *normative*-choice interpretation, ML requires that a good system of making social decisions not lead to $(\frac{1}{2}, 0)$ or $(0, \frac{1}{2})$ being chosen, and the weak Pareto principle requires that a good system not lead to the choice of $(1, \frac{1}{2})$ or $(\frac{1}{2}, 1)$. So nothing can be chosen, and there is no good system of choice in the required sense.

IV. Restrictions, extensions, and reformulations

The impossibility of the Paretian liberal is based on the inconsistency of three conditions, namely unrestricted domain, the weak Pareto principle, and the condition of minimal liberty. To avoid the inconsistency, at least one of the conditions has to be dropped or weakened in some substantial way. In the literature on the subject, each of these avenues has been extensively explored.

Weakening unrestricted domain amounts to ruling out certain configurations – "profiles" – of individual preferences, so that with the remaining profiles the conflict cannot occur. Examples of this line of reconciliation include assuming that the actual preferences show "tolerance" in the sense of the individual's being *indifferent* over pairs belonging to other people's recognized personal spheres (Seidl, 1975), or "empathy" in the sense of the individual's *mirroring* other people's preferences over their respective private spheres (Breyer and Gigliotti, 1980), or being "nonmeddlesome" or "liberal" in the sense of the individual's attaching greater importance to ranking the alternatives over his own personal sphere vis-à-vis ranking the alternatives in other people's personal spheres (Blau, 1975; Breyer, 1978, 1977), or satisfying some other adequate restrictions.[4] These explorations throw light on the nature of the underlying conflict and are possibly relevant for thinking about education and value formation.

Restricting the domain does not, however, amount to an adequate way out of the conflict, since it does not tell us what social judgments would be made (or

---

[4] Benevolence toward each other can do the trick (Bergstrom, 1970). So could – possibly more surprisingly – systematic malevolence, if one individual directs it against the preferences of all others.

what states should be chosen, or how decision mechanisms should be organized) in dealing with profiles that violate the required restrictions, when such profiles actually happen to occur. Nevertheless, corresponding to any domain restriction, ruling out some preference profiles, there exist related solutions that take the form of negating *either* the weak Pareto principle or the condition of minimal liberty *for each profile that does not belong to the permissible domain*. Meddlesome individuals could be "penalized" by the denial of their special authority over their own personal spheres (Blau, 1975; Campbell, 1976; Ferejohn, 1978; Gaertner and Krüger, 1981; Gibbard, 1974), or their preferences could be either ignored or "amended" in dealing with the weak Pareto judgment (Austen-Smith, 1982; Coughlin and Sen, 1981; Farrell, 1976; Hammond, 1982b; Sen, 1976; Suzumura, 1978). These modifications amount to weakening the minimal-liberty condition or the weak Pareto principle, respectively. Other ways of restricting these conditions have also been investigated – some of them helping to avoid the conflict and others leaving it unaffected (Aldrich, 1977; Breyer and Gardner, 1980; Gardner, 1980; Kelly, 1976; Mueller, 1979; Suzumura, 1981; Wriglesworth, [no date]).

While methods of resolving the conflict have received much of the attention in the literature on the subject, there has also been interesting work in extending and generalizing the conflict. Allan Gibbard (1974: 388–97) has shown that individual liberties can even turn out to be internally inconsistent if the condition of minimal liberty is strengthened, permitting the individual to fix one "feature" of the social state, no matter what the others choose and no matter how the individual chooses his feature. If I am decisive on my wall color given everything else (including your wall color) and you are decisive on yours given everything else (including my wall color), then we can have a cycle if, for example, I want to *match* your wall color, but you want to *differentiate* from mine.

To avoid this problem – the "Gibbard paradox" – either the assignment of rights has to be more restrictive (making them, to use Suzumura's expression, "coherent," e.g., as with ML), or rights have to be conditional on individual preferences satisfying a condition of "separability" (Farrell, 1976; Gibbard, 1974; Hammond, 1981; Kelly, 1978). Separability requires that my ranking of my "personal" features (e.g., the color of my walls) be independent of the choice of other people over their respective personal features. These restrictions, which avoid the Gibbard paradox, may in fact be quite justifiable within the rationale of giving people rights over personal choices. If I am trying to paint my walls in a color different from yours, my ambition is not quite a "personal" or "self-regarding" one, and it is not unreasonable to desist from insisting that the fulfillment of such contingent preferences be a necessary part of my personal liberty. Even when the Gibbard paradox is avoided (through having coherent rights *or* separable preferences), the impossibility of the Paretian liberal continues to hold (Gibbard, 1974; Hammond, 1982b; Suzumura, 1978), and some further restriction is called for to avoid that conflict.[5]

---

[5] Gibbard's own solution, referred to earlier, takes the form of "waiving" some individual rights.

In another important departure, introduced by R. N. Batra and P. K. Pattanaik (1972; Stevens and Foster, 1978; Wriglesworth, 1982), the impossibility of the Paretian liberal has been extended to show that the Pareto principle conflicts not only with individual liberty but also with *group rights* (e.g., rights given by "federalism" or "pluralism"), and for much the same analytical reasons.[6]

The ways of avoiding the conflict and those of extending it, discussed earlier in this chapter, operate within the general format of social choice theory. The legitimacy of that perspective on liberty has been disputed, and it has been forcefully argued that the very characterization of liberty in social choice theory is fundamentally misconceived. I turn now to that general question and also examine some alternative formulations of liberty.

V. Liberty, control, and social choice

Robert Nozick raised a question of importance when, discussing the impossibility of the Paretian liberal, he criticized "treating an individual's rights to choose among alternatives as the right to determine the relative ordering of these alternatives within a social ordering" (Nozick, 1974: 165). Instead, Nozick characterized rights in terms of giving the individual *control* over certain decisions, and "each person may exercise his right as he chooses." "The exercise of these rights fixes some features of the world. Within the constraints of these fixed features, a choice may be made by a social choice mechanism based upon a social ordering; if there are any choices left to make!" (Nozick, 1974: 166).

A similar criticism has been made by several other authors (Barry, 1986; Bernholz, 1974; Buchanan, 1976; Chapman, 1981; Gärdenfors, 1981; Grout, 1980; Hammond, 1982, 1981; Nozick, 1974, 1973; Perelli-Minetti, 1977; Roberts, 1976; Rowley and Peacock, 1975; Sugden, 1981), and the point has been put thus by Robert Sugden, commenting on the impossibility of the Paretian liberal:

The flaw in this ingenious argument lies, I suggest, in Sen's formulation of the principle of liberty. Although he claims (Sen, 1976: 218) that he is appealing to the same ideas of liberty as Mill did, there is a crucial difference between what Mill meant by liberty and what Sen means. Mill would have agreed that "there are certain personal matters in which each person should be free to decide what should happen"; but would he have agreed that "in choices over these things whatever he or she thinks is better must be taken to be better for society as a whole"? The first of these two propositions is a value judgment about procedures: it says that certain issues ought to be delegated to, or reserved for, individual decision-making. The second proposition is a value judgment about end states: it says, in effect, that the procedure of reserving these issues for individual decision-making invariably leads to the selection of the best feasible end states. But why should a liberal have to claim this? . . . So far as specifically liberal values are concerned, there is nothing inherently dignified or undignified about the act of reading *Lady Chatterley's Lover.* (Sugden, 1981: 196–7)

---

[6] For extensions in a different direction, see Albert Weale (1980: 13–19); Iain McLean (1980: 212–13).

The point is cogently argued, but it is based on taking an unduly narrow view of the possible content of "social preference" – of being regarded as "better for society." In fact, a social-preference statement may well reflect nothing more than a condition on the choice function, as was explained in section I. But even if the outcome-evaluation interpretation is considered, that need not be a judgment about the "inherent" goodness or badness of the states. In the context of the procedural judgment that Sugden attributes to Mill, social preference can be seen as reflecting the ranking – not necessarily complete – of alternatives in terms of consistency with the right procedures. There is nothing unusual about procedure-based judgments of the relative merits of different outcomes; there are plenty of such judgments made by Mill himself.[7] A judgment about anything need not be a function only of the inherent qualities of that thing. To take an analogy from a different field, contrast the following statements about the goodness of Mitterrand as a spokesman for France:

A. Mitterrand is the best person to speak for France, since he won the presidential election.
B. Mitterrand is the best person to speak for France, since no one else has his ability to interpret the soul of France.

Procedure-based judgments of the goodness of states are comparable to (A) rather than to (B).

When the outcome-evaluation interpretation of social preference is considered in the context of a purely procedure-based view of liberty, an outcome that is regarded as "better for society" from the point of view of liberty is so regarded precisely because that is what would be chosen by the person in question. Even "a value judgment about procedures" implies – given the behavioral parameters – judgments about what states *should* emerge, namely the consequences of the use of the right procedures. Social preference can be made to reflect that judgment.[8] So, even if it were the case that procedural judgments are adequate for fully characterizing liberty in social decisions (a view that I will presently dispute in section VI), even then the condition of minimal liberty can be correspondingly interpreted, and justified, within that framework. If a social state can emerge only through the violation of the right procedure, then an indictment of that state

---

[7] It should, however, be mentioned that although Mill did endorse procedural judgments of the kind referred to by Sugden, he did not, in fact, take a *purely* procedural view of liberty.

[8] In terms of Isaac Levi's (1982) distinction between "social value" and "social welfare," this interpretation of the condition of minimal liberty relates to social value rather than to social welfare. Levi himself confines his discussion to the interpretation that minimal liberty is a condition on social welfare (presumably associated with individual welfares rather than with any procedural condition of choice). The term social welfare in social choice theory does have this "welfarist" ring, but it *need not* have the "welfarist" *content* (Sen, 1970b: 33–4), and can well be seen in the same way that Levi sees "social value": "some standard of social value which evaluates social states with respect to whether they are better or worse" (1982: 240). As Levi rightly points out, even "rugged libertarianism" has implications for social value, requiring "modification of the standard of social value when its fit with libertarian choice mechanisms turns out to be poor" (1982: 242).

in that context is implicit in the procedure-based value system itself. And the impossibility of the Paretian liberal – under the outcome-evaluation interpretation combined with a purely procedural concept of liberty – is concerned with the inconsistency of the ranking based on such indictment (reflected in the corresponding interpretation of "minimal liberty") and the Pareto quasi-ordering.

If instead of the outcome-evaluation interpretation of social preference, the normative-choice interpretation is considered, then it is even more straightforward to see the condition of minimal liberty in terms of the perspective of liberty as control. It insists that the outcomes to emerge must not be different from what would be chosen if certain issues are delegated to, or reserved for, individual decision making. If that condition were violated, then of course there would be a violation *also* of the principle, as described by Sugden, "that certain issues ought to be delegated to, or reserved for, individual decision-making." The impossibility of the Paretian liberal under the normative-choice interpretation asserts, inter alia, that such a principle of choice procedure cannot be combined – for an unrestricted domain – with insistence on the Pareto optimality of outcomes.

These misunderstandings about the content of the social choice propositions are partly the fault of social choice theory itself. The language of social choice theory, though precisely formulated, has tended to be rather remote from the standard language of social and political philosophy, and the skill of the social choice theorist in obtaining technical results has not quite been matched by the inclination to discuss issues of interpretation. In particular, there is need to clarify the different substantive contents of a given result corresponding to the different interpretations of such concepts as social preference, and also to relate these different contents to the traditional issues of social and political philosophy.

It is also worth emphasizing that the conditions of liberty – such as Condition L and Condition ML – used in social choice theory do not attempt to present a comprehensive view of liberty; rather, only of some of its implications. This is adequate for the impossibility results, since the inconsistency of the Pareto principle with liberty can be shown by demonstrating its inconsistency with some *implications* of liberty, without having to characterize liberty fully.

For example, someone could insist that liberty requires *not merely* that the individual get what he *would* choose *but also* that he get it *through* choosing it himself. In this case there is an asymmetry in judging the liberty aspect of (i) his getting and (ii) his not getting, what he would choose. If we know that he has *not* got what he would choose, we know that his liberty has been violated, and that kind of deduction is all that is required for the impossibility of the Paretian liberal. On the other hand, even if we know that he has got what he would choose, the quoted view of liberty will not permit us to be sure of the fulfillment of his liberty, since his liberty *would have been* violated if, say, somebody else had chosen for him what he would himself choose. The quoted view is thus not denied, nor of course asserted, in deriving the impossibility of the Paretian liberal.

VI. Control and indirect liberty

I now take up the postponed question of whether liberty is concerned just with actual control. It certainly *is* concerned with control – that is not in dispute – but is it *just* control that it is concerned with?

First consider the case of a person, Ed, who has been injured in a car accident, but is fully conscious. The doctor tells him that she can treat him in one of two ways, A and B, and though both would be effective, she is certain that A would be very much better for him in terms of side effects. Ed says that he understands the options and accepts that A would indeed serve his welfare better, but he has some moral objection to treatment A (its development involved cruelty to animals) and would therefore prefer to have treatment B. It is easy to argue here that Ed's liberty is better served by the doctor giving him treatment B, even though his welfare would have been better served by A. I shall describe this as a case in which Ed's *direct* liberty is better served by B.

Now consider the case in which Ed is unconscious after the car accident, but his companion knows about Ed's moral beliefs and the strength of his convictions. The same choice arises with the doctor making the same assessment. The companion says that she is completely convinced that Ed *would have chosen* treatment B despite accepting that A would serve his welfare better. It seems reasonable to argue that, in this case too, Ed's liberty would have been better served by the doctor's giving him treatment B, even though Ed himself is not exercising any direct control over the particular choice. I shall describe this as a case of Ed's *indirect* liberty's being better served by B.

It is, of course, tempting to think that, in the second case, what is involved in the choice made by the doctor and Ed's companion is Ed's welfare. But the example was so specified that that presumption is not easy to entertain, since neither the doctor, nor Ed's companion, nor indeed Ed, can be taken to assume that B would serve Ed's welfare better. Quite the contrary. The argument for treatment B rather than A is precisely that Ed *would have chosen* it, and that is clearly a liberty-type consideration rather than a welfare-type consideration. What Isaiah Berlin calls "the extent of a man's, or a people's, liberty to choose to live as they desire" (1969: 70) does seem to require counterfactual exercises of this kind. To see liberty exclusively in terms of who is exercising control is inadequate.

The relevance of *indirect* liberty seems quite substantial in modern society. Police action in preventing crime in the streets may serve my liberty well – since I don't want to be mugged or roughed up – but the control here is exercised not by me, but by the police. (The fact that it may also serve my *welfare* well is, of course, a different consideration.) What is relevant for my indirect liberty in this case is the understanding that *if* I had control over the crime *specifically directed against me*, I would have exercised my choice to stop it. Of course, it is *conceivable* that a person would have chosen to be mugged or roughed up or hit by a car going the wrong way on a one-way street, but the presumption on which the consideration of *indirect* liberty is based is that he would not have so chosen.

There is a danger that in crudely identifying liberty with direct control – overlooking the counterfactual exercises involved in indirect liberty – a lot that is important might be lost. Society cannot typically be organized in such a way that each person himself controls all the levers related to his personal sphere.[9] But it would be a mistake to assume that considerations of liberty of a person are irrelevant in a particular choice if he himself is not making the choice. Giving the unconscious Ed treatment A – though acknowledged by all to be better for his welfare – is a violation of Ed's liberty in a manner that giving him treatment B is not. What a person *would have chosen* if he had control is an important consideration in judging the person's liberty.

The social-choice characterization of liberty compares what emerges with what a person *would have chosen,* whether or nor he actually does the choosing. This leaves out something that may be important to liberty, to wit, whether what he gets was actually *chosen by him* and not merely what he *would have chosen* (though not necessarily chosen by him). This is a gap, and although this gap does not affect the impossibility of the Paretian liberal in any way (as discussed in the last section), it can be important for a more general treatment of liberty (as opposed to that of just some of its implications). The gap can be closed only by enriching the description of social states in such a way that the agency of choice is incorporated in it. This involves a departure from the existing format of social choice theory, in which people choose between social states without the description of the choice being incorporated in the description of the states themselves, and I shall not pursue the problem further here. (See, however, Sen, 1982a, 1983.)

On the other hand, the characterization of liberty just in terms of "who actually controls what" is also inadequate. Although the impossibility of the Paretian liberal, appropriately interpreted, holds also for that perspective on liberty (as was discussed earlier), the social choice framework permits analysis of *indirect* liberty, but the actual-control framework does not.

VII. Preference, choice, and personal spheres

As was discussed in section II, the link between preference and choice over an individual's recognized personal sphere plays a rather crucial role in the social choice characterization of liberty. This assumption of "minimal preference-based choice" is much less demanding than the more common assumption of "universal preference-based choice" (as used by Arrow and others), but even the "minimal" assumption may well be questioned.

The force of preferring as a ground for choosing is altogether more powerful in decisions about one's personal life, which do not directly affect others, than in decisions of other kinds. One's desire is a good reason for choosing in one's own

[9] The question involves what Christian Seidl has called "the technological factors of liberalism" (Seidl, 1975: 260).

personal sphere, but less compelling for choosing in other people's personal spheres or even in public spheres.

To illustrate the contrast, take an example – the old decision problem of the person who prefers peaches to apples and encounters the fruit basket going round the table after dinner (Nowell-Smith, 1954: 102–3). There happens to be only one peach but many apples in the basket. The choice is not a purely personal choice for him, since his taking the peach would leave some with no choice at all. It is, of course, quite possible that our man at the dinner table will grab the peach with a sigh of relief that the basket got to him in the nick of time. But suppose he does not, and nobly chooses an apple. It is not clear yet that in this choice he is actually acting against his own preference or desire, since, despite his general preference for peaches over apples, he might in this case prefer to have an apple rather than the solitary peach, taking everything into account (morals, embarrassment, etc.). However, it is also quite possible that on balance he does, in fact, prefer or desire having that lovely peach. If under these circumstances he decides that he must not choose the peach despite his desire and thus acts against his own preference (defined in terms of desire rather than choice), then we would indeed see a violation of the assumption of "universal" preference-based choice. But not – and this is the important point here – of "minimal" preference-based choice; for his choice of fruit *in this case* cannot be seen to be in his personal sphere since it *directly* affects others, and that is crucial to his decision. The case is quite different from one in which there are enough fruits of each type for all.

The assumption of minimal preference-based choice demands only that individual choices be guided by the respective individual preferences over the *recognized* personal spheres given by the chosen condition of liberty. A recognized personal sphere of an individual will be just a *part* of his or her "personal sphere" in the more general sense, namely where others are not directly affected. Indeed it could be minute for two people and empty for others under the condition of "minimal liberty."

VIII. The Prisoner's Dilemma: Comparison and contrast

The individual preferences underlying the impossibility of the Paretian liberal have been compared with those in the Prisoner's Dilemma (Fine, 1975).[10] Though this is instructive to note, and the similarity is clear enough in the example involving *Lady Chatterley's Lover,* the analogy can be misleading in at least three respects. First, in the usual analysis of the Prisoner's Dilemma, no question is raised about the status of individual preference in determining the goodness of the outcome, and Pareto optimality is taken to be the obvious goal.

---

[10] Thomas Schelling commented in 1969 on the similarity in his response (prepublication) to my "Impossibility of a Paretian Liberal."

But that is precisely a central issue in the analysis of the impossibility of the Paretian liberal.

Second, in the Prisoner's Dilemma each person has a list of strategies to choose from (to confess or not to confess, say), and each person's strategy availabilities are independent of the actions of the other. This is similar to the "feature" or "issue" formulation of the liberty conditions, where each person fixes some feature of the social state (e.g., person i fixes whether he reads *Lady Chatterley's Lover* or not) (Bernholz, 1974; Gärdenfors, 1981; Gibbard, 1974; Levi, 1982; Nozick, 1974). But in the real world, such fully "independent" choice of individual features might not be "technologically feasible," even for those issues which are regarded as matters for personal decision *to the extent* to which independent choice is possible (Barnes, 1980; Seidl, 1975). For example, in the work-choice case, the overall employment opportunities are such that the feasible combinations are confined to four alternatives only, and this does not permit either individual to freely chose his employment independently of the other. On the other hand, to the extent that such a choice does exist – as it does for precisely one pair for each (each person has the option of working full-time or not at all *if* the other person happens to work half-time) – the consideration of liberty is taken to require that each person's options should be resolved by the person himself. This case illustrates the impossibility of the Paretian liberal, but it does not have the form of the Prisoner's Dilemma game.

Third, even when each individual can choose his personal "feature" or "issue" independently of the choice of others, the impossibility of the Paretian liberal can hold without the game's being a variant of the Prisoner's Dilemma.[11] Consider, for example, a variant of the work-choice case, with each person having the choice of working (1) or not (0), and being free to choose his employment as he likes. Person 1, whom I shall call the "envious worker," has the preference ordering: (1, 0), (0, 0), (1, 1), (0, 1), in decreasing order, and person 2 – the "egalitarian shirker" – has the ordering: (0, 0), (1, 1), (1, 0), (0, 1), in decreasing order. Compared with no one working, that is, (0, 0), person 1 prefers (1, 0), and, given that choice, would freely choose to work. Compared with (1, 0), person 2 prefers (1, 1), and he too – given that choice – would freely choose to work. Though each has made a prudent choice, given the choice of the other, and the outcome (1, 1) is a "Nash equilibrium," it is Pareto-inferior to (0, 0), which completes a Pareto-liberty cycle. It is, in this case, impossible to combine the Paretian judgment with equilibrium of individual preference-based choice over the respective personal spheres.[12] But the game is not a Prisoner's Dilemma – indeed person 2 has no dominant strategy.

---

[11] The former has a wider domain than the latter. In fact, Kevin Roberts (1976) has established and analyzed an impossibility result that works on a domain that is wider than that of Prisoner's Dilemma but narrower than that of the impossibility of the Paretian liberal.

[12] In such cases as well as in cases corresponding to the Prisoner's Dilemma, the equilibrium property of the Pareto-inefficient outcome is based on each person taking the other's strategy as *given*. Neither has indeed any incentive to change his strategy given that of the other. Isaac Levi

IX. Solution by collusion?

Irrespective of whether or not the game form coincides with the Prisoner's Dilemma, given the Pareto-inefficient result of individual exercise of rights, neither person can bring about a Pareto improvement based on his own action. But potentially the individuals *together* can, of course, bring about a Pareto improvement through collusive action, thereby resolving the Pareto inefficiency of the libertarian outcome. In order to permit such collusive action, the characterization of individual rights has to permit "marketing" of rights. For example, in the work-choice case, each person may make a commitment not to use his right to accept more employment, in exchange for the other's making a similar commitment.

Some authors (e.g., Buchanan, Gärdenfors, Barry) have seen in this possibility a "solution" to the impossibility of the Paretian liberal. I believe this is not a solution, but the possibility of such collusive action to move away from Pareto-inefficient "liberal" outcomes must be considered. In fact, the possibility of such a move away was already noted in the original presentation of the impossibility result, where it was pointed out that the so-called liberal solution is "not merely not Pareto-optimal, it is also a point of disequilibrium" and that quite possibly "the market will not achieve the Pareto-inoptimal 'liberal' solution either" (Sen, 1970b: 84).

Why does this line of reasoning not provide a solution to the impossibility of the Paretian liberal? There are several distinct barriers to this "solution," and here I shall present only a brief discussion of the main issues involved (see also Sen, 1982b). There are four distinct questions to deal with:

1. *The legitimacy issue:* Will the scope of individual rights admit such marketlike contracts?
2. *The Pareto-end issue:* Will the individuals actually try to get away from the results of individual exercises of rights, to a Pareto-superior state?
3. *The contract-means issue:* If the only way of getting to such a Pareto-superior state is through a binding contract, will the individuals still try to get there?
4. *The instability issue:* If the individuals do try to move to such a Pareto-superior state through a binding contract, will they be able to sustain the contractual outcome?

Questions can indeed be raised about the legitimacy of a contract that requires both parties to renounce their freedom to choose within their personal spheres (e.g., to accept employment), and such questioning may even get some support

---

(1982) has considered the case in which the individuals do not know what the other has chosen. With that assumption and the further assumption that each person's belief about the other person's strategy is a function of his own strategy, Levi shows that the Pareto inefficiency of the outcome of individual choice can be avoided, provided the beliefs are of the right sort.

from John Stuart Mill's argument that "the principle of freedom cannot require that the person be free not to be free" and that "it is not freedom to be allowed to alienate his freedom" (Mill, 1965: 348). But Mill was dealing with the rather extreme case of slavery in making these remarks, and the argument clearly does not readily apply to, say, mutual employment-denying contracts.

There is, however, the somewhat different issue whether such contracts should be publicly enforceable, even if there is nothing illegitimate in making such a contract. The distinction, as Rawls has argued, can be important. The role of an enforcer checking whether you have broken your contract not to accept employment (or ascertaining whether the prude has broken his agreement to read *Lady Chatterley's Lover* every morning) is morally problematic, aside from being deeply chilling.

The Pareto-end issue raises a question of a different type. The fact that a Pareto-superior state is higher in everyone's preference scale is certainly *an* argument for trying to get to such a state. On the other hand, the status of preference – either in the form of desire or of satisfaction – is by no means above moral questioning. John Broome has argued that preferences do need rational assessment (Broome, 1978), and it is of course quite possible that some types of envy-based preferences – such as those against the other person's employment in the work-choice case – may fail to pass such assessment. Questions can be raised about "nosey" preferences too – for example, being more concerned with other people's reading habits than with one's own. Though a preference may be seen to be "irrational" even by the person holding it, it does not by any means follow that his preference will actually change – immediately or ever – and cease to have that quality. In such a situation it would not be unreasonable for a person to decide that he must be guided not by his actual preferences only, but also by his "metarankings" reflecting what he would like his preference to be (Baier, 1977; Harrison, 1979; Hirschman, 1982: ch. 4; Hollis, 1979; Sen, 1979b, 1974; van der Veen, 1981).

There is a further question here. Even if the person is perfectly at peace with his preferences and finds them by no means irrational, he might still wish to discriminate between different parts of his preferences. He could agree with Mill that "there is no parity between the feeling of a person for his opinion, and the feeling of another who is offended at his holding it," and that "a person's taste is as much his own peculiar concern as his opinion or his purse" (Mill, 1965: 331). There is nothing inconsistent, or even peculiar, in being sure about the rightness of one's preference and at the same time not wanting it to "count" (Sen, 1976: 235–7, 243–4) when it happens to deal with other people's personal lives (e.g., "I would have preferred if you were not to do this, but it is *your* life, not mine, and I would ask you to ignore my preference").

My point here is not that it will be wrong for a person to seek a Pareto improvement of the kind under discussion if he considers such a move to be good, but that he may well not consider such a move to be good. The person's *decisions* in such fields involving other people's personal lives should not be taken for granted even when there is no uncertainty as to what his *preferences* are.

Turning now to the contract-means issue, even when each person would like the other person's life to be run differently from what that person wants, neither person might nevertheless want to achieve that result *through* an enforced contract. This is a traditional problem in matters of love and friendship, but it can arise in other types of situations as well, and the worth – and indeed the nature – of an outcome might well be taken to be sensitive to how it is brought about. I don't know how important this type of means-based consideration might be – it obviously would vary from case to case – but it is an issue that has to be faced in seeking solution by collusion.

Finally, ignoring all these difficulties, consider the case in which all the parties do try to have a Pareto-improving contract and it is agreed that such a contract is perfectly legitimate for them to have. Would this solve the problem? Indeed not, since the incentive to break the contract *remains*. The important point about the possibility of the Pareto-improving contract is that it disequilibrates the Pareto-inefficient outcome resulting from the individual exercise of rights (Sen, 1970b: 84), but it need not make the contracted arrangement itself an equilibrium. Indeed, in a situation exemplifying the conflict between the Pareto principle and individual liberty, there might exist no equilibrium at all – with some states being rejected by the Pareto-improving contract and the others being rejected by individual decisions over their own personal spheres. The difficulty of enforcing contractual behavior in personal lives is daunting, and doubts about the moral legitimacy of enforcing such contracts, noted earlier, do not make the problem any easier.

The impossibility of the Paretian liberal, interpreted in terms of descriptive choice, leads to a game with an empty core. The instability problem can be shown to be deeply ingrained in the nature of the conflict (Aldrich, 1977a,b; Gardner, 1980; Green, 1980; Miller, 1977), and there seems to be a general confluence of the possibility of Pareto-improving contracts on the one hand, and the existence of cyclical or intransitive group decisions, on the other (Bernholz, 1980, 1976; Schwartz, 1977).

The Pareto-improving contract is not so much a "solution" of the impossibility of the Paretian liberal as a part of the "problem" itself. Consider first the *descriptive-choice* version. *Without* such contracts, the stable outcomes may well be Pareto-inefficient, and with them there may well be no stable outcomes at all! It is, of course, quite possible that in some particular cases of the conflict, such contracts will be sought, made, and successfully enforced, and the outcomes will happen to be stable. But such a contingent occurrence, dependent on the variety of circumstances discussed above, can scarcely count as a general solution of the impossibility of the Paretian liberal.

With the *normative-choice* interpretation, these difficulties do, of course, remain. But further questions are raised about the normative relevance of such exchanges and their enforcement, even when they do take place and produce a stable outcome. It is important to note that the normative problems – both of *choice* and of *outcome evaluation* – may be viewed not merely from the position of outsiders, but also from the position of the involved individuals themselves. In that context, the individual's choice behavior cannot, obviously, be taken as given. The question that has to be faced then is: "Should I seek such a contract?" and not whether others have any reason to object if I were to seek such a contract. To try to "solve" this problem by invoking one's preference as the great arbitrator is surely to beg an important moral question.

Indeed, the status of preference is one of the central issues involved in the impossibility of the Paretian liberal (Sen, 1979c). It can be seen as showing the impossibility of giving priority to preferences over personal spheres while accepting the priority of unanimous preference rankings. In the context of the morality of personal choice, this conflict has to be faced. The possibility of a Pareto-improving contract does nothing to resolve it.

X. Concluding remarks

I have argued that there are several distinct interpretations of "social preference" in social choice theory, and correspondingly, of "liberty" in that framework. The impossibility of the Paretian liberal holds under each of these interpretations, but has correspondingly different, though related, contents. Outcome evaluation, normative choice, and descriptive choice are examples of alternative interpretations.

Second, I have also argued that the formulation of liberty in terms of the individual's having actual *control*, independent of the nature of the *outcomes*, is fundamentally inadequate. What has been called here "indirect liberty" is systematically ignored by the "control view" of liberty.

Third, the conflict between the Pareto principle and individual liberty holds also under the control interpretation, and the issue of the inadequacy of that interpretation does not, therefore, have a decisive bearing on this *particular* conflict.

Fourth, the possibility of Pareto-improving contracts does not, contrary to some claims, eliminate (or "resolve") the impossibility problem under any of the alternative interpretations.

Finally, there is nothing much to "resolve" anyway. The impossibility of the Paretian liberal just brings out a conflict of principles – a conflict that might not have been immediately apparent. There are, of course, many such conflicts. The really interesting issues relate to the implications of the conflict.[13] There are implications both for evaluation of outcomes and for choice of decision procedures. I have tried to discuss some of these implications.

---

[13] See the literature cited in sections IV and V.

References

Aldrich, John. (1977a). "Liberal Games: Further Comments on Social Choice and Social Theory." *Public Choice* 30: 29–34.

—— (1977b). "The Dilemma of a Paretian Liberal: Some Consequences of Sen's Theorem." *Public Choice* 30: 1–21.

Arrow, Kenneth, J. (1963). *Social Choice and Individual Values.* 2nd ed. New York: Wiley.

Austen-Smith, David. (1982). "Restricted Pareto and Rights." *Journal of Economic Theory* 26: 89–99.

Baier, Kurt. (1977). "Rationality and Morality." *Erkenntnis* 11: 197–232.

Barnes, Jonathan. (1980). "Freedom, Rationality and Paradox," *Canadian Journal of Philosophy* 10: 545–65.

Barry, Brian. (1986). "Lady Chatterley's Lover and Doctor Fischer's Bomb Party: Liberalism, Pareto Optimality, and the Problem of Objectionable Preferences." In Jon Elster and Aanund Hylland (Eds.), *Foundations of Social Choice Theory.* Cambridge: Cambridge University Press.

Batra, Raveendra N., and Prasanta K. Pattanaik. (1972). "On Some Suggestions for Having Non-binary Social Choice Functions." *Theory and Decision* 3: 1–11.

Bergstrom, Ted. (1970). "A 'Scandinavian Consensus' Solution for Efficient Income Distribution among Nonmalevolent Consumers." *Journal of Economic Theory* 2: 383–98.

Berlin, Isaiah. (1969). *Four Essays on Liberty.* New York: Oxford University Press.

Bernholz, Peter. (1980). "A General Social Dilemma: Profitable Exchange and Intransitive Group Preferences." *Zeitschrift für Nationalökonomie* 40: 1–23.

—— (1976). "Liberalism, Logrolling, and Cyclical Group Preferences." *Kyklos* 29: 26–37.

—— (1974). "Is a Paretian Liberal Really Impossible?" *Public Choice* 19: 99–107.

Blau, Julian H. (1975). "Liberal Values and Independence." *Review of Economic Studies* xlii: 395–402.

Breyer, Friedrich. (1978). *Das Liberal Paradox.* Meisenheim am Glan.

—— (1977). "The Liberal Paradox, Decisiveness over Issues, and Domain Restrictions." *Zeitschrift für Nationalökonomie* 37: 45–60.

Breyer, Friedrich, and Roy Gardner. (1980). "Liberal Paradox, Game Equilibrium, and Gibbard Optimum." *Public Choice* 35: 469–81.

Breyer, Friedrich, and Gary A. Gigliotti. (1980). "Empathy and the Respect for the Right of Others." *Zeitschrift für Nationalökonomie* 40: 59–64.

Broome, John. (1978). "Choice and Value in Economics." *Oxford Economic Papers* 30: 313–33.

Buchanan, James. (1976). "An Ambiguity in Sen's Alleged Proof of the Impossibility of the Paretian Liberal." Mimeograph, Virginia Polytechnic.

Campbell, Donald E. (1976). "Democratic Preference Functions." *Journal of Economic Theory* 12: 259–72.

Chapman, Bruce. (1981). "Rights as Constraints: Nozick versus Sen." Mimeograph, Westminster Institute for Ethics and Human Values.

Coughlin, P., and Amartya K. Sen. (1981). Unpublished notes, Institute of Economics and Statistics, Oxford.

Farrell, M. J. (1976). "Liberalism in the Theory of Social Choice." *Review of Economic Studies* 43: 3–10.

Ferejohn, John A. (1978). "The Distribution of Rights in Society." In Hans W. Gottinger and Werner Leinfellner (Eds.), *Decision Theory and Social Ethics: Issues in Social Choice*. Dordrecht: Reidel.

Fine, Ben. (1975). "Individual Liberalism in a Paretian Society." *Journal of Political Economy* 83: 1277–82.

Fishburn, Peter. (1973). *The Theory of Social Choice*. Princeton, N.J.: Princeton University Press.

Fountain, John. (1980). "Bowley's Analysis of Bilateral Monopoly and Sen's Liberal Paradox in Collective Choice Theory: A Note." *Quarterly Journal of Economics* 94: 809–12.

Gaertner, Wulf, and Lorenz Krüger. (1981). "Self-supporting Preferences and Individual Rights: The Possibility of Paretian Libertarianism." *Economica* 48: 17–28.

Gärdenfors, Peter. (1981). "Rights, Games, and Social Choice." *Noûs* 15: 341–56.

Gardner, Roy. (1980). "The Strategic Inconsistency of a Paretian Liberal." *Public Choice* 35: 241–52.

Gibbard, Allan. (1974). "A Pareto-Consistent Libertarian Claim." *Journal of Economic Theory* 7: 388–410.

Green, E. T. (1980). "Libertarian Aggregation of Preferences: What the 'Coase Theorem' Might Have Said." *Social Science Working Paper* No. 315. California Institute of Technology.

Grout, Paul. (1980). "On Minimal Liberalism in Economics." Mimeograph, Birmingham University.

Hammond, Peter. (1982). "Utilitarianism, Uncertainty and Information." In Amartya Sen and Bernard Williams (Eds.), *Utilitarianism and Beyond*. Cambridge: Cambridge University Press.

——— (1981). "Liberalism, Independent Rights and the Pareto Principle." In J. Cohen, (Ed.), *Proceedings of the 6th International Congress of Logic, Methodology and Philosophy of Science*. Dordrecht: Reidel.

Hansson, Bengt. (1968). "Choice Structures and Preference Relations." *Synthese* 17: 443–58.

Hare, Richard. (1952). *The Language of Morals*. Oxford: Clarendon Press.

Harrison, R. (Ed.). (1979). *Rational Action*. Cambridge: Cambridge University Press.

Herzberger, Hans. (1973). "Ordinal Preference and Rational Choice." *Econometrica* 41: 187–237.

Hicks, John. (1939). *Value and Capital*. Oxford: Clarendon Press.

Hirschman, Albert. (1982). *Shifting Involvements*. Princeton, N.J.: Princeton University Press.

Hollis, Martin. (1979). "Rational Man and Social Science." In Ross Harrison (Ed.), *Rational Action*. Cambridge: Cambridge University Press.

Kelly, Jerry S. (1978). *Arrow Impossibility Theorems*. New York: Academic Press.

——— (1976). "The Impossibility of a Just Liberal." *Economica* 43: 67–76.

Levi, Isaac. (1982). "Liberty and Welfare." In Amartya Sen and Bernard Williams (Eds.), *Utilitarianism and Beyond*. Cambridge: Cambridge University Press.

McLean, Iain. (1980). "Liberty, Equality and the Pareto Principle: A Comment on Weale." *Analysis* 40: 212–13.

Mill, John Stuart. (1965 [1854]). *On Liberty*. Reprinted in M. Lerner (Ed.), *Essential Works of John Stuart Mill*. New York: Bantam Books.

Miller, Nicholas. (1977). "Social Preference and Game Theory: A Comment on 'The Dilemma of a Paretian Liberal,'" *Public Choice* 30: 23–8.

Mueller, Dennis C. (1979). *Public Choice.* Cambridge: Cambridge University Press.

Nowell-Smith, Patrick H. (1954). *Ethics.* Harmondsworth: Penguin.

Nozick, Robert. (1974). *Anarchy, State and Utopia.* Oxford: Blackwell.

——— (1973). "Distributive Justice." *Philosophy and Public Affairs* 3: 45–126.

Perelli-Minetti, C. R. (1977). "Nozick on Sen: A Misunderstanding." *Theory and Decision* 8: 387–93.

Plott, Charles. (1976). "Axiomatic Social Choice Theory: An Overview and Interpretation." *American Journal of Political Science* 20: 511–96.

Roberts, Kevin. (1976). "Liberalism and Welfare Economics: A Note." Mimeograph, St. Catherine's College, Oxford.

Rowley, Charles K., and Alan T. Peacock. (1975). *Welfare Economics: A Liberal Restatement.* London: Martin Robertson.

Schwartz, Thomas. (1977). "Collective Choice, Separation of Issues, and Vote Trading." *American Political Science Review* lxxii: 999–1010.

——— (1976). "Choice Functions, 'Rationality' Conditions and Variations on the Weak Axiom of Revealed Preference." *Journal of Economic Theory* 12: 414–27.

Seidl, Christian. (1975). "On Liberal Values." *Zeitschrift für Nationalökonomie* 35: 257–92.

Sen, Amartya. (1983). "Evaluator Relativity and Consequential Evaluation." *Philosophy and Public Affairs* 12: 113–32.

——— (1982a). "Rights and Agency." *Philosophy and Public Affairs* 11: 3–39.

——— (1982b). "Liberty as Control: An Appraisal." *Midwest Studies in Philosophy* 7: 207–21.

——— (1979a). "Personal Utilities and Public Judgements, or What's Wrong with Welfare Economics?" *Economic Journal* 89: 537–58.

——— (1979b). "Informational Analysis of Moral Principles." In Ross Harrison (Ed.), *Rational Action.* Cambridge: Cambridge University Press.

——— (1979c). "Utilitarianism and Welfarism." *Journal of Philosophy* 76: 479–87.

——— (1977). "Social Choice Theory: A Reexamination." *Econometrica* 45: 53–89.

——— (1976). "Liberty, Unanimity and Rights." *Economica* 43: 217–45.

——— (1974). "Choice, Orderings and Morality." In Stefan Körner (Ed.), *Practical Reason.* Oxford: Blackwell.

——— (1971). "Choice Functions and Revealed Preference." *Review of Economic Studies* 37: 307–17.

——— (1970a). "The Impossibility of a Paretian Liberal." *Journal of Political Economy* 78: 152–7.

——— (1970b). *Collective Choice and Social Welfare.* San Francisco: Holden-Day.

Stevens, Dana N., and James E. Foster. (1978). "The Possibility of Democratic Pluralism." *Economica* 45: 401–6.

Sugden, Robert. (1981). *The Political Economy of Public Choice.* Oxford: Martin Robertson.

Suzumura, Kataro. (1981). "Equity, Efficiency, and Rights in Social Choice." Discussion Paper No. 155 (revised).

——— (1978). "On the Consistency of Libertarian Claims." *Review of Economic Studies* 45: 329–42.

van der Veen, Robert J. (1981). "Meta-Rankings and Collective Optimality." *Social Science Information* 30: 345–74.

Weale, Albert. (1980). "The Impossibility of Liberal Egalitarianism." *Analysis* xl.1, 185: 13–19.

Wriglesworth, J. L. (1982). "The Possibility of Democratic Pluralism: A Comment." *Economica* xlix.

(n.d.). "Solution to the Gibbard and Sen paradoxes Using Information Available from Interpersonal Comparisons." Mimeograph, Lincoln College, Oxford.

2. The contractarian explanation of the state

Jean Hampton

How do governments originate? How are they maintained? These are two causal questions about how states originate and persist through time that have always been of interest to anthropologists and historians. To answer them, however, one also needs to know the answer to a conceptual question: What is a state? This chapter attempts to answer all three questions by using ideas drawn from the social contract tradition. Together the answers constitute what I will call an explanation of the state.

It may seem fantastic to some that the social contract argument could provide plausible answers to the two causal questions. Doesn't the contract argument make the state's creation and maintenance the result of each subject's contractual consent to it? And isn't this a wildly inaccurate explanation of virtually every state's origin and continued existence? As Hume wryly observes:

> were you to ask the far greatest part of the nation, whether they had ever consented to the authority of their rulers, or promis'd to obey them, they wou'd be inclin'd to think very strangely of you, and wou'd certainly reply, that the affair depended not on their consent but that they were born to such obedience. (1978 [1739–40]: 548, sec. III, ii, viii)

In response to such ridicule, supporters of the contractarian methodology have tended to back away from claiming that their contract talk has any explanatory import. The contracts in the argument are generally represented as "hypothetical" occurrences and not historical events. The theorist is, on this view, using the contract talk not to give any dubious history lessons but merely to justify the state in terms of what people *could agree to* in an equal and impartial setting.

However, I do not want to give up on the idea that the contract methodology has explanatory power. In this chapter, I will construct an explanatory theory that I will argue is implicit in the traditional social contract argument but that does not make use of the literal notion of contract. I will conclude by considering first, in what sense this is a *contractarian* model given that it incorporates only an attenuated notion of agreement, and second, whether or not the explanation is true, and thus usable by an historian or anthropologist exploring the origins and histories of particular states, or by a political or legal theorist attempting to understand the nature of the institution itself.

It is important to stress that as I attempt to answer these questions, at no point will I be discussing the justificatory force that contractarians have believed their argument has. Whether or not one can construct a social contract argument justifying the state's authority (and in this essay I take no position on that issue), I am arguing that this form of argument can at least offer a partial explanation of what kind of institution the state is. I leave for another day a discussion of how much justificational force the social contract might have in political contexts.[1]

Solving the leadership selection problem

There are a variety of social contract arguments concerned with the justification of the state. My claim that we can distill from all of them a single explanatory theory of the state means that I believe they share, despite their differences, a common causal account of the state's creation and maintenance, and a common conceptual analysis of the state. It is one of the difficulties of my project that I must isolate these two common threads even while acknowledging the differences that divide members of this tradition.

We can find the end of that common thread by reflecting on the fact that those who present an argument in which people in a state of nature create a government are assuming that political subordination is not a natural feature of our social world. In contrast, those who believe that political subordination is natural will insist that one has no more reason to explain the subjugation of a human population to their ruler than one has to explain the subjugation of a group of mares to a stallion. Such subjugation is understood as inevitable, either because the natural masters are born with the power to dominate the natural slaves, or because the natural slaves are, for psychological or intellectual reasons, incapable of assuming the leadership role.

However, someone can believe that there is a hierarchy of talents and abilities that *ought* to be, but frequently is not, respected in the structuring of existing political societies. Or, more radically, he can deny that any such hierarchy exists and insist, as the traditional contractarians did, that human beings are similar enough in talent and abilities to make them equal, such that any of them could be leader. Either view is consistent with the contractarian methodology insofar as each accepts the fundamental tenet of that methodology, namely, that the state is an "artificial" institution (to use Hume's term) created (albeit perhaps not intentionally) by the actions of the human beings who would be rulers or subjects in it.

---

[1] The project of developing a contractarian explanation of the state may, however, help one to understand how social contract talk can have justificatory force. It is hard to understand how an appeal to a nonexistent promisorial agreement to create the state can provide a foundation for the legitimacy of that institution. On the other hand, if we can develop a theory that explains in what sense citizens really do "consent" to the states that rule them, it may be easier to understand how that consent could justify the institution.

(However, note that the second view would make not only political power but also the *reasons* entitling anyone to hold that power a human creation.) Most members of the contract tradition also believe that the state is not only created but also *maintained* by human action. The model I will present aims to clarify the nature of this maintenance activity.

If states are not only created but also maintained by the people, then this suggests that the people want them. In order to persuade his readers of the desirability of political society, the contractarian paints life without government in a "state of nature" as conflict-ridden, and presents people concluding that the state is a remedy (either the best or the only remedy) for that conflict. In the process of telling that story, the contractarian constructs a psychology that explains both why people tend to engage in conflict in a natural state, and why they would prefer to leave this state of conflict and enter political society. The psychologies of the traditional social contract theorists, and the reasons they give for state creation, have varied considerably over the years. But if one looks closely one sees that although their arguments differ on the questions of why the state is desirable and what kind of state people have reason to generate, all of them contain roughly the same account of how the state is created and maintained.

I want to propose that the reason why contractarians share a common explanation of the state is that, despite the use of different psychologies and ethical theories that justify the institution of different kinds of political regimes, each believes that the generation of the state involves solving the same game-theoretic problem. In order to make this claim plausible without going into taxing detail describing every contract argument in the tradition, I will sketch how it is true for the two most important members of that tradition, Hobbes and Locke. If this common element exists in their importantly different arguments, then we have at least the basis for a claim that it is definitive of the contractarian explanatory strategy.

Let us start with Hobbes's theory. People in his state of nature are largely, but not exclusively, self-interested, and pursue above all else their self-preservation. Their desire for this latter goal, along with their desire for glory, generate violent competition for objects that leads to a climate of distrust precipitating more violence. Hobbes presents the institution of a sovereign as not only a sufficient but also a necessary condition for peace. The people in his state of nature believe this, and hence desire to institute a sovereign. But they still face considerable disagreement on the question of *who* should be sovereign. What precisely is the nature of their disagreement?

To specify it exactly, suppose there are three people in Hobbes's state of nature who are unable to resolve Prisoner's Dilemma problems and who are therefore inclined to aggress against one another. Suppose further that these individuals accept the Hobbesian argument that the warfare in this state can be remedied only by the institution of a sovereign. To simplify the problem for the time being, let us also suppose that they agree with Hobbes that the state will operate best if sovereignty is invested in one person, so that they aim to create an absolute monarch. Their preferences over the various possible outcomes in this situation are as follows. First, each party will rate lowest the situation in which he is not a member of the state while the other two are, because here he is a lone individual in a partial state of war facing a unified group of two who can likely beat him in any conflict. Each of them will rate the partial state of war in which he is a subject in a two-person state higher than this, because here he would enjoy the increase in security that association with another person brings. He would prefer even more being subject in a state in which all three of them are members because in this situation peace finally prevails. Hobbes also tells us (1968 [1651]: ch. 15, para. 21) that individuals would rather be rulers than subjects in any state; hence, each would prefer being ruler of a two-person state rather than a subject in it, and each would prefer even more being ruler in a three-person state. But the importance of avoiding war and immanent death or injury is such that (assuming these people are not badly vainglorious) each individual would prefer being a subject in a three-person state to being the ruler in a partial state of war. So the question to be settled is, "Who shall reign?"

This situation is actually a kind of conflict-ridden coordination game much discussed in the game-theoretic literature called "the Battle of the Sexes" after Luce and Raiffa's (1957: 90–4, ch. 6) unfortunately sexist example of a husband and wife who each prefer different evening activities (he prefers a prize fight, she prefers a ballet) but who would also rather go with the other to his or her preferred evening activity than to go to his or her own favorite alone. A two-player version of this game is shown in Table 2.1.

It is important to note that this type of interaction is a *coordination* rather than a conflict problem because it has coordination equilibria. Coordination equilibria are defined as those situations where the combination of the players' actions is such that no one would be better off if any one player, either himself or another, acted differently (Lewis, 1969: 24). In the Table 2.1 matrix there are two coordination equilibria (AA and BB), which come about when A and B choose the same person as ruler. Each prefers either of these outcomes to the outcomes that result when they choose different leaders, because their disagreement prevents them from installing a government. For a population of n people in the state of nature, the matrix representing their deliberations will be n-dimensional, with n coordination equilibria, but that game will be closely analogous to this two-dimensional game.

So the major problem people with these preferences face in their efforts to create a commonwealth is a coordination problem with considerable conflict of interest on the issue: How shall we be governed? I call this the "leadership selection problem." And it really has two components. In the example above, the players agreed that only one of them would rule – their decision amounting to an agreement to create a state with an absolute monarch. But of course there can be a dispute over whether to invest sovereignty in one person or a group of persons, which is, in effect, a dispute over what form of government to institute. Resolving this dispute involves determining how many leaders will rule them, and what

Table 2.1. *The convention game of leadership selection*

		B	
		Choose A as ruler	Choose B as ruler
A	Choose A as ruler	3,2	1,1
	Choose B as ruler	1,1	2,3

power he/she/they will have, and it too would likely have a battle of the sexes structure.[2]

After resolving these matters, the people must decide (as in the example above) *which* person or persons to choose as leader to fill whatever offices in the government they have defined. If there is no disagreement on these questions, the people's dilemma is an easily solvable coordination problem with only one coordination equilibrium. Disagreement makes the coordination problem conflict-ridden, but unless it is so severe that people would rather remain in the state of nature than accept someone other than their favorite candidate as ruler (a preference driven by the desire for glory that Hobbes would condemn as irrational), it will not destroy the coordination character of the game.[3] As long as irrationality is not widespread, there should be sufficient support for achieving some resolution to generate an institution powerful enough to coerce any recalcitrant glory seekers into submission. Later I will discuss procedures, such as voting, that help to create a salient solution to this kind of coordination problem, which could be used to generate the state (Hampton, 1986: ch. 6).

Does Locke's argument for the state also assume that a conflict-ridden coordination game describes the problem of creating government? It does: Consider that unlike Hobbes's people, Locke's people can be motivated not only by self-interest but also by God's "Fundamental Law of Nature," which directs them to preserve the life, health, and possessions of others as long as their own preservation will not be compromised by doing so (1960 [1690]: 311, *Second Treatise,* sec. 6). Were people to act strictly in accordance with God's law, the state of nature would be a state of peace. But warfare is precipitated by irrational members of society, who either harm others for their own gain ("In transgressing the Law of Nature, the Offender declares himself to live by another Rule, than that of Reason and Common Equity" [1960: 312, sec. 8]) or fail (because of personal

---

[2] Kavka (1986: 188) agrees, noting that people may also agree at this stage on a constitution, explicit legislation, procedural safeguards to be followed in the regime, and so forth.

[3] Gregory Kavka (1986: 180ff) cites passages from *Leviathan* (ch. 18) in support of a similar analysis of the game-theoretic structure underlying the state's creation, but he does not go on to stress the way in which that structure underlies a convention-based rather than a contract-based explanation of the state.

bias) to interpret the Fundamental Law of Nature correctly, especially when they use it to justify the punishment of offenders. In virtue of the violent or uncooperative actions precipitated by this irrationality and self-bias, "nothing but Confusion and Disorder follow."[4] Reason directs men to pursue peace, but like Hobbes, Locke believes they can do so only by instituting a government:

I easily grant, that *Civil Government* is the proper remedy for the inconveniences of the State of Nature, which must certainly be Great, where Men may be Judges in their own Case. . . . the State of Nature is therefore not to be endured. (1960: 312)

Hence, for self-interested, religious and moral reasons, men "are quickly driven to [political] Society" (312).

Locke argues that political society remedies the disorder by providing impartial bodies that can fairly interpret the Fundamental Law of Nature and impartially adjudicate disputes using that law, and also by providing agencies that enforce the law effectively through punishment:

Mankind in general, may restrain, or where necessary, destroy things noxious to them, and so may bring such evil on any one, who hath transgressed that Law, as may make him repent the doing of it, *and thereby deter him,* and by his Example others, from doing the like mischief. (1960: 213, sec. 8. Emphasis added)

In other words, Locke believes that the use of fear can control the actions of those who refuse to live by the law of reason; on his view only the state can effectively and fairly generate that fear.

Given that this is the solution to their problems, what difficulties do Locke's people face creating that solution? Let us again consider our three-person state of nature, this time described in Lockean terms, and assume once again that they each prefer that only one of them rule. Consider that because Locke's people want the state in order to promote greater respect for a divine law that defines their obligations to one another, they desire political power not only for self-interested but also for moral and religious reasons. For all three reasons, each person would prefer least being a lone individual facing a unified group of two, because outside the state a person does not enjoy the enforcement of his rights according to this law. Locke would represent being a subject in a two-person state as better than this insofar as it would allow a person to enjoy some enforcement of rights and an increase in security (both of which are, at least in part, moral goods). Better still would be membership in a three-person state; here the person would enjoy a cessation of violence (or at least, depending upon the effectiveness of the ruler's enforcement, a lower threshold of violence). What about preferences for being ruler rather than subject in a two- or three-person state? Locke is not as committed as Hobbes is to the idea that each person would rather be ruler than subject, so it is theoretically possible that everyone would

---

[4] Locke writes, "it is unreasonable for Men to be Judges in their own Cases . . . Self-love will make Men partial to themselves and to their Friends. . . . Ill Nature, Passion and Revenge will carry them too far in punishing others" (1960: 316).

have the same favorite candidate, making the selection of a ruler easy. But if there were disagreements, Locke is clear that because it is highly desirable to institute government for moral as well as self-interested reasons, each would prefer being subject in a three-person state to being ruler in a two-person state.

So, once again, we have battle-of-the-sexes preferences, although these preferences are a function of both the moral, religious, and self-regarding interests of the people. The game-theoretic situation underlying the creation of the Lockean state is therefore the same as that underlying the creation of the Hobbesian state.[5] Locke also believes that there can be reasonable disagreements over the form that government should take, as well as over who should be ruler in it (although he himself argues for a government with divided powers and legislative dominance). But again, note that as long as each party does not prefer a continuation of war to compromise on a nonfavorite form of government, their disagreement will have a battle-of-the-sexes structure, and thus present them only with a conflict-ridden coordination game.

So we have actually discovered the two common threads running through the Lockean and Hobbesian arguments. First, both assume that the preferences of people regarding the creation of government in the state of nature give rise to a series of coordination games (most likely conflict ridden) which must be solved and maintained to generate and sustain that institution. So in answer to the causal question, "How is a state created and maintained," both say, "Through the generation and maintenance of conventions." Second, both see the state's role as primarily that of resolving, preventing, or punishing conflict among the people (although they disagree about exactly what reasons people have for desiring to create an institution that plays this role). And it is this role that they would regard as fundamental to understanding what a state is.

Granted that coordination games underlie the state's creation, and not Prisoner's Dilemmas, how are games of this kind solved and a desirable coordination equilibrium reached? Are contracts necessary to do so?

Creating leadership conventions

Although the word "contract" is sometimes used loosely to mean any sort of agreement, it is generally understood to be a certain kind of agreement, one in which one or more promises figure. The American Law Institute defines a contract as "a promise or set of promises for the breach of which the law gives a remedy, or the performance of which the law in some way recognizes a duty" (Atiyah, 1981: 28). The species of contract that the traditional contractarian

---

[5] Only if considerable numbers of people believe that there is *no* candidate (outside of their favorite) to whom it is better to be subjugated than to remain in a total or partial state of war is the conflict so great that the battle-of-the-sexes character of the game is destroyed. But given the way in which Locke believes government secures peace, such radical preferences are not defensible on his view on either moral or self-interested grounds, and he does not take seriously in his political writings the possibility that people could come to have them.

Table 2.2. *The strategic structure*
of bilateral contracts

		B	
		Action x	Action y
A	Action x	3,3	1,4
	Action y	4,1	2,2

invokes is known as a bilateral contract, in which "a promise, or set of promises by one side, is exchanged for a promise, or set of promises by the other side" (Atiyah, 1981: 32).[6] Contracts are made when parties to an agreement believe that the performance of the actions to be agreed upon is only collectively and not individually rational for each of them, such that an exchange of promises among them (i.e., a contract) to perform the actions seems necessary to secure performance. The Prisoner's Dilemma nicely represents the game-theoretic structure of this situation, and is depicted in Table 2.2.

In circumstances such as the state of nature, in which no law exists to enforce the contract, performance would only occur if the parties to it were able and willing to keep their contractual promises.

So if people in a state of nature needed a contract to institute the state, this would be because there were one or more Prisoner's Dilemmas associated with its institution, and that institution would only occur if people had the ability to keep a contractual promise to perform collectively rational but individually irrational actions. But we have seen that Prisoner's Dilemmas do not underlie the institution of the state in Hobbes's or Locke's theory. Although they are the sort of problem *precipitating* conflict for which the state is supposed to be a solution, they are not the problem that must be solved to create that solution. Another and more easily solved problem underlies the state's creation: the conflict-ridden coordination game. Might contracts, nonetheless, be necessary to solve these games?[7]

---

[6] There is also a species of contract that involves unilateral and not bilateral promising, but that species is not relevant to our concerns here.

[7] In his book *Hobbesian Moral and Political Theory* (1986), Gregory Kavka sends conflicting messages about how this question ought to be answered. He agrees that the battle of the sexes game characterizes the problem people face when they want to create a commonwealth, but he characterizes Hobbes's theory of the social contract as follows: "commonwealths are formed by institution, when a number of independent individuals create a common power over themselves by mutual agreement. This state-creating pact, or social contract, is pictured by Hobbes as having a complex structure. It is not really a single agreement, but a set of bilateral agreements linking each contractor with every other. Hence, a single party can rightly demand fulfillment of the agreement by each of the others. Each of these bilateral agreements surrenders the individual's right of self-rule to, and authorizes all the actions of, a sovereign person or assembly to be elected later by the parties by majority vote. In this two-stage process, the actual sovereign is selected only after the

The idea that a promisorial agreement is necessary for the state's creation is puzzling, because promises aren't usually taken to be either necessary or desirable for the solution of any coordination dilemma – even those with conflict. Consider that the task of the participants of such a dilemma is to realize only one coordination equilibrium. An effective way of doing so, if circumstances permit, is to communicate with one another so as to *reach an agreement* to pursue only one of the equilibria (e.g., players in a traffic coordination dilemma might specifically agree with one another to drive on the right rather than the left). Such agreements work as solutions to these problems because they give each party the "common knowledge that each prefers to conform to [the equilibrium chosen] conditionally upon conformity by others involved with him in [the game]" (Lewis, 1969: 83). How does that common knowledge help to effect a solution to this dilemma? I propose the following answer.[8] The fact that the agreement is commonly known causes each player to make a high assessment of the likelihood that the other player(s) will choose the agreed-upon equilibrium, such that an expected utility calculation performed by each of the players will dictate the action realizing that equilibrium by each player. Henceforth I will call such agreements *self-interested* or SI agreements, because self-interested rational calculation, rather than the sense of "duty" arising out of a promise or fear of a coercive power, is the motive for each person's performance of the act agreed upon.

But as David Lewis (1969: 35) explores, SI agreements might not be necessary for the resolution of a coordination problem. What is needed for its resolution is the generation of a *convention* governing which equilibrium to realize, and that convention can be generated even without agreement if there is an obviously salient equilibrium, one that stands out from the rest by its uniqueness in some conspicuous respect. If it is common knowledge that this equilibrium stands out in an obvious way, each will estimate the probability that they will perform the action leading to that equilibrium as higher than the probability that they will perform any other action, so that an expected utility calculation will dictate the pursuit of that equilibrium. In such situations it is "as if" there were an agreement on the pursuit of that salient outcome; hence it is common to hear people speak of there being a "tacit agreement" in these situations. Literally, of course, no one explicitly agreed with anyone on anything, but each did act by making reference to the beliefs and preferences of the others in the pursuit of this particular outcome, just as she would have done if there had been an explicit

parties are joined into a social union by overlapping mutual agreements. The parties bind one another to confer on whoever is elected their combined power and authority, in hopes thereby of achieving protection against foreigners and one another. The sovereign is not, qua sovereign, a party to the social contract and is therefore not constrained by it." (p. 181). Kavka's language here clearly signals that he sees this contract as not just an agreement but a promisorial agreement – one that binds and constrains.

[8] Lewis doesn't answer this question. My general answer to it in this chapter is given in more precise form in my *Hobbes and the Social Contract Tradition* (1986; ch. 6, 142–5).

agreement among them to pursue it. If this coordination problem persists and is repeatedly solved in this way, the participants have developed (without explicit agreement) a *convention* to solve their coordination problem.

So in order to solve their leadership problem, people who want to create a state must generate a leadership convention. As we shall discuss, either of the strategies involved, or some combination of the two, could be used to do so. Moreover, *something like* a contractual process *could* produce it. If each member had explicitly agreed with the others on who should rule and how, where that agreement involved a compromise by members of the group whose favorite outcome was not selected, then the conflict in the situation would be resolved and coordination achieved. However, notice that this compromise agreement *would not literally be a contract* because promises would not be necessary to keep it. Once the agreement was made it would already be in each party's interest to realize the coordination equilibrium agreed upon. This agreement would only be more difficult to make, requiring capitulation or compromise by some or all of the parties.

Another more historically plausible scenario used by Hobbes to explain the institution of a sovereign involves voting,[9] a method that is actually used by democratically organized states to select their rulers (although they use it in a situation where there is already a convention on how these leaders will rule, what powers they will have, and how long their term of office will be). Consider the problem facing any political party of selecting a viable candidate to represent the party in a general election. All members of the party realize that it is overwhelmingly in their interest to select someone from among their ranks to represent them, but there is often considerable disagreement as to who shall do so. Political parties such as the Democratic Party in the United States or the Labour Party in Britain resolve this controversy by holding successive elections (either in different geographical areas at different times, or successively at one national party convention), with those who get the majority of the votes staying in contention, and those who get small percentages of support dropping out. As the process continues, there is a gradual snowball or bandwagon effect, with one person usually emerging as the clear-cut favorite. The snowball effect in these elections is a clear indication that they are tactics for effecting a solution to a conflict-ridden coordination problem. The results of each successive election give people a way to determine the probability that their favorite leader will be able to receive support from the rest of the electorate, and thus allow them to calculate whether or not it is rational for them to hold out for that leader's selection. Those people who find themselves supporting candidates with little or no support from the rest of the electorate will find it rational to switch to a more popular candidate they prefer less, in the interest of getting a resolution to this coordination problem.

---

[9] Explicit mention of voting and democratic choice procedures occurs in Tönnies (1928: 198–9). Kavka thinks it is also suggested in *Leviathan*, chapters 18 and 20, but I do not see the idea explicitly present there.

If this election technique ever fails to effect a solution to a leadership selection problem, it is because a significant number of those whose favorite candidates lose refuse to accept that their candidates are effectively out of contention for selection, in just the same way that the loser of a coin flip might repudiate that coin flip as a strategy for solving this sort of problem. Such a refusal in a political context can produce stalemate and even civil war, but Hobbes would insist that this refusal is generally irrational. Holding out for a better deal means risking no solution to the problem, and thus a return to the state of war; it is a risk that an expected utility calculation in the state of nature would likely tell one not to take (unless, of course, the winning candidate posed a threat to one's life).

Historically, people have not been so rational or so moral, and have frequently resorted to warfare to choose their leaders and their governmental structures. But warfare is another device for achieving a resolution to a battle of the sexes problem relying on natural saliency rather than SI agreements. To see this, imagine a prepolitical situation in which war has gone on for some time and consider the plight of a very unsuccessful inhabitant. Unless he is badly vainglorious, such a person knows that he will never score a complete win over all the others in this state. Such a person is ripe for the following offer by a more successful inhabitant whom I will call a *sovereign-entrepreneur*. This entrepreneur says, "Look, you're getting nowhere on your own. But if you join forces with me and *do my bidding* (so that I am your ruler), then you will have more security than you now have." If this person doesn't accept this rather attractive-looking positive incentive by the sovereign-entrepreneur, he might be "offered" the following negative incentive: "Do my bidding or else I'll harm you!" And this threat will be real since, as we said, the sovereign-entrepreneur is a better warrior.

In general, both of these incentives are important tools for successful warriors to use in attracting subjects. The advantages of submission to this sovereign-entrepreneur are substantial: The subject will receive greater protection from other members of the confederacy, he will have a greater chance of warding off attacks from outsiders if he is allied with this leader than he would have on his own, and he might receive a share of the spoils of any victory achieved over the forces of these outsiders. However, negative incentives are useful as a method of encouraging some reluctant members of the state of nature to "give in" and accept the sovereign-entrepreneur as leader. Hence, the threats help to resolve the battle of the sexes problem over who should be declared ruler.

As entrepreneurs attract subjects in these ways, a certain number of powerful confederacies may emerge. But with their emergence comes a real market choice for the people in this state, as Robert Nozick actually noticed in his own attempt to construct a scenario of the creation of government (Nozick, 1974: 16ff).[10] In Nozick's scenario the forces of the two competing "protection agencies" do battle. One of these agencies will emerge as the usual or continual winner of

---

[10] Nozick actually constructs three scenarios, but the second and third are not sufficiently different from the first to merit discussion here.

these battles. And since the clients of the losing agency are ill-protected in conflicts with clients of the winning agency, they leave their losing agency to "do business" with the winner. Eventually one confederacy emerges as winner over all others and is thus the "best buy" in protection for everyone in this state. So the inhabitants of the state of nature looking for a protection agency are in a market. Heads of different confederacies essentially say to them: "Buy me if you want protection." And the confederacy that wins more often than any other will be the best buy for the people in that state.

There are two important points to notice about this scenario. First, coordination on who should be leader is being achieved *not* via explicit agreement among the inhabitants of the state of nature, but via a series of independent choices of a salient sovereign candidate by each inhabitant. Second, the negative incentives in this scenario are particularly useful in solving the *sort* of coordination problem that leadership selection presents. In particular, it breaks the conflict over who should rule (and how). Nor does the sovereign-entrepreneur have to threaten *everyone* in the state of nature. He need only threaten enough people to get a cadre of support enabling his confederacy to dominate in the state of war. Thereafter his confederacy will be the "best buy" in the state of nature and, as such, the salient choice for subjugation by everyone else.

The fact that warfare is not generally regarded as a *legitimate* way to solve this type of conflict-ridden coordination problem doesn't alter the fact that it can succeed in effecting a solution to it. Nonetheless, most social contract theorists haven't used this warfare scenario in their argument because it does not serve their justificatory interests. Any theorist interested in showing what kind of state we *should* create and maintain does not want to use stories of state creation such as the warfare scenario in which the mightiest, but not necessarily the most just leadership faction would prevail. It is natural to present a just government, which takes account of the rights of each individual subject, as the product of an agreement process in which those rights are respected. But Nozick's scenario has other advantages. In my restatement of his scenario I attributed to people the intention to leave the state of nature and create a government. But I needed to attribute to them at each moment only the intention to subjugate themselves to the best confederacy leader at that moment, and given the structure of the situation, this intention on the part of each of them would more than likely lead to the creation of a confederacy leader with a monopoly of power. Insofar as this "invisible hand" explanation need only make use of this limited intention, it not only has certain desirable explanatory features,[11] but may also be closer to what

---

[11] In Nozick's words: "Invisible-hand explanations minimize the use of notions constituting the phenomena to be explained; in contrast to the straightforward explanations, they don't explain complicated patterns by including the full-blown pattern-notions as objects of people's desires or beliefs. Invisible-hand explanations of phenomena thus yield greater understanding than do explanations of them as brought about by design as the object of people's intentions. It is therefore no surprise that they are more satisfying." (1974: 18–19).

actually occurred in the generation of existing political conventions than explicit-agreement scenarios.

The fact that traditional contractarians all resorted to the notion of an explicit agreement to construct a scenario of the state's creation has obscured the two causal explanations of the state that their arguments are making: namely, that states are created via the generation of a leadership convention, and second, that states persist through time for as long as this convention is maintained. As noted above, this convention can be generated without the people having the explicit intention to create a state. So despite what Nozick himself says, he is not any less of a "contractarian" because he uses in his argument a story in which the leadership convention is not generated by explicit agreement; instead, his successful use of a nonagreement story simply points up the fact that creating and maintaining a government involves the generation and maintenance of a conventional solution to a (probably conflict-ridden) coordination problem.

Empowerment

Thus far, this model makes the creation and maintenance of government a result of people's participation in a convention empowering rulers in a certain form of government. But we still do not know what participation in a leadership convention involves, such that the state is created and maintained. What actions must people take such that someone becomes their ruler?

Consider that a person is only a ruler – that is, only has *power* when his subjects do what he says, so people presumably make someone a ruler when they (or at least most of them) obey his commands. According to the contractarians, each subject gives the ruler the power of command over him: in Locke's words, "the first *Power, viz. of doing whatsoever he thought fit for the Preservation of himself,* and the rest of mankind, *he gives up* to be regulated by Laws made by the Society" (1960 [1690]: 397–8, *Second Treatise,* sec. 129). But what does it mean to be "regulated by laws made by the society"?

At the very least, it means being subject to the ruler's power to punish violations of these laws. In the *Leviathan* (ch. 28), Hobbes suggests that a subject grants the ruler punishment power when he does three things:

1. The subject must be disposed to obey the punishment orders of the person or group chosen as ruler.
2. The subject must surrender his right to come to the aid of another who is being punished by the ruler (although not, some might think, his right to defend himself).
3. The subject must oblige himself to assist the ruler in punishing others (but not, some might say, himself).

Regarding the first action: If we assume that the situation underlying the creation of a ruler is a battle-of-the-sexes dilemma, then once the subjects have agreed (implicitly or explicitly) that a certain person or group will be their ruler, obeying that person's punishment commands is identified as the way to achieve coordination in this situation; hence to the extent that obeying the punishment commands of any other person or group would disrupt this coordination, they have good reason not to do so.[12] Regarding the second action, it would seem that, in general, people are able to refrain from interfering with their government's punishment of people other than friends and relatives. Hobbes would point out that such punishment does not threaten their own well-being and insofar as allowing it to happen is a way of instituting a remedy to the warfare in that natural state, it is desirable to let it occur. Locke would point out that people are generally supportive, for moral as well as self-regarding reasons, of punishment of those who do not live by the law of reason and hence deserve the infliction of pain (indeed they support such punishment in the state of nature). Thus, any problems generated by those who do attempt to intervene on behalf of criminals for whom they care are small enough to be easily handled by a ruler who has sufficient police force to help him carry out the punishments.

But this brings us to the third action: In a community of any significant size the government will need help enforcing its edicts: police, judges, and jailers will all be required to make effective enforcement of the laws possible. Therefore, some percentage of persons in the community must be willing to carry out these jobs in order that the government have power. If (as Locke contends) people have the capacity to act in other-interested ways even at some cost to themselves, the ruler could appeal to them to volunteer their services. If (as Hobbes contends) they have no such capacity, a natural way for the government to receive their services would be to make individual contracts with each of them to become part of that cadre, giving them goods in exchange for service. Moreover, such a contract would not require either the ruler(s) or the members of the cadre to be fine, upstanding promise-keepers: it would only require that they be self-interested and smart enough to see the repetitive PD nature of the agreement (Axelrod, 1984). That is, because the government will stay in power only for as long as this cadre functions, it is in its interest to pay cadre members in order to ensure their future service. And because members of the cadre will only get that pay if they do what the government wants, it is in their interest to follow its orders. So we can expect these cadres to develop, and it is in the other subjects' interest not to interfere with their formation. The upshot of this discussion is that *no general social contract* is necessary for a government's empowerment.

But is this all that is necessary for a state to exist? Some legal theorists have argued it is not; on their view the state not only has the power to punish but also

---

[12] Of course, the state is continually threatened by those who claim to be a higher authority than the ruler, e.g., religious figures. Hobbes was particularly contemptuous and hostile toward the Christians of his day who maintained their right to disregard the commands of their ruler because a higher authority (e.g., the pope, a Protestant leader, even their own consciences informed by God through prayer and Biblical revelation) permitted them to do so.

the authority to rule.[13] What is state authority? Philosophers such as Anscombe (1981), Green (1988), or Raz (1979) understand it to be that which a state has, such that members of it believe they are obligated to obey its directives. So on this view, if I am a subject of a political system, then I obey a command of the state not only because I am fearful of the sanction if I don't and I am caught, but also (and more important) because the command is authoritative for me. "I have to do this because it's the law!" I think to myself. The exact definition of state authority is the subject of controversy, but one recent philosopher argues for the following definition: "α has authority over β if and only if the fact that α requires β to ϕ (i) gives β a content-independent reason to ϕ, and (ii) excludes some of β's reasons for not-ϕ-doing" (Green, 1988: 31).

Students of positivist legal theory know that it is important not to mistake a claim of authority for a claim of justification. As Hart was at pains to stress, to say that states have authority over their citizens is to make a purely descriptive statement, not a normative one. Whether or not a subject is right to obey the state, and whether or not a state deserves to have the obedience of its subjects, Hart claims that a coercive regime is only a state (as opposed to a group of gunmen coercing a population through the use of physical power) if the people accept a rule granting the regime the right to issue commands they will regard as binding upon them (i.e., that they will believe give them a content-independent reason for following them simply because they are issued by this regime).[14]

Now there are some who deny that states possess authority, even when this is understood in a purely positivist sense. But for those who believe it exists, the traditional, explicitly contractarian interpretation of the social contract argument might seem to promise an analysis of it. In the same way that my doctor has authority to take out my appendix if we have contractually agreed that she should do so, so too does it seem that my state has authority to dictate how I should behave in certain areas if we have contractually agreed for it to do so. Locke's appeal to promisorial consent is therefore explanatorily useful if one reads it as part of an explanation of how the state comes to have authority to command me. Someone who believes this may therefore want to supplement or replace any

---

[13] In my book *Hobbes and the Social Contract Tradition* (Hampton, 1986), I failed to emphasize sufficiently the extent to which states have authority, and not merely coercive power, over the ruled. This discussion aims to correct that oversight.

[14] Indeed, one might believe that a state can only be properly said to have punishment power (as opposed to the mere physical power to coerce) if it is the authoritative command-giver in the society. I will not take up here to what purpose a state ought to punish; this would be part of a moral theory of the state's legitimate role.

Notice how much Hobbes suggests the idea that states have (and ought to have) not merely power but authority of this kind in the following passage: "And when men that think themselves wiser than all others, clamor and demand right Reason for judge; yet seek no more, but things should be determined, by no other mens reason but their own, it is as intolerable in the society of men, as it is in play after trump is turned, to use for trump on every occasion, that suite whereof they have most in their hand."

convention-based model of the state with an explicit appeal to an authority-giving contract between the ruler and the people.

But is this explanation of authority any good? Over and over again, from David Hume to Ronald Dworkin, the contract tradition has been ridiculed for failing to provide anything like a plausible explanation of the state's authority using the idea of a promisorial contract. Just when, asks Hume, have most of the world's population undertaken this contractual obligation? People, he notes, generally obey the state because they think they are "born to it," not because they have promised to do so. What about the notion of tacit consent? If tacit consent is understood simply as the acceptance of benefits, then it is hard to know why it obliges us (it certainly wouldn't do so normally in a court of law – acceptance of benefits rarely, if ever, counts as making a promise), or why it obliges us members any more than it obliges any foreign traveler who enjoys the benefits of the state while she is here. And if we interpret this kind of consent such that it is more explicitly made and more explicitly promisorial, then it becomes increasingly difficult to argue that all or even most citizens of regimes around the world have ever given it.

Well then, might political authority be explained contractually if the contract explaining it is hypothetical rather than actual in nature? But here Dworkin (1974: 17–18) has the appropriate rejoinder: "A hypothetical contract is not simply a pale form of contract; it is no contract at all." We are not obliged by make-believe contracts, but by real ones. Hence, whatever excellent use a hypothetical contract has in defining justice or legitimating the state, a contract that never really took place cannot explain real authority.

I still think that there is something about a contractarian approach to state authority that is right, but I want to argue that this "something" can be best captured only by using the convention-based explanation of the state. The reason why explicitly contract-based explanations of the state's authority invariably fail is that they rest on a false history of the state.[15] But one can use the more plausible convention analysis to explain the state's authority by arguing that the process of generating a leadership convention involves not only the creation of rulers who have a virtual monopoly on force, but also (and perhaps more important) rulers who have authority to command. As Anscombe suggests, to create the state is to create *an authoritative office*.[16] An umpire in baseball has his authority by virtue of holding that authoritative office (required if the game is to be played), and not by virtue of any contract between him and the players that explicitly gives him the right to command them. Similarly, it is the nature of their office, and not any real or make-believe contract, that explains why our rulers have authoritative power. But that office is nonetheless one that, on the Conven-

---

[15] For this way of seeing the issue I am indebted to Alan Nelson, "Explanation and Justification in Political Philosophy," *Ethics* (1986).

[16] "Authority arises from the necessity of a task whose performance requires a certain sort and extent of obedience on the part of those for whom the task is supposed to be done" (Anscombe, 1981: 134).

tion Model, the people create and maintain through their participation in a certain kind of convention.

Now perhaps that participation is unwitting. A people who decide to regard a certain person as their queen because they believe that God has authorized her to rule and thus obey her, are in fact giving her both power and authority through their obedience as a result of their interdependent acceptance of her as leader – so that God doesn't authorize her, they do. The fact that their consent to her rule is unwitting; that is, their not knowing that it is they who are responsible for her holding that kind of office, which exists because of their need for it, might be greatly to her advantage. In particular, it might give her more security of reign because her subjects would not see that they in fact have the ability and indeed good reason to strip her of her authority to command them if her performance as ruler were poor. Nonetheless, she gets both her power and her authority by virtue of their unwitting convention-generating activity.

If one adds to one's analysis of the state the idea that the state is an institution whose rule is ultimately authoritative in the community ("the final court of appeal" as Rawls puts it),[17] one is accepting a Hartian (1961) approach to the nature of a legal system, rather than an Austinian approach. Insisting that Austin was wrong to suppose that a legal rule could be binding simply because the rule-giver has the physical power to coerce people to obey it, Hart maintained that a binding rule can only be created by one who has the authority to give the people such a rule. And this authority, he argues, can only come from another rule accepted by the people which he calls the "Rule of Recognition" (see the discussion in Dworkin, 1977).

I want to argue that if the contractarian chooses to do so, she can give an account of the state that dovetails nicely with the Hartian legal theory.[18] On the convention analysis, the leadership convention created by the people generates rules that together constitute the Hartian Rule of Recognition. First, the convention defines governmental offices and establishes limits on the powers and duties of these offices. These powers and duties constitute what I will call the "operational" rules of government. Second, the convention bestows on some of these offices the authority to command, which involves giving the officeholder the power to make a command that the people will believe they have a prima facie reason to obey simply because these officeholders have made it. Call these "authority-bestowing" rules; they entitle the officeholder to make directives that are binding on the people, and making them is actually part of the process of defining the offices of government. (What kind of authoritative directives a particular officeholder can make is determined by the leadership convention.) And finally, there are rules that specify the process of filling these offices, such that the person selected by the process is entitled to the office.

---

[17] Rawls (1971: 135) uses this phrase to describe the authority of the principles of justice upon which he believes rulers should act.

[18] The relationship between political analyses of the state and positivist and natural law theories of jurisprudence is badly underanalyzed. The discussion here is merely a start at such an analysis.

Creating the leadership convention involves generating these sorts of rules. Together they constitute an *impersonal* authority in the legal system, and I would argue that it is part of the conceptual analysis of the state that this impersonal authority exists. These rules are obligating not because they are themselves dictated by an authoritative officeholder (this puts the cart before the horse – these rules define what counts as an authoritative officeholder), but because they are accepted, via convention, by the people. Indeed, as Hart points out, these rules can exist and operate effectively even when there are many who are not terribly clear about the details of the authority of different offices of the government that the convention establishes. As long as there are some people who know the details, and these few are trusted by the rest to monitor the performance of any officeholder on the basis of these details, the convention can be said to be accepted by everyone (Hart, 1961: 111).

Let me stress again that on this approach to understanding the state's authority, the issue of whether the state is morally justifiable is irrelevant. This model offers an explanation of what the institution is, not a normative defense of it. If a moral theorist desires to pursue the justification of this institution, she will morally evaluate at the very least its use of negative sanctions to enforce its dictates, and perhaps also the moral legitimacy of the authority the state has over its subjects. If she believes the institution is morally justifiable, how would she defend it? She would do so using her favorite moral theory. Utilitarians, Kantians, and divine rights theorists will have different ways of defending (or attacking, if they choose) the state's legitimacy. And of course there are also contractarian ways of doing so. Contemporary philosophy has seen the rise of what I call contractarian moral theory, in which the notion of "what we could agree to" is understood to be central to evaluating actions, policies, and social institutions. There are a variety of contractarian moral theories that have been developed, and all of them are controversial. Embracing the Convention analysis of the state commits one to *none* of these views, because it is a nonnormative analysis. So of course, if one wants to legitimate the state one must supplement that analysis. Which theory one should choose, however, is a matter of independent philosophical assessment; there is no more reason to choose a contractarian defense of the state than to choose a contractarian defense of any institution or policy. One would only do so if one thought, on independent grounds, that this was the right moral theory to choose.

Summary

The Contractarian Explanation of the state can therefore be summarized as follows:

> The state is an institution whose primary role is to deter, prevent, and forestall conflict among people through the use of legislators, adjudicators, and coercive enforcers, and it is maintained by convention in which people are "in agreement" about what their government will be

and who will rule within it; specifically, it establishes the offices of government and procedures for filling those offices, and it grants punishment power to some of these officeholders. Participating in that convention means, at the very least not interfering with, and perhaps actively assisting in, the state's punishment activities – especially its formation and maintenance of punishment cadres. Hartian positivists will also argue that this convention is itself a complex set of rules entitling those selected by the procedures to hold office, obligating them to respect the terms of the office, and entitling them to make rules that are binding upon the people, so that it is an impersonal authority in the society by virtue of being accepted by the people.

The convention, once instituted, only exists for as long as the people maintain it, which involves their participation in the three punishment activities, and their continued acceptance and enforcement of the rules constituting it.

Note that the Convention Model presents the state as an institution whose primary role is to encourage cooperation and discourage conflict. For many this will be too limited a conception of the role of this institution, ignoring the way it may properly be engaged in the redistribution of assets in the name of justice, or in the education of its citizens, or in the promotion of cultural opportunities and endeavors. Contractarians can always argue for the addition of these duties to the state's agenda, but they would also argue that such additions do not change the fact that the state's power and authority to wield sanctions and issue binding commands are fundamental to understanding what it is, and how it is created and maintained.

What kind of relationship exists between the rulers and the ruled when the rulers' power is generated and maintained by convention? This is actually a complicated question, whose answer requires that we recognize that there is a hierarchy of what I will call (following Wittgenstein) "games" in a political society. First, there is the "political" game, in which the people are subordinated to government officeholders, who have the power to obligate them and to inflict sanctions upon them. So the relationship between people and ruler in this game is the relationship of a subordinate to a commander.

But second, there is the meta-game that creates and maintains this object-game, in which the people define and control the power of these offices and officeholders through their participation in the leadership convention. To understand the people's relationship with the rulers in this meta-game, let me use some of Locke's metaphors for a moment. Locke argued that creating the state involves the people becoming, after making contracts with one another, one unified entity – what he called a "political community." He then argued that the people, so understood, enter into contractual relations with the ruler. Of course literally there is rarely if ever such an explicit promisorial agreement between ruler and ruled, but if this language is metaphorical, it can be successfully cashed out using the Convention Model. That model places these parties in what I call an

Table 2.3. *The ruler–subject relationship*

Ruler	People	Ruler[a]	People[a]
	Keep in power	2	1
Govern according to terms of empowerment			
	Depose	4	3
	Depose	3	2
Ignore terms of empowerment			
	Keep in power	1	4

[a]Preferences for the outcome created after the people's second move (1 = highest, 4 = lowest).

"agency" relationship, which is not contractual either in nature or origin, but which is similar enough to actual agency relationships that are initiated by contract to make any metaphorical talk of a social contract between ruler and ruled forgivable. Just as a principal gives (usually via contract) a person known as her "agent" power to act by allowing her to wield a right belonging to the principal, so too do the subjects give a ruler political power through their generation of a leadership convention. And just as a principal can supervise the performance of her agent, and control the agent, by threatening to fire her if she does not use the principal's rights as the principal wished, so too can the people supervise the performance of the ruler-agent by threatening to depose him if he does not perform as the people wish. In Table 2.3 the game-theoretic structure of the ruler–subject relationship is presented.

Because the subjects in this game are able to make their move contingent upon how the ruler has moved, their possible moves, which are represented in the second column, are understood to be temporally posterior to the ruler's move. The numbers in the two right-hand columns correspond to the players' preferences for outcomes created by the combination of their possible moves.

This game is not a Prisoner's Dilemma, and hence does not require promises to bind ruler and people effectively. The ruler knows that if she rules against the people's wishes, they will fire her: Keeping her in power when she rules badly ranks lowest for them while their firing her when she rules badly ranks second highest for them. She also knows that if she rules well they will keep her "employed": Their keeping her employed when she rules well ranks highest for them; their firing her when she rules well ranks second lowest for them. So she has a choice between ruling well and staying in power (ranked second) or ruling poorly and being deposed (ranked last). So her best move is to rule well. But this is exactly the move by her that the people most want her to make. Their preferences and power in this situation force her to make a first move that allows them to achieve their favorite outcome, but the game is also such that she is able to retain power (a highly desirable outcome for her as long as she pleases them).

However, note that she is not completely powerless in this situation. Because the people need her to rule, she can be assured that her least favorite outcome (her doing the job and their deposing her) is also one of their least preferred outcomes. So she has enough power over them (at least for the time being) *because they need her* to secure a desirable outcome for herself (although not her most desirable outcome). Indeed, how well the agent needs to work is a matter of degrees: To stay employed she must work just well enough to make it more advantageous to the principal to keep her rather than incur the costs of firing her. (So in the end, the people who are the principal in this relationship will be unlikely to be able to demand and get exactly the performance from their ruler-agent that they would like.)

As I shall discuss in the next section, this analysis of the relationship between ruler and ruled is too simplistic, and I shall be discussing how to make it more sophisticated. However, one correction is easy to make, and making it allows us to cash out another Lockean metaphor. Insofar as the ruler's power is created through the generation of a convention, her power is the result of a lot of individuals determining that obeying the commands of only this ruler (in particular, her punishment commands) is rational. Hence a single entity called "the people" do not literally bestow or withdraw power; instead, whether or not a person rules depends upon a lot of individuals determining whether or not obedience or rebellion is in their best interest (where that interest is defined either by a moral or religious law or by their desires). Nonetheless, there is this much truth to the idea that the people institute and depose rulers: In order for individuals to institute a ruler, *each must coordinate (either explicitly or implicitly) with one another* on who the ruler shall be and what the scope of her legitimate areas of command are; and in order for individuals to depose a ruler, they must, once again, coordinate (either explicitly or implicitly) with one another on the idea that an alternative state of affairs would be better than the present state. So although Locke is saying something literally false when he says that the people contract with one another to form a unified political community that contracts with the ruler, nonetheless a state only exists when the individuals composing it are "in agreement" with one another, coordinating such that a leadership convention is established and maintained, and thereby becoming, collectively, the principal in an agency relationship with the officeholders.

One of the difficulties of coming to understand the state is that it is an enterprise constituted by two distinct games, in one of which the people are the controllers of the rulers, and in the other of which, the people are controlled by them. We are indebted to the social contract theorists for trying, albeit with metaphors, to make that double relationship clear.

Criticizing the Convention Model

How successful is this model? In this section I want to evaluate two criticisms someone could make of my claim that the social contract tradition generates an historically plausible, convention-based model of the state's creation and maintenance: First, one might object that the model, regardless of its success as an explanatory theory, is simply not generated by the social contract tradition; second, one might argue that it cannot be successful as an explanation because it is not historically plausible. I will discuss each of these criticisms in turn.

The Convention Model and the social contract tradition

To build the Convention Model out of Hobbes's and Locke's political writings using the resources of contemporary game theory strikes many as anachronistic at best, deeply distorting at worst. Are the language and tools that I use to state the model too dissimilar to the language and tools of the traditional contractarians to allow me to claim that it is nonetheless their model?

I do not believe so. We must resist the temptation to treat philosophical figures as museum pieces. Instead we should dissect, analyze, explicate, and respond to their arguments in order to see how far those arguments are right. Of course it is anachronistic to read game theory back into traditional contractarian writings – that is not the point. The issue to be decided is whether or not we learn anything of value about Locke's and Hobbes's understanding of the state if we do so, and I think we do. These philosophers were groping for ways of understanding the state not as the creation of God, not as ordained by nature, but as a human creation. The Convention Model explains how this is possible, and in the process, preserves two central ideas in the tradition, first, that there is a kind of agreement among the people that explains why the state exists, and second (although this point was contested by Hobbes), that there is an agreement between the people and the ruler setting out the terms of his rule. The first agreement is, on this model, a convention rather than an explicit promisorial agreement, whose generation could take many forms. The second agreement, on this model, is really an agency relationship between the people (who create and maintain the ruler's power for certain purposes) and the ruler (who must use that power to satisfy them or be deposed).

Still, I have made substantial revisions in the traditional contract argument by replacing talk of contracts with talk of conventions and agency relationships. I have argued that these revisions are consistent with and even required by the presuppositions of the traditional contractarians' arguments. By making these revisions have I vindicated the contractarian argument as an explication of the state, or have I refuted it?

Perhaps it really doesn't matter how one answers this question: What is important is the model itself and not its philosophical pedigree. Nonetheless, I tend to regard my analysis as a vindication of the contractarian argument. If one shows that the premisses of a political argument require a different conceptual representation of the state than the representation given by the original users of that argument, then it is appropriate to say that the revisionist conceptual representation has been implicit in the argument all along (albeit unacknowledged by its previous users). It is because the preferences of the people in the traditional contractarians' state of nature establish battle-of-the-sexes dilemmas rather than Prisoner's Dilemmas that it becomes right to say that, on a contractarian's view, the creation of government requires the generation of a convention.

Hume saw himself as an opponent of the social contract argument because he endorsed ideas which this analysis incorporates. But I would argue that he should be seen only as an opponent of the traditional contractarian's persistent use of the idea of contract, an idea that my analysis shows is not implicit in the argument itself and that, if inserted into it, damages the argument's operation as an explanation of a ruler's political power. Indeed, I would argue that both Hume and I are "revisionists" only in the sense that we are revising, and improving upon, the standard interpretation of the social contract argument.

Is the model right?

Critics may worry about the extent to which the Model can be empirically verified. I think such worries have merit, but before I explain why, I want to show that it does have some real explanatory power.

First, do the preferences of real people match the coordination-game preferences of Locke's or Hobbes's people on the question of whether or not to enter civil society? This is an empirical question to be answered by empirical study, but given that these philosophers show why moral, religious, and self-interested motivations give rise either to pure or conflict-ridden coordination game preferences on the question of instituting the state, this suggests that a wide range of real people, with any of these motivations, would nonetheless have preferences that fit the Convention Model.

This model can also be used to illuminate the actual reasoning processes of people who are considering whether or not to rebel against their government. Consider Gregory Kavka's intriguing discussion of what he calls the paradox of revolution. In Kavka's words, the paradox goes as follows:

exploited citizenry are apparently in a multiparty prisoner's dilemma situation with respect to participating in a mass revolt. Collectively they have the power to overthrow their oppressors, and would probably be better off if they did so. But an individual's participation in a revolt is dangerous and will have only a minute effect on the prospect of the revolt succeeding, while the individual can expect to reap most of the benefits of a successful revolt (should one occur) without participating. Hence, rational individuals will not participate, and mass revolts of rational citizens will never occur even against tyrannical, repressive, or exploitive regimes. This odd conclusion – that the rationality of the members of a society prevents them from overthrowing a despised government – is called *the paradox of revolution*. (1986: 267)

Kavka contends that the paradox shows that people are in a multiparty Prisoner's Dilemma (PD) with respect to the question of revolution, and as all students of this dilemma know, rational actions by rational people will lead to a suboptimal outcome in a PD – in this case, the outcome of continued submission. But in stating the paradox in argument form, Kavka does not explicitly mention any game-theoretic situation. He presents it as follows:

(1) Rational individuals act so as to maximize expected payoffs.
(2) In a potentially revolutionary situation, the expected costs of participation are higher than the expected costs of nonparticipation, and there are no sufficiently compensating expected benefits of participation.
(3) Therefore, rational individuals in a potentially revolutionary situation will not participate in a revolution. (1986: 268)

Of course, the argument cannot establish that revolution will never occur, because, as Kavka notes, people sometimes act irrationally, and thus irrational motives might explain revolutionary activity throughout history. Moreover, "the possibility of others irrationally joining a revolt may influence the cost-benefit analysis of *rational* potential revolutionaries" (268). With this in mind, Kavka proposes what he calls the "dynamic-maximizing" solution:

rational agents' expected utility calculations about participation in revolution will *change* as they observe others joining the revolutionary struggle. In particular, as a first approximation we would expect agents' estimates of the probability of the revolution succeeding to go up, and their estimates of the probability of being punished for taking part in the revolt to go down, as the number of people they observe taking part in the revolt increases. These changes in probability will in turn raise the expected benefits associated with participation (since the receipt of many such benefits is contingent upon the revolt succeeding) and decrease the expected costs (e.g., the risk of being punished for participating). It is also possible that the intrinsic payoffs of participation, such as the pleasure of taking part in a mass enterprise, and the intrinsic costs of nonparticipation, such as the guilt one may feel over being a free-rider, will increase as the number of others participating increases (273–4).[19]

So the idea is that as confederacies enlarge, more and more people will find it rational to participate. In particular, any individual will join the revolution when his or her "revolution-participation threshold" is reached. "Whether a revolution will occur will depend upon the distribution of revolution-participating thresholds among the members of a population" (Kavka, 1986: 274). It is possible that a population will have thresholds distributed such that revolution is essentially impossible, but it may also have thresholds distributed such that it is inevitable.

I like Kavka's solution to this paradox, but I want to argue that it is only a solution because in fact the citizenry are *not* in a multiparty prisoner's dilemma with respect to the question of revolution. This should be evident because, in a real PD, it doesn't matter how many of my fellow players are disposed to choose the cooperative action – *I* am still rational to refrain from cooperation. The fact that Kavka's solution has it that people will find cooperation in the revolution rational with increasing numbers of rebels shows that they are in a different kind of game.

As I have argued at length elsewhere, problems can seem "PD-like" even though they have a different game theoretic structure (Hampton, 1987), and that is what is going on here. In fact, parties are in a coordination game with respect

---

[19] Kavka proposes three possible solutions to the paradox. The first two are in Kavka's eyes problematic, and he is most pleased with the third. Hence this is the one I concentrate on here.

to the question of revolution. Just as creating a state involves solving a host of potentially conflict-ridden coordination problems, so too does changing it. Imagine that I am a disgruntled citizen who would like a new ruler. What reasons do I have for maintaining what I take to be a bad convention? Consider the reasons I have for maintaining any convention, for example, the convention to drive on the right. If there is no law requiring me to respect this convention I will respect it anyway if I believe, (a) that I am in a coordination dilemma; (b) that in fact driving on the right is the conventional solution to that dilemma; (c) that it is a convention that enables the community to achieve a desirable coordination equilibrium, so that it furthers the interest of those in the coordination dilemma; and most important, (d) there is no other convention on a different coordination equilibrium that it is rational for me to pursue (given the costs and benefits of doing so) by (in part) not obeying the convention. Note reason d presupposes that by acting so as to respect a convention, I also help in a very small way to maintain it through my respect for it.

These four considerations are also central to explaining why and when a citizen has reason to obey her ruler. I have reason to respect a leadership convention about who should rule, and thus obey the ruler, when (a') I am in a (conflict-ridden) coordination dilemma about who should rule; (b') in fact this ruler is the conventional solution to that problem; (c') it is a convention that enables us to realize a coordination equilibrium, so that it furthers the interests of those in the coordination dilemma; and (d') there is no other leadership convention that would realize a different coordination equilibrium whose adoption I believe it rational for me to pursue (given the costs and benefits of doing so) by (in part) not respecting this convention. Again, this last point presupposes that when I act so as to respect the leadership convention and obey the ruler's commands, particularly his punishment orders, I help in a small way to maintain this convention and keep him in power.

Now what happens when a subject believes a' and b', but denies c' – judging the convention to be bad either because it fails to realize a coordination equilibrium at all (so that, barring exorbitant costs, changing should be Pareto efficient for everyone), or because there is a better coordination equilibrium available to the group (although perhaps not better for everyone). In either case he concludes that people have made a mistake, and would be better off, on the whole, deposing the present leader and replacing her with another ruler. He therefore wishes to take from her the authority to rule which this bad convention grants her. If they come to agree that they have a better alternative (so that for each of them d' is no longer true), then (as we discussed above) neither he nor they will believe they should obey her, and will rebel. But if they do not agree with him, then his unilateral action in support of another candidate will be useless. *In fact* in this situation, a convention, albeit a bad one, does exist. And it is this fact that he is forced to take into account in his calculations. He might still draw the conclusion that he should obey the ruler if, for moral or self-interested reasons, the consequences of acting to change the convention will be worse than the consequences of acquiescing in the bad convention. He may make this judgment when he finds the present government bad but believes (given what he knows) that so few others agree with him that an attempt to change the convention by refusing to obey the ruler would be futile, or when he believes that they do agree with him that the present ruler is bad but disagree among themselves about what convention should replace it.[20]

However, there is one other reason why someone might obey a convention even when he judges it to be bad, and that is when there is no common knowledge of how the government is evaluated by the citizenry generally. Kavka gives a model for how this kind of situation inhibits revolution in his Paradox of Perfect Tyranny. As Kavka explains, a tyrant who is universally disliked can, paradoxically, remain in power, when the situation is such that the people obey the tyrant out of fear of one another. That is, each citizen is obedient

out of fear that some of his fellow citizens would answer the ruler's call to punish him if he were not. So citizen A obeys out of fear of citizens B, C, et al., B obeys out of fear of A, C et al., and so on. In this situation, the beliefs of rational citizens that their fellows will punish them for not following the ruler's orders constitute a network of interlocking mutual expectations, a "net of fear," that provides each citizen with a sufficient motive of obedience (Kavka, 1986: 257).

Kavka's remarks here fit with my analysis, given earlier, of sovereign empowerment through the citizenry's decision to obey or respect his punishment commands. This is, in effect, the decision by which people generate the leadership convention. Once in place, that convention yields considerable power for the ruler. But it is always power that, in the last analysis, can be traceable to the decisions of the individuals who are participating in the punishment process. Thus if the frail and universally disliked ruler can inhibit the passing of information among the disgruntled citizenry, their knowledge of the convention's existence, and their uncertainty about receiving support from others, will likely make it irrational for them to risk opposing the ruler.

In this situation the people are "mastered" by their ruler, despite the fact that they empower him by their obedience to him. To be *mastered* is *to be subject to the use of coercion in a way that disables one from participating in the process of creating or changing a leadership convention.* Because there are degrees of disablement, there are degrees of mastery. The use of coercion against blacks in South Africa, against left-wing Chileans by Pinochet, and against Tibetans in China, is substantial enough to inhibit such activity severely, rendering these people mastered to an extreme degree. But techniques of mastery are present in all Western democracies, as anyone whose name is on file at the FBI knows. A ruler has, and must have, significant coercive power over her citizens. That

---

[20] Hobbes argued that it was against reason for a subject to rebel against her government, but I have argued (Hampton, 1986; ch. 8, 9) that the premises of his argument commit him to the rationality of rebellion in certain circumstances. That discussion runs along roughly the same lines as the discussion here.

power makes her disproportionately more powerful than any of her subjects (or even fairly large groups of those subjects), and she may be able to use this power to disable, partially or totally, one or more of them from participating in or changing the leadership convention. And it is so tempting for rulers to do so, that there probably never has been (nor ever will be) a regime in which such disabling doesn't go on to some degree or other.

Even worse, a portion of the population may approve of the mastery of the rest of the population and actively support their ruler's use of power to disable that portion from participation in the leadership convention. Those who are disabled may even be in the majority if the ruler and his supporters are clever enough to keep important technology from them, rendering them badly unequal (e.g., in South Africa).

So there are really two forms of political domination that our discussion has revealed: the domination of a master, and the domination of a "hired" protection agency. The contractarian story, which presupposes that every person involved in the creation of the state is the equal of every other, results only in the creation of the second form of domination. But if, as seems true in the real world, equality cannot be presupposed because of technological (if not natural) superiority, then mastery can and does exist. Indeed, insofar as the very empowerment of a ruler destroys equality by making her more powerful than those who are ruled by her, the seeds of political mastery are planted in the very act of generating a leadership convention.

A pure form of mastery in a human community is very unlikely. Given human frailty and technological limitations (Superman and James Bond movies to the contrary) no ruler can hope to master people all by himself: He needs supporters to do so, and this means there must be at least an agency relationship between him and his supporters. In this sense Pinochet, Stalin, and Idi Amin, despite their mastery of subject populations, have all been agents; the power relationship within the ruling clique supporting them fits the contractarian's agency analysis of a political regime.

On the other hand, a pure form of agency seems just as unlikely. Aside from the fact that a portion of the population may approve of the mastery of others, and actively support their ruler's use of power to disable the rest from participating in the leadership convention, a ruler is always able to take advantage of the fact that the punishment power granted to him makes him disproportionately more powerful than any of his subjects (or even fairly large groups of those subjects) in order to partially or totally disable one or more of them from participating in or changing the leadership convention. For better or worse, when people create a state, they create a monster, over which it may not be easy to maintain control.[21]

Given both the reality and the limitations of technological dominance, the

---

[21] Thus many polities (e.g., the United States) rely on separation of powers to prevent any one individual or office from achieving significant degrees of mastery.

explanatory truth about political regimes would seem to be that they are mixtures, to various degrees, of the agency and mastery forms of domination. So what the contractarian "explains" with his convention model is only one aspect of our political reality: that is, the extent to which rulers have power, and perhaps also authority, through some or all of the subject's participation in a leadership convention. The Convention Model fails to accommodate the reality of the nonagency aspects of subjects' relationship with the regimes that rule them.

But even if contractarians have overemphasized the agency aspect of our political life, let me conclude by speculating that this may be because they have intuitively sensed that probably only the agency aspect can be morally justified. The Convention Model gives us the form of domination we would create if we were and always remained equal, and even as that state of equality is more ideal than fact, so too is the kind of political regime it generates.

References

Anscombe, Elizabeth. (1981). "On the Source of the Authority of the State." In Elizabeth Anscombe, *Collected Papers,* vol. 3: *Ethics, Religion and Politics.* Minneapolis: University of Minneapolis Press.

Atiyah, P. S. (1981). *An Introduction to the Law of Contract.* 3d ed. Oxford: Clarendon Press.

Axelrod, Robert. (1984). *The Evolution of Cooperation.* New York: Basic Books.

Dworkin, Ronald. (1977). "Model of Rules I." In Ronald Dworkin, *Taking Rights Seriously.* Cambridge, Mass.: Harvard University Press.

(1974). "The Original Contract." In Norman Daniels (Ed.), *Reading Rawls.* New York: Basic Books.

Green, Leslie. (1988). *The Authority of the State.* Oxford: Clarendon Press.

Hampton, Jean. (1987). "Free-Rider Problems in the Production of Collective Goods," *Economics and Philosophy* 3: 245–73.

(1986). *Hobbes and the Social Contract Tradition.* Cambridge: Cambridge University Press.

Hart, H. L. A. (1961). *The Concept of Law.* Oxford: Clarendon Press.

Hobbes, Thomas. (1968 [1651]). *Leviathan,* edited by C. B. MacPherson (using the 1651 "Head" edition). Harmondsworth: Penguin.

Hume, David. (1978 [1739–40]). *A Treatise of Human Nature.* Edited by L. A. Selby-Bigge, revised by P. H. Nidditch. Oxford: Clarendon Press.

Kavka, Gregory. (1986). *Hobbesian Moral and Political Theory.* Princeton, N.J.: Princeton University Press.

Lewis, David. (1969). *Convention.* Cambridge, Mass.: Harvard University Press.

Locke, John. (1960 [1690]). *Two Treatises of Government,* edited by Peter Laslett. Cambridge: Cambridge University Press.

Luce, R., Duncan, and Howard Raiffa. (1957). *Games and Decisions.* New York: Wiley.

Nelson, Alan. (1986). "Explanation and Justification in Political Philosophy," *Ethics* 97: 154–76.

Nozick, Robert (1974). *Anarchy, State and Utopia.* New York: Basic Books.

Rawls, John. (1971). *A Theory of Justice.* Cambridge, Mass.: Harvard University Press.

Raz, Joseph. (1979). *The Authority of Law.* Oxford: Clarendon Press.

Tönnies, Ferdinand. (1928). *Elements of Law.* Cambridge: Cambridge University Press.

3.   Marx's two logics of capitalism

William James Booth

Writing at the end of the twentieth century, we hardly need to be reminded that much of the conceptual heart of Marx's political economy is now a dead letter. Ideas such as the labor theory of value, surplus value, and labor as its unique source have been consigned to the archives of the history of economic thought. Yet at the same time there has been a recognition of another dimension to Marx's political economy, one that moves at a different level than the concepts just enumerated. Here Marx emerges as one of the founding figures trying to think through the project of a political economy: to set out the relationship between state, capital, and labor; to see in this economic formation not merely the production of goods and services, but the making of the entire mesh of social relations and more basically still to chart an economic approach to human behavior generally. It is in the light of an understanding of that level of Marx's work that we can, I think, grasp for example Robert Bates's recent call for a return to Marxian political economy as well as earlier (and perhaps more grudging) expressions of some (modest) affinity with this or related elements of his project, e.g., those of Gary Becker and Douglass North (Bates, 1990: 48–9, 51; Becker, 1976: 9; North, 1981: 61). It is also this very same dimension that has led to critiques of Marx, critiques that tend to include him among those seeking an economic explanation of human action as well as according primacy to the economic sphere in his account of society (Baudrillard, 1975; Castoriadis, 1978; Dumont, 1977: 111, 169–70). Marx, that is, is taken to treat humans as *homo economicus,* on a market model of rationalizing, motivations, and so on, or to give too great a centrality to scarcity, needs, and production. I will here put to one side those critiques, not because their challenges are not serious, but because there is another issue to be settled first. And that is that in the governing traditions of Marxism, Marx is to be sure seen as a (or *the*) founder of the political economic approach, though of a special kind: committed to a teleological theory of history, in which capitalism has its role and, embedded within that secularized Hegelian story, a theory of capitalism virtually without a subject, that is, one in which collective actors move across the historical-social stage, their scripts in hand. More recently, efforts have been made to recover a "choice-theoretic" approach from Marx's analyses. Some, such as John Roemer's work, are conducted on a grand level of theorizing about class and exploitation; others are more narrowly focused, for example Raymond Boudon's discussion of perverse effects (Boudon, 1979: 202ff; Roemer, 1982a). It is within the horizon of that debate over the competing logics of Marx's explanations of capitalism that this paper moves.

In this essay, then, I want to map out what I take to be the two logics of Marx's explanation of capitalism. The one is a functionalist mode, committed to (among other things) an account of capitalism in which persons are agents, strictly speaking, of lawlike, end-driven processes working behind their backs: a variant of the invisible hand story, literal (or more so than the Smithian original), perverse and with a vengeance. The other is an account that explains capitalism in the light of optimizing choices made within a set of institutional and endowment constraints. Both logics are engaged, in the first instance, as modes of explanation. But they are also manifestly bound up with normative concerns, and indeed the latter almost certainly drive (in some considerable measure, though unnecessarily) twentieth-century Marxism's preference for the functionalist mode. As we shall see presently, the textual evidence from Marx is ambiguous and oscillates between functionalist and intentional explanations. This essay is in part an effort to sort out and make sense of those competing logics that do battle at the core of Marx's explanation of capitalism. Second, it is an attempt to read out the normative/critical threads interwoven in that explanatory project. And finally, proceeding from a reading of Marx's intentional logic I want to sketch how this reveals still more fundamental problems in his understanding of capitalism.

I

Let me begin with the most familiar Marxian picture, one that rests upon a basic theoretical syntax of a determinist/latent functionalist type (Boudon, 1979: 190, 270, 248, 252).[1] Here I want to extend the analysis of the range of functionalist explanation in Marx beyond its traditional loci, namely the theory of history and the analysis of the role of the state and other institutions in stabilizing capitalism, into the very heart of Marx's project, his political economy. This logic also has a powerful, though indirect, impact on our understanding of the normative component of Marx's writings inasmuch as it sets out one way of grasping a sort of unfreedom peculiar, he thought, to capitalist society. And it shows just how great a challenge to plain text Marxism is mounted by those who seek to recast its explanatory apparatus along methodological individualist lines. For if the dominant logic of Marxism is the functionalist one, rational choice Marxists appear to be led into a critique of both its methodological and normative core.

---

[1] In Booth 1989, I gave an exclusively functionalist reading of Marx. The present essay represents a rethinking of that argument and section I of this chapter is adapted from that article.

The argument grounding this first logic, then, proceeds from the observation that Marx's explanation of the capitalist economy (and his critique of that society) draws upon a basic theoretical syntax (determinist/latent functionalist) adapted to explanatory purposes and to critical/normative tasks. By way of a first cut at characterizing this syntax, we might say that Marx's work moves within what Raymond Boudon has called a determinist paradigm: explanations of human actions as being determined exclusively by anterior (logically or chronologically) events in which the goals/intentions of the subjects have little or no explicative value (Boudon, 1979: 237, 270). When I describe Marx as a determinist I mean that in its foundations his explanation of the capitalist economy does not accord significant place to choice, individual purposes or goals. These phenomena – intentionality or purposiveness – are said rather to be the efflux of an undergirding causal order in the sense that persons are assumed to be the agents, the creatures, of that order and its functionaries. The lawlike statements that express this causal order and that constitute the explanation of that society do not have intentional, microlevel foundations. There is, in brief, a causal chain anterior to the behaviors, intentions, or goals of individuals and only insight into that anterior world allows (according to Marx) an adequate theoretical expression of the phenomena.

To sharpen that broad description of the basic syntax of Marx's analysis, we can add that he worked within a determinist paradigm of a predominantly functionalist sort. For my purposes in this essay, it is not necessary to enter into the thicket of debates about the value of functional explanation in the human sciences or those concerning ways of reformulating it so as to meet its critics' objections (Cohen, 1982, 1978; Elster, 1983). A rudimentary characterization of functionalism will suffice: "The latent functions (if any) of an institution or behaviour explain the presence of that institution or behaviour"; this latent function is postulated without the need to invoke a purposive actor; last, that there is a beneficiary group in relation to which the thing or behavior to be explained is said to be functional. These functional processes Elster designates "objective teleology," a phrase that places in sharper focus two central features of explanations of this type: (a) The idea of the systemic goal-oriented functional process is at the center of the explanation of the behavior and properties of the moments of the process, hence objective teleology, rather than a manifest function in which the actors' intentions are the major explanatory factor (Elster, 1983: 55–58, 1982; Merton, 1957: 60–1). And (b): The end (the beneficial result for the postulated beneficiary group – typically, the total social system) is the cause of the events (the effective causes) that produce it.

If we allow for some considerable looseness of fit between Marx's method and any more tightly specified subtype of that paradigm, we may conclude that there is a presence within his political economy of something like latent functionalist explanation (Przeworski, 1985b; Van Parijs, 1981: 180–3). I say "something like" here for two reasons. First, apart from one brief (and for our purposes, not very valuable) discussion in the *Grundrisse* and scattered lines elsewhere there is no sustained, explicit discussion of his basic principles of explanation. In particular, what is absent is an elaboration of the sort of causal laws that Marx is invoking in his explanation of capitalism; this we are left to tease out of his applied analysis. Second, and allowing for the moment what will be demonstrated in the following pages, Marx's functionalist explanation of the capitalist economy has some markedly unusual features, when measured against the standard rudiments of such explanations outlined above. These features can be summarized thus: Although capitalist production is an unintentional, purposive (objective teleological) process, the goal or endpoint cannot without qualification be described as a beneficial result for a beneficiary group. Focusing on Marx's account of the internal workings of this economy, it can be said that its laws, while they do yield short-term benefits (crudely, profits) for some capitalists, nevertheless drive toward its weakening and collapse or, from a different perspective, they lead to a point at which that particular economic organization ceases to be the optimal form for society's productive activity. Unlike traditional functional explanations of social phenomena, which tend to point to the stabilizing effects of the institution or practice to be explained, Marx's analysis of capital's laws portrays them both as constantly revolutionizing (e.g., technological innovation and the dissolution of inherited social forms) and as driving toward their own (and their "functionaries") demise.

This process is perplexing, especially in its third element: It seems at once unintentional, purposive, *and* self-destructive. One possible way of clarifying this is to suggest that what seems perverse in the internal valuation of capitalism appears as functional, in the more conventional sense, when it is nested in the overarching functional explanation of history. Here, for example, the negative consequences of the technical innovation "demanded" by the capital process – that is, the increasing organic composition of capital and the falling rate of profit – give way to an account that rests instead on the progressive capacity of improved technology to free persons from the domination of nature and the necessity of drudge labor. In other words, by shifting the locus of the beneficiary group and by asserting a different set of benefits to be realized – from, let us say, capitalists or all the members of capitalist society, to humankind and from surplus value to the material prerequisites of human emancipation from nature – it is possible for the laws of the capitalist economy to be understood as one necessary episode in a larger functional story, that of the movement of history, having its own telos and laws. Needless to say, this alternative reading, while it may make these claims more consistent on one level, also raises still more troubling questions about the teleological aspects of Marx's theory of history and the way in which the latter permeate (to its detriment) much of his social analysis.

Indirect evidence for the objective teleological type of explanation that we have attributed to Marx is to be found in the analogies he invoked when describing capitalism. These are often drawn not from the world of the market, of contract and exchange, in short from spheres in which intentional explanation would appear to be most appropriate but from the study of natural organisms and of automated processes in the world of production. Part of the reason for doing so was no doubt to attack the implicit claims of the contract or market vocabulary concerning the freedom of the agents whose behavior was being analyzed. But it is equally clear that these analogues are meant to indicate certain lawlike characteristics that they share with capitalism and, consequently, certain important explanatory features that their sciences have in common with that of the capitalist economy. Thus, for example, Marx often refers to the "life process" of capital, its "metabolism" and compares its circulation to that of blood in the body. And he praises the Physiocrats for seeing the "bourgeois forms of production" as "physiological" and thus "independent of anyone's will or of politics. . . " (Marx, 1963: 44). This same pattern is also to be found in Marx's other dominant metaphor for capitalism, the automated factory.

The factory viewed as a microcosm of capitalist society differs from the latter in a number of important ways for Marx: Within its walls, compulsion takes the form not of the "silent" pressure of economic laws but of despotism, direct control with a human visage, the capitalist or his managers. Moreover, its workings are the efflux of a consciously planned process whereas those of the broader circuit of capital are not (Marx, 1977b: 476–7; 1976c: 287–8). Nevertheless Marx found the parallel between certain features of the production process and of the surrounding society so irresistible that he abstracted from the former's specific properties in order to draw out what he considered to be crucial features of capitalism. "The power of activity which creates value by value existing for-itself. . . . is posited, in production resting on machinery, as the character of the production process itself, including its material movements" (Marx, 1973: 693). In the machine workshop, Marx writes, the process of production is objective, a "vast automaton" whose governing subject is not labor but the "self-acting" mover, the steam engine (Marx, 1977b: 501–2, 544–5). It is the workings of the various machines, driven by another self-powered machine, that determine the activity of the human beings who are absorbed as "conscious organs" into the stages of the machine's operations. The automatic character of this process, the fact that the objective process determines both the relations between and behaviors of persons – in short, that purposiveness belongs to things, not humans – these are the traits of machine production that, Marx believes, make that process a visible exemplar of a broader end-driven social process, M-C-M′ (where M stands for money, C for commodity widely defined, i.e., something exchanged; and M′ for valorized money, the terminus and purpose of the economic cycle), whose "automatic subject" is value. One technical point of clarification: M-C-M′ denotes the valorization process in terms of money rather than underlying values and for that reason it was, for Marx, only an approximation of the capital circuit that nevertheless pointed to the underlying structure and purpose of that economic formation (Marx, 1977b: 255. For limitations of the M-C-M′ formula, see 1981b: 109–43, and 1977b: 266).

Marx's miniature portrait of the human community in the factory suggests the method appropriate for analyzing it and, by extension, for comprehending the society that it, in important respects, mirrors. In the machine workshop, the major determining factors are the characteristics of the machines and of their relationship to one another. The human beings act as their servants or guardians, but the motor force, the linkages, and so forth, are all those of the machines themselves. This community has only the appearance of being human; it is, in fact, a community governed by machines with persons as their agents. The workings of the system, including those involving its human inputs, can best be understood, Marx writes, "objectively," as a process "viewed in and for itself" and analyzed into its constitutive phases (Marx, 1977b: 501). The science that understands such a system will be "objective" because the "subjective" element, the humans involved as producers in its workings, plays little or no role in determining the nature of the process (Marx, 1977b: 502). The laws of nature shape the design of the automated process and expressed in the form of science they are the means by which it is to be understood. For my immediate purpose, it is sufficient to make the point that a community (the automated factory) whose laws are those of the objective elements and relations of machine production is not usefully studied by a method that has as its centerpiece concepts of the intentionality of the actors in the process. Rather, since the phenomena of the factory exhibit key features of natural phenomena generally, something like a natural (and not a human) science provides the proper set of analytical instruments. And so too with the science of capitalism: its laws, those of the M-C-M' circuit, are "material," which means not the result of the will, and purposive without that purpose being the result of design. The political economy of bourgeois society presents its analysis as one of objective processes and in doing so it speaks accurately, or so Marx argues in this variant of his logic of capitalism (Marx, 1977b: 169; 1975b: 227; 1963: 44).

"In all forms of society," Marx writes, "there is one specific kind of production which predominates over the rest. . . . It is a general illumination which bathes all the other colors and modifies their particularity" (Marx, 1973: 106–7). M-C-M', which is the shorthand for that "specific kind of production," captures the *differentia specifica* of capitalism and indicates the sort of explanation appropriate for such a world – one that is "objective" or "material" (i.e., not the product of the will) and purposive, that is driven by a goal or end. We should now take a closer look at some of the ways in which that theory is specified. Consider Marx's analysis of time and production under capitalism. The reason that capitalism is driven to economize on time is that (according to Marx's labor theory of value) M' in fact amounts to embodied surplus labor time, and it is the expansion of that time that is the driving purpose of capitalist production. There are, in Marx's account, two basic ways in which the growth of surplus labor time can be ensured: absolutely (the extension of the working day or the intensification of the labor process) or relatively (the introduction of technology). It is of course true that both techniques are the creations of human beings, of capitalists who seek to compel their workers to longer hours in the factory or who select improved technology for their physical plant. These individuals act, Marx says, "consciously" and "willingly" – they want profits, choose to put pressure on their labor force, or buy technology. Some select mistaken strategies and fail;

others are more prescient and succeed. But are these conscious and willing agents what they appear on the surface to be, that is, actors whose behaviors can be accounted for by invoking intentional-level explanations?

The answer drawn from Marx's first logic of capitalism would be no. The capitalist is an agent, the "bearer" of the economic laws of capital: "The *functions* fulfilled by the capitalist are no more than the functions of capital – viz. the valorization of value by absorbing living labor – executed *consciously* and *willingly*" (Marx, 1977a: 989, 1051; see also 1980: 1604). The actual subject or moving force of the process is capital itself, a conclusion that is scarcely surprising in light of the preceding analysis of the M-C-M' circuit (Marx, 1977b: 255). One of the consequences of viewing persons not as a causally central part of the explanation of capitalism but as being among its derivative or determined features is that in his explanation of absolute surplus value, Marx makes it clear that the story does not lie in the good or bad will of the capitalists, who compel longer working days, but in capital's laws, which drive its agents toward the production of expanded surplus labor time (Marx, 1977b: 381). And so too in the case of the introduction of labor-saving technology (relative surplus value): Technological innovation is the consequence of the capital circuit's governing purpose, the maximization of surplus labor time. The capitalist's purpose is, however, not directly the increase of surplus labor time or surplus value (the internal purpose of M-C-M') and it certainly is not the promotion of the growth of human productive powers (the purpose of the historical process). Yet he is, Marx argues, an "agent" of both though he himself aims at neither (Marx, 1981a: 373; 1963: 270). The title of "agent," or "functionary" as Marx also calls the capitalist, suggests his necessary *and* subordinate role in the process: necessary in that he is the executor, the implementor; subordinate in that he is not the legislator, but acts in obedience to another, governing law.

Here are two questions that we might put to this thesis. First, what is the causal mechanism by which that dominant (systemic) end or purpose is achieved? Second, what is the mechanism (if any) that transforms the objective purposiveness of the capital process into behaviors suitable to its realization? I separate these two questions here (though as we shall see presently they are not distinguished by Marx) because on one evolutionary account of the workings of the capitalist economy, it is possible to model that economy in such a way that the motivations of individual actors are left out altogether: The survival conditions of the system cause that system to "adopt" successful players, even if those players have met the selection criteria not through motivated or purposeful adaptation but through chance or luck (Alchian and Demsetz, 1972: 213–14). The system drives toward ever more profitable firms by adopting those that meet its criteria and winnowing out those that do not, irrespective of whether those firms consciously set out to meet the selection criteria. In Marx's analysis, competition fills both roles: It is the source both of motivated adaptation to the circuit's requirements and of ensuring that among the adaptive strategies chosen by actors, only those that meet its criteria will survive.

The capitalist, in this story, need not be (and typically is not) conscious of the underlying, purposive circuit of value. Rather his goal is profit, and labor-saving technology offers him the prospect of selling his goods below their market price. For those less innovative than this capitalist, competition forces the new technology upon them since without it they will be unable to meet the lower prices of their more intrepid brethren. Survival and growth through expanded profits thus come to be the motivation for innovation in a competitive market. Buying cheap and selling high in the search for expanded profits may well be what directly determine the capitalist's behavior but lying behind these phenomena is, in Marx's political economy, the expansion of surplus value. The latter, the determining telos of the circuit, is most likely not visible to the capitalist, but the mechanism of competition reshapes that invisible tie between surplus value and profit (essence and appearance) into a motivating force for the capitalist who fulfills his role as agent by unwittingly advancing the former goal while consciously aiming only at the latter. Relatedly (for Marx), competition serves to weed out maladapted profit-expanding strategies and in so doing to ensure increasing rates of surplus value – that is, to promote its objective, regardless of whether optimization (or that type of optimization) is something sought by the actors involved.

What I wish to do now is to use a simplified version of natural selection explanations of behavior in order to show how Marx could embed the idea of market competition (which, on its face, seems much more amenable to individual actor/intentional types of explanation) in this variant of his logic of capitalism. Such evolutionary/natural selection analogies have long been attractive to economic theorists, Marxist and non-Marxist.[2] In the preceding pages of this essay, I have suggested one reason why Marx would be drawn to models of explanation taken from fields in which agents, their purposes and strategies are not granted a fundamental causal part in the account of the phenomena. That is, he sought to find principles adequate to the explanation of a society whose governing economic process operated in a lawlike manner independent of the wills of its agents. One critic of the use of this type of analogy in economic science has suggested, indirectly, another possible motivation of Marx's. She writes that the appeal of evolutionary analogies stems in part from "a persistent yearning to discover 'laws' that determine the outcome of human actions, probably because the discovery of such laws would rid the social sciences of the uncertainties and complexities that arise from the apparent 'free-will' of man. . . ." (Penrose, 1952: 818). As it stands, this proposition is not accurate in relation to Marx. Nonetheless in its juxtaposition of free will and economic laws it does intimate what in Marx is the intertwined nature of the functionalist explanation of the capitalist economy and the critique of that society. We shall return to the normative implications of Marx's functionalism at the conclusion of this section; for the present, let us see how the natural selection analogy can be used to make sense of the Marxian idea of competition as a moment within an overarching economic process.

[2] See Nelson and Winter, 1982: 33–45.

The immediate manifestations of natural selection occur at the individual level; for example, a fight between two male animals for the privilege of mating with the female (Dawkins, 1976. The following story draws freely on Dawkins's work). What motivates these creatures has nothing to do with the survival of genes or of the species. Most likely it is their pleasure, the tangible, sexual rewards of dominance within the herd. But their actions cannot be fully explained if what is focused on is their individual intentions. It is not a full explanation because the animals are "survival machines," vehicles for genes 'seeking' to increase their number in future gene pools. Their combat, and the immediate purposes that drive them in that behavior, serve another, determining purpose: Fighting sorts out winner and loser genes and, over time, washes the latter out of the pool by denying them reproduction. This battle is thus one regulating moment, key but subordinate, both in the world and in explanatory power. Similarly with Marx's analysis of competition: At the level of history, it is an element in the broader (teleological) process of the growth of human productive powers, the spur to their further development. Internally, that is within the M-C-M' process, it enforces the laws of capital and translates them into the subjective purposes of individual agents. A complete explanation of competition requires that we embed it first in the objective purposiveness of the valorization process and that process in turn in the overarching theory of history. A more modest project involves only the first explanatory nesting, but in no case can competition be grasped independently of it.

Two points, flowing from the preceding observations, need to be underscored. (1) To the extent that Marx specifies a causal mechanism that purports to show how the functional M-C-M' circuit operates, competition is it. Marx's argument here, where competition is taken as an analogue to natural selection, bears some very distant resemblance to the use of evolutionary theory in economics. These latter efforts often extensively qualify the applicability of biological models to economic phenomena and even then they are the subject of forceful methodological criticism. The version that I have reconstructed from Marx's writings is far more primitive and I advance no claims that such a theory of competition adequately explains its object. What I do assert is that it adds to the demonstration that one of Marx's modes of political economic explanation was functionalist and that Marx saw the need to unpack the black box, to show the mechanism that links the end and its causes even if, in its execution, that project failed. (2) Competition is *only* that mechanism. It is subject to and is merely the executor of another higher-order, law-governed and law-generating process, M-C-M'. Competition, Marx writes, "does not establish [capitalism's] laws, but is rather their executor. . . . Competition therefore does not *explain* these laws rather it lets them be seen. . . ." (Marx, 1973: 552. Emphasis in the original).

In the preceding pages, I have set out Marx's functionalist analysis of the role of competition in capitalist production. I shall now sketch the manner in which Marx turns that analysis into a critical tool to be used against the method of classical political economy. Consider the following passage from his *Notebooks* of 1861–3: "in competition, the immanent laws of capital, of capitalist production, appear as the result of the mechanical actions of capitals upon one another, that is, upsidedown and stood on its head. What is effect appears as cause, the changed form as the original one. Ordinary political economy therefore explains everything that it cannot understand by using the idea of competition; that is, the statement about the appearance in its most obvious form serves it as knowledge of the law itself" (Marx, 1980: 1630–1). This passage suggests a number of ideas of interest to us: It points (again) to a deep causal structure, with the surface phenomenon (competition) as its efflux *and* it advances a critique of a mode of explanation that does not accord primacy to that underlying causal order.

Let us look briefly at each of these in turn. The first point addresses the question of where the governing causal mechanism is to be located: whether it is to be discerned in the interactive behavior of capitalists seeking to optimize within a given set of constraints or whether that behavior is itself the result of a deeper causal order. Marx used two analogies to illuminate this distinction, both again drawn (revealingly) from nature: the heavens and the workings of the body. The movements of the planets have an apparent independence that conceals their "real motions." So too does the outer form of the body conceal its inner structure and life-sustaining functions, which are not visible to the eye (Marx, 1977b: 433, and 1968: 165–6). The imagery is misleading in that it does not draw out the important enforcement role played by competition. But it does suggest that the surface movement of the stars or limbs is the result of, and conceals, an underlying structure. And just as the actions of the planets are determined by mechanisms governing their motions and just as the form and action of the human body are the result of its metabolic processes and internal structure so too are the phenomena of capitalism the consequence of a deep causal order. It is that order, functional in nature, whose general formula is M-C-M', that Marx first sets out, only subsequently to move to its efflux, the "surface" of the bourgeois world.

The second point above speaks to the meaning of this distinction between deep structure and surface phenomena for the question of method and explanation. Recall the passage from Marx cited above: "the *apparent motions* of the heavenly bodies *are intelligible* only to someone who is acquainted with their *real motions,* which are not perceptible to the senses." This excerpt forms a part of Marx's discussion of why a scientific analysis of competition and capitalism as a whole is "possible only if we grasp the inner nature of capital." Competition is the phenomenal form (the "form of appearance") of the latter, but it conceals the reality of things (the "real motions") from the everyday observer. Competition is an illusory and superficial standpoint from which to explain capitalism and it dominates classical political economy because, Marx argues, it mirrors the way in which the capitalist sees the world: Cost, profit, and market competition, in short the surface, determine his well-being and that is reflected in his theorizing about the economic order of which he is a part (Marx, 1981a: 338, and 1968: 218–9). And so one of the threads running through Marx's critique of Adam Smith is that he had an "exoteric" and an "esoteric" political economy. The former was concerned with the external phenomena of capitalism (for Marx, principally those of competition); the latter, Marx, writes, using the biological imagery he so often employed in writing about capital, grasps the "physiology," the inner nature of capital. Political economy must, then, set for itself a scientific foundation: It must discover the hidden, inner laws of capital, the deep structure (Marx, 1971: 515).

The principal conclusion of this section is that in one of its variants Marx's political economy draws heavily upon a functionalist mode of explanation in its analysis of capitalism. That explanation, schematized as M-C-M$'$, understands the capitalist economy as a purposive (M$'$), law-governed process, which determines the significant behavior of the persons who occupy its various moments. This way of understanding capitalism identifies, according to Marx, its central distinguishing characteristic, what marks off this formation from its predecessors and successor: in a word, the autonomy of the production and exchange processes from human control. Functional explanation is thus the historically appropriate form of analysis for an economy of the capitalist type precisely because the latter's purpose and mechanisms, its causal laws, are independent of and have a priority over the wills and purposes of human agents. Pre- and postcapitalist formations require a different type of explanation since their governing purpose is the satisfaction of need determined by the community (or, under communism, by individuals: "to each according to his need") or its dominant class (Booth, 1991a, b). In short, the political economy of an embedded production process would have at its core, as Marx argues ancient economics did, the intentions of persons. That the political economy of capitalism has at its heart the idea of an autonomous, self-moving and regulating process indicates the peculiar nature of capitalism and of the science required for its comprehension. On this reading of Marx's analysis, then, the search for microfoundations is illusory; the intentions and behavior of agents, however specified, are rendered intelligible only against the background of that deep structure, the functional circuit of capital. From that theoretical standpoint, attempts to see in Marx a methodological individualist but one of a different stripe – that is, as a theorist who does not axiomatically posit instrumental, maximizing rationality as the core of agency but who looks instead at individuals and social properties as the "outcomes of practices" appear likely to fail.

I have also argued that Marx does not simply point to a beneficial end-result and then without any specification of a linking mechanism assume that its antecedent causes can be explained by that result. That linking mechanism is competition, which forces the objective purposiveness of the process upon individual actors, compelling them to make that goal (the maximization of surplus value) their subjective purpose (in the phenomenal form of profit). Competition serves too as the process's regulator by eliminating dysfunctional (suboptimal) technologies and, presumably, by removing from the process those "functionaries" less well adapted to achieving the circuit's goal. Competition, on this rendering of Marx, is a mechanism, a part of a broader and underlying process and is inexplicable apart from an understanding of its role within that capital circuit.

Recall that at the beginning of the essay, I suggested that the functionalism of Marx's political economy is related to the normative element of his work. This relationship will be sketched here under these two headings: autonomy and class. Marx's generic description of precapitalist economic formations: C-M-C (or variations thereupon: C-C = barter economies; or C [now reading *C* as consumption goods rather than commodities] which we might designate as the exchangeless autarkic household economy) and M-C-M' can be read not simply as schema for two sorts of production process, precapitalist and capitalist, but also as pointing to two different kinds of unfreedom. In the former, unfreedom is not mediated through contracts or markets and so it takes the form of direct coercion, of personal power, the imposition of one will upon another. In the latter, the source of unfreedom is "objective" or material, rooted in the autonomous economy whose dominant subject is self-valorizing value and not human beings. When Marx writes in the *Grundrisse* that capitalism is the "last form of servitude," he means that it is this special type of servitude, one in which the "violence of things" has taken the place of the violence of humans (Marx, 1973: 749, and 1976: 78–9). It is that thought which underpins Marx's theory of alienation and its literary expression: the language of Goethe's *Sorcerer's Apprentice* used to describe capitalism as "the sorcerer who is no longer able to control the powers of the nether world whom he has called up by his spells" which makes of that theory a (perhaps exotic) way in which to speak about freedom and the historical novelty of capitalist constraints upon it (Marx, 1976a: 489). And it is clearly that thought which led him to see in society's ex ante regulation of the economy the remedy to the ills of the bourgeois world. This idea of the *differentia specifica* of compulsion in capitalist society, central to Marx's critique of liberalism and to his vision of communism is so closely tied to his functionalist portrait of the capitalist economy that a critique of that method would appear to do considerable damage to the normative component of his work. So likewise with Marx's idea of class.

Thus far I have considered class as an embedded component of M-C-M', in which persons appear as agents, "functionaries" or "personifications" of their respective moments in the valorization cycle of capital. Class here is taken to be a way of explaining patterns of behaviors and interests in the production and market spheres, and in light of a background theory of functions in the M-C-M' circuit. But that is clearly not a complete deployment of the concept of class, for it is also an idea designed to account for solidarity relations, conflict and historical change, and constraint under markets. For those purposes, M-C-M' cannot be exhaustive, though it does remain basic: It sets out the forces patterning key relations of conflict and solidarity, but does not fully explain the translation of those patterns into the phenomena of conflict. That is, the reproduction cycle of capital, in Marx's account, creates some of the main underpinnings of classes as collectivities-in-struggle (to use Adam Przeworski's phrase). The valorization process of capital produces, according to Marx, the spatial concentration of workers and establishes communication among them; it levels out skills and wages, thereby helping to end conflict within the working class. And since the M-C-M' circuit is at its core a cycle of the productive consumption (exploitation) of labor, the central conflictual dynamic of capitalism is established there at the gross level. It is instantiated at the micro level in, for instance, "domination at the point of production" – the discipline of the factory, a relation that flows from the valorization terminus combined with one peculiar quality of labor as an input to production, namely its reluctance to deliver its services at full intensity.

If we unfolded in detail these various claims, we would see the ways in which, drawing on this version of Marx's logic of capitalism, the M-C-M' process provides the foundation for an explanation of the emergence of collectivities-in-struggle. What it does not do is to fill in the moves from that background or foundation to the phenomenal foreground of conflict, and in particular it does not speak directly to the role of politics. Consequently, throughout the history of Marxism, from Kautsky to Lenin, Luxemburg, and Gramsci, the problem has been posed of the relationship between classes as moments of the M-C-M' cycle and their expression at the political level. This issue, more than a little stale after some one hundred years of debate, does not interest me here. What is worth observing in it, though, is that however the mechanism is specified linking M-C-M'-generated classes to classes as social-political actors, the shared assumption is that it mediates between, on the one side, groups of persons who are agents, "bearers" of their respective locations in the valorization circuit of capital, and political outcomes on the other side. Class is the primordial unit of analysis and it is an expression, the efflux, of place-holding in the structure of capitalism.

The normative/critical content of Marx's second logic of capitalism is also played out at the level of the concept of class. To be a member of a class, on this reading, is to be a functionary in the sense now of not having freedom or choice; it is in short a "situation of being assigned [*Angewiesensein*]" (Marx, 1973: 96; Marx and Engels, 1976a: 77). Class is here a way of speaking about a radical unfreedom and the passivity of the person in the face of the "forces" of capitalism is central to this variant of Marx's claim. Reflect once more on his use of the factory as an analogue to capitalism. The relations among persons in that institution, their manner of cooperation, their arrangement in the space of the workplace, and so forth, are determined by the objective structures of the factory, by for example the layout of the machinery, a layout itself determined by the technology being employed. That structure as we observed is analyzable independently of its place-holders. More strongly, it has an explanatory primacy over the analysis of relations among them. Intentionality, choice, and so forth play as little or as derivative a role in the understanding of classes as they did in the explanation of the economic behaviors of capitalists and workers, in the narrower gauge application of M-C-M'. And to repeat: The critical gloss on that same reality is, for Marx, that class position denotes the fact that we are overdetermined by the valorization process of capital, and thereby rendered unfree.

II

In the preceding pages I ventured an analysis that made Marx into a functionalist of a sophisticated sort, one who sought to unpack the black box causal mechanisms uniting the ends and the behaviors producing them. Now I want to discuss Marx's second logic of capitalism. Here rather than a two-tier causal account of capitalism, the "laws of capital" on the one hand and their executive branch on the other, we will attribute to him a single-layered story in which it is the market as an institution (a set of constraints), its agents, and the consequences of their interactions under constraint that together warrant a lawlike picture of the phenomena. The language of surface and inner phenomena, of the exoteric and esoteric aspects of the economy, is replaced by the idea that the laws of capitalism are not located in some hidden domain or deep structure but rather are the efflux of (ex ante) uncoordinated decisions in a context of interdependency: "The laws of capital are in fact nothing other than the general relations of this movement [of competition among capitalists], its result on the one side, its direction on the other" (Marx, 1980: 1603, my translation; 1981a: 365; 1973: 157, 197). These general relations are amenable to an analysis of a lawlike kind because they are describable in a patterned (rule-governed) causal way, a causality that Marx expresses as the compulsion that those interconnections (in the form of competition) exert upon individual agents. Stated in plainer language, competition among capitalists directs them to pursue (choose) those ends that are at the heart of capitalism and the means appropriate to them and it weeds out maladapted choices/strategies. Similarly, Marx maintained that competition among workers in the labor market acts as a lawlike determinant of their behavior until the development of capitalism on the one side and the growth of trade unions on the other reduce the salience of the material bases of that competition (Marx, 1977b: 254, 381, 433; 1976a: 492–3; 1973: 413, 651, 657; and 1976d: 225).

What Marx wants to say in speaking of the "laws of capital" is that the processes of the capitalist market, while they are composed out of the acts of market agents, nevertheless appear to display in their totality an independence from these same persons, compelling or better directing them to act in certain ways. That property of unregulated but interdependent activity is, in one sense, truly independent of individuals, because it constrains them, and generates unintended consequences. It would, however, be wrong to imagine these laws as independent of humans in the same way as, for example, the laws of nature. For the "laws of capital" are the product of human hands, the results of an uncoordinated social economy. Perhaps Marx's use of the strong language of underlying causal forces determining the surface phenomena of the market was meant to convey the first of the preceding points and to undermine the idea that the market is a sphere of freedom because its particular moments are the decisions of individuals. But a careful laying out of the threads of Marx's analysis demonstrates that he did not need to leave the market sphere in order to make the arguments he did.

Marx's account of the generation of ("independent") laws out of interdependent but unregulated economic activity captures a part of what he understands by the emergence of lawlike forces from an anarchical (in the ex ante sense, i.e., not planned) market. Another part, indeed a crucial one, as we have seen, of his theory of the law-governed character of the capitalist market is the purposiveness of its processes. It is not simply that market competition constrains persons to act in certain ways, or that the actions of those individuals produce unforeseen consequences. Rather, these constraints and consequences are, in their varied ways, bound up with the overarching purpose of a capitalist economy: the creation of M' (Marx, 1977a: 1051; 1977b: 254). This can be read, as we did above, as Marx writing as if that purpose resided somewhere else than in the persons who act within the constraints of the market, and that it was, by a process unspecified (and perhaps unspecifiable) instantiated in the consciousness of capitalists, whereupon it becomes their "subjective purpose." (See Marx, 1977b: 254, 433.) What I want to venture now is the notion that Marx is seeking to draw out a thought much more credible than the idea that there is an "objective" purposiveness that is translated into a subjective one. And this is that competition in the market requires that individuals choose strategies, for example, cost cutting, introduction of labor-saving technology and so forth, which are best adapted to economic survival and expansion, that is to the creation of M'. This it does by, for instance, imposing penalties on counteradaptive decisions and rewarding the appropriate ones and leaving the decision between them to rationally motivated actors.

When Marx set out to analyze markets of the capitalist type, the portrait that he finally drew had the following central features: (a) markets are structured by the class position of their members, where by class position is understood their (unequal) endowments. (b) These markets are also structured by a pattern of entitlements, which in a pervasive capitalist market economy can be expressed as a money entitlement, that is, the power to purchase and sell. (c) Beyond these two initial premises, the market is structured in the sense that its operations consist of individual choices with no ex ante coordination at the level of the economy as a whole. (d) Those individual choices in an interdependent (or "social" as Marx sometimes calls it) economy interact with one another and set in motion lawlike processes. (e) These processes are lawlike in three senses: (1) they can be described in regular, causal pattern language. (2) They are like natural laws in that they bind or act as a force of compulsion upon persons, and appear to have an existence independent of them. In reality that independence of the laws of capital is partly fact, partly illusion – the former because those laws are not the product of human design, the latter because they are of human making. (3) They are end-directed in the sense that the various operations of the market compel its leading agents to pursue profit and it adjudicates between those who are successful in this and those who fail. The first species is preserved, the second perishes. It is this combination of traits that Marx thought defined the particularity of the capitalist market and that together set the foundation for the critical conclusions of this second logic of capitalism, the coexistence of individual choice and unfreedom in the market – arguments to which we shall now turn, in the form of an examination of the idea of class.

Let us see how this second logic of capitalism plays out in Marx's concept of class. Marx claims that the relation between buyer and seller in the (labor) market is shaped by their respective class positions (Marx, 1981b: 115; 1977a: 1015; 1977b: 723–4). Before they even meet in the market they are proletarian and capitalist; market behavior is determined, not in its detail but in its broad and defining structure, by class. The market is thus embedded in – shaped by – class and it reproduces those classes. Following on the first section of this essay, we might read this as an analogue, at the level of social analysis, to Marx's distinction between deep structure and epiphenomena. On this view, classes are not composed out of individuals, their behavior (preferences), and the constraints on them but, like a Marxist equivalent of the Platonic forms, they seem to stand above these persons, mold them and are analyzable independently of them. And as we have observed Marx's language often supports just such a construction: class membership is like a fate, something that descends upon one: It is a "situation of being assigned." Marx's manner of writing is here meant to convey a point, and I will return to that presently. Taken too literally, however, it can give a fundamentally inaccurate (and theoretically inferior) picture of what Marx understood by class.

We can begin by considering Marx's story concerning capital's "original sin": the history of the beginnings of capitalism in large-scale expropriation, the appropriation of unpaid labor, servility as a consequence of expropriation and the violent circumstances which created that servility. Putting to one side the issue of violence and the presence of the state, what it amounted to was a fundamental shift in the pattern of basic economic endowments, a different distribution of the "social elements" of production or, in plainer words, of labor and the other core means of production (Marx, 1981b: 462). Labor power becomes fully the property of its natural owner, who is under no juridical obligation to alienate (sell) it to an employer; it also, Marx maintains, becomes virtually their sole endowment. The means of production, such as a factory, likewise come under private ownership: To be operated, laborers mast be hired to run these various moments of the production process. This is, needless to say, a highly stylized and simplified picture and I use it only to capture a part of what Marx means when he writes that class precedes and structures the market. And that is that there is nothing Platonic or supramundane about this claim, which amounts to the assertion that market agents in a capitalist economy have different endowments. Those endowments may be traced along a number of lines, but a fundamental one, for Marx, is the possession of labor power alone and those who, having effective control over the instruments of production, but no direct control over labor, must now engage it in a market, for a price and from its proper owner.

This pattern of endowments constitutes one aspect of what Marx intends by class. And it explains a part of why buyers and sellers appear in the labor market: Given this pattern of endowments, individuals of both classes need each other – the one to secure income (wages) that are now the only recognized entitlement to commodities in the market, including sustenance, the other to create and maximize surpluses. Their appearance in the market, the fact that only there can they arrange both to create and to share in social wealth, in short their need for one another sets up the vital relational dimension of the Marxist definition of class. But notice how this relational aspect emerges: It is a consequence of a pattern of initial endowments (how that pattern itself is arrived at makes no difference for its impact on class formation) coupled with the optimizing behavior of the agents involved. The first part of this argument, the ownership or effective control over the means of production is, from the Marxist standpoint, a noncontroversial element of the definition of class as structuring markets. The second component, that individuals become capitalists or proletarians as they seek (choose) to optimize under a wealth constraint, that in other words the completion of class formation occurs in the market as these endowments are exchanged against one another, is less obviously a part of the Marxist tradition. Yet the particular novelty and brilliance of this position, set out in magisterial fashion by John Roemer, is that it is able to reproduce something very much like the classical Marxist typology of classes on microfoundations. That is, it is able to generate class position out of a standard model of markets, endowments, and preferences, rather than postulating such entities in advance. And that is (among other things) what gives it an atypical appearance (Roemer, 1982a: 14, 77; 1982b: 1; 1981: 202; see also Elster 1985: 326ff).

The value of the Roemer construction of class for the reading presented in this section lies in its unpacking of the mechanism by which classes are generated by markets under certain assumptions about the initial endowments of agents. And though I am not interested here in defending Roemer against the received orthodoxy (much less the reverse), it is important that Marx's analysis can in fact be reconstructed in a way that takes us close, unexpectedly perhaps, to Roemer-type classes. We have seen Marx claiming that class is anterior to market behavior and that assertion would appear, on its face, to rule out the Roemer approach and to sustain the Platonic version. But we also saw that when fully deployed, Marx's claim amounted to the proposition that the endowments (labor power and capital) of market agents were set before they appeared there and that they constitute one of the factors necessitating and shaping market exchanges. Marx also provides the material for the second element of the market behavior theory of class: optimising under constraints. This might seem at first to be fundamentally at odds with the canonical Marxist story according to which "compulsion" drives both capitalist and worker. Here again, a close examination of the substance of

Marx's argument yields a more finely inflected picture than does his often florid choice of words. The worker, Marx writes, is forced through his own interest to sell his labor power; he is compelled by his needs. For the capitalist, on the other hand, it is the creation of surplus value in the context of a competitive market which acts as a force compelling certain behaviors from him (Marx, 1977a: 1051; 1977b, 381–2, 932; 1976b: 118; 1976c: 174, 183; 1973: 245, 413).

Allow me to pursue some of the normative consequences of this move from a functionalist to an intentional logic of capitalism. In a sense, as we have observed, persons in a capitalist market economy could be said to choose their class position, and that claim is, I imagine, among the most counterintuitive from a Marxist perspective (Przeworski, 1985a: 95; Roemer, 1986: 90; 1982a: 81). This is the case because that argument might be taken to echo the thought that occupation and income differences, loosely speaking, class position, are the reflection of preferences, for instance for security over risk taking, or for leisure over monetary income. The element of constraint, so important to the Marxian critique, would seem to be reduced here to the exercise of preferences. And it would therefore become exceedingly difficult to make sense of Marx's repeated references to the "illusion" of freedom in the market and to the "veiled slavery" underlying it. In fact, however, the idea of choice under constraint captures handsomely Marx's argument and its shadings. Recall that according to that argument, external compulsion is absent from capitalist relations, meaning that power emerges from market transactions but has no (theoretically interesting) ex ante existence. The presence of persons selling (in the present) their labor power and of others buying it cannot be explained by coercion or status position. The worker, Marx writes, has a "wide field of choice," governs and is the proprietor of herself; she is not commanded or forced by some other person to sell her labor power. Yet it is essential to the Marxist definition of class that she be constrained to sell her time and activity, for otherwise class position would in fact be strictly a function of preferences (Cohen, 1978: 72; Elster, 1985: 324ff).

This is one of the central paradoxes of capitalism for Marx: that "external" or direct coercion is absent but not compulsion altogether, and that compulsion is not incidental but is rather central to the capitalist market economy (Marx, 1976c: 174, 183). Agents in a capitalist economy choose to engage in their various economic activities but they do so in a context of constraints, for example, survival of the enterprise in a competitive market or money-based entitlements to food and other consumption goods, and initial endowments. Those constraints are sufficiently powerful that no "external compulsion" is required in order to have workers deliver their services: the market, its constraints, and the endowments of individuals active in it, replace the more direct and personal form of coercion characteristic of the premodern world. Not only does it replace them, but it is more effective than they were in generating wealth-creating activity. The compulsion at work here is, Marx says, "silent," meaning not emanating from a person. He also describes it as "material" or objective and therefore difficult to perceive, theoretically, for a (liberal) way of looking at the world accustomed to thinking of coercion in its premodern and personal forms (Marx, 1982: 2131; 1977a: 1027–28n, 1031; 1977b: 899; Marx and Engels, 1976a: 78–9). It thus appears freer than economic behavior in the premodern world for two reasons: because of the absence of a visible master commanding it and because, relatedly, it must be free-willed, the object of choice. It is, however, as constrained a way of life with this important difference: that the constraints are no longer the master's whip but a highly restricted and unacceptable choice set. To repeat the central points: (a) the presence of that choice set is in fact one of the marks distinguishing the bourgeois from the premodern world; (b) the presence of that choice set gives the (misleading) appearance of a society without unfreedom, or none at least of a morally relevant sort.

Consider one of Marx's illustrations of this, chapter 33 of *Capital,* volume 1, entitled "The Modern Theory of Colonization." Those pages, despite their title, have little to do with colonization, being rather an attempt to illuminate the nature of compulsion in capitalist society. The argument is presented in this manner. In the developed bourgeois world, the compulsion underlying the (labor) market is hidden: voluntary contracts are the means by which labor is bought and sold, and whatever element of restraint may be visible in it appears as something "natural" in the sense of not emanating from any particular will. But in the colonies, where land is cheaply (or freely) available, migrants decline to participate as laborers in the industries being founded there. They prefer instead – and the feasible choice set enables them – to return to the condition of independent producers. In the end, Marx concludes, those circumstances that, in the European world, "naturally," that is, without the assistance of the state or of any authority whatsoever, populate the labor market with applicants must, in the new world, be artificially instituted through legislation, for instance by a mandated increase in land prices. The core of Marx's argument here is the notion that only as a result of a highly constrained choice set, "the labor market . . . or the workhouse," does the labor contract, so essential to capitalism, occur at all. Alter the boundaries of that set, and people exit the market (Marx, 1977b: 936).

The market is thus an institutional shelter for bilaterally voluntary exchanges in comparison to the ways of appropriating labor typical of slave or serf societies. But Marx maintained that if we add two further assumptions to this depiction, entitlements to all goods in a capitalist market depend on effective demand and a certain pattern of initial endowments, the end result is a severe set of constraints on choice. There is a third assumption at work here that, though not stated so boldly in Marx's writings, is a theme underlying his philosophy of history as the growth of human productive powers. That additional claim is this: that in order for this argument to function as a critique, the parameters of the choice set have to be malleable under some feasible alternative arrangement. Underdeveloped economies, the members of which live at the lower threshold of calorie consumption required for the sustaining of life, may also face severely restricted options, but if those restrictions are incorrigible they do not constitute the groundwork for a critique, even under the wide parameters of critique allowed by Marx, for example, where the constraints need not emanate from a will or an unjust act in order to be counted as wrongs.

Following the path laid out by this second logic, we can see that it is possible to recover central Marxian notions such as class by building from the microfoundations of intentional explanation. We have also seen that key critical propositions are sustainable on this new foundation. To that extent, Marx's analysis and critique of capitalism lose nothing in the move from the first to the second logic. Indeed, I would suggest that, whatever the debates about the value of rational choice theory, the elimination of the reifying language of forces, fate, and of unanalyzed collective actors is unequivocally positive inasmuch as it allows us to go beyond the antique, and bad metaphysics, which saturate parts of Marx's corpus. Attempting to understand phenomena of interest to Marxism against a background theory of constraints, choices, and their outcomes is both more challenging and more likely to be fruitful than an approach which renders many such questions (apparently) unnecessary by designating persons as agents and executors of forces independent of them.

III

Let us assume that central issues for Marxism, alike in its critical and explanatory undertakings, can be reconceptualized using this second logic. If that is not so, and the functionalist logic is in fact inextricably interwoven with the conceptual fabric of Marxism, then so much the worse for it. However, even on the optimistic assumption ventured here, namely that it can be so reconstituted, profound problems remain. Or, more accurately, they are induced by this shift in foundational logics. Here I shall point to one of them: class and identity. We saw that according to Marx's second logic of capitalism class could be understood as shared optimization patterns among a group of persons, who optimize in a similar manner because they are endowed with roughly similar assets and facing common institutional constraints. In that sense they can be said to choose their class position (Przeworski, 1985a: 95). I urged that this approach was more sound than the agent or functionary model. Nevertheless, once choice is introduced into the explanation of class, the question arises as to why choice is understood to be exercised only or even primarily over alienable market-type assets and within one dominant set of constraints – those associated with the market. Granted that they choose their (class) position: Why are we to assume that they choose within those boundaries alone? The preceding specification applies easily enough to narrowly economic behavior, and especially to that sphere of greatest interest to Marxism, that is, the labor market. But there are severe difficulties with this if what we (and Marx) want from the idea of class is something more, for example a theory of identity formation, of collective action and conflict. For our endowments and the constraints within which we deploy them are by no means strictly economic. We are not simply sellers and buyers of labor power within a market. Numerous possibilities other than those which generate Marxian-type classes and markets seem available to structure our choices, identities, and our collectivities: gender, ethnicity, and race are just a few candidates and, as Adam Przeworski has shown, which of these becomes operative is, in the same moment, something independent of our wills and something chosen.

Why then did Marx focus on one set of institutions and on the choices made within them, those that generate classes/collectivities-in-struggle purely out of the economic sphere? The answer to this goes deep into the heart of his portrait of capitalism, and here I shall offer no more than a summary version of it. I want to approach this by reflecting on a challenge to Marx's idea of class put forward by Przeworski. His counter to Marx can be expressed in this fashion: Classes are not "prior to" politics but are organized and defined within the political sphere. Marx was wrong, Przeworski concludes, to conceive of capitalism as a system of "isolated cycles of production," that is, as iterations of the M-C-M' circuit bounded on the one side by an historical (political) act of transfer, the expropriation of the direct producers, but self-operating (and in that sense nonpolitical) thereafter.

This critique can be used to place in bolder relief Marx's claim that characteristic of capitalism (in contradistinction to earlier social or economic formations) is the dominance of the economy over politics. Here are some of the main elements of that characterization: (a) Given an initial pattern of endowments (those separated from the means of production and the owners of those means), the market is a robust institution, capable of producing and reproducing exploitation relations of the capitalist form without (direct) state intervention. Force (politics) is the market's midwife (in capitalism's "original sin"), and it must tend over the markets' first emergence. After that, no midwife is needed. (b) This leads to a second core element: market neutrality, a thesis also brought to the fore by Przeworski's critique. Once the market becomes the pervasive mechanism for allocating goods and persons (labor) across society, its operations are neutral with respect to the political sphere – that is, it makes no noneconomic distinctions between persons. The often repugnant language of Marx's *The Jewish Question* is meant to express just that thought: Jews, who suffer under civil disabilities in the political sphere, are the equals of their political oppressors in civil or economic society. This is so because capital, unlike political institutions, is neutral in relations to its holders; the only passion it knows is the drive for more of itself. In its world, discrimination along religious, social, or gender lines has no place. Neutrality may be formulated, in the canonical language of liberalism, as the juridical equality of persons as self-owners. Marx accepts the neutrality description, but recasts it as the indifference of capital toward all (non-economic) distinctions. For Marx to agree that classes are formed within a political process would be to dilute a central element of his (and, interestingly, liberalism's) claim that the market is blind to (extraeconomic) differences among its actors, and that the market is the pervasive institution through which individuals in a capitalist society interact.[3]

(c) By way of that last point, we are brought to a third (and for us the most crucial) reason for Marx's turn away from the political sphere, generally and in his discussion of class formation – the dominance of civil society over politics. When Marx described Locke as the great ideologist of bourgeois society, he intended among other things, that Locke had envisioned the shrinking of the political and the corresponding growth of civil, or private society: the dominance, in short, of the market over all other realms. Conversely, the modern reincarnation of the republican tradition, in imagining that a restoration of something like the ancient primacy of politics and citizenship was possible, committed a basic error. Bourgeois society is simply not compatible with the intensely political world of antiquity (Lukács, 1971: 92; Marx, 1977b: 444n; Marx and Engels, 1976a: 409; 1976b: 122). Here once more the *Jewish Question* provides a key to Marx's thinking: not only does the political sphere not penetrate civil society, but it is in fact civil society that dominates, a point that Marx makes (perversely) by stating that the Jewish community, denied the political rights of the most ordinary Gentile citizen, nevertheless rules through its economic power. Notice that Marx is yet again developing a mirror image of the familiar liberal account: The state is indeed minimal because it has been, as it were, expelled from civil society, a possibility in turn opened up by the effectiveness of the market mechanism (after the initial distribution is set) in enforcing the behaviors required for the reproduction of capital. (See Marx, 1975a: 166–7, 170ff). Observe further that the market also appears as a sort of forum for freedom, standing in normative contradistinction to unfreedom in the state: Jews, Marx argues, were freer in the economic sphere, which is neutral and therefore blind also to religion. The standard Marxian reversal of this part of the liberal story is that the depoliticization of the economy sets in motion not autonomous agents but persons who, having lost their varied, ranked status positions, now come under the impersonal forces of the market and acquire, in that process, a new hierarchical ordering, new in that it is the consequence of the different functional roles they occupy in the reproduction of capital (Marx, 1977b: 719; 1976b: 118; 1973: 96; Marx and Engels, 1976a: 77).

The core of the preceding argument is Marx's acceptance of the broad-brush assertion that capitalism, in its most developed form, takes politics out of civil society and emancipates its agents, at least in relation to the world before capitalism. The state is a minimal one because its operations are no longer necessary to surplus creation. Politics or, more generally, nonmarket organizations reappear in a variety of guises only when the market fails. What is important to remark is that Marx clings to a view of the capitalist economy largely free from political institutions and that, accordingly, one of the defining properties of classes is that

---

[3] Recent literature on women's place in the economy shows just how ill-founded was the optimism of Marx (and the liberals) on the neutrality of the market. For some contemporary observations on the continued ascriptive structuring of the labor market, see Offe, 1985: 13, 36.

they must emerge (in all but the first instance) from the workings of the economy and not, as with status groups, as a function of the political realm. To assert that classes are constituted in the political sphere would be, for Marx, to reintroduce the political into civil society, to weaken the fundamental explanatory and normative propositions tied to the thesis of the autonomy of the economy under capitalism and to upset the ironic reversals that Marx was venturing against liberalism. More generally, to assert that we face a panoply of constraints and with varied endowments (not all located in or transacted through formal markets), and that therefore the identity we "choose" can have a manifold of locations in social-economic space – these propositions challenge central elements of Marx's picture of capitalism. And that challenge is not diffused but is rather brought on by the move from the bad metaphysics of Marxian functionalism to an intentional level of explanation. Marx's concept of class captured a set of constraints that we face and in so doing showed the limits of the classical liberal notions of the freedom and equality of the person. But in Marx's argument, class, understood as emerging from a cluster of constraints, endowments and choices located strictly in the production and market spheres, was all. And that was because the M-C-M′ circuit was not just the cycle of the reproduction and expansion of capital but the expression of modernity: of the hegemony of the market and the corresponding (relative) absence of the state, of the decline of noneconomic gradations among persons, for example, status, race, gender, and so forth, of the reduction of direct relations of domination, and of the fabulous wealth of this society expressed in commodities and not leisure or the pursuit of noneconomic goods. Marx thought that Aristotle's view that we are political animals made great sense in the world before capitalism, and that accordingly a book called the *Politics* might display before us the essential structure of such a society. (See Marx, 1973: 104 and contrast to Marx and Engels, 1976: 409, 412, 414). It tells us much about Marx's project that his masterwork on modernity was entitled *Capital*. Among other things, it tells us why he was wrong.

References

Alchian, Armen A., and Harold Demsetz. (1972). "Production, Information Costs, and Economic Organization." *The American Economic Review* 52: 777–95.

Bates, Robert. (1990). "Macropolitical Economy in the Field of Development." In James E. Alt and Kenneth A. Shepsle (Eds.), *Perspectives on Positive Political Economy.* Cambridge: Cambridge University Press.

Baudrillard, Jean. 1975. *The Mirror of Production.* Translated by Mark Poster. St. Louis: Telos Press.

Becker, Gary. (1976). *The Economic Approach to Human Behavior.* Chicago: University of Chicago Press.

Booth, William James. (1991a). "Economies of Time. On the Idea of Time in Marx's Political Economy." *Political Theory* 19: 7–27.

(1991b). "The New Household Economy." *American Political Science Review* 85: 59–75.

(1989). "Explaining Capitalism. The Method of Marx's Political Economy." *Political Studies* 37: 612–25.

Boudon, Raymond. (1979). *Effets pervers et ordre social.* Paris: Presses Universitaires de France.

Castoriadis, Cornelius. (1978). "From Marx to Aristotle, from Aristotle to Us." *Social Research* 45: 667–738.

Cohen, Gerald A. (1982). "Functional Explanation, Consequence Explanation and Marxism." *Inquiry* 25: 27–56.

(1978). *Karl Marx's Theory of History. A Defense.* Princeton N.J.: Princeton University Press.

Dawkins, Richard. (1976). *The Selfish Gene.* Oxford: Oxford University Press.

Dumont, Louis. (1977). *From Mandeville to Marx: The Genesis and Triumph of Economic Ideology.* Chicago: University of Chicago Press.

Elster, Jon. (1985). *Making Sense of Marx.* Cambridge: Cambridge University Press.

(1983). *Explaining Technical Change.* Cambridge: Cambridge University Press.

(1982). "Marxism, Functionalism and Game Theory." *Theory and Society* 2: 453–82.

Lukács, Georg. (1971). "The Changing Function of Historical Materialism." In *History and Class Consciousness.* Translated by Rodney Livingstone. Cambridge, Mass.: MIT Press.

Marx, Karl. (1982). *Zur Kritik der politischen Ökonomie (Manuskript 1861–1863).* In Vol. II.3.6 of *Karl Marx. Friedrich Engels Gesamtausgabe (MEGA).* Berlin: Dietz Verlag.

(1981a). *Capital.* Vol. 3. Translated by David Fernbach. New York: Vintage Books.

(1981b). *Capital.* Vol. 2. Translated by David Fernbach. New York: Vintage Books.

(1980). *Zur Kritik der politischen Ökonomie (Manuskript 1861–1863).* In Vol. 11.3.5 of *Karl Marx. Friedrich Engels Gesamtausgabe (MEGA).* Berlin: Dietz Verlag.

(1977a). *Results of the Immediate Process of Production.* Translated by Ben Fowkes. New York: Vintage Books. (Appendix to *Capital.* Vol. 1.)

(1977b). *Capital.* Volume 1. Translated by Ben Fowkes. New York: Vintage Books.

(1976a). *Manifesto of the Communist Party.* In Vol. 6 of *Karl Marx and Frederick Engels. Collected Works.* New York: International Publishers.

(1976b). *The Poverty of Philosophy.* In Vol. 6 of *Karl Marx and Frederick Engels. Collected Works.* New York: International Publishers.

(1976c). *Zur Kritik der politischen Ökonomie (Manuskript 1861–1863).* In Vol. II.3.1 of *Karl Marx. Friedrich Engels Gesamtausgabe (MEGA).* Berlin: Dietz Verlag.

(1976d). *Wage Labour and Capital.* In Vol. 9 of *Karl Marx and Frederick Engels. Collected Works.* New York: International Publishers.

(1975a). *The Jewish Question.* In Vol. 3 of *Karl Marx and Frederick Engels. Collected Works.* New York: International Publishers.

(1975b). *Comments on James Mill.* In Vol. 3 of *Karl Marx and Frederick Engels. Collected Works.* New York: International Publishers.

(1973). *Grundrisse.* Translated by Martin Nicolaus. New York: Vintage Books.

(1971). *Theories of Surplus Value.* Vol. 3. Moscow: Progress Publishers.

(1968). *Theories of Surplus Value.* Volume 2. Moscow: Progress Publishers.

(1963). *Theories of Surplus Value.* Vol. 1. Moscow: Progress Publishers.

Marx, Karl, and Frederick Engels. (1976a). *The German Ideology.* In Vol. 5 of *Karl Marx and Frederick Engels. Collected Works.* New York: International Publishers.

(1976b). *The Holy Family*. In Vol. 4 of *Karl Marx and Frederick Engels. Collected Works*. New York: International Publishers.

Meikle, Scott. (1986). "Making Nonsense of Marx," *Inquiry* 29: 29–43.

Merton, Robert K. (1957). *Social Theory and Social Structure*. New York: The Free Press.

Nelson, Richard W., and Sidney G. Winter. (1982). *An Evolutionary Theory of Economic Change*. Cambridge, Mass.: Belknap Press.

North, Douglass C. (1981). *Structure and Change in Economic History*. New York: W. W. Norton.

(1977). "Markets and Other Allocation Systems in History: The Challenge of Karl Polanyi," *Journal of European Economic History* 6: 703–16.

Offe, Claus. (1985). *Disorganized Capitalism*. Cambridge Mass.: MIT Press.

Penrose, Edith T. (1952). "Biological Analogies in the Theory of the Firm." *The American Economic Review* 42: 804–19.

Przeworski, Adam. (1985a). *Capitalism and Social Democracy*. Cambridge: Cambridge University Press.

(1985b). "Marxism and Rational Choice." *Politics and Society* 14: 379–409.

Roemer, John. (1988). "On Public Ownership," Working Paper Series, No. 317. Department of Economics. University of California, Davis.

(1986). "New Directions in the Study of Class." In John Roemer (Ed.), *Analytical Marxism*. Cambridge: Cambridge University Press.

(1982a). *A General Theory of Exploitation and Class*. Cambridge, Mass.: Harvard University Press.

(1982b). "Why Labor Classes?" Working Paper No. 195, Department of Economics, University of California at Davis.

(1981). *Analytical Foundations of Marxian Economic Theory*. Cambridge: Cambridge University Press.

Slaughter, Cliff. (1986). "Making Sense of Elster." *Inquiry* 29: 45–56.

Van Parijs, Phillipe. (1981). *Evolutionary Explanation in the Social Sciences*. Totowa, N.J.: Rowman and Littlefield.

PART II

Comparative politics

4. Structure, culture, and action in the explanation of social change

Michael Taylor

This chapter carries on an argument begun in an earlier essay (Taylor, 1988a) in which I used the explanation of social revolution to help pin down some general arguments about the roles of action and structure in explaining social change and about the scope of application of rational choice theory. My starting point in the earlier essay was the methodological point of view so lucidly exemplified in Theda Skocpol's (1979) *States and Social Revolutions.* Explicitly committed to a "nonvoluntarist, structural" explanatory perspective, Skocpol set out to explain structural outcomes directly in terms of structural causes. There was to be no role for intentional action or for individual goals, desires, and beliefs.

I. Explaining the origins of social structures

Against this position, I argued for the desirability of inserting actions between structural preconditions and structural outcomes. Of course, these actions must be explained in the usual way by the actors' desires and beliefs, and the obvious retort that can be and has been made by structuralists of this kind (and by others) is that if these desires and beliefs are in turn explained by their bearers' locations in social structures, then the structures are after all doing the real explanatory work or, as it were, taking the explanatory strain; the "actors" are mere conduits for these structural causal forces. (I take it that causal relations are between *events* whereas explanatory relations are between *facts,* but although everything

Drafts of parts of this essay were tried out in seminars at the European University Institute (Florence), the Institute of Political Science at the University of Aarhus (Denmark), the Department of Government at the University of Sydney, and the Department of Political Science and Philosophy at the Australian National University. I benefited (though probably not enough) from discussions at these seminars and in these institutions, particularly with Brian Barry, Geoffrey Brennan, John Burnheim, Jesper Grolin, Philip Pettit, Michael Smith, and Richard Sylvan; and from comments by Alan Carling, Sara Singleton, and the members of the Editorial Board of *Politics & Society,* especially Erik Olin Wright.

in the chapter can be written without loss or distortion so as to be consistent with this, I shall not always burden the prose with the appropriate locutions.) Against this reply, I want here to insist on three simple points. I shall do this mainly through discussion of historical examples, and this, together with a limited attempt at theoretical argument, will certainly not amount to a general theory of social change or of the origins of social structures or of norms. Nor will it amount to a general solution to the problem of the relations between structure, culture, and action – a solution I'm not sure exists.

The first point I want to insist on is that the causal origins of beliefs and desires are not always purely structural. The best explanations of desires and beliefs are not always in terms of facts about their bearer's locations in social structures (or, more properly, about the individual's *experience* of being in such structures). Changes in desires and beliefs can be (at least partly) the direct result of intentional actions – of their own bearers or of other actors – and sometimes the result may even be intended.[1] In section II of this chapter, I shall look at some examples of important historical changes in desires and beliefs that were brought about in this way. Barrington Moore reminds us that "to maintain and transmit a value system, human beings are punched, bullied, sent to jail, thrown into concentration camps, cajoled, bribed, made into heroes, encouraged to read newspapers, stood up against a wall and shot, and sometimes even taught sociology. To speak of cultural inertia is to overlook the concrete interests and privileges that are served by indoctrination, education, and the entire complicated process of transmitting culture from one generation to the next"; or, more briefly, that "human attitudes and beliefs fail to persist unless the situations and sanctions that reproduce them continue to persist or, more crassly, unless people get something out of them" (Moore, 1966: 486, 335, quoted in Barry, 1970: 96–7). There is often much truth in this (especially if his "situations" include social structures). But more typically, not only social structures but also other desires and beliefs of the agent in question and (unless we take an almost infinitely elastic view of "social structure") other environmental and situational conditions would have a place, along with intentional actions, among the proximate explanatory antecedents of (changes in) desires and beliefs.

Second, if desires and beliefs are explained (wholly or partly) by facts about social structures, social structures (facts about their origins, and so on) in turn have explanations. Though usually (but not always, as we shall see) intended by nobody, they are the residues or precipitates of many past intentional actions and are maintained or transformed by actions. This fact does not make structures explanatorily irrelevant; but then the fact that actions are explained by desires and beliefs that are the products of structures (among other things) does not make *individuals* and their actions, desires, and beliefs explanatorily irrelevant.

I find it very hard to see how it can plausibly be denied that social structures

---

[1] By "intentional action" and "intentional explanation," I mean roughly what Jon Elster (1983a: ch. 3) means in his *Explaining Technical Change*.

are (at least in part) the products of action. But since it is a notion that is subversive of theoretical perspectives that are still common (especially among sociologists and Marxists), I devote a section of this paper to showing how the peasant community that Skocpol (rightly in my view) took to be an important necessary condition for the French and Russian revolutions, survived and indeed was flourishing on the eves of these revolutions as a result of intentional actions.

A similar argument could be made for Skocpol's other preconditions of social revolution. Viewing them all as "structural," as she did, seems to me to be somewhat strained, but in any case they are states of affairs that were brought about by intentional actions. For example, the three revolutions she examines would not have occurred, on her account, if the states in question had been able to respond more effectively to intensifying military competition with foreign states. That they were unable to do so was in large part because, unlike their competitors, they presided over backward agrarian economies. But this state of affairs was the product of intentional actions. This should be obvious. To show it in detail would amount almost to writing the entire histories of these countries (and of their competitors), but I shall make a few remarks about one critical aspect – the contribution to economic underdevelopment made by the survival of communal institutions in the agrarian economy – in the light of the earlier account of the making of the peasant community.

So, third, it should be clear (if it wasn't already) that neither facts about individuals nor facts about social structures provide "rock-bottom" or "ultimate" explanations of social change. I am therefore rejecting both one-sided methodological individualism or "voluntarism" and any approach to explaining social change that sees individuals – their actions, desires, and beliefs, and even their very identities – as explicable solely in terms of their locations in social structures or that tries to explain, in some cases without reference to individual action at all, structural and other sorts of change in terms of facts about structures (*other* structures in the manner of Skocpol, or other parts of the same structure, or contradictions in and other characteristics of a system of structures). I am likewise rejecting the two analogous approaches to *culture* (about which more in section II) and the explanation of change.[2] But, more important, I want to reject a currently popular view (among writers *about* social explanation) that also refuses explanatory primacy or autonomy to either action or structure but then

---

[2] Most readers will be familiar with examples of strong "structuralist" and "individualist" positions. For examples of generally lopsided "culturalist" positions, in which culture tends to be seen as explanatorily primary and as possessing a great deal of autonomy, see Clifford Geertz (1973), Marshall Sahlins (1976b), and especially Sahlins (1976a). Anyone interested in seeing how Sahlins's approach works out in practice can try to explore the jungles of his *Islands of History* (1985). Once again: recognizing with Sahlins that the desires and beliefs taken as given by what he calls "utilitarianism" are (sometimes) culturally derived neither removes the necessity of providing an intentional explanation of action (which is what the "utilitarians" do) nor proves the primacy or autonomy of the cultural. I should add that earlier works by these two writers are exempt from this line of criticism.

goes on to claim not only that social relations are internal relations (the relata not being even definable independently of their relations) but that structures and agents are *mutually constitutive*.[3] With no analytical separation between the two (or between culture and action), I do not see how it is possible to unravel the causal interaction of action and structure (or action and culture) over time and hence to explain social change. I think this will be much clearer after the discussion below and in section II of a number of actual cases of important structural and cultural change, none of which could be accommodated within this "structurationist" framework.

The focus of section II is on the explanation of the origins of or changes in beliefs. My main examples concern *normative* beliefs, beliefs about how things ought to be or ought to be done. In some cases, the beliefs can reasonably be said to be constituents of ideologies or to form ideologies. I have three purposes in looking at how beliefs of this kind originate, in addition to the general purpose of endorsing and illustrating a general view of the explanation of social change which, though it too refuses explanatory autonomy or primacy to facts about individuals *or* structures *or* cultures, is, I believe, the only workable alternative to the structurationist approach of Giddens and his followers. (I emphasize that I am *not* assuming, as some philosophers have argued and many sociologists have supposed, that to have a normative belief, to make a moral judgment or any other sort of normative judgment, or to recognize or embrace a norm, is already to have a motivation to act in accordance with it, so that norms alone, without any of the sanctions that usually back them up, are capable of getting people to do things they would not otherwise do, such as contribute to the provision of a public good when it is not in their interest to do so.)

My first purpose in looking at normative beliefs concerns Skocpol's account of the origins of social revolution. Given her commitment to a "nonvoluntarist, structural" methodological approach, it is hardly surprising that she should have found no role in the explanation of the origins and courses of social revolutions for ideology or any sort of normative beliefs. Apart from the methodological difficulty she would have had in accommodating ideology or other normative elements in an explanatory framework from which individual actions, desires, and beliefs have been banished (although they do appear, as they must, in her narratives of the three revolutions[4]), she has a substantive reason for excluding them, which is essentially that revolutionary outcomes are never those envisioned in the ideologies of revolutionary leaders. But from this it does not follow that ideological intentions have no role to play in explaining the outcomes of revolutions (still less their origins), any more than it follows from the fact that any other sort of outcome was not intended by the actors producing it that it was

---

[3] This line has been developed most insistently by Anthony Giddens (1984). See also Roy Bhaskar's (1979) *The Possibility of Naturalism*. Many have followed them: see, e.g, recent books by Peter Manicas and Christopher Lloyd and the survey by Wendt (1987).

[4] Skocpol seems now to have disavowed the full-blooded structuralism of the methodological/theoretical program in *States and Social Revolution*. See Skocpol (1985).

not the product of intentional actions. So far as the *origins* of social revolutions are concerned, I think Skocpol (1979: 170–1) is largely right to claim that elite ideologies should play little or no explanatory role.[5] But she is quite mistaken if she believes that ideological or at any rate normative beliefs held by peasants played no role in the peasant rebellions that were crucial in the revolutions she studied or in peasant rebellion generally.

In addition to the problem she would have in accommodating such beliefs in an explanatory scheme in which structural outcomes are explained *directly* by structural preconditions, she is handicapped here by her apparent belief that the only sorts of ideology that might be relevant to explaining peasant rebellion are "radical visions of a desired new national society" – as she rightly says, peasants participated in these revolutions without becoming converted to such visions – and by her explicit belief that, since exploitation is "a constant feature of the peasant condition," it cannot be used as "an explanatory variable" (1979: 114–15). But if this last claim were correct, it would be hard to make sense of all those peasant rebellions (as well as more localized disturbances) that have occurred when there has been no change in state coercive capacity or in peasant capacities for collective action. (I agree with her of course that rebellions do not amount to revolutions.) We cannot understand these rebellions – and we cannot fully understand the rebellions at the heart of Skocpol's three revolutions[6] – without reference to what James Scott calls "the moral economy" of the peasant or something like it. Whether this "moral economy" amounts to a peasant ideology (I believe it does), normative beliefs are certainly an integral part of it.

Ideological and normative frameworks are things that are widely held to be an embarrassment to rational choice theorizing, to be either beyond its scope or incompatible with it. From reading Samuel Popkin's (1979) attack in *The Rational Peasant* on Scott's (1976) *The Moral Economy of the Peasant,* one might come away believing (as Popkin himself seems to believe) that these two approaches are incompatible with each other, that a peasant with a "moral economy" could not also be a rational peasant. This would be mistaken. There is in fact nothing in Scott's argument that cannot be integrated into the sort of explanatory framework I am endorsing here.[7] Showing this is my second purpose in section II.

<hr />

[5] Sewell's (1985) critique of Skocpol's treatment of ideology does little to weaken *this* claim, since what he says concerns only the course and outcome of the French Revolution, not its origins. But it is hard to deny the relevance of elite ideologies in explaining the courses and outcomes of the French, Russian, and Chinese revolutions and harder still to deny their relevance to the explanation of most later revolutions. I do, however, share Skocpol's (1985) lack of enthusiasm for Sewell's "cultural-anthropological" approach to ideologies.

[6] Skocpol acknowledges (121–2) the disastrous decline in the French peasantry's (and urban artisans' and laborers') welfare in 1788–9 and that "the short-term subjective exacerbation of specific grievances . . . may well play a precipitating role, accounting for the timing of particular rebellious acts" (115), but she seems determined to ignore these facts in explaining the origins of the French Revolution.

[7] Popkin's valuable, positive contribution in *The Rational Peasant* is his account of the role of

Rational choice theorists have often been berated for taking desires and beliefs as given and unchanging. This is seen as a grave limitation, if not a fatal failing, of their approach. It is true that most of them have taken little interest in the genesis of desires and beliefs. But all explanation has to take *something* as given; the explanatory buck has to stop *somewhere*. Recognizing that an intentional explanation is only a part of the explanatory story and that the explanation of the desires and beliefs that it takes as given need not be intentional (though in some important cases it is, as section II will show) neither obviates the need for intentional explanation nor somehow renders it trivial (as anyone will know who has, for example, studied genuinely strategic interaction). It is also untrue that rational choice theory can account only for "marginal decisions" within given social structures and cultures and cannot help explain "structural transformations." This hoary old charge is repeated in a recent study of "structural transformation" of political culture – David Laitin's (1986) *Hegemony and Culture* – whose historical details (as we shall see) nevertheless show how the transformation was brought about intentionally by self-interested actors! But while I argue here (and this is my third purpose in section II) that some aspects of culture are the direct products of intentional actions, I do *not* believe that there are good rational choice explanations of the origins of *all* aspects of culture. Sometimes, as in Scott's account of the "moral economy" of the peasant, it makes good sense to see cultural features as arising directly out of the individual's location in or experience of social structures. (On my account, "culture" includes ideologies and normative beliefs, such as those of the "moral economy.")

Since the only good explanatory rational choice theories we have at present are founded on an assumption of *thin* rational choice, I shall conclude this essay by looking briefly at the *scope* of thin rational choice explanation and arguing (in an extension of remarks made in "Rationality and Revolutionary Collective Action") that certain kinds of action – including much culture-producing action – are not explained well in this way.

Return now to Skocpol's "nonvoluntarist, structural" explanatory perspective.

"political entrepreneurs" in facilitating peasant collective action. His attack on Scott is in my view overstated. Though Scott has nothing to say about "rationality," he does not deny that the peasant is a rational actor, and, as we shall see, he does have a great deal to say about peasants' reasons for action – their desires and beliefs – and his account of peasant rebellion presupposes individual rationality of some sort. Much of what he says about the "moral economy" is compatible with an assumption that peasants maximize expected utility with strong risk aversion. He recognizes that his argument is "probably not applicable" to rich peasants, who are less risk averse. (Compare C. J. Bliss and N. H. Stern (1982), a careful and detailed study that found peasant choice to be consistent with an expected utility maximization model exhibiting a strong risk aversion that declines with wealth.) It is also worth noting that it is *not* an implication of the moral economy approach that "there is a community orientation whereby the free-rider and leadership problems are easily overcome by proper socialization to norms" (Popkin, 1979: 25). In fact, as I argued (Taylor, 1988a), some villages *can* overcome free-rider problems, not through socialization to norms but through individual rationality, *just because* they are strong communities – but this argument is strangely absent from *The Rational Peasant*.

In applying this approach to social revolutions ("rapid, basic transformations of a society's state and class structures . . . accompanied and in part carried through by class-based revolts from below" [1979: 4]), Skocpol argued that "the sufficient distinctive causes" of the social revolutionary situations beginning in 1789 in France, 1911 in China, and 1917 in Russia could be found in certain structural conditions. There must first be a weakening of the state's repressive capacity sufficient to provide an opening for peasant revolt. This Skocpol sees as being initially the product of a political crisis whose causes lie in the state's relations to other states and to its own domestic classes: the state is pushed by intensifying economic and military pressure from economically more advanced and militarily more powerful nations into attempting to carry out reforms and extract extraordinary resources from its population rapidly in order to catch up economically and compete militarily, and when its efforts in this direction are impeded by a backward agrarian economy and by a powerful landed upper class, it loses the support of many of those on whom it depends, and eventually collapses. Then, the peasant revolts, which take advantage of this initial collapse and hasten it, can be successfully mounted and sustained only under certain social structural conditions: The relations between peasants must be locally those of a strong community with considerable autonomy from upper classes and the state. (In my view, the latter is a condition of the former, since strong community requires, among other things, that relations between its members are relatively direct – not mediated by, for example, local landlords and state officials.)

Of these structural preconditions for social revolution, I focused in the earlier essay on the peasant community and argued that it was precisely because peasants lived and worked in communities (in the cases of France and Russia at least) that it was individually rational for them to participate in the sustained revolutionary collective action that succeeded in overthrowing the old order in the countryside, and that supplying this motivational link between structural conditions and structural outcomes made for a better explanation.

Now, if social *changes* (especially rapid ones like revolutions) are to be explained, and if social structures are sets of relations that are fairly *stable* over relatively long periods of time (which they are in Skocpol's account), then it should be obvious that the changes cannot be explained only by purely structural preconditions. For this reason alone, we should not be surprised that Skocpol, when she turns from her general theoretical and methodological recipe to histories of the three revolutions, does not live up to her rigorous structural manifesto.

But simply inserting motivational links between structural preconditions and structural change still will not do. If the outcome is the product of actions, each of which is intentionally explained in terms of desires and beliefs (or causally explained by individuals coming to hold these desires and beliefs), and *if* the desires and beliefs are causally explained in terms of locations in social structures (or more properly by the individual's experience of being in such structures), then we have changes supposedly being explained solely by unchanging desires and beliefs.

Social changes are produced by actions; social *changes* require *new* actions. New actions require changed desires or beliefs or both. So either one or more of the explanatory structures must change (in which case perhaps they should not be called structures, at least while they are changing) or, if structures are (relatively) unchanging, as on most definitions they must be, the changes in desires and beliefs must have some other source. There are, as I've suggested, several possible kinds of such sources.

Skocpol's explanation of peasant revolt could be elaborated so as to have something like the following form. As a result of their locations in (or experiences of) social structures (the relations between classes, the internal structure of their class, including the form of the village community, and their relations with the state), the peasants, before the revolution, had certain desires and beliefs, including desires for more land and lower dues, taxes and tithes, and beliefs about, for example, the state's current repressive capacities. These desires and beliefs explain their revolutionary *in*action before the state's collapse. Then, certain events, which in Skocpol's account begin with foreign wars, cause peasants to modify some of these desires and beliefs (in particular, their beliefs about the repressive capacities of the state and about any new state's probable attitudes to, for example, peasant seizures of land); as a result actions that were not rational before become rational. (It is natural to say that peasant rebellions took advantage of new *opportunities* that became available as a result of the state's collapse. But note that these lead to action *via* peasants' [changed] beliefs about them. Similarly, the explanation of peasant revolutionary collective action might be thought to require reference to peasant *capacities* for collective action – in particular the collective capacity that is the product of community [Taylor, 1988b] – as well as to their desires and beliefs; but again these explain action *via* individual beliefs about them – beliefs that arise from the experience of living in the village community.)

This would be one way of filling out Skocpol's structural account. Even if we say, as perhaps Skocpol would have done, that the events – such as foreign wars – that led to changed desires and beliefs are somehow the products of structures, the resulting account is surely no more (or less) a structuralist explanation than an individualist one. But in any case, as I said earlier, I would not want to assume that locations in social structures are the only sources of desires and beliefs; usually (always?) *other* prior desires and beliefs (as well as other external causes) are among the proximate explanatory antecedents of (changes in) desires and beliefs. Nor would I want to assume that, where there is a strong causal link from social structures to desires and beliefs, there is no "slippage" in the transmission – that structures are transmitted predictably and automatically into desires and beliefs. For between social structural and other causal "inputs" and the "final" desires and beliefs that are the proximate causes of action, certain "interior" processes may intervene – processes of judgment (in the interpretation and application of the requirements of one's own social roles, for example), critical reflection (on one's own desires and beliefs, including normative beliefs), self-evaluation and self-modification (of the pattern of one's first-order judgments and reflections), as well as, perhaps, the operation of the emotions.[8]

To explain social change, then, we clearly need to refer to more than stationary structures. But just as there are explanations of change that are purely structural, so there are accounts of social change that explain change directly in terms of events without recognizing that the effects of these events on social change (which must be via action) often depend on (the experiences of individuals located in) social structures. The effects of such events are refracted through structures. Thus, the same events can produce quite different social changes in places with different social structures, because the structures will determine in part the rational responses of differently situated individuals to the events in question. (This is the methodological burden of Robert Brenner's argument [1982, 1976] against explanations of economic development in terms of the "external" stimuli of population growth, the rise of trade, and the appearance of new productive forces, which do not give proper recognition to the mediation of the events by the structure of property relations. The *content* of Brenner's argument is also relevant to the origins of social revolution and I shall return to it later.)

A great deal of the argument on all sides of the continuing debates on the explanatory roles of structure, culture and action has clearly been too general, abstract and disembodied to be persuasive. (And where, occasionally, theoretical reflection has been combined with detailed historical study, general methodological positions have been staked out that are not compatible with the author's own version of historical events. Skocpol and Laitin are examples.) So in trying here to contribute to this debate I have thought it essential to make my case through a fairly detailed discussion of historical examples. I turn now to the first of these: the construction of the peasant village community in prerevolutionary France and Russia.

---

[8] That human beings, probably uniquely, possess these reflexive capacities is enough for some writers to put them beyond explanation. But if, as I believe, we have no good reason to deny that the sources and workings of these capacities and processes themselves have causes (however dimly they are presently understood), is there then no room left for *agency?* It would certainly seem so, if for agency we require that the agent be (in Roderick Chisholm's words) a "prime mover unmoved." The urge to see human beings in this way – the urge to save them uniquely from being a part of the causal flow – seems to be driven by a vastly too crude conception of causation and by the thought that the alternative is to "reduce" human beings to the level of creatures whose behavior is triggered by environmental stimuli in the simplest, most direct way. But of course human beings do not (always) respond in this way. Between their environment and their actions may come reflexive, self-evaluating and self-modifying processes of the sort referred to above. And though all these capacities – and variable individual propensities to exercise them – have causal ancestries, they are enough, it seems to me, to enable us to distinguish agents "sufficiently within the causal fabric" and hence to save human beings from being *just* another link in the causal chain or a *mere* conduit of the causal flow. For a full and for me persuasive defense of this view, see Daniel C. Dennett, *Elbow Room: The Varieties of Free Will Worth Wanting* (1984).

The making of the peasant village community

"Rationality and Revolutionary Collective Action" (Taylor, 1988a) was about the explanation of action in terms of *given* social structures. Here, I take one of these structures, the peasant village community – which Skocpol rightly took to be an important necessary condition of the French and Russian revolutions – and try in turn to explain *it*, to show why it was the way it was on the eve of each of these revolutions.

In the French and Russian cases, the peasants were able to take advantage of the breakdown of the state and spontaneously mount large-scale effective insurrections because they already lived and worked as members of strong village communities. In China, on the other hand, spontaneous insurrections did *not* occur, according to Skocpol, because such preexisting communal solidarity was absent. Eventually the Chinese peasantry *did* mount a successful assault on the landlords, but only after it had been organized painstakingly by the Communist Party, whose cadres, in effect, acted as "political entrepreneurs" to strengthen and extend what community there already was. Skocpol, in my view (Taylor, 1988a), sees too little preexisting community in the Chinese countryside: The Chinese Communist Party would not have succeeded there unless it had found *something* to work on. But she could hardly have failed to see that the greatly strengthened communities and new organizations that eventually formed the foundations of the peasants' fight against the landlords and opposing armies were *constructed*, mainly by the intentional actions of Communist cadres.

That the peasant village communities that were already in place in France and Russia on the eve of revolution were also constructed is less obvious. This is no doubt because in part they evolved very slowly and came to be the way they were at those times as a result of enormous numbers of individual actions over very long periods of time. I do not intend to try to sketch this history, which is what would be required for a full explanation of the state of these communities on the eve of the revolutions. I shall look at only a part of the story, though an important part, which shows why the peasant community was still vigorously alive as late as 1789 in the French case and 1917 in the Russian, when processes had been in train during the preceding centuries that left to themselves would have greatly weakened if not dissolved the village community as they had done elsewhere, most notably in England.

In tracing the evolution of French and Russian peasant communities, I am dependent on the secondary sources. In the case of France I rely especially on recent work by Hilton Root (1987), who has carried out the most detailed studies of this question.[9] In the case of Russia, fortunately, there seems to be little

---

[9] The role of states in creating peasant communities was mentioned by Samuel Popkin in *The Rational Peasant* (see mainly pp. 39–40). I am not as sure as Popkin seems to be about the generality of this element in the origins of peasant communities and will confine my discussion here to the cases of France and Russia. For an account of a different (but still intentional) path to peasant community formation and strengthening, see Stern (1983).

disagreement among historians about the broad outlines of the evolution of the peasant community and in particular about the extraordinary role in it of state action. The actions of state managers, we shall see, played a large direct part in constructing, strengthening, and preserving peasant communities, down to the eve of the revolutions. This turned out to be doubly fateful for the prerevolutionary state. For the preservation of communal arrangements in the rural economy almost certainly did much to impede economic development in these two countries and hence to bring about that relative economic and military backwardness that was a precondition of the state crisis from which the revolutions emerged, and then provided the social basis for the peasant collective action that, taking advantage of the state's collapse, revolutionized relations of production in the countryside.

France

We can begin the story for France in the fifteenth century, when the crown, in its efforts to build a centralized state and form a unified nation, sought to undermine the authority and influence of the lords. In pursuit of this goal, it set about confirming peasant property rights and strengthening them in law (thus preventing landlord appropriation of land abandoned during the demographic decline of the fourteenth and fifteenth centuries) and developing, among other things, its own system of courts to which the local seigneurial courts were to be subordinate. Village communities were encouraged to make use of these courts and were accorded formal recognition as corporate legal actors. At the same time, the corporate identity of these communities was strengthened when the crown began to tax peasants directly but, lacking the control and the resources to assess and collect taxes from individual peasants, assessed their communities instead and made each of these communities collectively responsible to the crown for apportioning the tax burden among its members and collecting the taxes from them. The crown adopted and developed this method from the seigneurs, who had earlier helped to strengthen communities or even to introduce communal organization as an aid to controlling and dealing with the peasants generally and ensuring a regular flow of income in particular.

Then, with the rise of the absolutist state in the seventeenth and eighteenth centuries, these communal rights and responsibilities of the peasants were further strengthened by the crown. Behind the state's activities here, we find once again geopolitical-military competition. To meet the escalating costs of fielding large standing armies and keeping up with the new military technology, the state needed to extract increased tax revenues. To do this without bringing on a fresh wave of the rebellions that tax increases had induced in the recent past, the crown chose a set of policies that had the effect of strengthening the village community. In order to ensure that taxes got paid more regularly and that a higher proportion of the peasantry's surplus income went to the state, the crown had first to make villages more solvent and reduce their debts to private creditors. Famines, epidemics, and especially a century of intermittent warfare had by midseventeenth century reduced many peasant communities to insolvency. They had sold off communal lands and woods and other possessions to seigneurs and others with wealth and had contracted considerable debts. From the crown's point of view, the payments on these debts, and the taxes that some communities were obliged to levy on their own members to meet community expenses, simply siphoned off peasant income that could have gone to the crown, and the loss of communal lands had in many cases so weakened the peasant economy that communities had difficulty in meeting their obligations. So the crown, wishing to increase its revenue without further impoverishing the peasantry and increasing the risk of rebellion, set about (from 1659) restoring to the communities all the woods and meadows and other commons they had sold off since 1620. The purchasers had to be compensated by the communities over a ten-year period. Furthermore, seigneurs who had at any time since 1630 exercised their right to take a third of any common lands that were divided were obliged to return them. At the same time, the crown liquidated and repaid the communities' debts. And finally, in edicts issued in the 1680s, the peasant communities were forbidden to alienate communal property in the future (Mousnier, 1979: 559–61).

In order, moreover, to keep the lords on the crown's side, their tax-exempt status had to be preserved. So the state could raise money from them only by borrowing it; and in order to give prospective investors confidence in the state it had to persuade them that peasant communities were solvent – which in any case they had to be if the state was to service the debts.

Part of the cohesion of the rural community derived, of course, from the shared opposition of its members toward the lords, whose depredations engendered among the peasants a defensive unity that overcame their internal differences. (See, for example, Bloch, 1966; Soboul, 1956.) The strengthening of this oppositional cohesion was another by-product of the state's actions in this period. To ensure that the fiscal policies described were implemented in the countryside, the king appointed intendants, whose jurisdiction in the villages became so extensive that in time the traditional administrative and political village role of the seigneur was undermined. Having still to pay seigneurial dues as well as royal taxes, and having access as communities to the royal courts, the peasants were now encouraged to challenge their seigneurial obligations in the courts; but since they usually lost these cases, the experience served only to intensify their opposition to the seigneurs and so strengthen their own unity.

The French state, then, driven especially by the fiscal demands of international competition, pursued in the century after 1650 policies whose effect was to strengthen the rural communities. In fact, it rescued and preserved them; for it seems likely that, if the state had not intervened, if the erosion of the common property resources and communal rights that were their lifeblood had been allowed to continue, the communities, with the help of the seigneurs and townspeople who were buying their properties, would have broken themselves up by the time of the Revolution.

In the final decades before the Revolution, the state did, however, come to see rural communalism in a new light and, in a *volte-face* similar to the reversal of Russian policy embodied in the Stolypin reforms (see below), began from mid-century onwards to try to dismantle the peasant communities. Intensifying international competition, especially with England, and France's drastic losses in the War of the Austrian Succession (1740–8) and the Seven Years' War (1756–63) in particular, strengthened the hand of those who felt that the old (community-strengthening) policies, whatever their merits in Louis XIV's time, must now be abandoned. Instead, the crown must now generate economic growth (and hence increased tax revenue) by promoting economic individualism. The community's collective responsibility for taxes would have to go, common lands would have to be partitioned and enclosed, collective control of individuals' activities and rights would have to be abolished, and generally the individual members of the communities, especially the more prosperous individuals, were to be given a freer hand to become efficient capitalist farmers.

But the royal edicts that legislated this agrarian reform were to have little effect. This was above all because most of the intendants in the villages, believing that the changes would make it impossible for them to collect the taxes and difficult for the peasants to pay them, obstructed the implementation of the legislation. They continued to hold communities collectively responsible for taxes, they declined to initiate partitions and enclosures, and in general they allowed the peasants to continue in their old collective ways.

The upshot was that on the eve of the Revolution the peasant community was scarcely diminished in its vigor and in its capacity for collective action. I think it is reasonable to conclude that this state of affairs had been brought about largely by the intentional actions of state managers, at least in the sense that if they had not acted in the way they did, the rural community would have been much weaker in 1789.

Russia[10]

Any group of neighboring cultivators *could* constitute a community (Taylor, 1982), though perhaps in a weak sense, even if it held no resources in common and collectively refrained from regulating in any way the use to which individuals put their privately possessed resources. If, however, the members of a group held some resources as common property – woodland, pasture, and water, for example – and together directly regulated individual use of them, then there had to be some degree of community among them. The degree of community would tend to be greater still if, as in an open-field system like that of prerevolutionary France, there were also a certain amount of collective regulation of the use of important resources, like arable land, that were in private possession. In much of

---

[10] The following account draws especially on Atkinson (1983); Gerschenkron (1965); Pipes (1977); Shanin (1972); Watters (1968); and particularly Blum (1971a, b, 1961).

prerevolutionary Russia, communal control went even further than this, for the distinctive features of the commune were its practice of periodically repartitioning its arable land so as to roughly equalize the amounts held by its member-households and its collective responsibility to the government for the payment of taxes. It is to these two features in particular that we must pay attention if we are to account for the peculiar strength of the Russian peasant commune – and hence its exceptional capacity for collective action – as late as 1917.

The land-equalizing repartitional commune, or *obshchina*, did not become widespread until the eighteenth century, but the village commune – a weak community with little autonomy – had emerged during the fifteenth and sixteenth centuries. Long before that, during the Kievan period, what had probably been an extended patriarchal family unit or "great family commune" had given way to the "territorial commune" (*volost*) that regulated the use of pastures, forests, and fisheries held in common among neighbors and assumed responsibility for apportioning the tax burden and collecting the taxes from its constituent households, while leaving them free, in their isolated farmsteads or hamlets, to run their private holdings more or less as they saw fit.

Then, beginning in the fifteenth century, three developments got under way that were no doubt causally interrelated, though the exact timing and causal connections are not entirely clear. First, there was a movement away from the isolated farmsteads and hamlets that hitherto had characterized the settlement pattern as peasants began to come together in villages. (The proportion of settlements that were villages was to reach almost 78 percent by the mid-nineteenth century.) Second the authority and autonomy of the territorial commune declined, and the *volost* was displaced by the village commune, as the seigneurs, who had in increasing numbers received from their sovereigns grants of land that cut across the territorial commune boundaries, undermined the authority of the *volost*, imposed ever greater restrictions on the individual peasant's use of his holding (using the village commune and its officials as their agents), and, over the century beginning around 1550, with the backing of a series of laws made by a cooperative state, gradually reduced their tenants to the status of serfs. Third, bound up with this movement toward the village commune was the introduction, probably beginning in the fifteenth century, of the open-field system.

The advent of open-field cultivation in any locality would of course have required a much closer cooperation among the peasants, and this would have indicated the establishment of villages if these did not already exist. The growth of hamlets into villages could also, of course, have resulted in part from mere population growth. In the steppe provinces, concentration into villages would have been a rational defensive reaction to the constant threat of raiding by nomads. But Jerome Blum also speculates that in other areas the peasants were brought together to live in communities *by the lords* to make it easier for the lords to control them and exact obligations (Blum, 1961: 506). Similar building and strengthening of village communities by seigneurs occurred much earlier in many parts of Western Europe.

The final development of communal repartitional land tenure, however, did not take place until the eighteenth century (though in a few exceptional places it seems to have emerged in the seventeenth or even the sixteenth century). The manner in which the repartitional commune was introduced varied, but in most cases it is clear that intentional action by state managers and landlords played a significant part. Consider first the category of seigneurial peasants. The spread of collective repartitional tenure among the serfs seems to have resulted from actions taken by the serf owners, which in turn were precipitated by the introduction by the state of the soul tax in 1724. This new tax required payment of the same amount by every adult male serf. Since most of a peasant's income derived from his own allotment of land, the peasants with little land would have found payment of the tax much more difficult than would those who were better off. And since the lord was made responsible for collecting the tax, it was in his interest to see that every one of his peasants was in a position to pay up. He set about doing this by allotting to each "peasant labor unit" (*tiaglo,* which usually consisted of a man and a woman, though sometimes it was larger, so that a peasant homestead would typically possess more than one *tiaglo*), an equal amount of land, or rather taking account of the variable productiveness of the land, so much land as to enable each *tiaglo* to produce the same amount. (It has to be remembered that the *obshchina* did not *farm* collectively: Individual households cultivated their own allotment separately and were the owners of what they produced, net of rents and taxes.) Since the number of productive individuals (and hence the number of *tiagla*) in each household changed over time for normal demographic reasons, this equality of landholdings could be maintained only by periodically redistributing the community's land. The serf owner handed over responsibility for this to the peasants themselves, who knew far more about the variable quality of the land than he did. And so was born the repartitional commune.

In the origin, at a later date, of the repartitional commune among the nonseigneurial peasantry, the state often had a more direct hand. It was concerned, as always, to ensure that every peasant had the wherewithal to meet his tax obligations; it probably also believed that egalitarian land redistribution made rural discontent less likely and reduced the probability of peasant violence. The state itself directly introduced the repartitional commune later in the eighteenth century and in the early nineteenth century among the so-called black peasants (those living on land to which private upper-class landowning had not been introduced) and among peasants living on court-owned land. In other areas, the peasants themselves introduced it, usually as a result of pressure from the community's poorest members, who in some cases appealed successfully to the government (Blum, 1961: 514–23).

The next and near-final stage in the construction of the Russian peasant commune was ushered in by the Emancipation Edict of 1861. The effect of this, a consequence intended by its authors, was to preserve the land-equalizing repartitional commune where it already existed, and even to strengthen its communal character, and to introduce it in areas where it was not already established.

In view of my earlier discussion of the international background to social revolution, it is interesting to note that the desire on the part of state managers to free the serfs and their belief that the time was ripe for it were the products of Russia's defeat in the Crimean War. In the first place, the tsar and his advisers concluded, with good reason it would seem, that Russia's economic (and hence military) backwardness had something to do with the defeat and that the institution of serfdom had something to do with the backwardness of the overwhelmingly agrarian economy. A few no doubt concluded that it was not serfdom per se that was the sole or main barrier to a more productive rural economy but rather communal tenure and the practice of repartition, which reduced the individual peasant's incentive to husband his allotment with an eye to the future and invest in its improvement, and the want of sufficiently large, enclosed holdings to make investment and innovation rational. If so, their fears were overridden by the political and fiscal considerations that seem to have been uppermost in state managerial minds. Above all, there was the desire for political stability fueled by fear of peasant unrest. (And perhaps peasant disturbances during the war also helped to persuade some that serfs did not make a good foundation for an effective modern army.)

If the serfs were to be freed in the interests of political stability, then for the same reason it was imperative that something take the place of the erstwhile authority and order-maintaining powers of the lords. This role, it was thought, could be carried out by the *mir*. But the *mir* owed its effectiveness to the *obshchina*. And besides, the *obshchina*, through its land-equalizing repartitions, assured all its members a subsistence, and, as long as it survived, no rural proletariat would emerge. For these reasons too, then, the *obshchina* was viewed as a bulwark against peasant unrest. Finally, if serfdom was to go and the flow of tax revenue to the state was to be maintained, then the freed serfs must be guaranteed the wherewithal to meet their tax obligations – which of course would be accomplished by continued membership in an *obshchina* – and the taxes must be collectible – which again would be facilitated by having the peasant kept in place on the land under a strong *mir*. This was to be assured by the system of redemption payments devised by the legislators, which had the additional merit, from the state's point of view, of maintaining for some time to come the lords' supply of labor and income and hence their ability to meet *their* obligations to the state.

What the Emancipation did was to grant the individual member of a village commune the formal freedom (after an initial period) both to separate out his strips of land from the *obshchina* into a (possibly consolidated) private holding and to leave the commune altogether, but to make either of these moves virtually impossible in practice. These formal freedoms were to take effect after an initial period of nine years during which the peasants were to be obliged to remain in place and pay quitrent or fulfill labor obligations, as before, for the use of their land. After that, the peasants would have to make redemption payments over many years before the land became theirs. The *mir* was made responsible for meeting the redemption obligations, which would be made to the lord by agreement, or, failing agreement, to the state over a period of forty-nine years. The separation of a peasant's land from the commune's land before the redemption obligation had been discharged could occur only with the consent of the commune – unless the individual householder paid up the whole of the remaining redemption debt for his land (or paid half of it if the remaining members of the commune agreed to pay the other half). Very few peasants were in a position to do this; and the commune would be loathe to let them go, since it needed every householder it could get to share in the collective redemption. The principle of collective responsibility thus effectively bound the individual to the *obshchina* and tended in fact to strengthen its communal element.

As if this were not enough, the Emancipation Act put further obstacles in the path of a peasant wishing to leave the commune. He had to relinquish forever his rights to communal land allotments and of access to the commons, discharge all outstanding tax payments for his entire household, and obtain the consent of his parents.

Where land tenure was not communal, households could redeem their land individually, but now the whole village was henceforth to be collectively responsible for the payment of taxes. In this way, the principles of the *obshchina* were extended to areas where previously they had not been practiced.

In thus strengthening the peasant community, the Emancipation helped to prepare the way for the abortive 1905 Revolution and, since the Stolypin reforms of 1906–10 had (as we shall see) only limited success in weakening the communes, for the 1917 Revolution as well. It is worth noting in passing that the Emancipation probably helped to prepare the Revolution in another way: Its provisions were a bitter disappointment to the peasants (following the Edict there were hundreds of disturbances requiring intervention by government troops), and this served both to intensify the peasants' desire for more land and to bring about a long overdue disenchantment with their tsar.

In the years between the Emancipation and the 1905 Revolution, the state actually took steps to further buttress the village commune. Although its abolition of the poll tax in 1885 should have weakened one presumption in favor of land-equalizing repartition, the state then immediately proceeded with various Acts that had the effect of protecting and even strengthening the hold of the commune over its members – for example, the Act of 1886, which decreed that any household wishing to divide its property between its members must first obtain the consent of two-thirds of the village gathering (*skhod*); the Act of 1893, decreeing that there should be at least twelve years between repartitions (often interpreted in practice as a twelve-year *maximum* interval!) but also that between repartitions the *mir* could not take back any of an individual's allotment (which had the net effect, apparently, of inducing the adoption of repartition in areas where it had not been practiced); and the Act of November 1893, which stipulated that an individual peasant must now also obtain a two-thirds majority of the gathering if he wanted to redeem his land before the commune had redeemed all of its land and further prohibited the sale of allotment land to anyone not a legally defined peasant.

It was not until 1905 that the government finally abandoned its faith in the commune as a bulwark of political stability. In the widespread peasant violence beginning in that year and continuing into 1906 and 1907 – including destruction of manor houses, seizures of estate land and property, and strikes by agricultural workers (Perrie, 1972) – "the Russian peasant commune dramatically revealed its additional latent function as a generator of egalitarian ideology and as a school for collective action of a kind capable of turning into revolt overnight" (Shanin, 1972: 37). The government's response was first to announce in November 1905 that redemption payments would be reduced by 50 percent in 1906 and abolished altogether as of January 1, 1907, and in autumn 1906 to decree that peasants would no longer be subject to passport control by the commune. Then, with the appointment of Stolypin as prime minister in July 1906, came a determined attempt at a wholesale attack on the peasant commune. Stolypin initiated a series of reforms (from November 1906 to 1911) designed to break up the commune and to promote capitalist farming. The reforms were supposed to end collective responsibility for taxes and to make it easier for the individual peasant (especially the richer peasant) to withdraw from the commune and to become established as an independent owner of a consolidated farm.

But it seems that the reforms had only limited success. The peasants were uncooperative, and in the relatively brief space before the Revolution (in which the peasants in effect reversed Stolypin's reforms and reestablished the commune where it had been broken) only a small percentage of land was separated from the communes and enclosed.[11]

So that, on the eve of the 1917 Revolution, the peasant village commune was still a strong, flourishing institution. Over several centuries, especially the two that preceded the revolution, it had been *constructed*. It was the precipitate of past intentional actions – those of the peasants themselves of course, but especially those of the lords and above all those of state managers.

Excursus: social structure and economic backwardness

The peasant community, whose existence was a precondition of social revolution in France and Russia because it provided the social basis for sustained, rational, revolutionary collective action, played a central role in another of the preconditions for revolution in these two countries. The peasant insurrections took advantage of – and would certainly not have succeeded without – the breakdown of the old-regime states. These state crises developed as a result of "intensifying military competition with nation-states abroad that possessed relatively much greater and more flexible power based upon economic breakthroughs to capitalist industrialization or agriculture and commerce" (Skocpol, 1979: 50). A central reason,

[11] This seems to be the general view now. See Shanin or Pipes (1977: 19).

then, why these old regimes were not competing successfully and were unable to mobilize extraordinary resources sufficiently rapidly to meet the new military threats that preceded the revolutions was that, unlike their principal competitors, they presided over backward agrarian economies.

A full explanation of the origins of these two revolutions, one that went behind the immediate precipitants and triggers of the revolutionary events, would therefore ideally provide an explanation of the economic backwardness of these countries relative to their principal competitors. At any rate, a "nonvoluntarist, structural" account of the causes of social revolutions, such as Skocpol claims to provide, would presumably have to explain this economic underdevelopment without reference to intentional action. I cannot take this possibility seriously. Of course, the intentional actions that constitute economic development or result in underdevelopment must themselves be explained, and the desires and beliefs that explain them could no doubt in large part be structurally explained (in particular, by structures of property relations, about which more in a moment), but, once again, *these* structures in their turn have to be explained.

The village *community* constituted one aspect of the rural social structures of prerevolutionary France and Russia that almost certainly gave rise to desires and beliefs resulting in action uncongenial to economic development. This has been noticed by many historians and, as we saw earlier, it was recognized by experts and politicians and even some state managers themselves in the decades leading up to their respective revolutions. In both countries, the development of large, enclosed holdings, separated from the common lands and/or freed of communal control, was thought to be a necessary condition of rural economic development. In Russia, the practice of periodical land-equalizing repartitioning was reckoned to be especially unconducive to development, since it diminished any incentive the individual peasant might have to husband his allotment and invest in its long-term improvement.0

Now of course the communal institutions of the agrarian economy are only a part of the social structure, and they are not the only part that is relevant to the explanation of economic development or underdevelopment. They are in fact a part of the structure of what Robert Brenner calls property relations, defined as "the relationships among the direct producers, among the class of exploiters (if any exists), and between the exploiters and producers, which specify and determine the regular and systematic access of the individual economic actors (or families) to the means of production *and* to the economic product" (Brenner, 1986: 26. Emphasis in original). Brenner has argued that these "property relations will, to a large degree, determine the pattern of economic development of any society" and in particular will explain the origins of agrarian capitalism and the first breakthrough to sustained economic development in England and the underdevelopment of the French economy relative to the English in the same period (Brenner, 1982, 1976 [reprinted in Aston and Philpin, 1985]. On the French case, see also Hoffman, 1988).

In its general *form,* Brenner's argument about economic development illustrates well the approach (or at any rate an aspect of the approach) to explaining social change sketched earlier. The (economic) actions that individuals (here producers and exploiters) find it rational to pursue are to be explained in terms of "specific, historically developed" property relations (in particular, capitalist property relations provide the conditions under which individuals find it rational and possible to act in such a way as to sustain continuous economic growth, whereas precapitalist property relations prevent development); and the emergence of a new structure of property relations (in particular, the transition to capitalist property relations) must be explained as an unintended consequence of intentional actions.

Substantively, Brenner's argument leads him to conclude that a transition to capitalism was least likely where the peasants possessed *collectively*, as communities, their means of subsistence while such a transition was most likely where the peasants possessed their means of subsistence *individually*. Where *communities* possess the means of subsistence (land above all) or control its allocation, they are most unlikely to allow individuals to alienate their land or separate it off from the community's holdings (Brenner, 1986). And (as we saw, in the last section, in the case of prerevolutionary France and Russia) the lords, too, would generally act to maintain the community and its control over its members, and even to reconstruct the community where it had decayed.

This analysis, if correct, provides part of the explanation for why England had made the breakthrough to capitalist property relations and hence to sustained economic growth well before the time of the French Revolution while most of France had not and why, despite a crash program of industrialization around the turn of the century, Russia still had an essentially precapitalist agrarian economy at the time of the 1917 Revolution and was economically underdeveloped relative to her principal military competitors. We would of course still need an explanation of how (for example) peasant possession and control of access to land came to be and to remain in large part communal in France in the centuries leading up to the revolution, while in England communal possession and control had long since largely given way to individual ownership. Part of such an explanation was sketched in the previous section, where we saw how intentional actions, above all by state managers, helped to construct peasant communities in France and Russia and to preserve them from decay and dissolution.

A final methodological point about Brenner's approach (see also Brenner, 1977). In criticizing explanations of the origins of modern economic growth based on technological innovation, the rise of trade, and especially the growth of population (which is the dominant approach in the historical literature), Brenner wishes to deny not that these things, especially population growth, are important, but only that they determine social change directly. Rather, they cause economic development (if at all) only *through* the existing structure of property relations. Putting the point in the language used earlier, social change (e.g., economic development) is brought about by *actions;* the rational course of action for an individual (what to produce and how) depends, *via* his desires and beliefs, importantly on his location in social structures (say, in the structure of property relations). It follows that how an individual economic actor responds to some external stimulus – like population growth, the emergence of new opportunities for trade or of new productive forces – depends on the structure of property relations in which the actor is embedded and the actor's location in it. Thus, the same external stimulus may lead to different forms of change, because it is refracted through different structures – as, for example, population growth had different consequences for economic development in different parts of Europe in the late medieval and early modern period because it was refracted through different structures of property relations.[12]

II. Explaining the origins of norms

In this section, I consider the explanation of desires and beliefs, which rational choice explanations characteristically take as given (and also, usually, as changing). My discussion is by no means exhaustive or systematic; it tries only to exhibit examples of both structural and intentional origins of desires and beliefs, to show through these examples how rational choice explanations of action need to be and can be complemented by structural and cultural explanations of desires and beliefs, but also (paralleling the argument in the second part of section I) to argue that culture itself has to be explained and that a key part of the explanation must be intentional. A general implication of these arguments, taken together with those in "Rationality and Revolutionary Collective Action," is (as I argued in section I) that neither structure, nor culture, nor action has explanatory primacy or autonomy.

My main examples (for reasons given in the introduction to section I) concern normative beliefs – beliefs about how things ought to be or ought to be done. In two of the examples, the beliefs could reasonably be said to constitute or at least be central components of *ideologies*. The first example is drawn from the work of James Scott and shows how the desires and beliefs making up a part of what he calls the "moral economy" of the peasant, which can be accommodated

---

[12] The general point here is also nicely illustrated by Skowronek (1982). He shows how a systematic transformation of state organization took place in the United States between 1877 and 1920 as a result of three "environmental stimuli"; namely domestic and international crises (the end of Reconstruction, the Spanish-American War, World War I), class conflict (between labor and capital, between factions of capital), and "the evolving complexity of routine social interactions" (e.g., population growth and concentration and technological growth). But Skowronek emphasizes that the structural or institutional changes did not flow automatically from these stimuli, for they were (indeed had to be) carried out by individual actors – above all by occupants of government offices – and how these people responded to the external stimuli depended on "the institutional and political arrangements that define their positions and support their prerogatives within the state apparatus." In particular, although officeholders had to respond to these external developments, they tried to do so in a way that preserved their positions and the powers that flowed from them. As in Brenner's argument, then, existing structures mediate or refract the impact of external changes.

without strain within the methodological framework I have advocated and should, *pace* Skocpol, play a role in the explanation of peasant rebellion,[13] are the products of locations in (or, more precisely, experiences of) social structures. The subsequent examples provide illustrations of the way in which ideological or normative beliefs can change as a direct and indeed intended result of intentional actions.

On some accounts, the values and beliefs (or propositional attitudes), including the *normative* beliefs, actually held by a group of people *are* its culture. On this view, the explanation of the origin and evolution of *culture* is the subject of this section of the essay, and one of my arguments here is that intentional actions must be a key part of the explanation of cultural change. On some other accounts, culture refers to the propositions themselves, to those things about which people have or could have desires and beliefs. On the first account, the standard folk-psychological explanation of action is of course directly in terms of culture (or cultural facts). On the second account, culture must enter in an obvious way into the explanation of the desires and beliefs that explain action, and hence it is relevant to the explanation of cultural change. But clearly it cannot alone have causal power. Part of a culture, in this sense, cannot be explained in terms of other parts or by its relation to the whole, and relations between the parts of such a cultural system – underlying polarities, contradictions, or whatever – cannot in themselves propel or explain cultural or any other sort of social change. Culture is not self-generating. Although what follows is mainly about normative *beliefs*, it has obvious implications for the explanation of culture in this second sense.[14] I emphasize that I shall not be attempting either a general characterization of "culture" or a (general) theory or explanation of cultural change.

Before discussing some examples of the emergence of norms in the real world, a brief aside is in order on some recent theoretical work that looks set not only to generate new interest in this subject among political scientists but also to start them down the wrong road. The work I have chiefly in mind is Robert Axelrod's (1986) "Evolutionary Approach to Norms" and related work by James Coleman.

Axelrod begins with an *n*-person Prisoners' Dilemma (PD) game. In what he calls the "basic norms game," each player must first choose between cooperating and defecting in this PD; then, any player who sees a defection (which he or she does with a given probability) may choose to punish the defector, but at a small cost to himself or herself. So players' payoffs are determined by the outcomes of

---

[13] Alan Knight (1986, especially 1: 150–70) has argued persuasively for the importance of peasants' ideological or normative beliefs for an understanding of at least the Mexican Revolution. He stresses, too, the important role played by the peasant community in providing the organizational cell of revolution – the social basis of revolutionary collective action – but again parts company with Skocpol in seeing the developments that precipitated the revolution as largely endogenous.

[14] There are many other usages of culture. The word is unfortunately used for a hopeless variety of things and often to cover simultaneously (or variably!) a variety of different things, some of them ill-defined. To be analytically useful, its usage clearly must be restricted and stable. It should in my view *include* normative beliefs or at least *shared* normative beliefs.

the PD and by whether they punished defectors and/or, if defecting themselves, were punished by others. In repeated plays of this game in a computer simulation, high-scoring individuals have more "offspring" in the next round, and low scorers are eliminated. A "norm" is then said to have been established if few defect in the underlying PD and many punish those who do defect.

This "basic norms game" was then extended to a "metanorms game," in which it was additionally possible for each player to punish anyone who did not punish a defector in the PD game.

Recent work by James Coleman (1986) proceeds in a similar way: First equating a norm with "the set of sanctions that act to direct the behavior in question," then (bizarrely) taking mere cooperation in an iterated PD to be "equivalent to obeying a norm," and finally introducing a two-stage game in which the players first make choices in a PD, then decide whether to sanction those who chose to defect in it (and in which, presumably, a norm would be said to have emerged when players cooperate in the PD and sanction those who don't).

Axelrod's and Coleman's work, then, is not about norms but about sanctioning systems.[15] These two must in my view be kept distinct if we are to make any progress in answering the old (and still unresolved) question of whether and to what extent norms have independent causal efficacy or motivating force (hence in particular whether norms can solve collective action problems). If we are to get clear about these things, we must separate normal *practice* from ideals or normative *beliefs* (beliefs about how things should be or should be done) and distinguish both of these from sanctioning systems. It is, of course, to norms as ideals or normative beliefs that we must pay attention if we are ever to decide the question of whether norms can compel action that is not in the actor's self-interest.[16] On Axelrod's definition, "a norm exists in any social setting to the extent that individuals usually act in a certain way and are often punished when seen not to be acting in this way." This equates a norm with normal *practice* (how

---

[15] Earlier, Toshio Yamagishi (1988a,b; 1986) had made experimental studies of the emergence of just such a sanctioning system, beginning also with a first-order PD game but not using Axelrod's – to my mind dubious – "evolutionary" approach and with no confusion of sanctioning systems and norms. In his experiments, players were given money that they could keep or contribute to the provision of a public good; additionally, some groups were given the opportunity of developing a negative sanctioning system, which punishes the member of the group who cooperates least in the (first-order) public goods game and which is therefore itself a (second-order) public good. The amount of punishment was determined by the total contributions to the sanctioning system. The findings were, as expected, that where there was no opportunity to develop a sanctioning system, cooperation was greater in groups consisting of individuals who had been found to be "high-trusters" than in groups of "low-trusters"; but, interestingly, when subjects were presented with an opportunity to develop a sanctioning system, it was found that (1) low-trusters contributed *more* to the punishment than did high-trusters; (2) the amount of *first-order* cooperation was greater than when no sanctioning system could be developed; and (3) the effect of the sanctioning system on first-order cooperation was greater among the low-trusters than among the high-trusters. These results give some empirical support to Hobbes's argument.

[16] In the few paragraphs I devoted to norms in *The Possibility of Cooperation* (1987: 29–30), I wasn't entirely clear about this.

people usually act) *together with* a system of *sanctions*. It makes no reference to ideals or normative beliefs, which in my view are the essence of norms. It is, of course, very difficult in many cases to separate the effects of sanctions from the effects of norms per se. Often, subtle informal social sanctions are at work, or there are sanctions operating in a different arena at some remove from the normatively required action, which may then function merely as a signal that one would act properly in the other arena.

Axelrod himself states (without argument or evidence) that "an established norm can have tremendous power," that "norms . . . govern much of our political and social lives," that "norms have virtually wiped out colonialism . . . and retarded the spread of nuclear weapons" (!) and so on. That systems of (sufficiently severe) *sanctions* can have such powers is not in doubt. We also know that we can "internalize" social disapproval and suffer from feelings of guilt without being shamed, and this, or its prospect, can have motivational force. But this still leaves unanswered the interesting question of what motivational force, if any, normative belief or subscribing to a norm can have.

Many philosophers have argued, in a variety of ways, that there is a conceptual or constitutive or analytic link between making a normative (or at least moral) judgment or having a normative (or moral) *belief* that one should perform some action and being *motivated* or possessing a motivating reason to perform it. (The motivation could of course be just one of several, possibly competing, motivations simultaneously influencing the individual, so that even if having a normative belief necessarily is to have or necessarily engenders a motivation to act, the action will not necessarily be performed by someone having the belief or of subscribing to the norm.) There are, for example, those who argue that to have such a belief *is* nothing other than to have the appropriate desire (to say that you think some end is morally good or right is just to say that you value it); or that to make an evaluative judgment is to be disposed to favor a certain action and such a disposition is a kind of desiring. There are those who argue that recognizing a normative truth rationally requires one to have the appropriate motivation. And there are those who argue that one could not have *come to make* a normative judgment (there would be no point in trying to reach such a judgment) without also coming to have, in some degree, the corresponding motivation. But there are many other philosophers who are not persuaded that there are any of these or any other conceptual or constitutive or analytic connections between normative belief or judgment and desire or motivation, and I agree with them (which is not to deny that as a matter of fact people very often are motivated to act in accordance with their normative beliefs).[17]

This problem is not the focus of what follows, but it brings out the importance of separating systems of sanctions from ideals or normative beliefs. It is to the

---

[17] Some notable defenses and discussions of these various positions are Ayer (1937), Hare (1952), Foot (1978), Frankena (1958), McDowell (1978), Nagel (1970), Railton (1986), and Smith (1988, 1987). I am grateful to Michael Smith for guidance here.

origins and evolution of the latter (in the real world) that the rest of the essay is devoted. Let us first consider two cases in which it makes sense to see social structures as providing the main source of normative beliefs (the first example) or *changes* in social structures as providing the main impetus to *changes* in normative beliefs (the second example). Then, in the following section, we will consider two examples of intentional explanation of changes in normative beliefs.

Explaining culture structurally

The moral economy of the peasant

Though James Scott (1976) has not been alone in describing and insisting on the explanatory importance of the "moral economy" of the peasant (or of the poor, or the crowd),[18] his account, besides being the fullest, has brought out most clearly its social-structural sources, which are my main concern here.

At the center of peasant politics, in Scott's view, is the peasant's overriding concern with obtaining a secure subsistence for himself and his family. This concern derives from his precarious position, which is in turn the product of a shortage of land, capital, and outside employment opportunities. If there is insufficient relief from the state, the owner of the land he rents, or his other creditors, and insufficient help from his kin and others in his community, then a bad harvest can mean starvation or, if this is to be avoided, dependence on others or sales of land and livestock resulting in reduced ability to subsist in the following years.

Fear of such a subsistence crisis leads the poor peasant to be highly averse to risk. Rather than trying to maximize average return, he will adopt "safety first" policies that he believes will minimize the probability of a disaster. To this end he follows the local traditions of seed varieties and methods of cultivation "designed over centuries of trial and error to produce the most stable and reliable yield possible under the circumstances" (Scott, 1976: 2) and he spurns new varieties and techniques promising higher average yields if they are attended with greater probability of failure to produce a subsistence in any one year.

Together with these technical arrangements, the peasants maintain certain social arrangements that also serve to reduce the probability of a subsistence crisis for each family or to cushion the blow if it comes. They include the practice of reciprocity and work sharing, especially among kin; the use of a variety of informal social controls to bring about a little redistribution of the wealth of the village's better-off members, who are expected to display greater generosity in giving to their less fortunate kin and neighbors and in sponsoring religious rituals and supporting other village activities; and the retention by some villages of communal land that can be allotted to the neediest members of the village or rented out for their benefit. Informing these practices, in Scott's view,

---

[18] See also, most notably, Thompson (1971) and Moore (1978).

is the principle or norm that whenever the village's resources are sufficient, it should guarantee every family a subsistence minimum.

Fear of a subsistence crisis and the concomitant aversion to risk governs the peasant's attitudes to much else. He would rather be a smallholder than a tenant and a tenant rather than a wage-laborer, because although smallholders are often poorer than tenants and tenants often poorer than wage-laborers, the smallholder usually has more secure access to means of subsistence than the tenant, and both the smallholder and the tenant, who consume their own crops, are less vulnerable to market fluctuations than is the wage-laborer. The peasant also wants a land-tenancy arrangement that guarantees him a subsistence every year, not necessarily one that maximizes his average income; so he prefers a system in which the landlord assumes some of the risk (as in a sharecropping arrangement that gives the peasant a fixed *proportion* of the crop) or better still *all* of the risk (as in a "feudal" system of tenure giving all the profit to the landlord but guaranteeing a minimal return to the peasant) to an arrangement that, though it gives him all the profit, burdens the peasant with all the risk (as in a fixed-rent tenancy guaranteeing the landlord a fixed return). And similarly, the peasant wants a system of taxation by the state that is sensitive to his subsistence needs; so he prefers a system that taxes him only in years when he has a surplus over subsistence to one that takes a fixed proportion of his resources, and both of these to a fixed tax that must be paid regardless of the size of his harvest.

The "safety first" attitude that informs these practices and preferences does not imply that no peasant ever takes risks. If a new seed variety or new method of cultivation seems to promise substantial gains with little risk to subsistence security, even a poor peasant may try it. Richer peasants, of course, will be even more willing to take risks with a part of their production; and since they are less risk averse, they are also less likely to have the attitudes toward social arrangements for insurance against subsistence failure and the preferences among systems of land tenure and taxation that are shared by the great mass of their fellow peasants with little land and income.

The peasant's overriding concern with subsistence security is reflected, finally, in his conception of justice and his beliefs about when he is being *exploited* by landlord and state. In his view, he has a right to subsistence. For him this is a moral principle. It is joined to a second moral principle, the *norm of reciprocity*, by which he judges his relationships with others. Even in his most unequal relations – with state, landlord, or patron – the peasant has definite expectations about what is owed him in return for his taxes, rents, labor, and loyalty, and at the minimum he is owed a subsistence or the freedom to obtain one. So what he believes to be his right to subsistence sets a lower bound to the norm of reciprocity. When it is infringed, when the relationship in question is therefore not even minimally reciprocal, only then does he feel the relation to be exploitive. It is not how much is taken from the peasant, or how unequal the resulting distribution is per se, but how much is *left* to him that determines whether he believes himself to be *exploited*.

This account of the world of the poor peasant shows how certain preferences and beliefs, especially normative beliefs, are the products of his location in (or experience of) social structures, in this case mainly relations of production. It is the essential background to Scott's contribution to the explanation of peasant rebellion. For in his view, it is a rapid increase in the exploitation of a large body of peasants, a sudden massive violation of their "moral economy," that generates an explosive situation of potential rebellion.

In his case studies of rebellion in Vietnam and Burma in the 1930s, Scott shows in detail how there had been a steady deterioration in the position of the peasants under the colonial regimes and then a very rapid worsening on the eve of the rebellions. With the growth of the colonial state, more taxes had been collected more efficiently, including the hated fixed taxes that bore no relation to the peasants' subsistence needs. The concurrent commercialization of agriculture had exposed an increasing number of peasants to the insecurities of the market, producing even greater fluctuations in their incomes. The two developments together rendered the village less autonomous and less of a community, more fragmented and less able to maintain the social arrangements that helped to insure and protect the individual peasant against subsistence crises. The peasant also increasingly lost, under the impact of colonial policy and population growth, access to forest, wasteland, and common pastures, which fell into private owner-ship. Finally, the peasant's exploitation by his landlord increased, as population growth, the peasant's loss of common lands, the weakening of village redistribu-tive mechanisms, and the fluctuation of market prices all enhanced the bargain-ing power of the landlord relative to his tenants and laborers, while his claims against them were increasingly backed by the colonial state.

All these developments had made the peasant more vulnerable to world market fluctuations. And when, as a result of the world depression, the price of rice collapsed in 1930, the colonial government in Vietnam tried to make up for lost customs revenue by leaning harder on head taxes while landlords tried to com-pensate for their loss of income from rice sales by putting an end to the loans they formerly gave their tenants to enable them to pay their head taxes and meet production costs.

What followed – la terreur rouge in Cochin China, "the most massive popular revolt the colony had witnessed" in northern Annam, the Saya San rebellion in Burma – is described in detail by Scott.

Now a change in peasants' beliefs about their exploitation – leading presum-ably to changes in their assessments of the courses of action open to them, including participation in rebellion – is of course only (at best) a necessary condition for rebellion. Scott recognizes that whether peasant anger is translated into rebellion may depend on other conditions, such as the strength of the peasant community, the "repressive capacity of elites," and the unavailability to the peasants of opportunities for adapting incrementally to their deteriorating condi-tions. Let us assume, as Scott's discussion seems to warrant, that these condi-tions were not changing at the time of the outbreak of rebellion, or rather (since this is what matters in explaining whether peasants chose to rebel) that the peasants' desires and beliefs about these things were not changing. *Some* preference or belief, however, must change if revolutionary or rebellious actions are to become rational where they were not rational before. In Scott's account, these changes are in the peasants' beliefs about their exploitation. (This is, of course, in striking contrast to Skocpol's account in which, as I have emphasized, we have to *insert* the changes in beliefs – quite different beliefs – and the consequent actions, in order to provide the necessary links between structural preconditions and structural outcome.) It makes no substantial difference to my argument whether we say *either* that these changes were the product of changed social structures (notably the relations of production) *or* that the relevant structures did not change (the actors were still in the same sort of *relations* of production, even though there had been changes in the specific *interactions* "within" and sustaining these relations – the *terms* of A's tenancy agreement with B, and so on) and the changes that proximately caused rebellion were in desires and beliefs, including peasants' beliefs about their exploitation, which were brought about by "exogenous" developments (population growth, the depression, etc.) refracted through the existing social structures and assessed by the preexisting unchanged standards or norms of the peasants' "moral economy." (Of course, the exogenous developments were themselves the aggregate products of intentional action, even though their repercussions in Vietnam and Burma were hardly intended: agriculture is commercialized by *people;* demographic pressure increases because *people* have "too many" children, usually for good reasons; and so on.)

What Scott has given us, then (though this is not the way he puts it) is first an explanation, in terms of (experiences of) social structures, of certain peasant desires and beliefs, amounting perhaps to an ideology, certainly including normative beliefs; second, a convincing argument that these beliefs play an essential role in explaining peasant rebellion[19]; and third, an account of how "exogenous" developments, working "through" social structures and existing normative beliefs, lead to *changes* in desires and beliefs – an account of the sort that Skocpol needed to connect her structural preconditions with structural outcomes (though in her case other kinds of exogenous developments and changes in desires and beliefs would have to be considered).

Nothing in this argument of Scott's is incompatible with the explanatory scheme endorsed here. It is an example of the sort of explanation of the desires and beliefs informing action that must typically complement rational choice explanations. In Scott's examples, the normative beliefs are given a "structural" explanation, and it is not these beliefs whose change precipitates rebellion. In later examples we shall see how norms themselves may change, and change, moreover, as a direct and even intended result of intentional action. To find good accounts of such change, I have had to go outside the literature on revolution and rebellion.

[19] For another good example, see Knight (1986).

The evolution of inheritance norms and kinship ideology among the Toka

For a good example of how changes in social structures can lead directly to changes in normative beliefs, consider some recent work of Ladislav Holy (1986) describing an important change in norms of inheritance – from uterine to mainly agnatic inheritance – among the Toka, a Tonga-speaking people of the Southern Province of Zambia. The Toka are sedentary agriculturalists. Their chief domestic animals are cattle, although fishing provides their main source of meat. For subsistence crops, they grow bulrush millet, sorghum, and maize (which is also a cash crop, their only one).

Traditionally, Toka inheritance norms, both their usual practice and their ideas about how things should be done, were matrilineal. According to these rules, all the members of a man's matrilineage had a claim on his estate, though one of them was designated his principal heir. But recently a new norm, according to which a man's son should be his main heir, has emerged. The precipitant of this change was the introduction of a new technology, which made changes in certain of the relations of production desirable.

A standard "explanation" of the demise of matrilineal inheritance is that it results from a change from production for subsistence to product for exchange, for a concomitant of the latter is competition for scarce resources and this is incompatible with the wide distribution of resources engendered by matriliny. But there is no "mechanism" in this account to show how the change comes about, or rather how it is brought about. Instead, it is seen as an automatic adjustment in one part of a system of functionally interrelated parts that have come into structural contradiction (as between, for example, the family and the matrilineal descent group). A great virtue of Holy's account is that it shows *how* the change comes about.

Every Toka is both a member of his or her mother's *mukowa* and a "child" of his or her father's. A *mukowa* (plural *mikowa*) is a subdivision of a clan and consists of the geographically localized matrilineal descendants of one ancestress. It has a male head.

Under the old system of inheritance, when a man died, his social position as well as his material goods were passed on. The successor to his social position, who inherited his spirits or shade and his kinship duties, was ideally and usually his sister's son, though occasionally it was a uterine brother or a more distant matrilineal relative. His material goods, however, were divided among his kinsmen and affines, nearly three-quarters of the estate going to the members of his own *mukowa* (with the successor always being the main beneficiary), about a quarter to the members of his father's *mukowa,* and only a token going to affines and nonkinsmen. (This distribution itself is not normative; it is the average outcome of the practice of giving a share only to those who attend the final mourning ceremony, and, as a result of the spatial distribution of *mikowa,* members of the dead man's own *mukowa* usually get more.)

The development that precipitated the demise of the norm of matrilineal inheritance was the introduction of the plow, beginning in the 1920s and becoming widespread in the 1930s. Oxen and labor are scarce resources. Even the all-steel plow introduced in the 1930s requires four oxen, and the plowing and sowing behind the plow are done cooperatively and require three or four people. Most households, lacking sufficient labor and sufficient oxen, must cooperate with other households. There are two rules here: that a man without oxen should help to plow the fields of a man with oxen, who then uses his oxen to plow the fields of the former; and that close kinsmen should plow together. But in practice the first rule cannot be met because the distribution of plows to people is uneven, and the two rules together, sometimes invoked and sometimes ignored, are only two of many considerations that enter into the constitution of the plowing teams. Among the others are variable natural conditions affecting the timing of sowing and social relations other than those of close kinship, including relations of friendship and neighborliness. The rules are in fact subservient to the Toka's long-term goal, which is "to produce enough wealth to secure . . . a comfortable life in a dry brick house with a zinc roof furnished with pieces of European furniture." In practice, when putting together a plow team, a Toka will "strategically exploit" distant kinship and affinal relations as well as close kinship ties and in doing so will assess "the strategic importance of each particular kinship link, and the spatial proximity or distance of the relative in question, as well as the character, nature and intensity of previous interactions between them" (Holy, 1986: 66, 69).

Since residence is usually virilocal, the relationship that is in fact most important in recruiting plow teams is that between parent and son. The son is recruited at an early age (from nine or ten) into his parents' plow team, usually stays in the village after marrying, and continues to cooperate with his parents. When his father retires, the son becomes the plowman, assisted by his wife and mother, with the father occasionally lending a hand. The son shares in his father's right of disposal over the oxen and hence can use them to plow for money.

This new form of cooperation is taken by Holy as the outcome of the pursuit of economic self-interest by father and son. The father secures provision for his old age. The son *could* pursue his long-term economic goals independently of his father by buying his own cattle or borrowing oxen, but this is not compatible with his father's strategy. Of course, the father *could* get by without his son by recruiting a replacement into the plow team, but he would have much less control.

What has happened here, then, is that a technological development – the introduction of the plow – brought about, or more precisely made it rational for the crucial actors to bring about, a restructuring of the relations of production.

This new structure of relations – or at any rate this new pattern of interactions, which, if it endured long enough, would qualify as a new structure – led in turn to the emergence of new norms of inheritance and succession. The effect of conformity with the old norms, as we have seen, was to disperse a man's estate among his matrilineal relatives, the main heir being the successor to his social position, who was typically his sister's son. Under this system, then, a man's son would not have benefited from the wealth that, under the new relations of production, he had helped his father create through cooperation in plowing, and such cooperation would not then have been a rational strategy for the son.

Given that the new form of cooperation was, on introduction of the plow, desirable, it also became desirable that the old norms be modified. And that is what happened. The new norm of inheritance seems to be that, although the deceased's estate is still widely disbursed among his matrilineal kin, his *son* is the main heir, inheriting a large part of the estate and, most important, the plow and much of the herd.

Although the new norm of (mainly) agnatic inheritance emerged as a product of the self-interested pursuit of economic advantage, it was, says Holy (1986: 86), also *justified* by appeal to the belief traditionally held by the Toka that helping to produce a man's wealth entitled one to a share of it when he died, and this belief was itself a norm. No normative system exists in isolation. A norm is in general part of a system of more or less compatible norms. In some cases, then, changing or modifying one norm would make adjustments of other norms desirable. And even if events (like the introduction of the plow and the changes in relations of production it precipitated) did not make it desirable to change *several* norms, either directly or indirectly through a chain of adjustments (as they appear not to have done in the Toka case), the existence of other related norms would in general still be relevant to an explanation of the emergence of a new norm. For acceptance of a new norm among a group of people, especially by those whose material interests are not strongly affected, would often be eased by appeal to other normative beliefs they hold.

Many other cases could be mentioned in which norms have changed as a result of the emergence of new relations of production, which in turn have been brought about by technological changes. This pattern of change, it could be argued, conforms to the classical form of historical materialism. But it is not the only pattern. Norms do not evolve only in response to changes in the relations of production induced by development of the forces of production – as the following examples will show.

Intentional explanation of changes in normative beliefs

An individual's desires and beliefs, including normative beliefs, can change as a direct result of his or her own intentional actions. People can and do intentionally change their own goals, wants, and the like; and they can and do intentionally act to modify their own beliefs, particularly in order to reduce cognitive dissonance. (Cognitive dissonance, we can say, gives them preferences over beliefs [Akerlof and Dickens, 1984; Elster, 1983: ch. III, IV, 1979: 77–86].) Changes in desires and beliefs can also be in part the unintended consequences of others' actions, and they can be the *intended* product of others' actions. This last possibility is perhaps the least familiar, and the implied view of culture as directly constructed by intentional actors is one that many writers on culture and structure might be at least comfortable with. Let us consider two examples (in enough detail, I hope, to be persuasive).

The transformation of marriage and kinship norms in Europe

My second example of norm evolution involves a quite different process, though it too concerns inheritance. It is taken from Jack Goody's (1983) study of the radical changes that occurred in a range of marriage and kinship norms in the early Christian era. On Goody's interpretation, the new norms (though they were never universally subscribed to) were introduced by the church, in its pursuit of economic goals.

Before the spread of Christianity, kinship and marriage practices in most of Europe did not differ from practices widespread around the Mediterranean and in the Middle East. In particular, marriages to close kin were encouraged, as were marriages to close affines or the widows of close kinsfolk, the transfer of children between families by adoption, and the taking of concubines. These were norms in the sense both of normal practices and of shared ideals or normative beliefs. A man was expected to marry a close kinswoman. A widowed woman was expected to remarry promptly, usually to her dead husband's brother. A man with no heirs was expected to provide one by adopting a child or by taking concubines. All these practices were rejected by the early church, which, in setting out to overturn them, opposed itself not only to Roman law and custom and its own holy scriptures but to long-established popular practice. Why did it do this?

Goody's answer is essentially that these practices all served to keep inherited property within the family; by overturning them the church made possible the transfer of family property to itself.

Exogamous marriage meant that any property inherited by the wife could be passed on at her death to people outside her natal family. By preventing this – by ensuring that daughters married within the family – a family could prevent this dispersion of its property when it had no male heirs. (Women, it should be remembered, could accumulate property, especially through the prevailing institutions of the dowry and, since women generally lived longer than men, the dower.)

But what if a couple had no children at all? Other "strategies of heirship" were available to deal with this: divorce and remarriage, adoption, and polygyny or concubinage. By turning to one or more of these, a man could hope to provide a male heir and thus keep his property within the family. Since on average about 20 percent of couples have no boys and a further 20 percent have no children at all, some 40 percent of families would have no immediate male heir if all these practices were prohibited. By the fourth century, the church had begun to forbid them all – even adoption, which thus disappeared for 1,500 years. (It was not until 1926 that it was legalized in the United Kingdom, for example.)

The church needed resources to look after not only the poor but also itself and all those who left the care of their kin to devote themselves to its services. The effect of prohibiting these practices was to leave large numbers of families without heirs, "real" or "fictional," and thus with property that could more readily be bequeathed to the church. And the church did not fail to encourage them to do this.

These norms – the ideals that the church sought to establish as practice – did not command universal assent. Unsurprisingly, there was much resistance (which is, as Goody says, hard to quantify). But it is certain that the church did somehow succeed in instilling in large numbers of people such a concern for their souls and a fear of eternal damnation that they were willing to part with a great deal of their property. For the consequence of this radical transformation in the norms and (in Goody's words) the "ideology of marriage" was that the church rapidly became enormously wealthy and powerful, not through tithes, taxes, and rents merely, but also through the transfer of title to land. In most European countries it became the largest landowner. In England, perhaps a quarter of all land was in the church's hands by the fifteenth century (and the church is *still* the largest landowner, despite Henry VIII's dissolution of the monasteries).

"Hegemony and culture" among the Yoruba

My final example of intentional culture formation is provided by a recent study by David Laitin (1986, 1985). The changes described by Laitin certainly involved changes in normal practices and presumably also in normative beliefs. But Laitin nowhere speaks of norms, only of "culture," of which norms are, of course, a part. His study is of special interest here because he claims – inadvisedly as we shall see – that what he has uncovered compels the social theorist to go "beyond rational choice." Rational choice theory, he says, may be of use in explaining "marginal decisions," but it cannot help us to explain "structural transformations" (1985: 303). It can, in his view, explain "marginal" choices within given social structures and cultures (including ideologies), but it cannot explain how these "givens" arise. This is an old claim. It has of course been one of the objects of this essay to show that it is mistaken.

Laitin's work provides a detailed illustration of how a restructuring of a group of people's political practices and ways of thinking about their political world – their political culture – can be brought about by the intentional actions of external powerholders, such as state managers and their local officers and advisers. It provides us in fact with the basis for an intentional explanation of just those structure- and culture-transforming processes that Laitin believes require us to go "beyond rational choice."

Laitin tells us that "culture orders political priorities" – that is, it shapes desires and beliefs – but also that "shared cultural identities facilitate collective action." If we recognize that political priorities – and desires and beliefs more generally – may have other sources besides "culture," this much is perfectly reasonable and of course conforms to the explanatory scheme endorsed in this essay. Because a shared cultural (ethnic, linguistic, religious) identity facilitates collective action, it may be rational for a person to modify his or her "cultural identity," for example, by emphasizing or even transferring his or her allegiance to a cultural group in order to take advantage of the group's greater success in obtaining collective goods, and it may pay a political entrepreneur to appeal to this shared identity when trying to mobilize a group of people for collective action. This idea flies in the face of those, like Clifford Geertz, who see cultural identities as "primordial," taken by the individual as given and unchanging and never to be questioned. But, as Laitin says, study after study of the "third world" has shown how these identities are malleable, how supposedly "primordial" groups have been *constructed* by political entrepreneurs, and how communal identities have been intentionally politicized and used in the pursuit of advantage, especially of benefits dispensed by governments. There is "overwhelming evidence that tradition is less a constraint on action than a resource for political engineering" (1986: 99).

But Laitin finds both "primordial" and "rational-actor" theories wanting, at least for the purpose of explaining his Yoruba materials. Since the late 1890s about 80 percent of the Yorubas (of whom there are some ten million in all), who dominate southwestern Nigeria, have been converted in equal numbers to Christianity or to Islam. *This* cleavage has not been politicized, and religion has not become the basis of political organization despite the fact that Christians enjoy definite economic advantages over Muslims; therefore there has existed ample scope for religion-based efforts by political entrepreneurs and an inducement for appropriate "identity investment" by ordinary Yorubas. Instead, Yorubas have organized themselves politically in terms of their membership of "ancestral cities" and, far from treating these as primordially given, have "for a long time strategically reformulated their ancestral city identities in order to position themselves for economic and political benefits" (1985: 286).

Ancestral cities are the erstwhile city-kingdoms that between them ruled the Oyo Empire (1600–1836). After Yorubaland was brought into the British Empire at the end of the nineteenth century, ancestral city identity should have atrophied and disappeared, for no sociocultural differences were correlated with ancestral city membership, and in time there were many Yoruba families who had not lived in their ancestral cities for generations. So why did the ancestral city become, as it still is today, "the central basis for political identity and mobilization within the Yoruba states of the Nigerian Federation," an identity sustained by now-traditional rituals and festivals?

The reason, Laitin tells us, is quite simply that the administrators of the British colonial state, wanting political control at low cost, intentionally revived and strengthened these ties! By reviving the fortunes of the old rulers of the ancestral cities as part of their policy of indirect rule, recognizing claims based on the ancestral cities, providing benefits to groups making such claims, defusing religious antagonisms while exacerbating those between ancestral cities, and so on, the British *self-interestedly constructed* the framework within which Yorubas would henceforth conduct their politics.

Although intentional explanation may have little to contribute to the study of the *formation* of the desires and beliefs of Yorubas acting within the framework created by the British, or of the desires and beliefs that informed the actions of the British in creating this framework, it is clearly an indispensable part, as the factual part of Laitin's account itself shows, of the explanation of these *actions* of the British. We do not need to "go beyond rational choice," as Laitin claims we must, in order to understand this part of the story – to understand what he himself calls "resource manipulation by the colonial state."[20]

III. Four concluding remarks

1. I have given illustrations of two kinds of causal origins of (changes in) norms; there are, of course, others. There is no single general theory or explanation of the emergence or evolution of norms (which is not to deny that some quite general things can be said about why we have norms and about why and in what circumstances they have motivational power independently of sanctions). There is not just one way in which norms can emerge or evolve, no single type of causal origin. Norms, and desires and beliefs more generally, can have structural, intentional, and cultural sources. (But recall earlier remarks about culture and note the fourth remark below.)

2. It should be clear from what I have said in this essay and its precursor that I am not committed to methodological individualism, at least not to that version of it according to which the properties of individuals alone provide "rock-bottom" or "ultimate" explanations. The proposition that explanatory chains "behind" an explanandum must always terminate at individuals is implausible. It is an equally implausible claim that social structures or cultures, or elements of them, should always provide the explanatory terminus. So too is the stronger claim that structures have their effects regardless of individual actions or desires and beliefs. I am rejecting, then, two widespread methodological views or programs: the one that views individuals – their actions, desires, beliefs, and even their very identities – as completely determined by, or explicable solely in terms of, their locations in social structures or cultures and that tries to explain structural and cultural change in terms of properties of the structure or cultural system itself, the individual being, in some structuralist versions, all but eliminable; the other that views culture and social structure as formed by and explained *solely* in terms of individual action and takes little or no interest in the explanation of the actions or the desires and beliefs that inform them.

But I am also rejecting another, currently popular view that, accepting that

---

[20] See Laitin (1985: 308–11) for other studies of deliberate action by colonial states to mold political structure and culture – all of them requiring us, in Laitin's view, to go "beyond rational choice," but all in fact perfectly consistent with the explanatory framework endorsed here.

neither action nor structure should alone have explanatory primacy or autonomy, seeks to conflate the two, claiming that they are *mutually constitutive* and that social relations are *internal* relations, the relata not being even definable independently of their relations.[21] There is some descriptive merit in this claim, but as an approach to explaining social change it is useless. To conflate structure and action is to rule out from the start the possibility of explaining change in terms of their interaction *over time*. It is hardly surprising, then, that none of the explanations I have used here for illustration, and no other detailed explanation of social change I am aware of, would be possible, given the premises of this "structurationist" program.

3. If intentional explanation is an indispensable part of all good (fine grained and "deep") explanation of social change, what form should the intentional part of the explanation take? The illustrations of intentional structure making and culture making discussed in this essay and its precursor all in fact conform to the standard "thin" theory of rational choice. On this account (which underpins almost all economic theory and its extensions into other social sciences, including the theory of collective action): (1) rational action is action that is *instrumental* in achieving or advancing *given* aims in the light of *given* beliefs; (2) the agent is assumed to be egoistic; and (3) the range of incentives assumed to affect the agent is limited.

But the thin theory of rationality does not *always* provide a good foundation for explanatory theories. (For example, the theory of collective action founded on the thin theory of rationality fails to explain *some* cases of collective action, though not as many as some suppose [see Taylor, 1988a, sec. VI for a brief discussion].) In "Rationality and Revolutionary Collective Action," I suggested four conditions under which behavior is most *likely* to be thin rational (and hence under which a thin theory is most applicable). Here, I want to restate these conditions (with one modification), provide some additional comment on them, and conclude with a remark about their implications for the explanation of cultural change.

The conditions are that (1) the options of courses of action available to the agent are limited; (2) at least some of the thin incentives facing the agent, or the (not necessarily monetary) costs and benefits attached to the alternative courses of action, are to the agent in question well defined, clearly apparent, and substantial; (3) much (for the agent) turns on the choice – that is, whether or not the agent realizes it when choosing, it matters (or will turn out to matter) a great deal to the individual which action is chosen (the "wrong" choice will be costly); and (4) prior to the choice situation there have previously been many similar or analogous occasions.

I did not claim that these conditions are either necessary or collectively suffi-

---

[21] See note 3. There is much *else* in the "structurationist" writings of Giddens and others that is perfectly consistent with what is said here, but the *distinctive* element in "structuration theory," which I have emphasized here, makes nonsense of it.

cient, only that, ceteris paribus, the more any one of them is satisfied, the more successful is a thin theory likely to be.

From the three characteristics of the thin theory of rational choice, we can see that a thin theory has explanatory power only where three sorts of motivations have little force: expressive motivations – the desire to be "true to one's self," to act consistently with one's deeply held commitments to principles, ideals, and so on; genuine altruism (beyond the family), as opposed to reciprocity; and motivation by "in-process" benefits or by what Tibor Scitovsky calls "pleasure." Since we can say, summarily and informally, that the conditions under which behavior is most likely to be thin-rational characterize situations of "scarcity" and "constraint," then moral self-expression, altruism, and "pleasure" are, as it were, luxuries.

Consider condition 1. It does not entail that action is determined. It says only that options are limited, but not that they are necessarily limited to one only. Like the other conditions, this condition alone is not sufficient. There are, as we shall see, choices between only two options (for example, between two possible spouses), which are unlikely to be made thin-rationally.

By "limited" in condition 1 is meant only limited numerically. That a thin theory is likely to get more explanatory purchase when the options are of limited *complexity* is implied by the first two parts of condition 2. In very many choices, including important ones that satisfy condition 3, such as the choice of a marriage or living partner, the goals and the connections between them and the available courses of action are not well defined and clearly apparent, so that, in these choices, the first two parts of condition 2 are not satisfied.

Notice next that the last part of condition 2 is not equivalent to condition 3. This is because the terms of condition 2 – the costs and benefits attached to alternative courses of action – are subjective, in the sense that the agent *sees* clearly what is at stake and thinks at the time of choosing that much is at stake (for him- or herself); but this is not entailed by condition 3. Think again of the choice of a marriage or living partner: what is at stake in choosing between the alternatives may not be apparent and may not be (subjectively) substantial at the time of choosing (so that condition 2 is not met), but it may soon become apparent that much *did* turn on the choice. Or more generally, the individual may not see a substantial offer or threat (or throffer) until some time after the choice has been made. Of course, it will often be the case that if condition 3 holds, then so too does condition 2, because the agent *recognizes* that condition 3 is true *and* is able to assess the costs and benefits. The agent is even more likely to come to this recognition if condition 4 also holds.

Condition 2, then, applies subjectively, to an agent's deliberations, whereas condition 3 applies objectively. The argument involving condition 2 holds because, if it is satisfied, deliberation is likely to yield rational choice; whereas the argument about condition 3 holds because, if it is satisfied, nonrational choice is likely to be eliminated. But rational choosing can thus survive such selecting or filtering only if the choice situation recurs. Hence condition 4. However, that prior to the choice situation in question there have been many similar or analogous occasions is not alone sufficient to filter out nonrational behavior if the survival or at least flourishing of the rational choosers or of rational choosing does not turn on choices of the type in question. Hence condition 3.

Thus, behavior is more likely to be thin-rational, the more each of conditions 3 and 4 is satisfied, *given* that the other is to some degree satisfied.

There are, then, clearly many choice situations in which behavior is unlikely to be thin-rational. Among others, they importantly include, first, a range of cases where, even though conditions 1 and 3 and in some cases perhaps 4 are met, the options are so complex or comprehensive that condition 2 is not met. These include choices on which a person's whole future flourishing might turn, like the choice of a spouse, of a career (though *some* people choose between careers by considering only the streams of income they are likely to provide), or between alternative jobs. In choices of this kind the problem is that the alternatives are *incommensurable*.

Such choices are made for reasons, but not as a result of calculation of benefits and costs or any other sort of calculation, nor even, in some cases, after deliberation. They nevertheless get made. And some of these choices between incommensurable alternatives are such that, however they are made (and whether thin-rationally or not), a person, having chosen (or finding him- or herself "in" or "with" one of the alternatives), cannot consider or would refuse to consider other alternatives (for example, alternative spouses, money or career in exchange for children, friendship, and so on); or, contemplating alternatives, cannot or would not view them as commensurate with whatever option he or she is already committed to. These involve what Joseph Raz (1986: ch. 13) has called "constitutive incommensurabilities."[22] Certain sorts of personal relationships and commitments to some kinds of projects and pursuits are in part *constituted* by such attitudes or incapacities: Lacking them, one cannot be said to *be* in such a relationship (to be a friend, for example) or be truly committed to such a project. The making of such commitments may not be explicable as thin-rational choice; in any case, having made or first accepted them, continuing to accept or affirm them will not be the product of thin-rational choice, will in fact put beyond the explanatory power of thin-rational choice theories an important domain of potential choosing.

4. What do these conditions tell us about the explanation of the origins and evolution of culture? Ernest Gellner has written: "The notion . . . that our life should be understood not in terms of constraints, operating through fear and hunger, but on the contrary, that what really guides social life are symbols and meanings and systems thereof, codes, etc., is extremely widespread . . . and is associated with slogans such as 'hermeneutics' and 'structuralisme'"; and elsewhere that "there are extensive aspects of human life, alas including those that

---

[22] Raz writes (1986: 334–5): "It is a mistake to think that if consequences are momentous they will translate into reasons for one action or the other which will make the choice determined."

seem essential for survival, where the actual sequence of events is determined not merely by the free play of some underlying [cultural] core mechanism (if indeed it exists at all), but by the blind constraints, shortages, competitions and pressures of the real extraneous environment."[23]

It's pretty clear in these essays what Gellner has in his sights, but not clear what he wants to put in its place. We cannot explain what people do and hence how social and cultural change come about by reference only to cultural systems or systems of symbols and meanings, by looking at the relations between elements of these systems or trying to discern some "underlying core mechanism" or "structure." Once again, to make a set of symbols or propositions or propositional attitudes (desires and beliefs) interintelligible, to make part of a system of such things intelligible or reasonable in the context of other parts of that system or of the system as a whole, is not, as so many writers suppose, to explain them. This much Gellner is certainly saying, and I agree with him.

Nevertheless, culture has a part to play in explaining action and hence social and cultural change. This is obviously so if culture is conceived of as a set of people's actual propositional attitudes, or desires and beliefs; but it is also true if culture is taken to be the propositions themselves – the objects of these desires and beliefs – and the relations between them. For in behaving and acting, people make use of the cultural materials (as well as other resources) that are already available, just as, in gaining a subsistence, building a house, or painting a picture, people make use of the available materials and technologies, which must therefore figure in the explanations of these activities. But (a very large literature, much of it structuralist or hermeneutic, notwithstanding) cultural elements

---

[23] These two quotations are from Ernest Gellner (1985: 160, 150) from his essays, "No *Haute Cuisine* in Africa" and "What Is Structuralisme?" In another essay in the same volume, "The Gaffe-Avoiding Animal, or A Bundle of Hypotheses," he has written (69, 71–3) that *Zweckrationalität*, or instrumental rationality, "presupposes that we can isolate, identify ends, aims, criteria of that which will satisfy us, which will warrant our treating the endeavour as having been crowned with success," or again that *Zweckrationalität* is possible only "within delimited areas" where "the criteria of success and the connections between available means and desirable ends are adequately defined . . . and efficiency is consequently identifiable . . . without undue difficulty." Gellner may be arguing here roughly that *Zweckrationalität* is possible only where the first two parts of my condition (2) are satisfied. Note that he seems to have in mind *any* sort of instrumental rationality, not necessarily thin rationality as I characterized it earlier, for he says that it is possible to be a *zweckrational* chess player, bridge player, and so on, as well as to be *zweckrational* at mountain climbing or moneymaking. Indeed it is. But note that these comments of Gellner's appear in an essay in which he argues that people in fact spend much of their lives not in the pursuit of aims but in the avoidance of gaffes. Gaffe avoidance, too, as Gellner realizes, can be viewed as an end whose pursuit can be accommodated within the *Zweckrationalität* model, but he resists such a move on the grounds that it courts the familiar danger of making *all* behavior rational, hence of turning the hypothesis of rational choice into a tautology. But if people try to avoid making gaffes because they want to win the acceptance and approval of others or at least to avoid their disapprobation, and if we assume that *this* general goal provides the only other type of incentive besides that of material or economic advantage (as in fact many explanatory rational choice models, including Olson's, do assume), then we certainly do not have a tautology. (Compare Taylor, 1988a: 66, and n. 5.)

(in the second sense of culture) and the relations between them do not by themselves move people to action, so cannot by themselves explain social and cultural change. Contradictions, for example, have no effect until they become the objects of inconsistent beliefs whose holders are moved to resolve the inconsistency. (They might be so moved by others – that is, by the desires and beliefs brought about by others, as in the Goody case discussed previously. They might resolve the inconsistency differently at different times, as it suited their interest at the time, as in the case of the Toka, where, although the old norm of inheritance was largely supplanted by the new one, with which it was inconsistent, it continued to be available, to be wheeled out by someone in support of his or her claims whenever it was convenient [Holy, 1986: ch. 10]. And such an inconsistency might be resolved by someone moved inter alia by preferences over their own beliefs to resolve their cognitive dissonance.)

Culture, then, enters into the explanation of action. But cultures, too, like social structures (see section I), have to be made (and into the explanations of the actions, of which cultures and social structures are the intended or unintended consequences or residues, culture and structure both enter). Much important culture making, and probably even more of structure making, should be explicable as thin-rational action, as I hope the examples discussed in this essay bring out. But it should also be clear, if my argument characterizing the conditions under which thin-rational choice theories are most likely to get explanatory purchase is correct, that many of the actions that directly create or cumulatively modify culture are not subject to scarcity and constraint and hence are *not* explicable in this way.

References

Akerlof, George A., and William T. Dickens. (1984). "The Economic Consequences of Cognitive Dissonance." In George A. Akerlof, *An Economic Theorist's Book of Tales*. Cambridge: Cambridge University Press.

Altham, J. E. J. (1987). "The Legacy of Emotivism." In Graham Macdonald and Crispin Wright (Eds.), *Fact, Science and Morality: Essays on A. J. Ayer's Language, Truth and Logic*. Oxford: Blackwell.

Aston, Trevor H., and C. H. E. Philpin (Eds.). (1985). *The Brenner Debate: Agrarian Class Structure and Economic Development in Pre-Industrial Europe*. Cambridge: Cambridge University Press.

Atkinson, Dorothy. (1983). *The End of the Russian Land Commune, 1895–1930*. Stanford, Calif.: Stanford University Press.

Axelrod, Robert. (1986). "An Evolutionary Approach to Norms." *American Political Science Review* 80: 1095–111.

Ayer, A. J. (1937). *Language, Truth and Logic*. Oxford: Blackwell.

Barry, Brian. (1970). *Sociologists, Economists and Democracy*. London: Collier-Macmillan.

Bhaskar, Roy. (1979). *The Possibility of Naturalism*. Brighton: Harvester Press.

Bliss, C. J., and N. H. Stern. (1982). *Palanpur: The Economy of an Indian Village*. Oxford: Clarendon Press.

Bloch, Marc. (1966). *French Rural History.* London: Routledge and Kegan Paul.

Blum, Jerome. (1971a). "The European Village as Community: Origins and Function." *Agricultural History* 45: 157–78.

(1971b). "The Internal Structure and Polity of the European Village Community from the Fifteenth to the Nineteenth Century." *Journal of Modern History* 43: 541–76.

(1961). *Lord and Peasant in Russia.* Princeton, N.J.: Princeton University Press.

Brenner, Robert. (1986). "The Social Basis of Economic Development." In John Roemer (Ed.), *Analytical Marxism.* Cambridge: Cambridge University Press.

(1982). "The Agrarian Roots of European Capitalism." *Past and Present* 97: 16–113.

(1977). "The Origins of Capitalist Development: A Critique of Neo-Smithian Marxism," *New Left Review* 104: 25–82.

(1976). "Agrarian Class Structure and Economic Development in Pre-Industrial Europe," *Past and Present* 70: 30–75.

Coleman, James S. (1986). "Social Structure and the Emergence of Norms Among Rational Actors." In Andreas Diekmann and Peter Mitter (Eds.), *Paradoxical Effects of Social Behavior: Essays in Honor of Anatol Rapoport.* Heidelberg/Vienna: Physica-Verlag.

Dennett, Daniel C. (1984). *Elbow Room. The Varieties of Free Will Worth Wanting.* Oxford: Clarendon Press.

Elster, Jon. (1983a). *Explaining Technical Change.* Cambridge: Cambridge University Press.

(1983b). *Sour Grapes.* Cambridge: Cambridge University Press.

(1979). *Ulysses and the Sirens.* Cambridge: Cambridge University Press.

Foot, Philippa. (1978). "Morality as a System of Hypothetical Imperatives." In Philippa Foot (Ed.), *Virtues and Vices and Other Essays in Moral Philosophy.* Oxford: Basil Blackwell.

Frankena, William K. (1958). "Obligation and Motivation in Recent Moral Philosophy." In A. I. Melden (Ed.). *Essays in Moral Philosophy.* Seattle: University of Washington Press.

Geertz, Clifford. (1973). *The Interpretation of Cultures.* New York: Basic Books.

Gellner, Ernest. (1985). "No *Haute Cuisine* in Africa," "What Is Structuralisme?," and "The Gaffe-Avoiding Animal or A Bundle of Hypotheses." In Ernest Gellner, *Relativism and the Social Sciences.* Cambridge: Cambridge University Press.

Gerschenkron, Alexander. (1965). "Agrarian Policies and Industrialization: Russia 1861–1917." In *The Cambridge Economic History of Europe.* Vol. 6. Cambridge: Cambridge University Press, pt. 2, ch. 8.

Giddens, Anthony. (1984). *The Constitution of Society: An Outline of the Theory of Structuration.* Cambridge: Polity Press.

Goody, Jack. (1983). *The Development of the Family and Marriage in Europe.* Cambridge: Cambridge University Press.

Hare, R. M. (1952). *The Language of Morals.* Oxford: Clarendon Press.

Hoffman, Philip T. (1988). "Institutions and Agriculture in Old Regime France," *Politics and Society* 16: 241–64.

Holy, Ladislav. (1986). *Strategies and Norms in a Changing Matrilineal Society: Descent, Succession and Inheritance Among the Toka of Zambia.* Cambridge: Cambridge University Press.

Knight, Alan. (1986). *The Mexican Revolution.* Vol. 1. Cambridge: Cambridge University Press.

Laitin, David D. (1986). *Hegemony and Culture: Politics and Religious Change among the Yoruba.* Chicago: University of Chicago Press.

— (1985). "Hegemony and Religious Conflict: British Imperial Control and Political Cleavages in Yorubaland." In Peter B. Evans, Dietrich Rueschemeyer, and Theda Skocpol (Eds.), *Bringing the State Back In.* Cambridge: Cambridge University Press.

Lewis, David. (1988). "Desire and Belief." *Mind* 97: 323–32.

McDowell, John. (1978). "Are Moral Requirements Hypothetical Imperatives?" *Proceedings of the Aristotelian Society* 52: 13–29.

Moore, Barrington, Jr. (1978). *Injustice: The Social Basis of Obedience and Revolt.* White Plains, N.Y.: M. E. Sharpe.

— (1966). *Social Origins of Dictatorship and Democracy.* Boston: Beacon Press.

Mousnier, Roland. (1979). *The Institutions of France under the Absolute Monarchy, 1598–1789.* Chicago: University of Chicago Press.

Nagel, Thomas. (1970). *The Possibility of Altruism.* Oxford: Clarendon Press.

Perrie, Maureen. (1972). "The Russian Peasant Movement of 1905–1907: Its Social Composition and Revolutionary Significance." *Past and Present* 57: 123–55.

Pipes, Richard. (1977). *Russia under the Old Regime.* Harmondsworth: Penguin.

Popkin, Samuel L. (1979). *The Rational Peasant: The Political Economy of Rural Society in Vietnam.* Berkeley: University of California Press.

Railton, Peter. (1986). "Moral Realism." *Philosophical Review* 95: 163–207.

Raz, Joseph. (1986). *The Morality of Freedom.* Oxford: Clarendon Press.

Root, Hilton L. (1987). *Peasants and King in Burgundy: Agrarian Foundations of French Absolutism.* Berkeley: University of California Press.

Sahlins, Marshall. (1985). *Islands of History.* Chicago: University of Chicago Press.

— (1976a). *Culture and Practical Reason.* Chicago: University of Chicago Press.

— (1976b). *The Use and Abuse of Biology: An Anthropological Critique of Sociobiology.* Ann Arbor: University of Michigan Press.

Scott, James C. (1976). *The Moral Economy of the Peasant: Rebellion and Subsistence in Southeast Asia.* New Haven, Conn.: Yale University Press.

Sewell, William, Jr. (1985). "Ideologies and Social Revolutions: Reflections on the French Case." *Journal of Modern History* 57: 57–85.

Shanin, Teodor. (1972). *The Awkward Class.* Oxford: Clarendon Press.

Skocpol, Theda. (1985). "Cultural Idioms and Political Ideologies in the Revolutionary Reconstruction of State Power: A Rejoinder to Sewell," *Journal of Modern History* 57: 86–96.

— (1979). *States and Social Revolutions.* Cambridge: Cambridge University Press.

Skowronek, Stephen. (1982). *Building a New American State: The Expansion of National Administrative Capacities, 1877–1920.* Cambridge: Cambridge University Press.

Smith, Michael. (1988). "On Humeans, Anti-Humeans and Motivation: A Reply to Pettit." *Mind* 97: 589–95.

Smith, Michael. (1987). "The Humean Theory of Motivation." *Mind* 96: 36–61.

Soboul, Albert. (1956). "The French Rural Community in the Eighteenth and Nineteenth Centuries." *Past and Present* 10: 78–95.

Stern, Steve J. (1983). "The Struggle for Solidarity: Class, Culture, and Community in Highland Indian America." *Radical History Review* 27: 21–45.

Taylor, Michael. (1988a). "Rationality and Revolutionary Collective Action." In Michael Taylor (Ed.), *Rationality and Revolution.* Cambridge: Cambridge University Press.

(1988b). "Community, Collective Capacities, and Freedom of Choice." Paper for Conference on Community and Liberty, Tucson, Ariz., June 1988.

(1987). *The Possibility of Cooperation.* Cambridge: Cambridge University Press.

(1982). *Community, Anarchy and Liberty.* Cambridge: Cambridge University Press.

Thompson, E. P. (1971). "The Moral Economy of the English Crowd in the Eighteenth Century." *Past and Present* 50: 76–136.

Watters, Francis M. (1968). "The Peasant and the Village Community." In Wayne S. Vucinich (Ed.), *The Peasant in Nineteenth Century Russia.* Stanford, Calif.: Stanford University Press.

Wendt, Alexander E. (1987). "The Agent-Structure Problem in International Relations Theory." *International Organization* 41: 335–70.

Yamagishi, Toshio. (1988a). "Exit from the Group as an Individualistic Solution to the Free Rider Problem in the United States and Japan." *Journal of Experimental Social Psychology* 24: 530–42.

(1988b). "The Seriousness of Social Dilemmas and the Provision of a Sanctioning System." *Social Psychology Quarterly* 51: 32–42.

(1986). "The Provision of a Sanctioning System as a Public Good." *Journal of Personality and Social Psychology* 51: 110–16.

5. Wages, strikes, and power: An equilibrium analysis

Peter Lange and George Tsebelis

A pattern and an introduction

One of the central features of neocorporatist systems is "labor quiescence . . . infrequent strike activity and wage restraint" (Cameron, 1984: 170). In countries with corporatist forms of interest intermediation, strike rates have been extremely low by comparative international standards (Cameron, 1984; Hibbs, 1978). These low rates of strike activity were preceded by comparatively high rates, but precipitous and seemingly permanent declines occurred sometime shortly before or after World War II (Hibbs, 1978). Even the occasional outbursts of labor agitation have been short-lived and low by international standards.[1]

Low strike rates in corporatist systems have generally been accompanied by very low rates of unemployment. They have also been associated with relatively stable control of government by political parties sympathetic to the labor movement, high rates of unionization, and a centralized trade union structure that carries on highly institutionalized and relatively centralized bargaining with employers. The government provides a high "social wage" to workers via transfer payments. The "fear of the sack" (Kalecki, 1971) is less trenchant than in most other of the advanced industrial democracies.

In neocorporatist systems, therefore, very low strike rates are associated with

A version of this essay was prepared for delivery at the 1988 Annual Meeting of the American Political Science Association. The essay was substantially revised while Lange was a Fellow at the Center for Advanced Study in the Behavioral Sciences supported by the National Science Foundation (#BNS - 8700864). George Tsebelis acknowledges the financial support of the Institute of Industrial Relations, University of California at Los Angeles. The authors would like to thank Brian Loynd for research assistance.

[1] Labor quiescence is an important part of the "virtuous circle" that characterizes economic performance in the corporatist countries: Political and institutional conditions foster labor quiescence, which, in turn, promotes improved economic performance, which, in turn, reinforces the favorable political and institutional conditions. A critical link in this chain is the low strike frequency and volume, for it creates a stable environment for investment behavior and economic growth. Without predictable and low strike rates, democratic corporatism would probably not work.

economic, political, institutional, and policy conditions that provide labor exceptional power resources it can bring to bear in bargaining with employers. This power is, however, rarely exercised in the form of strikes. How are these low strike rates to be explained?

One set of theories drawn from economics – which we discuss below as bargaining strength theories – hypothesizes a *positive* statistical association between the economic power of unions and/or the high wage expectations and militancy of workers and strikes. The theories capture the commonplace view that unions and workers are more inclined to strike when they feel relatively stronger and more secure. The kinds of variables adduced as indicators of labor strength, however, are those that are widespread in the corporatist systems. In its simple, linear form, therefore, this form of bargaining power theory of strikes cannot be correct.

Several types of alternative explanations have attributed the low strike rates precisely to the existence of very high levels of labor "power resources" derived not only from the economic position of workers but, critically, also from the labor movement's institutional and political power. Furthermore, these explanations often explicitly invoke a strategic view of unions as actors pursuing the (especially economic) interests of workers through both market and political activity in the most effective manner possible. Variables adduced in such explanations include the size of the welfare state, the presence of the political parties of the Left in government, the centralization, concentration, density, and "encompassment" of the union movement, the incorporation of union elites into state institutions, sustained full employment, and others.[2]

There is much merit in these power-based explanations. But there is a problem. We have multiple, sometimes inductive, sometimes deductive hypotheses proposing relationships between a dependent phenomenon and different independent variables that probably are related to each other, as well as to the phenomenon to be explained. What is needed is a theory of strikes that could include and order these variables and the various levels of analysis at which they move in a way which would be consistent with the empirical phenomena to be explained, and which would incorporate the strategic view of the actors that the bargaining power theories invoke.

As this suggests, we have rather specific goals for the theory we would like to develop. It should both identify the causal relationships between strikes and a variety of political and/or economically relevant real-world phenomena *and* specify the *mechanisms* that produce these relationships (Elster, 1983: part 1). In other words, what we are seeking is a theory of strikes that is empirically verifiable and has sustainable *microfoundations*.

---

[2] These explanations are discussed more fully below. For various versions, see Cameron, 1984, Hibbs, 1978, Korpi and Shalev, 1980, Lange and Garrett, 1985, and Panitch, 1979. While these authors differ in their specific interpretations, they share the view that when labor is very strong in both the market and political arenas, militancy is likely to be comparatively low.

By microfoundations we mean that the theory should be consistent with fully rational and strategic behavior on the part of the individual and collective actors involved; should treat collective bargaining outcomes, including strikes, as the product of the strategic, and therefore interactive, behavior of the actors; and should recognize that uncertainty or incomplete information may be a crucial factor in explaining when strikes occur. In this framework, we treat the strategies of the actors in an equilibrium context in which each behaves in a fully rational manner, given the information available to her at the time she reaches her decisions. Strikes, therefore, result from the rational pursuit of self-interest. They are not "mistakes," a notion that, as we will see, has been prominent in some explanations of them.

For this theory to be empirically verifiable, its theoretical terms, no matter how abstract, should have empirical referents, its propositions should be subject to empirical test, its implications should be consistent with known empirical phenomena on a cross-national basis.[3] Furthermore, as the data from neocorporatist systems suggest, the effects of variables outside the immediate collective bargaining framework on how that bargaining is pursued, and its outcomes, should be recognized.[4]

In the pages that follow we develop a model that uses a game-theoretic framework to analyze the bargaining relationship between unions and employers when both are considered to be fully rational, strategic actors. In order to introduce contextual and empirically meaningful factors in our model we will make use of the concept of nested games (see Tsebelis, 1990). The actors, employers and unions, interact with a series of other actors (government, nonunionized workers) and are subject to the pressures of their environment (more or less competitive international markets, high or low inventories, unemployment, etc.). So the bargaining game is nested inside a series of other national and international games, which will influence the payoffs, and therefore the strategies of the two main actors. Because of the nested games concept, our model is sensitive to variations of the same kind of parameters that are included in the bargaining power approach. In view of the empirical accuracy of the bargaining power models, we consider this similarity to be an advantage of our model.

One important difference between bargaining power explanations and our

---

[3] A good deal of the literature in economics seeking to explain strikes has been peculiarly applicable to the market-oriented industrial relations systems of the United States and Canada. Economists, therefore, have focused almost exclusively on the role of economic variables in explaining the strike decisions of unions. This is clearly unsatisfactory for other types of industrial relations systems (Cohn and Eaton, 1989; Shalev, 1980; Snyder, 1975).

[4] This formulation is intended to include strikes that are undertaken to improve wages and other monetary goals or goals that can be reinterpreted in monetary terms (e.g., hours of work), as well as in order to gain organizational recognition. It excludes, however, strikes that are undertaken for ends that no "reasonable" offer by the employer (perhaps in combination with the government) could satisfy (e.g., political goals such as government or regime overthrow; expropriation of the capitalist; reputation).

model should be underlined at the outset. For the former, changes in the environment have direct impact on the behavior of the actors. In our model, changes in the environment produce changes in the payoffs; these changes in turn produce changes in the strategies of the actors. However, what determines those changes in behavior are calculations of mutually optimal (equilibrium) strategies.

Thus, our model seeks to show why and how the economic, political, and institutional settings within which collective bargaining takes place affect the frequency of strikes through their impact on the actors' strategies. As we shall see shortly, existing theories either fail to provide an adequate theoretical account for the associations they discover between strikes and real-world phenomena, or do not provide theoretical models that adequately capture demonstrated empirical relationships and treat the actors in a consistently rational manner.

Power and information: A review of some literature

There are three primary theoretical approaches to the explanation of strikes in the current literature.[5] The first stresses the relative resources unions and employers can bring to bear as they bargain; we will refer to this as the *bargaining power* approach. The second focuses on the role of information in efficient (and possibly strike free) agreements; we will refer to it as the *information* approach. The third is the *game theory* approach. It stresses the interaction between bargaining parties in an equilibrium context but has not been systematically applied to the analysis of labor–capital relations with the possibility of strikes. All three provide useful insights into why strikes occur, but each has theoretical or empirical limitations. We discuss each of these in turn.

Bargaining power

The bargaining power approach as we are defining it includes all those theories that explain strikes as a function of the relative balance of resources (defined differently by different theories) that union and employer bring to the process through which they define the wage and other terms of the labor contract.[6] Such

---

[5] We concentrate much of our attention on the relevant literature in economics. Especially for the bargaining power approach, however, there is an extensive relevant literature both in sociology and political science, such as that devoted to resource mobilization. Only a small part of this work is devoted to strikes. See, for instance, Shorter and Tilly, 1974; see also Tilly, 1978. We are entirely ignoring the "pluralistic industrialism" approach to strikes that represented the mainstream only ten years ago. Our reasons for doing so is that recent work such as that of Hibbs (1978) and Korpi and Shalev (1980) has shown that the arguments found in this literature concerning strikes cannot be sustained.

[6] In keeping with other discussions (Cousineau and Lacroix, 1986), we are including the strike theory of Ashenfelter and Johnson within the bargaining power approach. While their theory is more deductive, the logic of their empirical work is consistent with a bargaining power approach as we define it, although the range of relevant variables they consider is narrow and they focus on their impact on workers' wage expectations. For a critique along these lines, see Shalev (1980),

approaches do not consider the strategic interaction between the actors. They also often use relatively ad hoc or inductive hypotheses about how different states of the world – economic, political, social – affect the expectations or tactical opportunities of the bargaining adversaries. These hypotheses are then tested through time series regression analyses of aggregate strike frequency. The best of these models explain very high degrees of the variance in strike frequency.

Shalev makes an important distinction between two streams of theory, both of which fall within the bargaining power approach as we define it. First, some theories – predominantly in economics and which we refer to as "bargaining strength" theories – stress the role of economic variables and their effects on wage expectations and employers' willingness to pay. Strikes result from failures in bargaining due to demands of workers that exceed the willingness of employers to pay.

The *locus classicus* of this type of theory is that of Ashenfelter and Johnson (1969). In their model, workers pressure their leaders – who must be responsive for organizational reasons – for a wage increase that exceeds, and that the leaders understand to exceed, the level of wages which the employers are willing to offer. If the employer judges the costs of a strike less onerous than paying the union's demands, a strike is the result. But the strike leads to a gradual reduction of the minimum wage workers are willing to accept until it reaches the level at which the strike can be brought to a close. Thus, strikes are the result of a "misalignment" between what workers expect from a contract and what employers are willing to give.

Operationally, strikes are expected to be more frequent when unemployment levels are low, for this will tend to increase wage expectations and decrease the costs of a possible strike. Employer profitability and past changes in real wages also enter the model via workers' wage expectations or employers' willingness to pay higher demands.[7] Thus, strikes result from economic conditions that make labor more aggressive, leading it to make demands employers cannot accept. The role of strikes is to realign workers' demands. The power of labor matters, but only because it leads to demands that are economically excessive given the economic condition of employers.

The second stream of bargaining power explanations of strikes is seen primarily in sociology and political science.[8] It emphasizes a far broader range of

---

who, however, wishes to include under bargaining power theories only arguments that stress the importance of political and institutional factors among the power resources available to capital and labor and that place less emphasis in explaining strikes on wage expectations. As will become evident, our approach is in sympathy with Shalev's stress on power, broadly understood, and on the importance of the tactical situation, but we find his explanation theoretically weakly founded.

[7] At the end of their article, Ashenfelter and Johnson recognize the possible effects of changes in the institutional framework within which bargaining takes place. These play a role, however, via their impact on wage expectations or the unions' rate of concession.

[8] For prime examples, see Cameron, 1984, Hibbs, 1978, Korpi, 1983, 1978, and Korpi and Shalev, 1980.

variables that are argued to affect the "power resources" of labor and capital. In these theories, manifest conflict becomes more likely as the power resources of labor – which is assumed under capitalism always to be the structurally weaker party – increase (Korpi and Shalev, 1980). As the balance of power becomes more favorable, unions are expected to exploit the tactical advantages to improve their economic situation which this affords. Whether they do so with strikes, however, depends on the relative advantage of pursuing demands within the market or political arenas. Thus, labor strength both in the labor market and in politics is expected to be associated with low strike rates (Korpi and Shalev, 1980).[9]

Some of the factors that influence the distribution of power resources overlap with the explanatory variables used in the narrower bargaining strength models: low unemployment, for instance. But political and institutional conditions enter fully into the range of variables to be considered so that factors such as the stance of government toward unions and employers and toward strike action, the density of unionization, the capacity of the unions for collective action, and the repressive capacity of the government need to be incorporated. Equally as important from a theoretical standpoint, manifest conflict and strikes are explained as a manifestation of the "continuous struggle for influence and advantage" (Shalev, 1980: 154) between labor and capital. Rather than directing our attention to the alignment of wage expectations with employers' willingness to pay, it underlines the importance of examining "how aggregate economic and noneconomic forces at any given point in time affect the interest and opportunities of unions and employers for initiating open conflict" (Shalev, 1980: 154), and the relative advantages of doing so through struggle in the political institutions and/or the market.

The broader formulation seems the more satisfactory.[10] Aside from the specific critiques of the work of Ashenfelter and Johnson made by Shalev (1980) which we will not repeat here, it seems more theoretically reasonable to recognize that it is not only what workers expect or would like to get from wage negotiations but their ability to pursue those expectations that should be considered:

wage expectations should not occupy the *central* place in aggregate models of industrial conflict . . . the desire to inflict costs on an opponent is of little practical importance absent the ability to do so. (Shalev, 1980: 155)

This is all the more the case since wage expectations themselves are likely to be influenced by the perception of the balance of powers between workers and employers.

The power resources form of the bargaining power approach directs our atten-

---

[9] Hibbs (1978) makes a similar argument, although based on somewhat different reasoning.

[10] A number of quantitative and more qualitative studies have demonstrated the power of such political and institutional variables in explaining variances in aggregate strike frequency, especially in contexts outside the United States (Hibbs, 1978; Korpi and Shalev, 1980; Shalev, 1980; Snyder, 1975).

tion to the importance of relative power and to a series of variables – political and institutional, and not just economic – that can be expected to influence the frequency of strikes via their impact on the relative power of the bargaining parties. Such variables should certainly be included in any model of strike behavior. The power resources approach to strikes, however, is not fully theoretically satisfactory.

The problem is rooted in what has been dubbed the "Hicks paradox" (Kennan, 1986). The paradox is a direct outgrowth of the theory of wage bargaining developed by John Hicks (1963). Hicks argued that the economic settlements arrived at through wage bargaining were entirely predictable. Using a simple deductive model relying exclusively on the economic considerations of the union and employer operating as a bilateral monopoly, he showed that settlements were the product of the interaction of the employer's desire to minimize the wage bill but willingness to make wage concessions in the face of a strike threat, and the union's desire to maximize some wage function and consequent resistance to wage concessions, counterbalanced by the costs of a strike. The intersection of the two curves expressing the union's and employer's trade-offs produces a determinate outcome on which the bargaining parties cannot mutually improve. The problem for an explanation of strikes is that, given any determinate solution, if the actors are rational and fully informed, strikes should never occur.

If they do, it must be "the result of faulty negotiation . . . adequate knowledge will always make a settlement [without a strike] possible" (Hicks, 1963: 147).[11] In turn, when labor and capital are considered rational, fully informed actors, it is not clear why their relative power, however measured, should affect the probability of strikes. The outcome reflective of the current balance of power resources should be attained without recourse to a strike,[12] which can only reduce joint net utility without altering relative payoffs. Thus, bargaining power theory, in all its variants, lacks microfoundations, despite its impressive macrostatistical results and the attractiveness of its conceptual orientation. It seems likely that political and institutional, and not just economic, variables affect the likelihood of strikes, but we do not have a satisfactory explanation of *why* and *how.*

Information theories, to which we now turn, operate at a level that could provide such microfoundations and thus address this question, but as we shall see, they both fail the test of empirical relevance and do not treat labor and capital as rational actors interacting with each other in pursuit of their interests.

[11] Actually, Hicks proposed two basic explanations for strikes in light of his model: private information or reputation building (1963: 146–7). We will see that the former has assumed a prominent role in the attempt to overcome Hicks's Paradox. As we have already indicated, we will not discuss the latter.

[12] Cousineau and Lacroix (1986: 377) make the same point when they write that if one assumes that "the parties involved in wage negotiations are informed about changes in the relative bargaining power . . . it would be reasonable to expect changes in relative bargaining power to be reflected in the terms of the wage agreements rather than in strikes."

Information models

Information models take the Hicks paradox as their starting point but seek to resolve it by loosening the perfect information assumption. They have principally argued either that strikes become more likely when the "informational environment" within which bargaining takes place becomes more uncertain or less tractable (e.g., Cousineau and Lacroix, 1986)[13]; or when one or both of the bargaining actors have private information to which the other actor does not have easy or immediate access (e.g., Hayes, 1984; Mauro, 1982).

While these theories are significantly dissimilar in many of their details,[14] they share some important features. First, all the theories within this approach seek to build up from microfoundations. Their hypotheses are derived from models of the expected behavior of individual bargaining agents, generally at the firm level. The issue, therefore, is the adequacy of these microfoundations both empirically: How well do they link to real-world variables? and theoretically: How well do they capture the processes they are trying to model?

Second, they all consider a relatively narrow range of variables in discussing the kinds of misinformation that lead to strikes. These approaches are relatively economistic in their interpretation of the variables that influence the bargaining positions and strategies of the actors. They focus on the collective bargaining dynamics internal to the firm (Cohn and Eaton, 1989). When they "recognize the role of bargaining power" (Cousineau and Lacroix, 1986: 377), only a relatively narrow range of economic variables is used, leaving political and institutional factors entirely aside.[15] Thus, they ignore uncertainty or incomplete information arising from the effects of changes in the political or institutional environment.[16] As we have already argued, this seems unsatisfactory.

[13] Cousineau and Lacroix (1986: 377) stress that "both the quantity and reliability of information needed to assess relative bargaining power do have significant value in predicting strike incidence."

[14] While all are basically deductive in their construction, for instance, Hayes (1984) relies exclusively on extensive formal modeling while most of the others construct models that are then given empirical referents and tested through regression techniques. Hayes's work (1984) stands out for its effort to explore the implications of asymmetric information for the logic of bargaining between capital and labor. Her analysis bears some similarities to the model we develop here, but there are significant differences, including the fact that in our model it is the employer, rather than the union, that is incompletely informed. This allows us to develop empirical referents for terms in our model that are both politically interesting and have correspondence with those employed in bargaining power analyses.

[15] The one exception here is the introduction of a dummy variable for Canadian wage control policies. Even these are interpreted in terms of their effects on the economic uncertainty in the bargaining environment (Cousineau and Lacroix, 1986: 383).

[16] It should be underlined that there is nothing inherent in these models that should restrict the range of variables they consider. It is unclear whether their restrictiveness is due to the narrowness of the authors' interpretations or to the fact that they work with data from settings in which there is little or no change in the political or institutional climate over the period of time considered. For a critique of the narrowness of these models, see Cohn and Eaton (1988).

Third, they share the view that strikes "result essentially from misjudgment in a world of imperfect information" (Cousineau and Lacroix, 1986: 385). This approach, then, directly addresses one of the principal critiques we previously raised about bargaining power theories by recognizing that the relative level or changes in the relative level of power resources cannot, if the actors are fully rational and informed, explain strikes.

For both theoretical and empirical reasons, uncertainty or lack of full information plays an important role in the explanation of strikes.[17] Yet, the information-based theories still fail fully to meet the requirements of a satisfactory theoretical treatment of strikes. In addition to their failure to incorporate the political and institutional environment and thus fully to capture the role of power, they also contain an underlying theoretical weakness.

These theories are all based on the idea that strikes are the result of misinformation. For instance, the employer's offer that triggers the strike reflects a misjudgment on her part of the offer that will gain the agreement of labor without a strike. The strike is the response to this "ill-informed" offer. "Since information is costly to obtain, correcting these misperceptions requires the use of resources. Strikes then become a method to transmit the information necessary to correct the parties' misperceptions about each other" (Mauro, 1982: 536). Strikes, therefore, are treated as mistakes, the results of misjudgments in the presence of incomplete information.

Such an explanation, however, is itself incomplete, for it fails to capture a critical distinction between a nonstrategic and strategic approach to the interactions between the players in bargaining. Strikes in the incomplete information models so far presented are "mistakes" in the sense that each actor would prefer that they did not occur and would act differently if confronted with the same situation again. They are not equilibrium outcomes produced by each actor undertaking appropriate strategic behavior, given the information available to her at the time she had to make her decision, decisions that the actor would necessarily repeat, and want to repeat, each time the situation itself was repeated despite the suboptimal outcomes that resulted.

This difference has a series of important theoretical consequences. First, in the information theories, imperfect information of the actors is treated solely as a source of error and suboptimal outcomes. In a more strategic understanding of the problem, however, the uncertainty or partial information of the adversary is not only a source of potential suboptimality; it can also become a resource in bargaining, a strategic opportunity better to advance one's interests. A clear example is the bluff in poker with a potentially good hand showing in one's face-up cards. In a more fully strategic and interactive framework, strikes would not be assumed to be the result of "faulty negotiation." In contrast to the implicit

---

[17] Cousineau and Lacroix provide evidence showing that economic variables reflecting instability in the informational environment of collective bargaining significantly explain interindustry differences in strike frequency "better than do interindustry differences in relative bargaining power or union militancy" (1986: 385).

assumption of information theories – the strike would not always be considered a way to communicate the truth.

A second limitation of how the actors and strikes are treated in the information theories is that they employ a restricted interpretation of the actors' rationality. In those theories, the actors do not behave strategically, in the sense that they try to maximize their interests, given what they can rationally expect the opponent to do, and vice versa. Instead, they react nonstrategically, seeking simply better to inform the adversary about their utilities and to gain information about the adversary's. There is no obvious reason, however, why this should be how rational actors would behave (Tsebelis, 1989). In fact, the implicit conception of the actors seems both naive and to contradict the notion of the rational maximizer that underlies the deductive logic of all these theories as well as theories of bargaining power.

We need, therefore, a more completely interactive way of modeling the actors' strategic behavior. This can be done by treating strikes as parts of an equilibrium strategy: calculated optimal courses of action on the part of all actors, given the information that they possess. Using this approach, we will be able to treat incomplete information as a resource and not just a limitation. We will also be able to incorporate fully the possibilities of strategic interaction between rational actors.

In addition, a strikes-as-equilibria approach will have an important additional advantage. It has the ability to answer conditional questions, leading to empirically testable predictions. If strikes are mistakes, it is difficult to specify the conditions that lead to these mistakes, and even more difficult to predict what would have happened if some of the parameters of the model were different. An equilibrium approach is designed precisely to answer such conditional questions – that is, to specify the conditions under which a certain behavior (in our case strikes) is the outcome of the interaction of rational agents. The advantages of an equilibrium approach to strikes, therefore, are considerable. Extensions of some contemporary developments in game theory allow us to pursue this approach.

Game-theoretic models

The third stream of literature relevant to the explanation of strikes is noncooperative game-theoretic models of bargaining. A first general remark concerning all these models is that, as in Hicks's argument, there is no possibility of strikes under complete information (if all players' payoffs are common knowledge), or, for that matter, of any kind of public disagreement between the bargaining players. The outcomes also are efficient: It is impossible to improve the situation of one player without making the other worse off. The reason is that only reasonable demands (justified by the payoffs of the player) are made, and so the demands are perfectly anticipated and met. The possibility of strikes or disagreements and inefficient outcomes arises only when one or both of the players do not know some of their opponents' payoffs. The situation then is resolved by trial offers (which are sometimes turned down), or, in the case of labor–management negotiations, by strikes. These models, like our model, focus on the micro level, and treat trial offers (or by extension strikes) not as mistakes, but as part of the equilibrium strategies of the players.

However, while these models are very precise in the description of the institutional features of the bargaining game itself (who makes the offer, who knows what at each point in time, etc.), they remain extremely abstract in terms of contextual and empirically relevant factors that, as the empirical literature indicates, influence the outcomes of the bargaining game. Furthermore, most of these models speak about bargaining in general, or about the interaction between seller and buyer, and, therefore, do not include explicitly the possibility of strikes.

The archetypical models of noncooperative bargaining are two models by Rubinstein (1985a, 1982), the first with complete information, the second with one-sided incomplete information (one players knows only her own payoffs, while the other knows the payoffs of both). Rubinstein (1982) solved the problem of the division of one dollar between two players. He noted that any division of the dollar is a Nash equilibrium (i.e., that any unilateral deviation from the partition is either infeasible, or undesirable). Since there is an infinite number of equilibria in the "divide the dollar" game, Rubinstein tried to find a partition with some characteristics of stability. He considered that each player is impatient, and that this impatience would drive the process of bargaining to its final outcome. Each player makes an offer, which is either accepted or rejected by the opponent. If the offer is accepted, the game ends; if the offer is rejected, the other player makes a new offer that is in its turn either accepted (game ends) or rejected (game continues). Rubinstein modeled impatience by a discount factor: in each period of time, the dollar was shrinking by a different percentage for each player. He proved that under perfect information this process converges to perfect equilibrium. The first player makes a specific offer that is immediately accepted.[18]

We will briefly discuss only two other models that provide important ideas for our own model, which follows. Shaked and Sutton (1984) introduce the idea of an "outside option." Their model is a bargaining model with complete information, where one or the other player has the possibility, if she wants, to choose an "outside option." If one player chooses the outside option, then with some probability p the game ends, and prespecified payoffs are distributed to the players; with a probability $(1 - p)$ the bargaining continues, and a player makes an offer that gets accepted (game ends) or rejected (the game continues), another outside option becomes available, it is taken or not, and so on.

---

[18] In a second paper, Rubinstein (1985a) introduced incomplete information (one of his players did not know the discount factor of her opponent). In this case, the first player's offer was not always accepted, and the negotiations could continue for several rounds. Crampton (1983) and Sobel and Takahashi (1983) produced similar bargaining models with one-sided complete information, where only one player could make the offers. Fudenberg and Tirole (1983) introduced a model with two-sided uncertainty, but with a finite number (two) of rounds.

We will use the concept of an outside option to model strikes explicitly. In our model, labor will have the outside option of a strike. If the option is taken, the government intervenes in the negotiation process with probability p, and gives some payoffs to the players. Empirically, this does not require that the government actually dictate the terms of the agreement between capital and labor, but only that with probability p government will intervene and thereby assure an agreement that will be more, or less, favorable to labor. The agreement itself could still be reached between the bargainers for capital and labor. If the government does not step in to terminate the game, the negotiations continue.

A second model, that of Grossman and Perry (1986), is very similar to the one we subsequently present. Its major innovation over those already presented is that it not only presents a bargaining problem with infinite rounds but introduces the possibility of one-sided or asymmetric information. The situation is that of a seller and a buyer, where the buyer's valuation of the transaction object is unknown. Grossman and Perry's model presents all the desirable properties of a labor management negotiation game, except for two: (1) It does not include the possibility of strikes and the strategic alternatives generated by this option; (2) it includes only one-sided uncertainty.

As we will see, the model we propose resolves only the first of these problems. Labor and Capital negotiate over the division of the economic output through negotiations at the level of the factory, the branch, or the whole country. Strikes are possible and the actors, especially labor, therefore have expanded possibilities for strategic action. Furthermore, capital will be considered to have incomplete information about the strength of labor. To simplify the presentation, we rescale the output so that the negotiation is, in the model, for one dollar.

In order to facilitate understanding, we present the model in three stages. We first discuss a bargaining model with complete information, basically following Rubinstein (1982); in the second stage, we introduce an outside option (the strike); and finally, we solve the problem of bargaining when strikes are possible and information is incomplete.

A model of strikes with one-sided incomplete information

Stage 1. The Rubinstein model

The first player makes a proposal of how to split the dollar; if the offer is accepted, the game ends; if not, the other player makes an offer, which can be accepted or rejected; if the offer is accepted the game ends. Both players are impatient, which means that the dollar shrinks in the eyes of each one of them in each period of time by different amounts. Call d_C and d_L the time discount factors of Capital and Labor, respectively. It means that one dollar in period one is worth only d_C to Capital and only d_L to Labor in the next period.

These time discount factors drive the negotiation process to its conclusion. Capital is pressed because of the potential loss of profits with the passage of time, so d_C of a firm can be conceptualized as such a potential due, for instance, to intense competition in the presence of high demand or the absence of inventories in the presence of the prospect of sales; in the case of national bargaining, d_C could represent the level of international competition: The more competitive international markets and the greater the possibility of lost sales if negotiation is prolonged, the more Capital is eager to conclude bargaining. Labor, on the other hand, is pressed to present concrete outcomes of the negotiation by its internal organizational structure. Leaders who do not produce desirable outcomes can face internal challenges and the possibility of their replacement or of organizational decay. That is why Labor has a time discount factor.[19]

This conceptualization of time discount factors permits us to introduce other actors into the model according to the nested game framework. When Labor, for example, increases its organizational discipline, or solidifies its jurisdictional boundaries, or, in Hirschman's (1970) terms, there is a reduction of the potential for exit or voice without a commensurate increase in the other, its time discount factor increases and, therefore ceteris paribus, its share of the output (of the dollar) rises. Or, when Capital faces a more competitive economic environment, its discount factor decreases, it feels pressure to conclude an agreement more quickly, and consequently, is willing to give up more in order to finish sooner rather than later.

How would Capital and Labor divide the dollar between them under these conditions? Consider that they have arrived at an equilibrium, and this equilibrium gives x to capital and $(1 - x)$ to Labor. If Capital receives x at time t, it would not accept anything less than xd_C in time $(t - 1)$, therefore giving Labor at the most $1 - xd_C$. If Labor receives at the most $1 - xd_C$ at time $(t - 1)$ then it would get at the most $d_L (1 - xd_C)$ in time $(t - 2)$, therefore giving Capital at least $1 - d_L (1 - xd_C)$. One can repeat the same argument interchanging the words "at the most" and "at least," and would conclude that Capital receives exactly $1 - d_L (1 - xd_C)$ in time $(t - 2)$. However, since by assumption we are at equilibrium, what Capital receives at time t and what it receives at time $t - 2$ should be the same. This argument leads to the division of the dollar the following way:

Capital receives

$$x = (1 - d_L)/(1 - d_L d_C), \tag{1}$$

and Labor receives

$$1 - x = d_L(1 - d_C)/(1 - d_L d_C). \tag{2}$$

Several remarks are in order. First, the equilibrium is obtained in the first round: Capital makes an offer where it keeps x cents from the dollar, and gives $(1 - x)$ to Labor, and Labor accepts immediately, because it knows that it cannot do any better. Second, the structure of the game, and the alternating offers were crucial for the calculation of the equilibrium. Third, the player who moves first,

---

[19] An alternative conceptualization is the level of control of the leadership over the organization. The higher this level, the less Labor leaders feel pressed rapidly to conclude negotiations.

in our case Capital, has an important advantage. Indeed, had Capital moved second, it would have received the share indicated by (1) multiplied by d_C, that is, a number less than (1).[20,21] Fourth, the player who is most impatient will give up more of her share in order to conclude the bargaining process sooner. It is easy to verify that $x_C(x_L)$ increases with $d_C(d_L)$, and decreases with $d_L(d_C)$. After these observations, we can proceed to step 2 of the model, and introduce the outside option.

Stage 2. Complete information and possibility of strikes

Before a player makes an offer, she can interrupt bargaining and choose an outside option. If she makes this choice, then the bargaining game stops, and each player receives, with probability p, a prespecified payoff of which both are aware; call these payoffs o_C for Capital and o_L for Labor. The bargaining continues with probability $(1 - p)$ and the player makes an offer. The opponent can accept, and the game ends; she can refuse, and choose the outside option; or she can make a new offer. If the outside option is chosen, then the game ends with probability p and the players receive o_C and o_L respectively. Otherwise, the bargaining continues.

How will the players bargain in the presence of an outside option? Appendix 1 calculates the equilibrium of this model. Here we will explain the logic of bargaining when such an outside option is possible. To simplify matters, we consider only the case where an outside option is available for Labor. That is, only Labor has the possibility of interrupting the negotiation for an outside option (strike). If a strike occurs, then the players receive the payoffs o_C and o_L respectively with probability p and they continue bargaining with probability $(1 - p)$.

Under these conditions, Labor will choose the outside option only if o_L is greater than the share it would receive according to (2). If it chose to take an outside option with value less than the share indicated by (2), Labor would run the risk (with probability p) of receiving less. So, although a strike is always an available outside option for Labor, it will be chosen only if its value is over a certain threshold. Knowing that, Capital will not be affected if the value of the outside option is less than (2) and the equilibrium will be described by (1) and (2). If, however, o_L is greater than (2), then Labor will always choose to strike when it is its turn. Knowing that, Capital has to make an offer that will be at least as attractive to Labor as the (discounted for impatience) combination of strike and possible counteroffer. Appendix 1 replicates the calculations of the Rubinstein model when an outside option is available to Labor.[22] Note that in every

---

[20] This asymmetry between the two players can, however, be rectified by appropriate algebraic manipulations (see Sutton, 1986).

[21] Another property of this equilibrium is that it can be shown that if the two players have time discount factors that tend to 1, then they divide the dollar into two equal parts, which is a division with normatively pleasing properties. More precisely, Rubinstein (1982) has shown that his equilibrium converges to the Nash bargaining solution (see Luce and Raiffa, 1957).

[22] The calculations replicate Sutton, 1986. The reader should consult that paper for more details.

case, despite the fact that there is the possibility of infinite bargaining, the player's impatience, on the one hand, and complete information on the other, terminate the process in one period: The first offer is such that it is immediately accepted, and the game ends.

Here we can report the results, and introduce terminology that will be useful in the next and final step. We will call "Strong Labor" (SL) the Labor player with an outside option big enough to be taken whenever the opportunity arises. We will call "Weak Labor" (WL) the Labor player with an outside offer smaller than she would get out of the bargaining process (and who, therefore, never selects the outside offer). The outcomes will be reported in the following way: x is the equilibrium share of Capital, and it will be indexed by the order the two players take turns to make offers.[23] As we have already said, although the logic remains the same, the bargaining equilibrium is sensitive to who made the first offer.

$$x_{C,WL} = (1 - d_L)/(1 - d_L d_C), \tag{3}$$
$$x_{WL,C} = d_C(1 - d_L)/(1 - d_L d_C), \tag{4}$$
$$x_{C,SL} = (1 - po_L - (1 - p)d_L)/(1 - (1 - p)d_L d_C), \tag{5}$$
$$x_{SL,C} = d_C(1 - po_L - (1 - p)d_L)/(1 - (1 - p)d_L d_C). \tag{6}$$

Equation (3) indicates Capital's share when it starts first and plays against Weak Labor. Equation (4) indicates Capital's share when Weak Labor starts the negotiating process. Equation (5) indicates Capital's share when it starts the negotiation process against Strong Labor. And Equation (6) indicates Capital's share when it receives an offer from Strong Labor.

Note again the advantage of the player who moves first. Note also the fact that the game ends in time period 1, even in the case of Strong Labor, because, since Capital can anticipate a strike, it concedes a bigger part of the dollar.

Again, the conceptualization of strikes as outside options presents the opportunity to introduce the impact of outside actors into the model according to the theory of nested games. For example, the existence of militant workers outside the union facilitates strikes for Labor, and so raises the value of the outside option. Further, the existence of a Labor government increases the value of the outside option, because it makes government intervention to end a strike in favor of Labor more probable.

This second stage of the model is richer and more realistic than stage 1 because it introduces the possibility that unions can undertake strikes. However, strikes never result. If Labor is weak, it is not a real threat to strike; if it is strong, its strength is anticipated and Capital makes an offer that heads off a strike. Moreover, the value of the outside option does not figure in the solution of the bargaining game between Capital and Weak Labor. The reason is that under perfect information both players know that such an option will not be exercised, so they disregard it. Stage 3 will introduce incomplete information, and not only the possibility but also the occurrence of strikes. Moreover, as we will see, the

---

[23] Labor will obviously receive the remainder of the dollar.

value of the outside option of Weak Labor enters in the solution, because it provides an opportunity for Weak Labor to bluff and pretend that it is Strong in order to extract more from Capital.

Stage 3. Bargaining with incomplete information

Consider now the case where Capital does not know the value of the outside option for Labor. That is, discount rates are common knowledge, and Labor knows the value of striking, but Capital knows the value of the outside option only as a probability. Labor has a probability w of being weak (value of outside option o_W) and $(1 - w)$ of being strong (value of outside option o_S). The model will examine in detail the case where o_W is less than the value indicated by (2) and o_S is more than (2). So Strong Labor would always strike, while Weak Labor would never strike. This is by far the most interesting case. In the final discussion we will examine several variations of the model, where some of the assumptions we will make here are relaxed.

The situation can be conceptualized as in Figure 5.1. Labor and Capital have to divide the dollar. Labor's share is measured from left to right, while Capital's share is the remainder and is measured from right to left. Strong Labor will strike a deal that is toward the right of the figure, while weak Labor will not be able to push the outcome very much to the right. According to our assumptions, o_W, the outside option of the Weak Labor, is less than it would obtain through negotiations $(1 - x_{C,WL})$. On the other hand, Strong Labor can obtain more $(1 - x_{C,SL})$ than Weak Labor through negotiations, and the value of its outside option o_S is even higher.

Appendix 2 presents the analytic solution of the problem. Here we will present only the logic of the model. Let us study the problem that each of the actors faces. Capital does not know whether it deals with Strong or Weak Labor. However, there is a probability w that Labor is Weak, and this probability is common knowledge. Capital knows that any offer that gives Labor less than $(1 - x_{C,WL})$ will be rejected by both Weak and Strong Labor, and so, because it is pressed for time, it will not make such offers. On the other hand, Capital knows that any offer that gives Labor more than what Strong Labor would get (that is, more than $(1 - x_{C,SL})$) would be accepted by both Weak and Strong Labor. Moreover, Capital knows that if it has to deal with Strong Labor, it will not be able to concede less than $(1 - x_{C,SL})$. In fact, if Capital's offer is any less than $(1 - x_{C,SL})$ Strong Labor will immediately go on strike. So Capital has to make an offer somewhere in between the two extremes, so that the offer will be accepted by both possible types of Labor, or at least by Weak Labor.

Strong Labor has easy choices. It knows that it can get $(1 - x_{C,SL})$, so it will accept nothing less. An offer will be accepted only if it grants this share; otherwise Strong Labor will go on strike.

Weak Labor faces a more complicated problem. If Capital knew that it was facing Weak Labor, it would give only $(1 - x_{C,WL})$. However, Capital does not

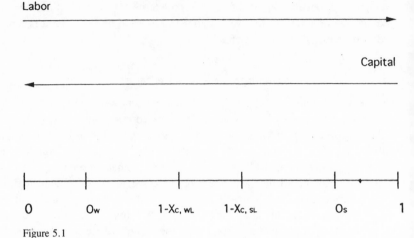

Figure 5.1

know which opponent it is facing, so there is a possibility for Weak Labor to bluff, and behave as if it were strong: That is, if offered anything that is considered unacceptable, strike first and then make the same counteroffer that Strong Labor would make. One could imagine that Weak Labor could behave exactly as Strong Labor and strike always unless it is offered $(1 - x_{C,SL})$. However, there are costs from such a behavior. As we said, if the outside option is taken, then there is a probability p that the outcome for Weak Labor will be o_W – that is, less than it could get through negotiation under perfect information. So Weak Labor's bluffing capacity is limited. If the offer is big enough, it will be better off accepting it than bluffing and striking.

Knowing all that, Capital will be able to make an offer that will make bluffing from Weak Labor costly. In other words, Capital will be able to make an offer attractive enough to be immediately accepted by Weak Labor. So, finally, Capital will have the choice between making an offer

$$1 - x_{C,L} - \max[\{po_W + (1 - p)d_L(1 - d_Cx_{C,SL})\}, \ (1 - x_{C,WL})], \qquad (7)$$

which will be accepted by Weak Labor and rejected by Strong Labor, or decide to give up, ignore the possibility that Labor is Weak and treat it as Strong, and therefore make the offer

$$1 - x_{C,SL} = 1 - ((1 - po_L - (1 - p)d_L)/(1 - (1 - p)d_Ld_C)), \qquad (8)$$

which will be accepted immediately by Labor, whether Weak or Strong.

Equation (8) leads to the same partition of the dollar as Equation (5), the equilibrium when Capital is facing Strong Labor, and makes an offer first. The calculation of equation (7) is given in Appendix 2. The logic that leads to this equation is to dissuade Weak Labor from bluffing. Weak Labor might be tempted to bluff if the first quantity in the right hand of (7) is greater than the second. In this case, Weak Labor is willing to take the risk of a strike (which is likely to have unfavorable results, (since o_W is by definition less than $(1 - x_{C,WL})$) in order to persuade Capital that it is Strong, and receive $(1 - x_{C,SL})$ in the next round. If the second quantity in the right-hand side of Equation (7) is greater than the first, then Weak Labor has no bluffing potential. If Weak Labor has no bluffing capacity and Capital wants to probe whether its opponent is strong or weak, it will make the offer $x_{C,WL}$. The willingness of Capital to test the strength of its opponent depends on the probability w that Labor is Weak, and its time discount factor d_C. The relation is the following: If

$$x_{C,SL} \geq wx_{C,L} + (1 - w)d_C x_{C,SL}, \qquad (9)$$

Capital will choose to treat Labor as if it were Strong, instead of gambling that it is facing Strong Labor. Capital will have to wait one round, and then give the advantage of the first offer to Strong Labor.

Equation (9) should be read in the following way: If the probability that Labor is Strong is high, or if the time discount factor for Capital is low, that is, if Capital is pressed for time, it will give in immediately, and make a proposal acceptable by both Weak and Strong Labor. If, on the contrary, the time discount factor is high, or the probability of facing a Strong Union is low, or both, then Capital will pay the price to probe whether the opponent is Strong or Weak.

To recapitulate:

1. If Equation (9) holds, Capital will treat Labor as if it were Strong with probability 1. It will offer $(1 - x_{C,SL})$, and the offer will be accepted immediately. Equation (9) indicates that an immediately acceptable offer becomes more likely when the probability that Labor is Strong is high, and when Capital is pressed for time.
2. If (9) does not hold, Capital will make an offer that will be rejected by Strong Labor, which will immediately strike, and accepted by Weak Labor. There are two possibilities:
   a. If the second term on the right-hand side of (7) is greater than the first, then, Weak Labor has no bluffing capacity, so the offer will be $(1 - x_{C,WL})$. Weak Labor will accept immediately.
   b. Otherwise, Weak Labor has bluffing capacity, so it has to be bought by a higher offer. Capital will make the offer $(1 - x_{C,L})$ of Equation (7), which will be accepted immediately by Weak Labor.

In this model, strikes occur only when Strong Labor faces an offer that is less than $(1 - x_{C,SL})$. The reason that Capital may make such offers is not some miscalculation, but the fact that Capital's time discount factor is sufficiently high, or the probability that Labor is Strong sufficiently low, so that it is in the interest of Capital to probe the strength of its opponent. Note also that in this model, Weak Labor never strikes. Its bluffing potential is anticipated and neutralized by Capital.

These formal characteristics of the model prompt some more general observations that serve as preliminaries to an examination of the model's empirical relevance. First, the distributional impact of incomplete information should be underlined. Because Capital is incompletely informed, it has to pay a price. Its offer has to prevent Weak Labor from pretending that it is strong; and if Capital's discount factor is low, or the probability of facing Strong Labor is high, it has to make an offer acceptable to Strong Labor, regardless of whether it is facing a Strong or a Weak opponent. No such implications about the distributional impacts of misinformation can be drawn from the information theory discussed earlier.

Second, because of incomplete information, Weak Labor is sometimes able to bluff and pretend it is Strong, and extract more concessions from Capital. Equation (7) is crucial in determining the bluffing potential of Weak Labor. If the first term in the right-hand side is greater than the second, Capital has to worry about the bluffs of Weak Labor. If Weak Labor can bluff, then the outside option can be used, and the solution of the game includes the value of this outside option. Note that in equilibrium Weak Labor never bluffs, because Capital makes a higher offer, in order exactly to prevent it from bluffing. But the absence of evidence of bluffing does not mean that the potential for bluffing, with its distributional consequences, does not exist. Both this potential and its distributional implications are entirely absent from information theories of strikes.

Third, the game does not necessarily end after the first offer, as was the case in the first two steps of the model. It is possible that Capital finds it more profitable to take the risk and probe the identity of its opponent. If it is facing a Weak opponent, the offer will be accepted; if the opponent is Strong, then a strike will result, and the bargaining game will end in the next round. Therefore, if Capital decides to probe, a strike results with probability $(1 - w)$. As we have already said, such a behavior is not a mistake, or a miscalculation, or the result of misinformation. It is the best course of action for each one of the actors, given the information that they possess.

Fourth, when a strike occurs, there is a resulting loss of welfare for both actors. In the models of perfect information the first offer is immediately accepted, so the two actors divide the whole dollar between them. In the model of incomplete information, there are three possible cases:

1. Capital makes an offer acceptable to both Weak and Strong Labor.
2. Capital makes an offer acceptable only to Weak Labor, and is actually facing Weak Labor.
3. Capital makes an offer acceptable only to Weak Labor, when it is actually facing Strong Labor.

Only in the first two cases do the players share the whole dollar. In the third case, there is a strike, which may end by government intervention which provides an outside option (with probability p), or by continuation of bargaining and loss to both actors because of their time preferences. So, in the third case, one way or the other, there is a loss of aggregate welfare. Again, this is the result of the best course of action that the players can take.

Fifth, it will be useful for our empirical examples to offer comments about the impact of variations of the six parameters of the model (d_L, d_C, o_S, o_W, p, and w)

on three characteristics of the outcome of the model: the share of Capital, the bluffing capacity of Weak Labor, and the first offer made by Capital. We remind the reader that Capital's first offer determines whether there will be a strike (with probability $(1 - w)$) or not.

- The bluffing potential of Weak Labor is directly related to Labor's discount factor (d_L), to the value of the outside options of both Strong and Weak Labor (o_S and o_W), and inversely related to the time discount factor of Capital (d_C), and the probability that the outside option will be introduced (p).
- When the bluffing potential of Weak Labor increases, the share of Capital shrinks, because it has to make an offer acceptable at least to Weak Labor. Moreover, when this potential becomes very high, it may be profitable for Capital to make an offer acceptable to both Weak and Strong Labor instead of probing.
- The share of Capital in general increases when its time discount factor (d_C) increases, and when the probability that Labor is Weak (w) increases, and decreases with increases in all of the other parameters of the model.
- Finally, whether Capital will make an offer acceptable just to Weak Labor (which results in a strike with probability $(1 - w)$) or to both Weak and Strong Labor, depends on how close the two offers are to each other, the time discount factor of Capital (d_C), and the probability (w) that Labor is Weak. Capital is more likely to make the offer that ends the game immediately than wait; the closer the two offers are to each other, the lower its discount factor (d_C), and the lower the probability that it faces Weak Labor (w).

Empirical applications

We began this essay with a discussion of the pattern of strike behavior in neocorporatist countries and with an assertion that an adequate theory of strikes should have both strong microfoundations and empirical relevance. The preceding section has developed a model of strikes that provides such microfoundations with assumptions that are relatively realistic, certainly more so than those found in the existing information theories. We turn now to a preliminary examination of the model's empirical relevance and ability to explain known phenomena related to strikes. Our discussion should allow us to show the power of the model as a source of explanations of a diverse set of phenomena that have had no unified and systematic analysis of microfoundations to date.

Empirical referents

To begin this discussion, it is worthwhile reviewing and elaborating on the empirical referents of the principal concepts employed in the model: the strength of Labor; the size of the outside option; and the strength of Capital.

1. The strength of Labor is treated as a function of two other variables: the size of the outside option and the degree of organizational control exercised by the union leadership over those for whom it bargains. We will discuss the factors that influence the size of the outside option separately.

The *degree of organizational control* is a function of the extent to which the union leaders with responsibility for contract negotiations feel secure from challenges from those for whom they negotiate and to whom they are putatively responsible and responsive. The greater such security, the less labor leaders discount the future, for the less they need to be concerned that failure to reach an early contract settlement will promote internal dissidence that might threaten their leadership, and the more they can feel assured of maintaining their leadership positions into the future regardless of how the negotiations proceed.[24]

Hirschman (1970) provides a useful scheme for analyzing the extent of such control. Factors such as the formal and informal rules of union elections (affecting the possibilities for "voice"); the extent of jurisdictional overlap and thus union competition for the same members (affecting the possibilities for exit); and whether bargaining units are open or closed shops affect relations of representation between leaders and rank and file. More generally, the degree of competition for jobs between unionized and nonunionized workers; and the degree of ideological, as contrasted to bread and butter, commitment to the union (affecting the likelihood of members exercising exit and/or voice) will all influence the degree of control.[25]

2. The size of the outside option is a function of the expected utility of a strike that is resolved through government intervention. It is the second factor to be considered in evaluating the strength of Labor. The size of the outside option is influenced by two parameters: the militancy of workers and the degree to which government is sympathetic to Labor and sensitive to the possibility that Labor might strike. The former affects the utility of the outside option because it indicates that government will have to impose a higher settlement in order to satisfy workers. The latter affects the probability that Labor will resort to the outside option: governments more sympathetic or sensitive to Labor will be more likely to intervene on Labor's behalf. It is the two *in combination* that determine the value of the outside option.

Empirically, the *militancy of workers* is likely to vary positively with the tightness of the labor market, as has been argued by bargaining power theorists. In addition, however, it should be underlined that the militancy of workers can

---

[24] Following much of the industrial relations literature, we are here assuming that union leaders have a preference function that places organizational maintenance and their own survival in office before other possible preferences. For a review of this literature, see Farber, 1986.

[25] For an extensive application of the Hirschman framework to unions in the context of explanations of neocorporatist wage regulation, see Lange, 1984a. As this study indicates, there are ample empirical materials for analyzing the degree of centralized control with some accuracy. See also Golden (1991).

also be influenced by factors other than labor market conditions such as ideology, or government conditions that reduce their fear of repressive responses to strike actions or encourage them to believe that the likelihood that a strike will be successful has increased. Sabel (1981), for instance, discusses the role of changing worker consciousness in explaining the militancy of migrant workers during different phases of their migration and Hibbs's work (1976) suggests that the presence of Communist workers may increase the proclivity among workers to strike. The literature on social mobilization and political opportunity structures discusses the ways that changes in the political environment may affect people's willingness to undertake collective action (Tarrow, 1983; Tilly, 1978). We do not need to elaborate further on this argument here other than to stress its central implication. The model we have developed can accommodate a far wider range of sources of worker militancy, wider than that found in many of the other explanations discussed earlier.

The *sympathy or sensitivity of government to Labor* can be a function of a number of factors. The most obvious and oft-discussed one in the literature is the extent of historical linkage or electoral dependency on the labor movement of parties in government. This is the factor generally employed in the literature on neocorporatism that we discussed earlier. As Przeworski and Sprague (1986) point out, however, most governments of the Left face difficult trade-offs at the margin between appealing to their "core" labor supporters and to middle-class voters whose support may be necessary to improve the chances of electoral victory. Thus, the extent to which even a government dominated by a labor party is likely, ceteris paribus, to intervene on behalf of Labor, thereby increasing the value of the outside option, is likely to depend not just on the ideology of the party or its institutional links with the labor movement but also on the specific characteristics of the electoral and institutional conditions in which the party – which is assumed to want to win and hold office – finds itself.[26]

Even governments that are not dominated by labor parties and in which such parties are not even present, however, can, under certain conditions, increase the value of the outside option for Labor. This will be the case if the government is particularly sensitive to the possibility that Labor might strike, whether for electoral or other reasons. Examples might be fear of a major strike just before a national election, or situations in which a strike might have severe consequences for the national economy – and probably thereby for the government.[27]

[26] For a similar argument, see Hibbs (1976) and our subsequent comments. This is a classic example of how the nested character of the Labor–Capital game comes into play. The structure and payoffs of the interparty game affect the payoffs a labor or other party can get from a strategy of accommodating unions, which, in turn, affects the size of the outside option in the L–C game and thus the strategies of Capital and Labor and the likelihood of strikes.

[27] One implication of the role of government sensitivity to strikes in the determination of the value of the outside option is that the scale or *economic impact* of a potential strike may assume considerable importance in some situations. Thus, other things held constant, the outside option should have a higher value where the industrial relations system is centralized and Labor is perceived to be able successfully to undertake a national strike if it receives an unfavorable offer.

3. The strength of Capital is determined in our model by the degree to which employers discount the future. Where Capital discounts the future more heavily, it will be weaker than where it is willing to wait out even a lengthy negotiation with, and possible strike by, Labor. We have already indicated that Capital can be expected to be more impatient, the greater the potential loss of profits with the passage of time and/or lost production due to a strike. Conditions in which such would be the case include intense competition for markets that could not easily be recouped if lost, and a shortage of inventories to cover production losses from a strike. Where bargaining takes place on a national level, one would, ceteris paribus, expect Capital to discount the future more heavily and thus be weaker in relatively small, open economies.

Even this brief review of possible empirical referents and operationalization of the critical concepts employed in our model indicates the extent to which it can incorporate variables central to the power resources form of the bargaining power approach. In our case, however, these variables are brought into consideration via their impact on the payoffs associated with different courses of action in different situations. Their effects on behavior are mediated by the way they alter the payoffs to, and thus the mutually optimal (equilibrium) strategies of, the actors, rather than through a direct impact on the actors' behavior. Therefore, our model provides microfoundations for many of the empirical results of the power resources approach to strikes. It identifies which variables in the environment of Labor and Capital are likely *to affect* when negotiations break down and strikes occur, and when the outcomes of negotiations without strikes are likely to be more or less favorable to Labor, but also *why* and *how* these variables have the effects they do.

Empirical applications

It is also clear, however, that the model should enable us to explain known empirical phenomena and associations, and it is to this issue that we now turn. We focus on the pattern of extremely low strikes found in the neocorporatist systems described at the outset of this essay, although we believe the model can be substantially generalized.

The application of our model to the neocorporatist cases is relatively straightforward, although some interesting implications emerge. As discussed, the likelihood of strikes declines as the probability that Labor is strong $(1 - w)$ increases and Capital discounts the future heavily (d_C is low). Labor's strength, in turn, is a function of its degree of internal discipline and of the value of its outside option. In the neocorporatist systems, all of these variables militate against strikes and they do so in a highly stable manner given the political and economic characteristics of the countries.

As is by now well known, labor unions in Sweden, Norway, and Austria have been highly centralized and concentrated, enjoy a relative monopoly of representation, and their leaders have enjoyed considerable legitimacy and job security.

The unions have also been able to convince their members to allow the leadership considerable leeway in bargaining with employers (Lange, 1984).[28]

The outside option can also generally be expected to have a very high value in these countries. On the one hand, a number of conditions favor high degrees of potential militancy on the part of workers. Among these are the generally tight labor market conditions, the very strong social wage and other programs which "decommodify" labor, and the extremely high rates of unionization. On the other hand, governments in these countries, generally dominated by parties of the Left, have been highly favorable to labor or sensitive to the potential costs of a strike. Capital in these countries has been highly sensitive to the costs of strikes. Operating in a relatively small, open economy, and thus highly vulnerable to fluctuations in international trade, it has generally had much to gain from concluding rapid and peaceful agreements with labor.

Taken together, these conditions reflect a relatively more favorable balance of power resources to Labor in these countries than elsewhere among the advanced industrial democracies. It is also noteworthy that these conditions have held over long periods of time. There is, therefore, little possibility for misunderstanding on the part of the actors of the strategic situation which they face: The probability that Labor is strong is quite high and is relatively stably so. Our model also allows us to explain why these power resources translate into extremely low strike rates. Put simply, given the combination of a very high probability that Labor is strong and Capital's structurally induced impatience, there is little reason for Capital to do other than make an offer to Labor that the latter should accept. Strikes should be extremely rare by international standards, and they are.

Contrast some of the implications of the explanation of the low strike rates in corporatist countries that our model provides with those offered elsewhere. First, in seeking to explain the low strike rates in neocorporatist countries, both Korpi and Shalev (1980) and Hibbs (1978) argue that the labor-supportive policies of Left governments in social democratic countries induce unions to shift their strategic focus from the labor market to politics and state policies. This account accords with the historical development of strike rates in these countries and treats labor as rationally pursuing its interests. It is not clear, however why labor should not maximize its gains through the use of its power in *both* the market and political arenas.

Hibbs (1978: 17), moreover, assumes that, if Labor were seeking to maximize its return from the market, it would strike more often and thereby improve its share. Thus, low strike rates must be the product of restraint on market aggressiveness (which may, or may not, be the product of rational calculation) by Labor. This excludes *by assumption* the possibility that Labor is doing as well as it can do, given the strategic context in which it is operating, and the offer it

---

[28] It should also be noted that over time the success of the leadership in gaining benefits for members works to create a culture within the union supportive of a considerable degree of leadership autonomy.

receives from Capital (also behaving rationally and also doing as well as it can do).[29] Yet this is precisely what our model suggests is the case.

A similar critique applies to the argument that labor parties act to discourage worker militancy (Hibbs, 1976: 1051). This could be the case for electoral reasons (labor wants to attract middle-class voters), the argument Hibbs tests, or because labor leaders are unwilling to use their power to pursue class interests to the fullest (Panitch, 1979). Again, however, both arguments assume that Labor would rationally have an interest in being more aggressive in the labor market but holds back because of political sympathies and/or pressures, or an absence of class will. As we have seen, this need not be the case. Labor's strength may be anticipated in Capital's offer, making a strike unnecessary, and in fact counterproductive.

But what evidence can be offered that labor is strategically optimizing? Here we offer only some suggestive indications that await subsequent detailed examination. First, Lange (1984a) addressed the relationship of union responsiveness to members in corporatist and noncorporatist systems. The null hypothesis was that the unions would have to be less responsive in corporatist systems if they were, in fact, keeping wages below the levels that workers, given their interests and market strength, could expect to get. The results, however, showed no relationship between corporatism and less responsive internal trade union structures. This suggests either that workers in these corporatist countries are peculiarly docile or, as our model would suggest, that the workers' and unions' strength is largely anticipated in capital's contract offers.

Second, an implication of our model is that the *outcome* of wage bargaining, as measured by Labor's share, should be superior in systems – like the neocorporatist ones – where the probability Labor is strong is high, the value of the outside option high, and Capital discounts the future heavily. This pattern should occur, not due to strikes, but as the result of the size of the initial offers that Capital makes, given the strategic situation that it faces.

Cameron (1984) provides some relevant data. In exploring the relationship between labor quiescence and a series of economic performance indicators, he finds that labor quiescence was very mildly and positively associated with a "higher proportion of domestic factor income received by employees" and with increases in labor's share from the mid-1960s to the early-1980s. The relationships are weak, however, and he concludes that

quiescence does not appear to produce any marked diminution of labor's share of income (contrary to what critics of wage restraint and 'corporatist collaboration' might suggest).

---

[29] An interesting problem arises here. What economic outcome for workers are the unions trying to maximize: the wage share resulting from the immediate contract or wages over time? Alvarez, Garrett, and Lange (1991), Lange (1984b), and Lange and Garrett (1985) have argued that conditions in the neocorporatist countries make such a choice of preferences possible and have suggested that choosing the former is likely to reduce the latter. Wallerstein and Przeworski (1988: 20) provide strong support for the argument that centralization of unions maximizes the aggregate welfare of union members.

And, conversely, militancy does not appear to produce any marked improvement in labor's share of income (as such critics might imply) (173).

It was also the case that there is a strong association between low strikes and higher social wage payments: "in short, labor was compensated – to some degree at least – for its quiescence" (173).

What these results suggest is that labor received an overall package superior to that found in systems with a greater number of strikes, but that the benefits did not arrive solely through wage bargaining – where the results were no worse, but also no better – but through some combination of market bargaining and government action. This raises an interesting implication we have not, so far, been able to examine more closely: that the strategic situation represented in the corporatist cases can involve relatively complex mixes of employer offers and government actions to produce the level of overall compensation and income and other security sufficient to gain labor's acceptance without a strike. Note, however, that even if this is the case, the absence of strikes in these countries is not the result of labor's unwillingness to pursue what it would be rational for it to seek, or of a shift in the locus of conflict, but rather of its pursuit of an equilibrium strategy, given the strategic context in which it is operating.

Conclusions

This essay has presented a model of wage bargaining between Capital and Labor that could provide microfoundations for frequently observed associations between political, institutional, and economic conditions affecting the power resources of labor relative to capital and the frequency of strikes. The problem addressed has been the extremely low strike rate in neocorporatist countries for which plausible macro explanations have been offered and empirically supported, but for which the microfoundations were weak.

In developing our model, we have sought to assure that we would capture the insights of the existing work on strikes while integrating these into a systematic, concise, and empirically relevant framework. From the literature using the bargaining power approach, we have wholeheartedly adopted the stress on relative power resources of labor and capital but have noted both the absence of microfoundations and the related inability to explain how the balance of power resources, by itself, could explain strikes. From the neoclassical economic literature on bargaining we have adopted the basic insight that strikes should be understood as the outcome of incomplete information but also pointed to the empirical and theoretical narrowness of the bargaining models employed and to the failure fully to incorporate the strategic rationality of the actors.

The model we have developed has relatively few parameters and each of these has accessible empirical referents that accord with those identified in much of the power resources literature. It is based on the fundamental assumptions that actors are fully rational, that their strategies are interactive, and that the outcomes of bargaining, including strikes, represent equilibria, which reflect the best the actors could do, given the situation they faced, and the strategic options of their opponent. In addition, the model incorporates incomplete information in the form of Capital's uncertainty whether Labor is strong or weak.

The critical theoretical consequences of adopting an equilibrium perspective for the analysis of strikes should be underlined. It certainly shows that strikes need not result from "mistaken" behavior. But perhaps even more important, it demonstrates that the absence of strikes by itself can tell us nothing about the power of labor alone, and, by implication, the power of labor alone can tell us nothing about the probability of strikes. We are critical, in other words, of any theory that forecasts outcomes based solely on changes in any parameter affecting one player alone. Such explanations are incomplete, for they fail to incorporate the possible reactions to the changed situation of the opponent who must also be treated as rational and strategic.

Our model was sufficiently complex to account for real-world situations, and sufficiently simple to make the logic of these situations intelligible. In particular the modeling was focused not on abstract problems, but on concrete questions having to do with specific political contexts and political institutions. For example, some one-sided information models assume that Capital is the unknown actor, and focus on the conditions prevailing in the market that are unknown to Labor who tries to understand them by observing Capital's behavior (Mauro, 1982). In our model, by assuming that Labor was the unknown actor, we were led to focus on politically important questions of labor organization, and the relationship between labor and government. Moreover, the theory of nested games enabled us to study how factors such as organization, market conditions, or government policies will affect the outcome of bargaining between Capital and Labor.

Using the model, we were able to explain a number of phenomena related to the pattern of Capital–Labor relationships in the neocorporatist countries. Our results here should be treated as preliminary. There are other phenomena that could be examined in these countries and the model should certainly be extended to the explanation of strikes and strike patterns more broadly.

There are also extensions of the model that would increase further its realism. One of the most interesting of these would be to improve on the way capital's uncertainty is modeled. In our model, we incorporated the assumption that the probabilities of Weak and Strong Labor could take on only two values. It is more likely, however, that capital is more accurately modeled as having a probability distribution of labor's possible strengths. If this was incorporated into our model, we believe it would increase the number of possible periods over which bargaining could proceed. In our current model, the bargaining process can end either in one or in two periods. If, however, the state of Labor strength is defined over a probability distribution, it is conceivable that the game would continue for more than two rounds. Again, this would add further realism to the model.[30]

---

[30] In fact, Grossman and Perry (1986) have investigated such a model with multiple rounds of negotiations.

The model presented here allows us to bridge the gap between two approaches, which have been too often either mutually ignored or hostilely confronted: that which stresses power and conflict and that which seeks to model political and social actors as rational and the outcomes of their interactions as reflective of equilibria. To the extent this exercise is successful, it should improve our ability to analyze politically relevant phenomena and to enrich and expand the study of comparative politics without losing what makes the field so interesting.

Appendix 1: Bargaining with outside option (strike) and perfect information

Notation

- Call x the share of Capital; x is indexed by the two players, with the player making the offer first.
- Call d_L and d_C the time discount factor of Labor and Capital, respectively
- Call o_S and o_W the outside option of Strong and Weak Labor respectively. Note that o_S is greater than the bargaining share, while o_W is less. As a result, o_S is always taken by Strong Labor and appears in the formulas, while o_W is never taken and never appears.

Case 1. Capital + Weak Labor; Capital moves first (Table A1.1). Assume that Capital at time 2 receives at least $x_{C,WL}$. This share is equal to $d_C x_{C,WL}$ at the previous time period. So, Weak Labor can receive at most $1 - d_C x_{C,WL}$ at time 1. Therefore, in the previous time period, Weak Labor can receive at most $d_L (1 - d_C x_{C,WL})$, which leaves at least $1 - d_L (1 - d_C x_{C,WL})$ for Capital.

The same argument can be made by interchanging the terms "at least" and "at most." So, Capital at equilibrium receives exactly $x_{C,WL}$. To calculate $x_{C,WL}$, we equate Capital's share at time 2 with time 0, and solve $x_{C,WL}$:

$$x_{C,WL} = 1 - d_L(1 - d_C x_{C,WL}) \Rightarrow x_{C,WL} = (1 - d_L)/(1 - d_L d_C)$$

[*Note:* In the next case, the table is presented, but the repetition of the argument is left to the reader.]

Case 2. Capital + Strong Labor; Capital moves first (Table A1.2). In equilibrium the initial offer of Capital should be equal with the offer after one round of negotiation. Solving for $x_{C,SL}$ gives

$$x_{C,SL} = (1 - po_S - (1 - p)d_L)/(1 - (1 - p)d_L d_C)$$

[*Note:* Capital and Strong Labor could have such attractive outside options that they are tempted to make unacceptable offers to each other, waiting for the government to intervene. In this case, the expected value for Labor will be

$$po_S + pd_L(po_S) + p^2 d_L^2 (po_S) + \cdots = po_S/(1 - pd_L) = O_S$$

and

$$po_C + pd_C(po_C) + p^2 d_{C2}(po_C) + \cdots po_C/(1 - pd_C) = O_C$$

In order to eliminate this implausible possibility, we assume

$$O_S + O_C < 1$$

Table A1.1

Time			$C \geq$ (at least)	$WL \leq$ (at most)
0	C	offer	$1 - d_L (1 - d_C x_{C,WL})$	
		accept		$d_L (1 - d_C x_{C,WL})$
1	WL	offer		$1 - d_C x_{C,WL}$
		accept	$d_C x_{C,WL}$	
2	C	offer	$x_{C,WL}$	
		accept		$1 - x_{C,WL}$

Table A1.2

		C	SL
C	offer	$1 - (po_S + (1 - p)d_L (1 - d_C x_{CSL}))$	
	accept		$(po_S + (1 - p)d_L (1 - d_C x_{CSL}))$ (strike)
SL	offer		$1 - d_C x_{C,SL}$
	accept	$d_C x_{C,SL}$	
C	offer	$x_{C,SL}$	
	accept		$1 - x_{C,SL}$

Moreover, we assume that $o_C < x_{C,SL}$ (otherwise Capital would choose to have a lock out before making its next offer).]

Appendix 2: Bargaining with outside option (strike) and incomplete information

Notation: In addition to the notation of Appendix 1, there is probability w that Labor is Weak and $(1 - w)$ that it is Strong.

The solution concept applied here is that of sequential equilibrium (Kreps and Wilson, 1982). Application of this concept requires that strategies are optimal responses to each other for the remainder of the game (subgame perfection) given the players' beliefs; and beliefs are updated along the equilibrium path by Bayes's rule. This concept is not restrictive enough (leads to too many equilibria), because how a player updates his beliefs off the equilibrium path is not specified. We will assume optimistic conjectures (Rubinstein, 1985a); that is, anytime Capital sees Labor making a choice off the equilibrium path, it infers that it is confronting Weak Labor. This restriction leads to a unique outcome.

Lemma 1. *Any offer greater or equal to* $1 - x_{C,SL}$ *is immediately accepted by Labor.*

Proof: See Case 2 in Appendix 1.

Lemma 2. *Any offer less than* $1 - x_{C,WL}$ *is rejected by Labor.*

Proof: See Case 1 in Appendix 1.

Lemma 3. *Strong Labor rejects any offer less than* $1 - x_{C,SL}$, *strikes and makes a counteroffer of* $1 - d_C x_{C,SL}$ *which is accepted.*

Proof: See Case 2 in Appendix 1.

Lemma 4. *If Weak Labor rejects an offer, it strikes first, and makes the counteroffer* $1 - d_C x_{C,SL}$.

Proof: The offer will be at least $1 - x_{C,WL}$ by Lemma 2. If Weak Labor rejects and reacts differently than Strong Labor (either does not strike first, or does not counteroffer $x_{SL,C}$ afterward). Capital identifies the opponent as Weak with probability 1. Consequently it will never offer more than $1 - x_{C,WL}$. However, several rounds have gone and the share is accordingly discounted.

Lemma 5. *An offer that is rejected by both Strong and Weak Labor is a dominated strategy for Capital.*

Proof: If both Strong and Weak Labor reject, Capital gains no information, and when it is its turn to make an offer, it finds itself in the initial situation while the dollar has been discounted by d_C^2.

Lemma 6. *There are only two undominated equilibrium strategies for Capital:*

1. Make the offer $1 - x_{C,SL}$ (pooling equilibrium)
2. Make an offer $1 - x_{C,L}$ which is acceptable by Weak Labor but not by Strong Labor (separating equilibrium).

Proof: (1) An offer more than $1 - x_{C,SL}$ is dominated because $1 - x_{C,SL}$ is accepted by Labor (Lemma 1). (2) An offer in the $((1 - x_{C,L}), (1 - x_{C,SL}))$ interval is dominated by $(1 - x_{C,L})$. Indeed, both these offers are accepted by Weak Labor and rejected by Strong Labor. (3) Any offer in the $[0, 1 - x_{C,L})$ interval is rejected by both Weak and Strong Labor (Lemma 5).

Theorem 1. *The value of* $x_{C,L}$ *is given by*

$$x_{C,L} = \max((po_w + (1 - p)d_L (1 - d_C x_{C,SL})), (1 - x_{C,WL}))$$

Proof:

	C	WL
C	$1 - po_w - (1 - p)d_L (1 - d_C x_{C,SL})$	
L		$d - d_C x_{C,SL}$
C	$x_{C,SL}$	

From this table it follows that the share of Weak Labor is

$$po_w + (1 - p)d_L(1 - d_C x_{C,SL}).$$

The rest of the theorem follows from Lemmas 2 and 5.

Theorem 2. *Capital offers* $1 - x_{C,SL}$ *if* $wx_{C,L} + (1 - w)d_C x_{C,SL} < x_{C,SL}$ *(pooling);* $1 - x_{C,L}$ *otherwise (separating)*

Proof: Capital has the option of making an offer $(1 - x_{C,SL})$ that will be accepted immediately; or an offer $(1 - x_{C,L})$ that will be accepted by Weak Labor (that is, with probability w), and rejected, followed by a strike and a counteroffer by Strong Labor (with probability $(1 - w)$). Capital chooses the expected utility maximizing option.

[*Note:* The belief of Capital is that Labor is strong with probability $(1 - w)$ in the beginning of the game; if Capital makes a separating equilibrium offer it immediately infers with probability 1 what type of Labor it faces. Off equilibrium beliefs act as a deterrent here so that no player deviates from his equilibrium strategy. Alternative off equilibrium belief formation would lead to less intuitive equilibria. For example, if Capital has pessimistic beliefs (inferred from any off equilibrium path move that the opponent is Strong Labor), then Weak Labor will have an incentive to deviate all the time, and therefore, the only equilibrium would be the pooling one.]

References

Alvarez, Michael, Geoffrey Garrett, and Peter Lange. (1991). "Government Partisanship, Labor Organization and Macroeconomic Performance." *American Political Science Review* 85: 539–56.

Ashenfelter, Orley, and George Johnson. (1969). "Bargaining Theory, Trade Unions, and Industrial Strike Activity." *American Economic Review* 59: 35–49.

Cameron, David R. (1984). "Social Democracy, Corporatism, Labor Quiescence and the Representation of Economic Interest in Advanced Capitalist Society." In John Goldthorpe (Ed.), *Order and Conflict in Contemporary Capitalism.* Oxford: Oxford University Press.

——— (1978). "The Expansion of the Public Economy: A Comparative Analysis." *American Political Science Review* 72: 1243–61.

Cohn, Samuel, and Adrienne Eaton. (1989). "Historical Limits of Neoclassical Strike Theories: Evidence from French Coal Mining, 1890–1935," *Industrial and Labor Relations Review* 42: 649–62.

Cousineau, Jean-Michel, and Robert Lacroix. (1986). "Imperfect Information and Strikes: An Analysis of Canadian Experience, 1967–1982," *Industrial and Labor Relations Review* 39: 377–87.

Crampton, P. (1983). "Bargaining with Incomplete Information: An Infinite Horizon Model with Continuous Uncertainty." Research Paper 680, Graduate School of Business, Stanford University.

Elster, Jon. (1983). *Explaining Technical Change: A Case Study in Philosophy of Science.* Cambridge: Cambridge University Press.

Farber, Henry S. (1986). "The Analysis of Union Behavior." In Orley Ashenfelter and Richard Layard (Eds.), *Handbook of Labor Economics.* Vol. 2. Amsterdam: North Holland.

Fudenberg, Drew, and Jean Tirole. (1983). "Sequential Bargaining under Incomplete Information." *Review of Economic Studies* 50: 221–47.

Golden, Miriam. (1991). "The Dynamics of Trade Unionism and National Economic Performance." Unpublished manuscript, Department of Political Science, UCLA.

Grossman, Sanford, and Motty Perry. (1986). "Sequential Bargaining under Asymmetric Information." *Journal of Economic Theory* 39: 120–54.

Hayes, Beth. (1984). "Unions and Strikes with Asymmetric Information." *Journal of Labor Economics* 2: 57–83.

Hibbs, Douglas A., Jr. (1978). "On the Political Economy of Long-Run Trends in Strike Behavior." *British Journal of Political Science* 8: 153–75.

——— (1976). "Industrial Conflict in Advanced Industrial Societies." *American Political Science Review* 70: 4, 1033–58.

Hicks, John R. (1963). *The Theory of Wages.* 2d ed. London: Macmillan.

Hirschman, Albert O. (1970). *Exit, Voice and Loyalty: Responses to Decline in Firms, Organizations, and States.* Cambridge, Mass.: Harvard University Press.

Kalecki, Michael. (1971). "Political Aspects of Full Employment." In *Selected Essays on the Dynamics of the Capitalist Economy.* Cambridge: Cambridge University Press.

Kennan, John. (1986). "The Economics of Strikes." In Orley Ashenfelter and Richard Layard (Eds.), *Handbook of Labor Economics,* Vol. 2. Amsterdam: North Holland.

Kohlberg, Elon, and Jean-François Mertens. (1986). "On the Strategic Stability of Equilibria." *Econometrica* 54: 1003–37.

Korpi, Walter. (1978). *The Working Class in Welfare Capitalism: Work, Unions and Politics in Sweden.* London: Routledge and Kegan Paul.

——— (1983). *The Democratic Class Struggle.* London: Routledge and Kegan Paul.

Korpi, Walter, and Michael Shalev. (1980). "Strikes, Industrial Relations and Class Conflict in Capitalist Societies." *British Journal of Sociology* 30: 164–87.

Kreps, David M., and Robert Wilson. (1982). "Sequential Equilibria." *Econometrica* 50: 863–94.

Lange, Peter. (1984a). *Union Democracy and Liberal Corporatism: Exit, Voice and Wage Regulation in Postwar Europe.* Ithaca, N.Y.: Center for International Studies, Western Societies Program, Cornell University.

——— (1984b). "Unions, Workers and Wage Regulation: The Rational Bases of Consent." In John Goldthorpe (Ed.), *Order and Conflict in Contemporary Capitalism.* Oxford: Oxford University Press.

Lange, Peter, and Geoffrey Garrett. (1985). "The Politics of Growth: Strategic Interaction and Economic Performance in the Advanced Industrial Democracies, 1974–1980," *Journal of Politics* 47: 792–827.

Lange, Peter, George Ross, and Maurizio Vannicelli. (1982). *Unions, Change and Crisis: French and Italian Union Strategy and the Political Economy, 1945–1980.* Boston: George Allen and Unwin.

Luce, R. Duncan, and Howard Raiffa. (1957). *Games and Decisions: Introduction and Critical Survey.* New York: Wiley.

Mauro, Martin (1982). "Strikes as a Result of Imperfect Information," *Industrial and Labor Relations Review* 35: 522–38.

Olson, Mancur. (1982). *The Rise and Decline of Nations: Economic Growth, Stagflation, and Social Rigidities.* New Haven, Conn.: Yale University Press.

Panitch, Leo. (1979). "The Development of Corporatism in Liberal Democracies." In Philippe Schmitter and Gerhard Lehmbruch (Eds.), *Trends toward Corporatist Intermediation.* Beverly Hills, Calif.: Sage Press.

Przeworski, Adam, and John Sprague. (1986). *Paper Stones: A History of Electoral Socialism.* Chicago: University of Chicago Press.

Rubinstein, Ariel. (1985a). "A Bargaining Model with Incomplete Information about Time Preferences," *Econometrica* 53: 1151–72.

——— (1985b). "The Choice of Conjectures in a Bargaining Game with Incomplete Information." In Alvin Roth (Ed.), *Game Theoretic Models of Bargaining*. Cambridge: Cambridge University Press.

(1982). "Perfect Equilibrium in a Bargaining Model." *Econometrica* 50: 97–109.

Sabel, Charles F. (1981). "The Internal Politics of Trade Unions." In Suzanne D. Berger (Ed.), *Organizing Interests in Western Europe*. Cambridge: Cambridge University Press.

Selten, Richard. (1975). "Reexamination of the Perfectness Concept for Equilibrium Points in Extensive Games." *International Journal of Game Theory* 4: 25–55.

Shaked, Avner, and John Sutton. (1984). "Involuntary Unemployment as a Perfect Equilibrium in a Bargaining Model." *Econometrica* 52: 1351–64.

Shalev, Michael. (1980). "Trade Unionism and Economic Analysis: The Case of Industrial Conflict." *Journal of Labor Research* 1: 133–69.

Shorter, Edward, and Charles Tilly. (1974). *Strikes in France, 1830–1968*. Cambridge: Cambridge University Press.

Snyder, David. (1975). "Institutional Setting and Industrial Conflict: Comparative Analyses of France, Italy and the United States." *American Sociological Review* 40: 259–78.

Sobel, Joel, and Ichiro Takahashi. (1983). "A Multi-Stage Model of Bargaining," *Review of Economic Studies* 50: 411–26.

Sutton, John. (1986). "Non-Cooperative Bargaining Theory: An Introduction," *Review of Economic Studies* 53: 709–24.

Tarrow, Sidney (1983). *Struggling to Reform: Social Movements, Resources Mobilization and Cycles of Protest*. Ithaca, N.Y.: Center for International Studies, Western Societies Program, Cornell University.

Tilly, Charles. (1978). *From Mobilization to Revolution*. New York: Random House.

Tsebelis, George. (1990). *Nested Games: Rational Choice in Comparative Politics*. Berkeley: University of California Press.

(1989). "The Robinson Crusoe Fallacy: The Abuse of Probability in Political Analysis," *American Political Science Review* 83: 77–91.

Wallerstein, Michael, and Adam Przeworski. (1988). "The Centralization of Bargaining and Union Wage Demands." Presented at the Annual Meetings of the American Political Science Association.

6. A game-theoretic model of reform in Latin American democracies

Barbara Geddes

Bureaucratic inefficiency, patronage-induced overstaffing, and outright corruption retard economic development and reduce public well-being in developing countries. They prevent governments from effectively carrying out the economic plans to which they devote so much official attention and deprive citizens of government services to which they are legally entitled.

The costs associated with bureaucratic deficiencies are widely recognized. Nevertheless, the initiation of reforms has proved difficult. This essay explains why reforms that are widely regarded as necessary and desirable often face such severe obstacles to their initiation. It finds the explanation in the interests of the politicians who must make the decisions that would promote or impede reform. The heart of the argument is that these individuals frequently face a choice between actions that serve their individual political interests and actions that would improve the long-run welfare of their societies; when this happens, individual interests generally prevail. Reforms only occur in political circumstances that render the individual interests of the politicians who must initiate them consistent with the collective interest in reform.

Struggles over administrative reform have developed in virtually all countries in which political competition preceded the establishment of a professionalized state apparatus. The initiation of reforms entailed as bitter a struggle in Britain and the United States during the nineteenth century as in Latin America during the twentieth century. Numerous case studies of the initiation of reforms exist – but few general explanations.

This article suggests a general explanation. It uses simple game-theoretic models to explore how different electoral and party systems affect the incentives of legislators to initiate reforms. Here I focus on one type of reform, the intro-

I am grateful to Robert Bates, Gary Cox, Bernard Grofman, Peter Lange, Ronald Rogowski, Kim Stanton, George Tsebelis, Michael Wallerstein, and John Zaller for making helpful comments and sharing hard-to-find information.

duction of merit-based hiring for civil servants, but I would expect the explanation to be applicable to a range of other reforms.

Merit-based hiring was selected for emphasis because the many administrative reform packages proposed during recent decades nearly always include it; because rules for merit-based hiring, unlike other kinds of reform, vary only moderately from country to country; and because the effects of laws requiring recruitment by exam are relatively easy to assess. Meritocratic recruitment is not always the most important aspect of administrative reform; but it is always at least moderately important, and it is the easiest element of reform to "measure" and compare across nations.

This study analyzes the legislative struggle over reform in South American democracies,[1] some of which have initiated reforms, and some of which have not. The choice of this set of cases holds roughly constant several variables that are often mentioned as possible causes of honesty and competence in government: culture, colonial institutional structure, and level of economic development. At the same time, it preserves sufficient variance in contemporary political institutions and reform outcomes to allow the testing of hypotheses.

The need for reform

Demand for reform in Latin America resulted from widespread recognition that the traditional use of government resources for partisan purposes had led to excesses. In Uruguay during the 1950s and 1960s, for example, so large a fraction of the budgets of many government agencies went for wages to pay patronage appointees that there were no funds left for operating expenses. In 1960, Montevideo newspapers reported that because the Ministry of Public Health had created 1,449 new jobs in public hospitals, no money was left to buy medicines and essential hospital equipment (Taylor, 1960: 222). The Ministry of Public Works hired 313 new employees during one seven-month period to repair equipment. Since no funds remained to buy spare parts, by the end of the period none of the department's many self-propelled road scrapers remained operable, and all work on the roads had ceased. The "entire budget was being used to pay personnel and none was left for fuel, equipment, and materials" (Taylor, 1960: 103, 178–9).

Overstaffing is only one of the forms government inefficiency can take. In 1983, a group of Peruvian researchers set out to acquire a license to operate a small workshop in Lima. Documenting every step and moving as expeditiously as procedure allowed, they found that it took 289 days to obtain the 11 separate

---

[1] Although bureaucratic incompetence and corruption also plague authoritarian regimes, I shall examine only democracies because, in this model, the incentives that determine whether political leaders will initiate reform depend on institutional features of the political system. Consequently, one would need a different set of arguments to explain reform in an authoritarian institutional setting.

licenses and certificates legally required. Along the way, they were solicited for bribes 10 times (de Soto, 1986: 173–5).

As governments in the region began trying to promote economic development and as state intervention in economies increased, the need for administrative reform to increase the effectiveness of developmental strategies became increasingly obvious and urgent. Technical experts claimed that intervention in the economy would not produce desired effects unless the individuals making and carrying out policies were better trained (e.g., Emmerich, 1972, 1960; International Bank for Reconstruction and Development, 1961), presidents regularly proposed administrative reforms as elements of their development strategies (e.g., Brewer-Carías, 1975a; Morcillo, 1975), political party leaders espoused support for reform (Brewer-Carías, 1975a; Groves, 1974; Urzúa and García, 1971), the press campaigned energetically against corruption and incompetence in the bureaucracy and called for reform (González, 1980; López Pintor, 1972; Taylor, 1960; Urzúa and García, 1971), and ordinary people expressed a desire for more competent and honest government in their answers to survey questions.[2]

Impediments to reform

In spite of widespread support, however, reforms have occurred only slowly and sporadically. Two groups have opposed reform: those who have found in bureaucratic jobs a "refuge from which to make a last-ditch stand for their right to a quiet, incompetent existence" (Hirschman, 1958: 154) and elected politicians and party activists. The opposition of employees who gained their jobs through patronage reflects the expected costs of reform to them. But perhaps less obviously, administrative reform is also costly to the politicians who must enact it. Traditionally, jobs in the bureaucracy and the multitude of contracts, subsidies, exceptions, and other scarce values distributed by bureaucrats have served as important electoral resources. Politicians and officials have been able to trade help in acquiring these resources for support (Biles, 1978, 1972; Singer, 1965; Valenzuela, 1977).

Administrative reform threatens to eliminate these political resources. Reforms that introduce merit as the main criterion for hiring and promotion decrease the ability of politicians and party leaders to reward supporters with jobs. Efficiency criteria applied to bureaucratic procurement procedures reduce political discretion in the awarding of contracts. The use of economic and technical criteria rather than partisan favoritism to decide who gets subsidized credit, access to foreign exchange, tax exemptions, and so on further reduces the resources politicians can exchange for support.

The cost of administrative reform to politicians and party activists is thus clear. Under certain circumstances, however, administrative reform may also provide

[2] See notes 6, 7.

them with benefits. If the national economy improves as a result of increasing the competence of officials and the effectiveness of their decisions, incumbent politicians and their party can claim credit for it in the next election. Moreover, politicians and their party may gain support from voters who favor reform. Politicians may gain a sense of satisfaction from having helped provide the country with more honest and competent administration. A final possibility is that, as the electorate grows, politicians and party leaders will prefer to switch from offering private goods in exchange for support to offering public goods, because, in a mass electorate, public goods cost politicians less per voter reached (Cox, 1986).

To explain why reforms have occurred at some times and places but not others, then, one must answer the question, Under what circumstances will the benefits of reform outweigh the costs to the politicians who must at least acquiesce in passing them?

The interests of legislators and party leaders

Whether politicians will initiate administrative reform depends on the incentives they confront. Only if the individual aspirations for power, status, wealth, or policy change on the part of political activists and politicians can be furthered by the provision of reforms will they be provided. A formalization of the incentive structures faced by South American politicians making a choice about whether to use their limited resources to consolidate political support in customary ways or to bring about more efficient administration will yield predictions of when such reforms should occur.

Two groups of political actors play a role in the struggle over reform: elected politicians and party leaders (who often hold no elected office). Simplifying somewhat, one can hypothesize that these individuals want, above all, to further their political careers. Given this first-order preference, their strategic second-order preferences will vary, depending on the specific possibilities available to them.

The interests of elected officials in Latin America resemble the interests of politicians elsewhere. They want to be reelected,[3] and they prefer some policies over others. Without doing them too much of an injustice, we can assume that for most politicians most of the time, the desire to be elected takes precedence over policy preferences (see Ames, 1987). For some, the desire for office and its perquisites truly overwhelms their commitment to particular policies. Others

---

[3] Presidents may appear to be an exception to the assertion that politicians care most about reelection, since, in most Latin American countries, they cannot be immediately reelected. They can, however, serve again after one or two terms have elapsed. Many do so (e.g., Fernando Belaúnde and Carols Andrés Pérez); and more hope to but are prevented from doing so either by military intervention (e.g., Eduardo Frei and Juscelino Kubitschek) or by ambitious competitors within their own parties (e.g., Carlos Lleras Restrepo). The incentives presidents face as they confront the reform issue are detailed in Geddes, in press, ch. 6.

may want to be elected only in order to enact preferred policies; but if they fail to be elected, they lose their chance of influencing policy outcomes. Thus, even for the public spirited, the preference for election will be strong since election grants the opportunity to achieve other preferences (see Mayhew, 1975).

This is not to deny that for some politicians, ideological commitments outweigh the desire to be elected. The electoral process, however, tends to weed out such individuals; they are elected less frequently than those who consider winning of paramount importance. This selection process also contributes to the predominance of electoral motives among those who have already achieved office. As an initial simplification, then, suppose politicians compete with each other in a zero-sum electoral game, and that for those who compete in it, the desire to win this electoral game overrides other goals.

Party leaders further their careers by increasing the electoral success of their parties and by achieving greater influence within their parties. Many of their goals will thus coincide with those of politicians in their parties, since both politicians and party leaders benefit from policies that give their party electoral advantages. In certain other respects, however, their interests diverge. Party leaders benefit from policies that advance the interests of the party as a collectivity over the long run, whereas, in some situations, individual candidates may be injured by such policies. Party leaders, for example, favor rules that enforce party discipline; but in some circumstances individual legislators may be able to improve their electoral chances by breaking ranks. Situations may thus arise in which party leaders have interests not shared by the average legislator. Party leaders must then deploy the incentives at their disposal to influence legislators' votes.

The importance of party leaders in the struggle over reform depends on how much they influence candidates' electoral chances. Virtually all Latin American countries elect legislators using systems of proportional representation. The factors that contribute to the probability that candidates will win elections depend on how candidate lists are selected and whether lists are closed (placement on lists being determined by party leaders) or open (determined by voters). In open list systems, the vote for candidates depends on the popularity of their positions on issues, voters' party loyalty, candidates' personal charisma, and constituency services, patronage, and favors – much as it does in winner-take-all systems such as the United States. In closed list systems, the candidate's probability of winning depends primarily on party loyalty and the candidate's position on the party list. Factors such as charisma, issue position, and constituency service affect the candidate's probability of winning by influencing party leaders' decisions about placement on the list, rather than by influencing the vote directly.

In systems in which party leaders' control over the list strongly influences who is elected, they exercise great power over the votes of politicians who have to be concerned about future reelection. In systems such as Brazil's (in which party leaders have virtually no control over who runs for office) or Colombia's during the National Front (in which party leaders lost control of the lists) they exercise

Table 6.1. *The effect of patronage on the probability of election*

		Politician II	
		Merit	Patronage
Politician I	Merit	v_1, v_2	$v_1 - x_2, v_2 + x_2$
	Patronage	$v_1 + x_1, v_2 - x_1$	$v_1 + x_1 - x_2, v_2 + x_2 - x_1$

Note: Politicians' utilities are assumed linear with the probability of winning the next election. v_i = the probability that candidate i will be elected if no jobs are distributed for political purposes. v_i rises and falls exogenously with normal political tides. $\Sigma\ v_i = 1$. x_i = the amount by which candidate i can increase his or her chances of election (at the opponent's expense), by rewarding supporters with government jobs. (It is assumed here that on average, each individual who works to maintain the candidate's political machine, get out the vote, etc., in the expectation of receiving a job will increase the candidate's probability of being elected by some positive, though possibly quite small, amount.)

little power. Where party leaders determine election chances, the calculations of legislators considering a vote for reform will focus on the vote's expected effect on the judgments of party leaders.

Meritocratic hiring rules and other reforms that introduce impersonal criteria for the allocation of government resources reduce politicians' and party leaders' discretion over the distribution of the jobs and favors that fuel political machines and thus influence the vote. No politician in competition with others engaged in trading jobs and favors for votes can afford unilaterally to eschew reliance on patronage. Some, however, might be willing to give up this resource if others did. Similarly, no party leader could afford for the party unilaterally to cease distributing patronage; but some might be willing if they could be assured that others also would do so.

The conditions under which legislators can be expected to favor reforms that deprive everyone of some valued electoral resources can be deduced from a simple game-theoretic model, as shown in Table 6.1. In this simplified world, each politician has some baseline probability of winning the next election, v_i, determined by voters' party loyalty, issue preferences, and so on. This baseline probability can be increased by the skillful use of political favors and decreased by his opponents' distribution of favors.

The payoffs in these matrices reflect the amounts of patronage to which a national party machine has access as a result of its participation in government. Because of the centralization of decision making and resources in Latin America, the patronage resources available to legislators depend more on their party's national position than on local resources.

The Table 6.1 matrix shows the incentives faced by candidates from different parties as they decide whether to use patronage to secure votes during an electoral campaign. The top left cell of the matrix shows the candidates' probabilities of

Table 6.2. *The effect of voting for reform on the probability of reelection*

		Legislator from minority party	
		Reform	Patronage
Legislator from majority party	Reform	v_1, v_2	$v_1 + e, v_2 - e$
	Patronage	$v_1 + x_1 - x_2 - e,$ $v_2 + x_2 - x_1 + e$	$v_1 + x_1 - x_2,$ $v_2 + x_2 - x_1$

Note: x_i and v_i are defined as in Table 6.1. e = the amount of credit a legislator can claim for voting for reform.

winning when neither distributes favors; these are just the baseline probabilities v_1 and v_2. In the lower left cell, Politician 1 uses patronage, gaining an electoral advantage of x_1 from it; the opponent, who does not use patronage, then suffers a decline in probability of winning of $-x_1$. The upper right cell shows the reverse situation. The lower right cell illustrates the prereform milieu in which both candidates rely on patronage.

If this pattern of incentives were the whole story, there would never be any reason for legislators to approve administrative reform. Each individual who relies on patronage is better off, no matter what others do and whether the game is repeated or not. If for any reason, however, legislators place a positive value on reform, no matter how small, the outcome of the game depends on the magnitude of the difference between x_1 and x_2 in relation to the expected political value of the reform. That is, if legislators value reform at all – if, for example, they think supporting reform would sway the votes of a small number of middle-class idealists or improve their standing by a tiny increment with party leaders – they might in some circumstances vote for reform.

Where popular demand for reform exists, giving legislators a reason to vote for it even though that reason rarely outweighs reasons to vote against, the incentives facing legislators as they decide how to vote are schematized in Table 6.2. The lower right cell is the same as in Table 6.1. Members of both parties vote against reform, so that neither can claim credit and neither is hurt by the other claiming credit. The reform fails since neither large party voted for it and members of both parties continue to rely on patronage during election campaigns. The upper left cell shows the situation when both parties vote for reform. Since both voted for it, the electoral advantage of voting for it cancels out. The reform passes and neither party can rely on patronage during future campaigns. The upper right cell shows the payoffs that would result if the majority party voted in favor of reform and the minority party voted against. The reform passes and neither party can use patronage in future campaigns; and the majority party reaps a small electoral advantage, e, at the expense of the minority party from voting for reform. The lower left cell shows what happens when the majority party votes against reform and the minority votes in favor. The reform fails to pass and both parties continue to distribute patronage. The minority party gains a small amount of credit at the majority's expense for its vote for reform.

Whether legislators will vote for reform when they face the incentives schematized in Table 6.2 depends on the relative magnitudes of x_1 and x_2. If $(x_1 - x_2) > e$, that is, if x_1 is any significant amount larger than x_2, the majority party will vote against reform, and it will fail. If, however, x_1 and x_2 are approximately equal, that is, if the two parties have approximately equal access to patronage resources, the majority party will vote for reform, and it will pass.[4] The minority party, as long as e has any positive value at all, will always prefer reform.

To reiterate in nontechnical language, in an election, all candidates can be expected to rely on patronage, as shown in Table 6.1. Members of a party disadvantaged by the distribution of patronage resources, however, would be better off if the merit system were imposed on everyone. Thus, they always have an incentive to support reform in the legislature. Giving up the use of patronage would make them better off as long as everyone else also gave it up. As many observers have noted, the reform issue generally appeals to the "outs" in politics.

Where patronage is equally distributed and politicians can gain even a small amount from a vote for reform, members of both parties have reason to vote for it. In this situation, patronage conveys no relative advantage, but voting for reform may improve electoral chances. Consequently, political interest dictates the passage of reform. The matrix demonstrates the logic underlying these conclusions for political systems dominated by two large parties or coalitions, but the same argument would hold if three or more parties played central roles in electoral competition. Then patronage would need to be distributed approximately equally among all the top parties before it would be rational for legislators in the larger parties to vote for it.

Members of a party with greater access to patronage have no incentive to vote for reform in the legislature and no reason to eschew patronage during the electoral campaign either. They can improve their chances of being elected by relying on patronage, no matter what members of the other party do and no matter how long the situation continues. Members of a party with more access to patronage, then, could be expected to opt for reform *only* if they thought other gains from voting for reform would outweigh the certain costs that the loss of patronage would entail. One can imagine a situation in which public outrage over bureaucratic incompetence and graft had become so vehement that politicians might fear that they would lose more votes by voting against reform than by reducing their ability to distribute patronage. If public outrage very often reached such proportions, however, legislators would be eager rather than reluctant reformers.

---

[4] Speaking of majority parties in the Latin American context involves a degree of simplification. In fact, legislative majorities are usually coalitions. This should not, however, affect the logic of the argument.

Descriptions of the reform movement in the United States suggest that public outrage over the assassination of President Garfield· by a disappointed office seeker played a catalytic role in bringing about reform (Van Riper, 1958: 88–94). Even in this case, however, the legislature voted to pass the reform only after the election of 1882. This election, more than a year after Garfield's death, gave Democrats a majority in the House and thus marked the end of the Republicans' post–Civil War dominance over patronage. A few months prior to the 1882 election, the House had "derisively and angrily refused to give a paltry sum and to aid a single experiment of reform" (Hall, 1884: 462). Immediately after the election, faced with the prospect of sharing the spoils in the immediate future, the same representatives who had ignored public opinion five months earlier passed the Pendleton Act by an overwhelming majority (Van Riper, 1958: 94). Most of the time, legislators and party leaders can afford to ignore the public's desire for reform because reform is only one of many issues that affect voters' choices and is rarely – perhaps never – the most important issue to most voters.

To summarize the argument so far, the payoff matrices imply a prediction that spoils will be outlawed in democracies when two conditions are met, namely, that the benefits of patronage are approximately evenly distributed among the larger parties, and legislators have some small incentive to vote for reform.

Such reforms may turn out to be fragile if access to patronage again becomes one-sided, a subject to which I will return below. For now, let us look in more detail at how the game-theoretic prediction fares when confronted with evidence from the Latin American democracies.

The effect of the distribution of patronage on reform

This section tests the predictions derived from the game-theoretic model on the universe of Latin American countries that have experienced fifteen or more years of consecutive competitive democracy since 1930: Brazil, Chile, Colombia, Uruguay, and Venezuela. Costa Rica was excluded because its legislators cannot be immediately reelected, so that the simplifying assumptions about the interests of legislators used here might not apply to them. The 1930 cutoff date was chosen because interest in state-fostered development (and hence in administrative reform) began in most countries during the Depression. Prior to that time, administrative reform was not typically seen as an issue having much importance for public welfare.

Of the five countries examined, three – Colombia, Venezuela, and Uruguay – passed initial civil service reforms during more-or-less democratic periods.[5] Brazil's initial reform occurred during the Vargas dictatorship in the late 1930s. Most attempts to extend the reform during the democratic period failed. No

---

[5] The categorization of Uruguay as a democracy at the time of the reform is somewhat dubious. The elected president had staged a coup and replaced the elected legislature. Still, two factions continued to function as the most important political competitors (Taylor, 1952). Since party competition continued during this period of modified democracy, Uruguay was retained in the small universe of democracies.

comprehensive civil service reform passed in Chile during its long period of democracy. In the following pages I examine the circumstances under which reforms occurred in Uruguay, Venezuela, and Colombia to see whether they are consistent with the predictions of the model. Then I discuss Brazil and Chile as contrasting cases.

In the real world there is no way to measure amounts of patronage or how much influence on the vote it has. In the case studies that follow, I deal with these measurement problems by relying on two plausible assumptions. First, all else equal, the distribution of jobs and favors increases the probability of being elected (otherwise politicians would not expend so much of their energy providing such services); the more a politician distributes, the better the politician's chances. Second, the amount of patronage to which a candidate has access for distribution depends on the party's control of elective and administrative offices at the national level, which in turn depends on the party's present and past electoral success. Electoral victories allow the more successful party to appoint its adherents to bureaucratic posts. These appointees become the source of the favors that influence later elections. (Generally, a waning party that has lost many of the seats it formerly held in the legislature will still be able to call upon loyalists in the bureaucracy for a number of years.)

These assumptions permit an approximate rank ordering of each party's access to patronage, a level of measurement sufficient for the simple model used here. They imply that if two parties control roughly equal numbers of seats in the legislature over a period of years, each party will have access to about the same amount of patronage. If, in contrast, one party dominates the legislature, we can assume that it also dominates patronage opportunities.

Colombia

Competition between the Liberal and Conservative parties for control of government and the spoils associated with control structured Colombia's political history prior to 1990. Until 1958, transfers of power from one party to the other were accompanied by large-scale turnovers of personnel and partisan violence (Solaún, 1980). Public welfare suffered from the inefficiency of a bureaucracy composed of patronage appointments as well as from periodic outbreaks of violence. As early as the 1920s, critics identified the parties' excessive reliance on patronage as one of the pathologies of Colombian life. Reforms have been undertaken, however, only during two time periods, both of which correspond to periods of approximate equality between the two parties.

Colombia's first experiments with merit-oriented administrative reforms occurred during the presidency of Enrique Olaya Herrera (1930–4). The Olaya administration marked the first electoral victory of the Liberal Party in the twentieth century. Olaya won by a slim margin, and the reformist Liberals' hold on government during his first two years remained tenuous. Several administrative reforms were passed at this time, the most important of which aimed at improving the performance of the Ministry of Public Works and other agencies responsible for the construction and maintenance of railroads and highways (Hartwig, 1983: 105–7).

By 1934, the Liberals had consolidated their electoral dominance, and Alfonso López won the presidency easily. He continued many of the new economic policies of Olaya but permitted the reassertion of partisan considerations in hiring. The Olaya administration's merit-based reforms quietly disappeared during the Liberal hegemony of 1934–46 (Hartwig, 1983: 106–11).

Colombia's next attempt to establish merit as the basis for recruitment to the civil service occurred in 1958. At that time, each of the major parties controlled exactly half of the legislature and half of the available administrative appointments. This was due to a pact, the National Front, between the Liberal and Conservative parties that established parity between the two traditional rivals in the national legislature, in departmental (i.e., state) legislatures, in municipal councils, and in administrative appointments. This pact, designed to end a decade of repression and partisan violence in which more than two hundred thousand people had been killed, was scheduled to remain in effect for sixteen years. Each party would receive 50 percent of the seats in legislatures and councils. The presidency was to alternate between the two parties. A career civil service was proposed as a means of removing key jobs from partisan control, and other administrative jobs were to be distributed equally between supporters of the two parties. In short, the pact established an equal sharing of power and patronage regardless of electoral outcome for sixteen years (Berry, Hellman, and Solaún, 1980; Dix, 1980; Hartlyn, 1988).

The pact called for the creation of a merit-based career civil service, but presidential and legislative action were required to initiate it (Groves, 1974; Morcillo, 1975). Individual legislators facing this decision about whether to forgo a portion of customary patronage would have to consider the electoral costs and benefits associated with patronage, as shown in Table 6.2. By law, each party could claim an equal share of patronage. Nevertheless, no individual legislator could afford to eschew the use of patronage unilaterally.

Two factors contributed to making a vote for reform more attractive than it might otherwise have been. The first was the interest of all politicians in reestablishing a democratic system, which depended on ending partisan violence. Administrative reform was expected to help end the violence by providing a fair means of distributing jobs and also by contributing to better quality economic policy. Leaders in both parties had committed themselves to agreements, including complicated parity arrangements as well as civil service reform, as a way of reducing the violence and reestablishing a competitive political system. Thus, party elites had managed to forge an enforceable cooperative solution to the prisoner's dilemma of unrestrained party competition. The career interests of high-level party leaders in reestablishing the competitive electoral system explain their support for the pact.

Legislators' second reason for voting for reform was the expectation that it would affect future placement on electoral lists. Party leaders in Colombia at that time could influence legislators' decisions with special effectiveness because of party cohesion and a closed list proportional representation system (see Duff, 1971). Although the proliferation of factions within Colombia's two major parties during the pact subsequently reduced the influence of party leaders over legislators, in 1958 both parties were still relatively cohesive (Archer, 1990).

Evidence from the Colombian case is thus consistent with the model. Reform occurred when access to patronage was distributed equally. Party discipline enforced by the closed list system provided legislators with an additional incentive to vote for reform.

Uruguay

In Uruguay, the career civil service was first mandated by the 1934 constitution. This constitution legalized a pact between two factions of the traditional dominant parties, the *terrista* faction of the Colorado Party and the *herrerista* faction of the National, or Blanco, party.

Uruguay has historically had a two-party system within which multiple factions have independent legal status and run their own lists of candidates in elections, thus creating a de facto multiparty system. Prior to the reform, Gabriel Terra, head of the *terrista* faction, had been elected president on the Colorado ticket. In the face of severe economic distress caused by the Depression, and an apparently insurmountable policy immobilism caused by Uruguay's collegial executive and powerful but factionalized legislature, Terra staged a coup d'état in 1933. Luís Alberto Herrera, caudillo of the most important Blanco party faction at the time, collaborated with Terra; and the two faction leaders entered into a pact to share government offices, excluding other factions of both parties (Taylor, 1960: 23–9).

The sitting legislature was dismissed. Terra and Herrera chose a Deliberative Assembly of ninety-nine members made up of approximately equal numbers of Colorado supporters of Terra and Blanco supporters of Herrera to act as a provisional legislature. They in turn elected a Constituent Assembly made up of Terra and Herrera supporters. The resulting constitution institutionalized the pact by mandating minority representation in the president's Council of Ministers and the equal division of Senate seats between the two most-voted lists of the two most-voted parties. The division of the Senate assured these two factions equal control of appointments of all important administrative positions, the boards of directors of state enterprises, Supreme Court justices, and members of the Accounts Tribunal (Taylor, 1960: 171). At the same time, it excluded other factions from access to spoils. In effect, it transformed what had been a de facto multiparty system into a two-party system with approximately equal access to patronage for both parties.

Traditionally, the Colorado Party had attracted more electoral support and controlled more patronage than had the Blancos. More popular parties usually have access to more patronage, but the pact resulted in an equal division of patronage in spite of electoral inequality. In this setting, the Constituent Assembly was able to agree to establish a career civil service, which would remove some appointments from the discretion of party activists. As in Colombia, the closed list system provided faction leaders with incentives they could deploy to affect the votes of members of the Constituent Assembly.

This brief period of relative equality between two factions was unique in Uruguayan history. The two parties achieved approximate equality in electoral strength in 1962 and 1971, but the largest factions within each party remained unequal (Fabregat, 1963: 31; Rial, 1985: 12–13; Venturini, 1984: 25, 50). No legislation passed to enforce the principle of meritocratic hiring in practice. Legislative and constitutional additions to the civil service law after the 1930s generally focused on providing job security, vacations, grievance procedures, and so on. In other words, later additions to the civil service laws were designed to benefit well-organized civil servants and thus contribute to electoral gains for legislators, not to require further sacrifice of electoral interests.

Venezuela

At the beginning of the democratic period in Venezuela, administrative reform seemed to be supported by everyone. Excessive corruption had helped discredit the dictator, Marcos Pérez Jiménez; and administrative reform was widely seen as needed, both to reduce corruption and to improve the state's ability to use oil revenues to foster development and increase social welfare. President Rómulo Betancourt expressed strong support for reform, foreign experts were hired to help formulate a reform and train Venezuelans to implement it, and a reform agency attached to the presidency was created (Brewer-Carías, 1975a,b; Stewart, 1978).

The agency completed its draft plan for civil service reform in 1960, and the president submitted it to Congress. The president had a coalition majority in Congress. Since party discipline in Venezuela is strong (in part because of party leaders' control of electoral lists), prospects for reform should have been good. Nevertheless, the civil service reform bill was never reported out of committee (Groves, 1967).

It continued, moreover, to languish in Congress throughout the Betancourt presidency and through that of his successor, Raúl Leoni. Venezuelan observers note that despite flamboyant public statements supporting reform, neither president really pushed the bill (Brewer-Carías, 1975a: 454–7). Throughout this period, the party *Acción Democrática* (AD) controlled the presidency and a strong plurality in Congress. The AD leaders had much more to lose from giving up patronage than had the other parties.

In 1968, Rafael Caldera of the Social Christian Party (COPEI) was elected president with 28.9 percent of the vote, as compared with the AD-led coalition vote of 28.1 percent. In the legislature, the vote was split between the two largest parties, with 25.8 percent for AD and 24.2 percent for COPEI (Ruddle and Gillette, 1972). The civil service reform was brought forward for consideration in Congress again, revised to make it congruent with recent constitutional and institutional changes, and passed in 1970 with support from both AD and COPEI (Brewer-Carías, 1975a: 475–9; Stewart, 1978: 39–40). Thus Venezuela's first merit-based civil service law also passed during a period of temporary equality between parties.

Brazil

Getúlio Vargas established a career civil service in Brazil during the dictatorship of 1937–45. The reform had made a fair amount of headway in imposing merit as the criterion for hiring and promotion by the time Vargas was overthrown in 1945. But after the return to democracy, earlier reforms were to a considerable extent undermined (Siegel, 1966: 148–75).

From the establishment of democracy until the military coup in 1964, the distribution of electoral strength and patronage in Brazil was quite unequal. The country had a multiparty system with open list proportional representation in the lower house and a majoritarian system in the Senate. The three most important parties were the *Partido Social Democrático* (PSD, a traditional, conservative party despite its name), the *Partido Trabalhista Brasileiro* (PTB, the Labor Party), and the *Uniao Democrática Nacional* (UDN, a middle-class reformist party). The PSD and PTB had developed from the traditional and labor wings of the political machine created by Vargas during the dictatorship (Oliveira, 1973; Souza, 1976). They were entrenched in the government bureaucracy prior to Vargas's overthrow, and their patronage resources remained impressive throughout the democratic period. In spite of apparently important ideological differences, the PSD and PTB formed frequent electoral alliances. The UDN, in contrast, developed in opposition to the Vargas political machine (Benevides, 1981). Over the years it achieved some access to patronage as a result of entering coalitions and winning some elections, but it never equaled the other parties.

During the 1950s and 1960s, as economic development became the most important goal of the Brazilian government, concern about administrative reform reached new levels. Presidents Getúlio Vargas (during his second administration), Juscelino Kubitschek, and Jânio Quadros all proposed reforms (Graham, 1968: 143–53). Public demand for reform, as expressed in the press and in answers to survey questions, was widespread. For example, a 1964 survey asked, "Which one of these do you think our country needs most: an honest government without corruption; a government that gets things done; a fair distribution of wealth; national unity; or individual freedom?" Even though the income distribution in Brazil was one of the most skewed in the world, 62 percent of those who answered chose "an honest government without corruption." The second most frequent choice was "a government that gets things done."[6] When

---

[6] This question comes from a survey conducted by the United States Information Agency in March 1964 (World Survey II: Attitudes toward Domestic and Foreign Affairs [$N=466$]), made available

asked to agree or disagree with the statement, "The only really important problem in Brazil is the problem of lack of character and honesty," only 15 percent of those who had an opinion disagreed. When asked the most important reason for their party preference, 44 percent mentioned honesty first, more than twice as many as mentioned party program or past record.[7]

Even in the face of such expressions of public opinion, however, legislators making the decision whether or not to vote for reform had to take into account the costs and benefits associated with patronage. Members of the UDN would have been better off if they had been able to pass a reform. Under these circumstances, it is not surprising that the UDN espoused "the struggle against the forces of administrative corruption that have been dominant for many years" (Pinto, 1960) in platforms, campaigns, and speeches. Individual members of the party could still improve their chances of being elected, however, by relying on promises of patronage during the campaign.

Members of the UDN behaved as would be expected, given the costs and benefits they faced. Most members relied on patronage and deals in electoral campaigns but advocated the passage of reform bills in Congress (Geddes, 1990). This stance, though rational, left them vulnerable to charges of hypocrisy from both idealists within the party and opponents outside.

In contrast, PSD and PTB legislators had no reason to vote for reform and every reason to continue relying on patronage during electoral campaigns. During the democratic period, the career civil service remained on the books; but control over new hiring returned, for the most part, to the realm of patronage. Congress reduced the status and powers of the *Departamento Administrativo de Serviço Público* (DASP), the agency in charge of enforcing civil service laws (Siegel, 1966: 148–72). Much of the time, exams were not held and appointments were made in the temporary and extranumerary (i.e., outside the merit system) categories of employment. The dividing line between merit-based career and noncareer civil servants was blurred by the passage of laws conferring career civil service status and perquisites on "temporary" employees who had not taken the exam but who had spent five years or more in public employment (Graham, 1968: 140–58).

Reform laws were proposed at various times; but only two kinds of civil service laws made it through Congress: those that granted benefits to civil servants and thus involved no electoral cost to legislators and those that extended meritocratic norms into agencies controlled by one particular party and thus involved gains rather than costs for the majority of legislators. In the realm of granting benefits, Congress increased the wages of civil servants and passed several laws granting job security and higher status to unclassified employees. The one exception to the overall decline in the merit-based civil service during

by the Inter-University Consortium for Political and Social Research (ICPSR 7048), University of Michigan.

[7] These questions come from a survey conducted by Júlio Barbosa et al. (Political Behavior and Attitudes in a Brazilian City, 1965–1966 [$N=645$]), made available by the Inter-University Consortium for Political and Social Research (ICPSR 7613), University of Michigan.

the democratic period occurred when Congress extended the merit system to cover the social security institutes. Thousands of jobs in these institutes had been used during the second Vargas and the Kubitschek presidencies to reward the presidents' Labor Party (PTB) coalition partner (Amaral, 1966: 17–19; Siegel, 1963: 6). Hiring in the institutes had, in effect, been turned over to Labor Party activists. By voting to include the institutes in the merit system, members of Congress from other parties could decrease the resources available to the Labor Party without incurring any cost themselves. Given the unusual circumstance of the existence of a group of agencies dominated by one particular party, the vote for reform did not depend on parity in the legislature.

Chile

During its long history of democracy, Chile never passed a comprehensive civil service reform. It had no civil service commission and no uniform system of recruitment and promotion (López Pintor, 1972; Valenzuela, 1984: 256). It did have some requirements for entry, such as completion of the tenth grade; but even these were violated in practice. Each agency controlled its own recruitment system. As a result, some agencies were highly professionalized, others extremely politicized (Ascher, 1975: 57–86; Urzúa and García, 1971: 175–8).

The Chilean party system was far more fragmented than those of the other countries discussed. Traditionally, the Radical Party had greatest access to patronage. Radical party dominance began to decline in the early 1950s, but no conjuncture occurred that gave approximately equal patronage to the largest parties in Congress (Valenzuela, 1985: 44–7).

Two characteristics of the Chilean democratic system further decreased the likelihood of passing a reform: the open list system of proportional representation initiated in 1958 and the fragmented party system. It might appear at first that in a fragmented party system such as Chile's, in which the "dominant" party often receives only 20 percent to 30 percent of the vote in legislative elections, several smaller parties could band together to pass reforms that would deprive the largest party of its disproportionate access to patronage. In this way, a group of smaller parties with less access to patronage could improve their ability to compete against the party with the closest ties to the bureaucracy.

In an open list system, however, incumbents' interest in maintaining their advantage over competitors in their own parties outweighs their interest in depriving members of other parties of access to patronage resources. In open list systems, the candidate's place on the list is determined by the vote the candidate receives. In other words, a candidate runs not only against candidates from other parties but also against other candidates from his or her own party.

Patronage thus becomes an even more valuable resource to the candidates who have access to it. Candidates can distinguish themselves from the candidates of other parties on the basis of programmatic appeals, offers of public goods, and ideology; but attention to casework and the distribution of private goods are among the few ways of distinguishing themselves from other candidates in the same party. Incumbents have a great advantage over other candidates in terms of their ability to distribute favors. Consequently, incumbents of all parties in an open list proportional representation system can be expected to be especially reluctant to give up patronage.

Had Chilean party leaders had an interest in reducing reliance on patronage, they might have succeeded in overcoming incumbents' reluctance to vote for reform. Despite the open list system, Chilean party leaders (in contrast to Brazilian) have substantial influence over the political careers of legislators. They influence them through control over who achieves a place on the list, whose name appears at the top of the ballot (and thus receives a disproportionate share of the votes of the unsophisticated), and who receives cabinet appointments, often a steppingstone to executive office. Given the unequal distribution of patronage among parties and the importance of patronage to the organizational survival of parties, however, party leaders had no interest in reform.

The fragmented party system necessitated government by coalition. Agreements on the distribution of spoils among coalition partners held these coalitions together (Valenzuela, 1978; López Pintor, 1972: 89). Even if the president's party had been willing to make an agreement with the opposition to eschew patronage, it could not have done so because disintegration of its governing coalition would almost certainly have followed. Such an agreement with the opposition would, in effect, constitute defection in the ongoing assurance game between the president and his coalition partners; and he could expect to be punished for defection by loss of support.

Given the fragmented party system, unequal access to patronage, open list proportional representation, and the need for coalitions in order to govern, the game-theoretic approach would predict no civil service reform in Chile; and none occurred. With regard to the occurrence or nonoccurrence of an initial reform, then, game-theoretic predictions seem to be consistent with events in all the countries examined.

The return to an unequal distribution of patronage

Up to this point, I have dealt with the situations in which the first step toward a merit-based civil service was taken. I turn now to consideration of whether these initial steps have been, or will be, followed by others. Given the notorious inefficiency of postreform bureaucracies in Venezuela, Colombia, and Uruguay, one must conclude either that civil service reform does not work in Latin America or that initial reforms were subsequently undermined.

Evidence suggests that professionalization does occur and does increase competence and public service orientations in the parts of the bureaucracy in which it occurs (Hartwig, 1983; Láfer, 1970; Schmidt, 1974; Vieira, 1967; Wahrlich, 1964) but that initial reforms affect only a small part of the bureaucracy. Where conjunctures favoring the passage of reforms have lasted only a short time, additional increments of reform have not followed initial reforms. Further, subsequent legislation and executive decrees have sometimes vitiated earlier reforms.

In Venezuela, when the AD returned to its then customary dominant role with the election of Carlos Andrés Pérez in 1973, nonpartisan administration suffered a setback. Pérez won the presidency with a strong plurality (48.4 percent, compared with 36.7 percent for COPEI). He was the first elected Venezuelan president to have an absolute majority in both houses of Congress (Karl, 1982: 182–4). He asked for, and eventually got, special powers to enact by executive decree a package of proposals aimed at controlling and using effectively the windfall of oil money threatening to engulf the nation. Included among these projects were several administrative reforms. Pérez expressed strong support for administrative reform, including professionalization of personnel. His actions, however, tended to belie his words.

Decree 211, issued by Pérez, allowed the administration to increase the number of nonclassified public employees (i.e., temporary and low-status employees who need not pass exams to enter the service) as well as the number of positions *de confianza* (high-status appointments in which loyalty is considered an appropriate criterion for recruitment). Employees *de confianza* in 1982 included all division chiefs, those employed in fiscal sections, buying, supplies, and document reproduction, and all secretaries in these areas. COPEI claimed that eighty thousand people had lost their jobs for political reasons during the administration turnover when Pérez came to power (Karl, 1982: 267). Pérez, in other words, took the opportunity provided by having a majority in the legislature, to build the political machine that would form the foundation of his second successful campaign for the presidency (Geddes, in press: ch. 6).

Some administrative reforms have occurred, however, since the Pérez administration. An anticorruption law, for example, was passed in 1982 when AD and COPEI each received 39.7 percent of the vote in legislative elections.[8] The problem of professionalizing personnel, however, remains unsolved (Brewer-Carías, 1985).[9] Partisan considerations still affect most hiring decisions, and turnover in the bureaucracy when a new administration comes into power is so high that administrative output falls noticeably (Cova and Hannot, 1986). Corruption continues to be a serious problem.

The situation in Uruguay resembled that in Venezuela, but in a more extreme form. After the end of the pact between Terra and Herrera, Uruguay never again experienced equality among the largest party factions. The 1934 constitution mandated that hiring and promotion be based on merit but did not establish an agency to conduct exams. Instead, each bureaucratic entity set its own standards. Some evidence about the strictness of these standards can be inferred from education statistics. Of public employees in the mid-1950s, 46 percent had not

---

[8] Ley Orgánica de Salvaguarda del Patrimonio Público (*Gaceta Oficial*, no. 3077, *extraordinario*, December 23, 1982). My thanks to Michael Coppedge for bringing this law to my attention.
[9] "Burocracia: Ciudadano" (Bureaucracy: Citizen), *El Diario de Caracas*, August 2, 1987.

finished primary school, and 70 percent had completed ten or fewer years of schooling (Taylor, 1960: 215–19). Entrance exams in many agencies guaranteed little more than literacy. There was one important barrier to entry, however; applicants were not permitted to take the test unless it was signed by the neighborhood *sublema* (i.e., party faction) boss (see Biles, 1978, 1972).

Most legislation regarding the civil service and additional provisions added to subsequent constitutions dealt with job security and grievance procedures. These issues involve no cost to legislators as long as the number of jobs keeps expanding and brings them electoral benefits in the form of support from government employees (estimated at 27.6 percent of the working population of Uruguay in 1956; see Taylor, 1960: 100).

As a result of this series of laws and constitutional provisions, by the 1960s it had become virtually impossible to dismiss government employees. The 1952 constitution provides that the Senate must approve the dismissal of a classified employee. Even the dismissal of temporary employees has led to serious political repercussions (Taylor, 1960: 215). As noted, such a large proportion of agency budgets was spent on wages that at times, agencies could not afford to buy equipment needed in order to carry out their functions and supply government services.

To summarize, in Uruguay's factionalized political system, legislators supported the elements of career civil service that could be converted into electoral advantage, especially job creation and job security. They did not provide for the imposition of merit as the criterion for hiring and promotion, which would have reduced the ability of factions to service their clients.

The pattern of implementation of the 1958 reform in Colombia resembles that in Uruguay. Once parity between the two major parties was established, competition among the factions within each party for shares of the party's half intensified. Struggles for patronage among factions of the same party became increasingly vitriolic over time. As in Uruguay, the party pact has led to a sharp increase in the number of government jobs.

All Colombian presidents during the early democratic period made some effort at administrative reform, and quite a few reforms gained legislative approval. Merit-based hiring has been an exception, however. By 1966 when Carlos Lleras Restrepo came to power, only 5 percent of public employees were included in the merit-based career civil service. Lleras mounted an aggressive campaign against corruption and patronage and for administrative reform. Congress, however, successfully blocked his proposed personnel reforms. Unable to extend the merit system to cover more jobs, near the end of his term Lleras issued a decree allowing public employees to enroll themselves in the career service without taking the exam, thus undermining the meritocratic element of civil service.

As the party pact neared its end, conflict between the parties increased and interest in administrative reform waned, even in the executive branch. With the failure to extend the merit system, civil service in Colombia, as in Uruguay, had become synonymous with inflexibility and the inability to fire incompetents

(Hartlyn, 1988). Misael Pastrana, the last president during the pact, showed little interest in reform, being more interested in consolidating his party's position before the first election unfettered by parity agreements. His successor, Alfonso López Michelsen, suspended the career civil service during a state of siege.

The general assessment by observers of the current Colombian scene is that professionalization of some key sectors of the Colombian bureaucracy has occurred but personnel reform in general has failed (Hartwig, 1983; Vidal Perdomo, 1982). In spite of considerable presidential support, campaigns against corruption in the press, and supportive public opinion, legislators in the factionalized party system have not found it in their own interest to extend the merit system. Since the end of the National Front, party parity has not occurred. Because of the ease of forming faction lists, party leaders failed to exert much influence over legislators' votes (Archer, 1990).

In brief, then, in all the countries examined, reforms initiated during periods of party equality or during a dictatorship suffered reverses when the distribution of power among the competitive parties became unequal. Even in the United States, when the election of 1896 resulted in renewed Republican dominance, the merit system was seriously threatened. President McKinley removed the exam requirement for ten thousand jobs. Further, during the McKinley administration Congress passed legislation excluding thousands of new appointments from the system (Van Riper, 1958: 171–5). If McKinley's assassination had not brought Theodore Roosevelt unexpectedly to the presidency, administration in the United States might look less different from Latin America than it does today.

Civil service reforms generally include two kinds of provisions: (1) requirements for merit-based hiring and promotion and (2) guarantees to employees of job security, fair treatment, union representation, and so on. In unequal or fragmented party systems, legislators have been reluctant to increase the number of jobs included in the merit system, since each new inclusion reduces the resources available to politicians and party leaders for use in their struggle with each other. Laws extending perquisites and job guarantees to larger numbers of employees have posed no problem for legislators, however, since they bring electoral benefits from grateful employees.

Implications for the future of reform

In the United States, where both parties enjoyed similar access to patronage from 1882 until 1896, civil service was gradually extended "by executive order, taking advantage of feeble statutory authorization" (Schattschneider, 1942: 138). By 1896 the merit system had been extended to cover about half of all appointments, which included "the bulk of the offices which it was then either legal or politically and administratively practical to place under the merit system" (Van Riper, 1958: 130). Most of these extensions occurred when the party in control of government had lost an election and expected the incoming party to dismiss its supporters (Skowronek, 1979). This pattern of incremental extension was possible because, in a system of two approximately equal parties, occasions recur when it is temporarily in the interest of one party or the other to extend the merit system. Over time, this series of instrumental decisions creates a professional civil service.

The same thing is likely to happen in South America but will take longer because of differences in party systems. The initial establishment of a merit-based civil service, an agency to administer it, and (usually) a school to train civil servants creates islands of competence within the bureaucracy and concentrates advocates of further reform strategically inside government. Though they lose many battles, they rarely disappear from the scene completely.

Reform continues to be strenuously advocated both within the executive branch of government and in the press. Elected officials, however, often feel reluctant to extend reform. Even in the two countries with two-party systems, the institutionalization of factions that run separate electoral lists has transferred the struggle for patronage from a struggle between parties into a struggle among factions within each party. This makes it extremely unlikely that equality can be maintained for any length of time, since it must be maintained among factions, not just parties.

Multiparty systems in Latin America have so far not produced lasting periods of relative equality among the most popular parties or coalitions. One party has usually tended to dominate, and it has not served that party's interest to extend the merit system. If two approximately equal parties were to emerge as the only serious competitors for power in a multiparty system, however (as seems quite possible in Venezuela), the game-theoretic model would predict further extensions of reform; and some extensions have occurred in Venezuela.

Conclusion

The very simple game-theoretic model proposed implies two predictions about when administrative reform should occur: (1) reforms are more likely to pass the legislative hurdle when patronage is evenly distributed between the strongest parties, and (2) initial reforms are more likely to be followed by further extension of reform where the electoral weight of the top parties remains relatively even and stable.

The rational actor assumptions on which the model is based also imply several predictions about the effects of certain institutions on the probability of reform. Open list proportional representation, for example, because it makes patronage a valuable resource to incumbents in their struggle against challengers within their own party, reduces the probability of reform. Electoral rules that result in the proliferation of candidate lists (e.g., minimal requirements for party qualification or easy formation of dissident electoral lists within parties) also reduce the probability of reform because fractionalization reduces the probability of an equal distribution of patronage among the larger parties. Institutional features of the party system that give party leaders more influence over legislators (such as control over placement on the list) can work in either direction. Where party leaders have an interest in reform, their ability to impose party discipline increases the probability of reform; but where party leaders have no interest in reform, their influence makes reform less likely.

The evidence I have examined has proved consistent with these predictions. All the instances of initial civil service reform in democracies occurred during periods of party parity with regard to patronage. Reforms did not occur in democracies with open list proportional representation. Factionalism seemed to undercut the ability of two-party systems to produce recurrent situations of equality. Finally, when the parties returned to their normal situation of inequality after a temporary period of parity, reforms were not extended and, in fact, were often cut back.

Moreover, evidence from these cases has proved inconsistent with other explanations of reform. It is, for example, sometimes suggested that administrative reform occurs when countries attain a level of economic development that makes the continuation of government incompetence economically costly. The dates of initial reforms in these cases, however (Uruguay, 1934; Brazil, 1937; Colombia, 1930–34 and 1958; Venezuela, 1970; and Chile, none prior to the 1973 Pinochet regime), offer little support for a direct link between development and reform. A related but more political argument hypothesizes that reforms occur when the demographic changes that accompany development give reformist parties supported by middle-class and manufacturing interests the chance to defeat traditional machine parties. Latin America offers few examples of victories by unambiguously reformist antimachine parties. The Christian Democratic Frei administration in Chile comes closest to what North Americans think of as a reform government. It did not introduce civil service; rather, the many administrative changes initiated by the Christian Democrats sought to monopolize offices for their own party. In contrast, the reforms that actually introduced meritocratic hiring (as demonstrated in the case histories) occurred when traditional machine parties found themselves forced to share power with other traditional machines.

In contrast to the arguments advanced to explain reform in the United States, Latin American specialists have sometimes suggested that the Iberian colonial heritage shared by Latin American countries predisposes them toward clientelism and against impersonal procedures such as meritocratic recruitment to civil service. There may be some truth in this argument, but it obviously cannot explain the very considerable differences among Latin American cases.

The game-theoretic model has thus proved sufficiently useful to deserve further research. Claims about its generality have to be somewhat cautious because of the small number of culturally and historically similar cases examined here. It may be that the domain of this model is limited to the Western hemisphere. Nonetheless, its implications are quite far-reaching. It suggests that administrative reforms will be difficult to achieve and maintain in democracies, especially democracies with fragmented party systems. Certain characteristics that are often thought of as increasing representativeness, such as multiparty systems that reflect a wide spectrum of interests and open list proportional representation, may paradoxically cause elected officials to be less responsive to the public interest.

One of the promises of democracy is that it makes government services available to all citizens regardless of wealth or status. The failure to professionalize public administration, however, makes that promise hard to keep. Stories abound in Latin America about the need for bribes or pull in order to get everyday services such as renewal of a driver's license. More seriously, inefficiency and incompetence in government agencies can be so extreme that clients' needs cannot be served at all. For example, Montevideo's *El País* reported in 1960 that the Fund for Pensions for Rural, Domestic, and Aged Workers was up to two years behind in the commencement of payments to nearly four thousand people (Taylor, 1960: 222). During the democratic period, Chileans eligible for pensions routinely sought the help of elected officials to avoid the months or even years of red tape involved for the politically unconnected to initiate payments (Tapia-Videla, 1969: 300–13; Valenzuela, 1977: 120–37). All but one of Brazil's many social security institutes had gone bankrupt, in part because of excessive employment of untrained Labor Party supporters, by 1964 (Malloy, 1979). In these instances (and many others could be cited) the failure of public service directly affects the quality of life of the ordinary people whom democracy is supposed to benefit.

It is ironic that the reforms that would improve efficiency and fairness in the provision of government services should be impeded by the same representative institutions whose manifest purpose is to reflect constituents' interests.

References

Amaral, Carlos Veríssimo do. (1966). *Política e administracao de pessoal: estudos de dois casos* (Politics and personnel administration: two case studies). Rio de Janeiro: Fundação Getúlio Vargas.

Ames, Barry. (1987). *Political Survival: Politicians and Public Policy in Latin America.* Berkeley: University of California Press.

Archer, Ronald. (1990). "Clientelism and Political Parties in Colombia: A Party System in Transition?" Presented at the annual meeting of the Midwest Political Science Association, Chicago.

Ascher, William. (1975). "Planners, Politics, and Technocracy in Argentina and Chile." Ph.D. diss., Yale University.

Benevides, Maria Victória Mesquita. (1981). *A UDN e o Udenismo* (The UDN and UDNism). Rio de Janeiro: Paz e Terra.

Berry, R. Albert, Ronald G. Hellman, and Mauricio Solaún (Eds.). (1980). *Politics of Compromise: Coalition Government in Colombia.* New Brunswick, N.J.: Transaction Books.

Biles, Robert. (1978). "Political Participation in Urban Uruguay: Mixing Public and Private Ends." In John Booth and Mitchell Seligson (Eds.), *Political Participation in Latin America,* Vol. 1: *Citizen and State.* New York: Holmes & Meier.

188   BARBARA GEDDES

(1972). "Patronage Politics: Electoral Behavior in Uruguay." Ph.D. diss., Johns Hopkins University.

Brewer-Carías, Allan-Randolph. (1985). *El estado incomprendido: Reflexiones sobre el sistema político y su reforma* (The Misunderstood State: Reflections on the Political System and Its Reform). Caracas: Vadell Hermanos.

(1975a). *Cambio político y reforma del estado en Venezuela* (Political Change and State Reform in Venezuela). Madrid: Tecnos.

(1975b). "La reforma administrativa en Venezuela (1969–1973): Estrategias, tácticas y criterios" (Administrative Reform in Venezuela: Strategies, Tactics, and Criteria). In *Reforma administrativa: experiencias latinoamericanas* (Administrative Reform: Latin American Experiences). Mexico City: Instituto Nacional de Administración Pública.

Cova, Antonio, and Thamara Hannot. (1986). "La administración pública: Otra forma de ver a una villana incomprendida" (Public Administration: Another View of a Misunderstood Villain). In Moisés Naím and Ramón Piñango (Eds.), *El caso Venezuela: Una ilusión de armonía* (The Venezuelan Case: An Illusion of Harmony), Caracas: Ediciones IESA.

Cox, Gary. (1986). "The Development of a Party-Oriented Electorate in England, 1832–1918." *British Journal of Political Science* 16: 187–216.

de Soto, Hernando. (1986). *El otro sendero: La revolución informal* (The Other Path: The Informal Revolution). Lima: Editorial El Barranco.

Dix, Robert H. (1980). "Consociational Democracy: The Case of Colombia." *Comparative Politics* 12: 303–21.

Duff, Ernest. (1971). "The Role of Congress in the Colombian Political System." In Weston Agor (Ed.). *Latin American Legislatures.* New York: Praeger.

Emmerich, Herbert. (1972). "Informe sobre un estudio preliminar acerca de posibilidades de mejoras en la Administración Pública de Venezuela" (Report on a Preliminary Study of Possible Improvements in Venezuelan Public Administration). In *Informe sobre la reforma de la administración pública nacional* (Report on the Reform of National Public Administration). Vol. 2. Caracas: Comisión de Reforma de la Administración Pública.

(1960). "Administrative Roadblocks to Coordinated Development." Prepared for the Expert Working Group on Social Aspects of Economic Development in Latin America. Mexico City.

Fabregat, Julio T. (1963). *Elecciones Uruguayas* (Uruguayan Elections). Montevideo: Corte Electoral.

Geddes, Barbara. (In press). *Politician's Dilemma: Reforming the State in Latin America.* Berkeley: University of California Press.

(1990). "Building 'State' Autonomy in Brazil, 1930–1964." *Comparative Politics* 22: 217–35.

Gonaález G., Fernán. (1980). "Clientelismo y administración pública" (Clientelism and Public Administration). *Enfoques colombianos: Clientelismo* 14: 67–106.

Graham, Lawrence. (1968). *Civil Service Reform in Brazil: Principles vs. Practice.* Latin American Monographs No. 13. Austin: University of Texas Press.

Groves, Roderick. (1974). "The Colombian National Front and Administrative Reform." *Administration and Society* 6: 316–36.

(1967). "Administrative Reform and the Politics of Reform: The Case of Venezuela." *Public Administration Review* 27: 436–51.

Hall, E. F. (1884). "Civil Service Reform." *New Englander* 43: 453–63.

Hartlyn, Jonathan. (1988). *The Politics of Coalition Rule in Colombia.* Cambridge: Cambridge University Press.

Hartwig, Richard E. (1983). *Roads to Reason: Transportation, Administration, and Rationality in Colombia.* Pittsburgh: University of Pittsburgh Press.

Hirschman, Albert O. (1958). *The Strategy of Economic Development.* New Haven, Conn.: Yale University Press.

International Bank for Reconstruction and Development. (1961). *The Economic Development of Venezuela.* Baltimore: Johns Hopkins University Press.

Karl, Terry. (1982). "The Political Economy of Petrodollars: Oil and Democracy in Venezuela." Ph.D. diss., Stanford University.

Láfer, Celso. (1970). *The Planning Process and the Political System: A Study of Kubitschek's Target Plan, 1956–1961.* Latin American Studies Program Dissertation Series 16. Ithaca, N.Y.: Cornell University.

López Pintor, Rafael. (1972). "Development Administration in Chile: Structural, Normative, and Behavioral Constraints to Performance." Ph.D. diss., University of North Carolina, Chapel Hill.

Malloy, James. (1979). *The Politics of Social Security in Brazil.* Pittsburgh: University of Pittsburgh Press.

Mayhew, David. (1975). *Congress: The Electoral Connection.* New Haven, Conn.: Yale University Press.

Morcillo, Pedro Pablo. (1975). "La reforma administrativa en Colombia" (Administrative Reform in Colombia). In *Reforma administrativa: Experiencias latinoamericanas* (Administrative Reform: Latin American Experiences). Mexico City: Instituto Nacional de Administración Pública.

Oliveira, Lucia Lippi de. (1973). "O Partido Social Democrático" (The Social Democratic Party). Master's thesis, Universitário de Pesquisas do Rio de Janeiro.

Pinto, Magalhaes. (1960). "Relatório político do Presidente Magalhaes Pinto" (The Political Statement of President Magalhaes Pinto). Archives of the UDN, Fundaçao Getúlio Vargas.

Rial, Juan. (1985). *Elecciones 1984: Un triunfo del centro* (1984 Elections: Triumph of the Center). Montevideo: Ediciones de la Banda Oriental.

Ruddle, Kenneth, and Philip Gillette (Eds.). (1972). *Latin American Political Statistics: Supplement to the Statistical Abstract of Latin America.* Los Angeles: University of California, Los Angeles.

Schattschneider, Emil E. (1942). *Party Government.* New York: Rinehart.

Schmidt, Steffen. (1974). "Bureaucrats As Modernizing Brokers?" *Comparative Politics* 6: 425–50.

Siegel, Gilbert. (1966). "The Vicissitudes of Government Reform in Brazil: A Study of the DASP." Ph.D. diss., University of Southern California.

——— (1963). "Administration, Values and the Merit System in Brazil." In Robert Daland (Ed.). *Perspectives of Brazilian Public Administration.* Vol. 1. Los Angeles: University of Southern California and Fundaçao Getúlio Vargas.

Singer, Paulo. (1965). "A Política das classes dominantes" (Politics of the Dominant Classes). In Octávio Ianni (Ed.). *Política e revoluçao social no Brasil* (Politics and Social Revolution in Brazil). Rio de Janeiro: Civilizaçao Brasileira.

Skowronek, Steven. (1979). *Building a New American State: The Expansion of National Administrative Capacities, 1877–1920.* Cambridge: Cambridge University Press.

Solaún, Mauricio. (1980). "Colombian Politics: Historical Characteristics and Problems." In R. Albert Berry, Ronald G. Hellman, and Mauricio Solaún (Eds.), *Politics of Compromise: Coalition Government in Colombia*. New Brunswick, N.J.: Transaction Books.

Souza, Maria do Carmo Campello de. (1976). *Estado e partidos politicos no Brasil* (The State and Political Parties in Brazil). Sao Paulo: Alfa-Omega.

Stewart, Bill (1978). *Change and Bureaucracy: Public Administration in Venezuela.* James Sprunt Studies in History and Political Science. Vol. 56. Chapel Hill: University of North Carolina Press.

Tapia-Videla, Jorge Iván. (1969). "Bureaucratic Power in a Developing Country: The Case of the Chilean Social Security Administration." Ph.D. diss., University of Texas.

Taylor, Philip B. (1960). *Government and Politics of Uruguay.* Studies in Political Science, No. 7. New Orleans: Tulane University Press.

    (1952). "The Uruguayan Coup d'État of 1933." *Hispanic American Historical Review* 32: 301–20.

Urzúa Valenzuela, Germán, and Ana María García Barzelatto. (1971). *Diagnóstico de la burocracia chilena (1818–1969)* (Diagnosis of the Chilean Bureaucracy (1818–1969)). Santiago: Editoral Jurídica de Chile.

Valenzuela, Arturo. (1985). "Origins and Characteristics of the Chilean Party System: A Proposal for a Parliamentary Form of Government." Working Paper No. 164. Washington, D.C.: Woodrow Wilson Center.

    (1984). "Parties, Politics, and the State in Chile: The Higher Civil Service." In Ezra Suleiman (ed.), *Bureaucrats and Policy Making: A Comparative Overview.* New York: Holmes & Meier.

    (1978). *The Breakdown of Democratic Regimes: Chile.* Baltimore: Johns Hopkins University Press.

    (1977). *Political Brokers in Chile: Local Government in a Centralized Polity.* Durham, N.C.: Duke University Press.

Van Riper, Paul. (1958). *History of the United States Civil Service.* Evanston, Ill.: Row, Peterson.

Venturini, Angel R. (1984). *Estadísticas electorales: Elecciones nacionales 1926–1982, elecciones internas 1982* (Electoral Statistics: National Elections 1926–1982, Primary Elections 1982). Montevideo: Ediciones de la Banda Oriental.

Vidal Perdomo, Jaime. (1982). "La Reforma Administrativa de 1968 en Colombia" (The 1968 Administrative Reform in Colombia). *International Review of Administrative Science* 48: 77–84.

Vieira, Astério Dardeau. (1967). *A Administraçao do pessoal vista pelos chefes de serviço* (Personnel administration as seen by agency heads). Rio de Janeiro: Fundaçao Getúlio Vargas.

Wahrlich, Beatriz. (1964). *Administraçao de pessoal: Princípios e tecnícas* (Personnel Administration: Principles and Techniques). Rio de Janeiro: Fundaçao Getúlio Vargas.

7.   Transitions to independence and ethnic nationalist mobilization

Hudson Meadwell

In this chapter, I want to examine three propositions about ethnic nationalist movements:

1. Ethnic groups fight for secession despite the economic costs of the transition to independence and of independence, once achieved.
2. When individuals support secession, it is because to do otherwise would violate their ethnic identity.
3. Ethnic groups are like extended families.

Together these three propositions underpin an important theoretical understanding of ethnic nationalism. In the first part of the chapter, I examine the logical structure of these propositions, and some of the evidence from developing nations that is used to support them. In the second and third sections, I present a formal model of ethnic mobilization that addresses some important features of the causal structure of situations of transition to independence under conditions that approximate the institutional contexts of the developed West.

Secession in developing nations

Let me begin with the first proposition. In one of the central arguments in which this proposition is presented, secession is defined to include movements aimed explicitly at an independent state and movements seeking increased territorial autonomy (Horowitz, 1981: 168). By secession, I mean the former but not the latter. I argue that these regional movements are very different from independence movements. Regionalists want to improve their position within institutional arrangements between center and periphery without losing completely those

The author acknowledges the financial support of FCAR (Fonds pour la Formation de Chercheurs et l'Aide à la Recherche, Quebec). This is a revised version of a paper presented at the Eighth International Conference of Europeanists, Palmer House, Chicago, March 27–29, 1992. I thank Elizabeth Crighton for her comments.

components of center–periphery relations they value (Meadwell, 1991b). Nationalists are sensitive to economic costs. This is why in some cases independence will be forgone in favor of some more limited form of decentralization.

The most straightforward reading of (1), and one that I think is usually intended when this proposition is suggested, is (A) that secession is supported, no matter how high the economic costs. This reading has a very strong implication, namely that individuals are entirely insensitive to economic parameters. Two other possible interpretations of this proposition should be rejected. The first assumes (B) a linear relationship between the costs of, and support for secession, so that support declines as costs increase. This is a reasonable argument on its own, but it clearly does not capture the meaning of the proposition. A second interpretation also assumes a linear relationship but, in this case, proposes (C) that support increases with costs. This is probably closer to the intention of the argument embedded in (1) than the other interpretation just outlined, but this second interpretation is still not quite right.

It might appear, however, that this proposition implies a more complex nonlinear relationship between costs and support than is captured in these two interpretations. This, too, should be rejected, even if it seems a plausible alternative. It should be dismissed because this proposition actually does not describe a relationship across a range of values of costs and support. Therefore, the proposition says nothing about a relationship, whether linear or nonlinear, between support and costs. It says only that when costs are present, so too is support, and this *despite* the costs.

But, for the sake of argument, suppose that there is a nonlinear relationship in which (D) support is high when costs are low *or* high, and support is lower in the medium range of costs. (See Figure 7.1.) This exercise clarifies two important points. First, proposition (1) is only about a very specific region (R) of this support–cost space.

Second, there is a peculiar asymmetry built into proposition (1). Its explanation for support when costs are high cannot account for support in other regions of the relationship where costs are low. If our position is that secession is supported in R despite the economic costs, we can say nothing about support where support is present because costs are lower. We are left with two different explanations for different regions of this support–cost space.

Two arguments that have been made in support of this proposition are also unconvincing. First, Horowitz has argued that "a great many regions that do manage to secede can be expected to have postsecession economic difficulties" (1981: 194; cf. 1985: 132). This argument makes an excessively strong assumption about the information sets of individuals: that there is no way an individual may reasonably expect some significant probability of postsecession improvement in his or her economic situation. Further, these "economic difficulties" must be compared to the anticipated stream of benefits and costs under the status quo if secession had not been supported. Horowitz has also pointed out that secessionist regions are "disproportionately unfavored in resources and per capita

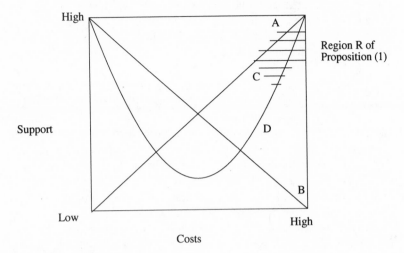

Figure 7.1. The support/cost space.

income" (1991: 11). But this does not rule out the possibility that individuals reasonably prefer independence because they hold out some prospect of doing better.

Before I move on to the second proposition, let me cut off one other possible escape route. A supporter of proposition (1) might argue that the world is structured in such a way that the economic costs of secession are not variable and are always high. Figure 7.1 is only a hypothetical space; the real space is region *R*. This is unconvincing.

Consider the proposition (2) that when individuals support secession despite the economic costs, they do so because to do otherwise would violate their identity. This cannot be a general explanation for secession, unless secession always involves economic costs so high that some special factor is needed to explain support. But if economic cost is the constraint on support for secession, surely we can expect support when secession is not costly or promises some reasonable probability of economic rewards. In these circumstances, we do not need identity to explain support. This demonstrates that the argument about identity is a special kind of explanation. It is a functional explanation: Identity is needed when the barriers to exit are so high that they could not be surmounted without it. Either these ethnic groups already are structured by the appropriate identity, or if they are not so organized, these identities must be invented. When collective identity is introduced into explanation for these circumstances, it cannot be used in the same way to account for support for secession when the latter is not (or is less) costly.

This proposition is even more peculiar. If individuals support secession despite the economic costs because to do otherwise would violate their identity, then the absence of support for secession is not caused straightforwardly by economic costs but by the absence of the appropriate collective identity. But once again, in these circumstances, we should not need to invoke the absence of the appropriate collective identity to explain the absence of support for secession. All we need in explanation are the economic costs.

Now, it may appear that my comments are nothing more than the application of a principle of parsimony in explanation. I do not believe that this is the case. Suppose we had two empirical cases: one in which secession is fought for, the other in which it is not. It is obvious that we cannot determine that collective identity was present and causally crucial in the first and absent in the second without examining the kinds of economic costs in the two cases. Clearly, given my earlier discussion, secessionist support in the first case may be associated with economic costs lower than the costs present in the second case.

It is likely no accident that the cases used to support propositions (1) and (2) are drawn often from developing nations, for a reasonable case can be made that the barriers to exit, in fact, are *lower* than in a contrastive class of cases such as the developed West. If barriers are lower, it is not clear that identity plays the explanatory role assumed in proposition (2).

A summary of relevant features of developing societies might include: (relatively) low levels of industrialization, low levels of per capita income, patrimonial states, often fairly recently formed, with insecure advantages in the means of coercion, and social structures in which tribal, kinship, and religious subsystems are important. Low levels of income are easier to replicate; patrimonial states are more likely to be corrupt, with bureaucrats subject neither to recall, nor to merit-testing. These states are more likely to be perceived to be alien, parasitic, useless institutions, and independent state-formation an improvement on them. States with only comparative advantages in the means of violence have more difficulty in preventing secession when the barriers to exit are lower, and raise the expected value of the use of force by secessionist movements. Secessionists can find financial and military support among third parties, and they can buy weapons in the international arms market to compensate for domestic disadvantage. Secessionists have sometimes shown remarkable ingenuity in raising resources to buy arms. Since they are often located in frontier areas (notably the case in Southeast Asia [McVey, 1984: 18]), smuggling (for example heroin and jade) often provides the necessary cash. They also can choose tactics that substitute for large numbers of supporters and that take into account states with significant comparative advantages in force. Finally, social systems structured by tribal, kinship, or religious subsystems also create ethnic groups with high carrying capacities. At the same time, political institutions are less likely to be open enough to provide the possibility of negotiating changes to the territorial distribution of power, including independence. (Consider, in contrast, the case of Quebec.) These institutional and structural features of developing nations should be *conducive* to secession, yet it is the developing nations that are used to argue that the barriers to exit are so high that individuals support secession despite the costs.

While Horowitz (1991: 11) has wondered why there are so many secessionist movements, given the apparent economic costs, McVey has asked in a discussion of armed separatism in Southeast Asia why there are not more. "With such shallow roots, with boundaries fixed by colonial rivalries as much as by cultural or national boundaries, flying in the face of ancient folkways and immediate individual interests – what glues the Southeast Asian state together?" (1984: 3). Her question nicely conveys how much is assumed in these two propositions.

This is a more serious problem than proponents of (1) and (2) have acknowledged. As I have demonstrated elsewhere (Meadwell, 1989a: 316–17), their argument takes a particular form. They assume that support for secession is higher than would be expected, given the myopic self-interest of individuals in an ethnic group. The residual between self-interest and support is explained by "nonrational" factors,[1] especially collective identity. This argument obviously depends on exhausting the explanatory power of rational action before invoking "nonrational" factors.

The following points are not presented as conclusive empirical evidence by any means, but they should raise some doubts about proposition (1) and suggest that some of these developing world cases of secession might be reinterpreted. In two prominent cases, seceding regions were relatively well-off. Katanga was the most resource-rich province of the Congo (Lemarchand, 1962); Biafra sat on the largest petroleum reserves in Nigeria (Nixon, 1972). In the case of Bangladesh, East Pakistan received less local currency at an equilibrium exchange rate for its exports and bought manufactured goods from West Pakistan at inflated prices because of high tariffs (Nafziger and Richter, 1976: 104; Rashid, 1990). "East Pakistan, poorer than West Pakistan at independence, became more disadvantaged over time relative to the West" (105). Political unification, in other words, produced few benefits, the local economy was tied to export markets for raw or semifinished production (jute and tea) that might be continued without significant dislocation after independence, and the region had a potential political class systematically excluded from public sector positions in Pakistan.

The Muslim separatist movement in the Southern Philippines was precipitated by intergroup competition for resources, as the Philippine government resettled peasants from Central Luzon to the island of Mindanao. The government introduced a system of land registration that worked to the advantage of new settlers, who often were able to evict Muslim residents from their homes and lands. Logging firms were granted concessions that often included land cultivated by Muslims. At the same time, a Christian militia force was formed to protect and extend Christian influence in the south (Bacho, 1987–8: 154). After the declaration of martial law in 1972 and an order to confiscate private arms, even as private armies continued to be tolerated, the Moros began to develop their own military force, supplied with arms by Libya and with access to a haven in Sabah in Malaysia. Secession was supported as the most appropriate means to protect

---

[1] Their construction of the problem mistakenly implies that rationality is never more than economic self-interest.

their communities in circumstances in which the government tacitly sanctioned land grabs by Christians and the private use of force. In this kind of case, in which a subsistence level is threatened, secessionist resistance in fact is an indirect consequence of risk aversion, because the economic and social changes in the south exposed peasants to a higher level of subsistence risk.[2]

While the goals of separation in the southern Sudan shifted between local autonomy and secession (Badal, 1976: 468), participants in the secessionist movement included skilled and semiskilled workers who had little prospect for promotion, despite their human capital. Foremen were typically northerners with no better qualifications or experience, other than fluency in Arabic. Southerners involved in the cash economy were aware that northern *jellaba* (settler-traders) had a trading and commercial monopoly (Badal, 1976: 470), which inflated prices of consumer goods. The educated intelligentsia, who also supported secession, were systematically denied employment opportunities in public administration at the central level because of nepotism and language-use (Arabic) (Raghavan, 1990: 133). "Southerners were little affected by Sudanization: only a handful of them were promoted to take responsible posts in government" (Badal, 1976: 472). The per capita product of the southern provinces was lower than the north (£14 Sudanese pounds in 1965 compared to £42 for the core northern provinces [Badal, 1976: 467]), but this hardly means that support in the South for secession was irrational. The tactics of the secessionist movement also took into account local constraints: Because the movement had no committed foreign power, "it could not risk open confrontation with the Sudan government, but continued to steer a middle course of protracted guerrilla warfare" (Badal, 1976: 471). These examples are not detailed, and they do not exhaust the relevant cases (see Horowitz, 1981: 171, Table I), but they suggest that the evidence used to support this proposition is not as strong as might first appear.

Having suggested that the political economy of developing nations may have consequences rather different than those anticipated in this proposition, I will now suggest that secession can be straightforwardly explained, even if economic costs are present, when a subset of the group expects political benefits after independence. Rent seekers, who expect to be able to control positions in the newly formed state, perhaps individuals excluded from the political class in the status quo or more generally individuals whose upward mobility is blocked, can support secession, and mobilize wider support through the manipulation of ethnic symbols and identities. Control of the state is an exclusionary mechanism that allows them to extract rents from the group. Not everyone *within* the group can have access to these rents, without dissipating their value, hence independence has redistributive consequences and it can leave others outside the privileged subset of the group worse off. This interpretation has two positive functions. It

---

[2] When an income level is less than a subsistence level, or marginally higher than a subsistence level but uncertain, many gambles, even at unfair odds, will have a higher expected utility than the status quo.

shows, first, that rationalist theories need not be economic. Second, the emergence of an independence movement in these circumstances is inexplicable if we do not give some theoretical space to rational choice. If rent seeking is a response to opportunity structures, and the manipulation or invention of an identity is a strategy to win through to a position of intragroup predation, we cannot do without rational choice theory.

Let me turn now to (3): Ethnic groups are like extended families (Connor, 1987; Horowitz, 1985; Smith, 1987). As a general statement about "ethnonationalism," this assertion is nonsense. Some ethnic groups literally are kinship groups, others are not. This proposition, however, is used to satisfy two theoretical needs. First, this supposedly universal feature of ethnic groups accounts for the emotional dimension of ethnic politics (Connor, 1987: 204). Second, "extended families" have distinctive carrying capacities that facilitate collective action. This first argument is dubious at best. The extended family is not the only source of emotion in political and social life. The second argument misunderstands the implications of carrying capacity. There is no direct relationship between a kinship-structured ethnic group and support for secession. Suppose the "family head" decides not to support secession. Authority relations in the kinship group then account for the enforcement of decisions within the "family," but kinship structure says nothing directly about the decision itself. It is also obvious that kinship structures actually can weaken the carrying capacity of secessionist movements that span different tribes or clans, as among the Kurds (Koohi-Kamali, 1992: 178) or Moros (Gopinath, 1991: 133).

These three propositions form the core of an influential set of arguments about ethnic nationalist mobilization. Their essential implication can be summarized in a different theoretical logic, which I will now develop. Let I_I and I_{SQ} refer to benefits for an individual under independence and in the status quo. Suppose that I_{SQ} is certain, but that I_I is risky. The individual has some chance (p) of receiving I_I and some choice $(1 - p)$ of receiving benefits under independence less than I_{SQ} (I_I'). The expected value of independence is

$$pU(I_I) + (1 - p)U(I_I'). \tag{1}$$

The expected value of the status quo is

$$U(I_{SQ}).^3 \tag{2}$$

When (1) = (2), risk-acceptant individuals prefer (1), risk-averters prefer (2), and risk-neutral persons are indifferent between them. Risk-neutral individuals will choose (2) when (2) > (1) and (1) when (1) > (2). Risk averters of course will always prefer (2) when (2) > (1). But unlike risk neutrals, they do not necessarily prefer (1) when (1) > (2). They will prefer (1) only for some values of the inequality, depending on the exact shape of their utility functions. (More exactly, it depends on the degree of concavity of the utility function. Risk neutrality is the lower limit of risk aversion.) Risk acceptors will always prefer

---

[3] For a discussion of nonlinearity in the probabilities, see Machina (1990).

(1) when (1) > (2), unlike risk averters, who prefer (1) only under some conditions. Unlike risk neutrals, risk acceptors do not necessarily prefer (2) when (2) > (1). There is some range of values that satisfy this inequality, under which risk acceptors prefer (1). This range depends on the shape of the utility function of risk acceptors, more specifically the degree of convexity of the function.

The theoretical argument of the three propositions, which I outlined at the start, does not assume that individuals are risk averse. Nor is it a theory of risk neutrality. It cannot be this because the argument assumes that secession involves economic costs, which means that (2) > (1). Under risk neutrality, an individual would never choose (1), given this inequality. But, of course, this is the choice which this theoretical argument assumes. These three propositions thus are built on an assumption of risk acceptance in an ethnic group.

It is important to be clear about what this assumption means. It does not mean that individuals prefer independence because they have poor information sets. If this were the case, individuals would change their preferences with better information. Two meanings of this assumption, however, are consistent with the thrust of these propositions. First, estimates of expected value are subject to cognitive or motivational biases of which individuals are unaware. Second, risk acceptance, when independence is fought for despite the economic costs, can also mean that individuals are aware of costs, believe that the probability that costs will be present is very high, and are willing to bear these costs. This latter interpretation is clearly stronger than the second, for it may be the case that individuals will change their preferences, if there are biases that are brought to their attention.[4] In a postindependent state, individuals who fit the first description may come to regret their prior preferences, although such regret may be subject to some form of rationalization. Individuals who fit the last description should not regret their preferences and therefore will not be prone to rationalization.

It is surprising that this theoretical framework does not take risk neutrality and risk aversion more seriously. The argument of proposition (1) does acknowledge that economic costs (transitions to independence and economic viability, if independence is achieved) are a constraint on support for independence, because some special factor is needed to overcome them, but then goes on to propose that these costs never actually constrain support.

These three propositions do not stand up all that well to critical scrutiny, even when their "critical cases" are examined. How would these propositions fare in a contrastive class of cases, such as the developed West? I will argue that they do no better. What I propose to do in the remainder of this chapter is to develop a

---

[4] Note that this argument is stated in terms of *preferences*, not directly in terms of individual *action*. But collective identity, at least in the propositions I am discussing, is both a source of preferences and a motivational set for action.

simple model of ethnic nationalist mobilization that takes up the problems of transition and viability.

In specifying the distinctiveness of nationalist politics, I emphasize the centrality of the goal of political independence. This is obviously not to say that all ethnic nationalists support independence. What I mean is that political independence is a distinctive feature of a particular political form, nationalism, and that other political forms have their own discourses and practices. From this understanding of nationalism, I draw two simple conclusions. First, there is a distinctive feature of ethnic nationalist politics: the problem of transitions to political independence and the economic viability of the ethnic group, if independence is achieved. Second, nationalism can give rise to factional politics defined around the duality of independence and autonomy in ethnic nationalist organizations. An appropriate model of ethnic nationalist mobilization should address both transitions and factionalism, yet no current discussion does. There are occasional discussions of either or both of these features, but they tend to be case-specific (e.g. Levy, 1990; Luis de la Granja, 1991; O'Leary, 1989; Pinard and Hamilton, 1986). This is what I propose to do.

The model of nationalist mobilization that addresses these concerns identifies conditions that both enable and constrain nationalist mobilization. The enabling condition is counterhegemony, understood as a process of institution building and identity formation. The constraining condition is the cost of transition to independence and the economic viability of the group if political independence is achieved. These enabling and constraining conditions are summarized in the next section. In the later sections, a simple model of mobilization, which incorporates these conditions, is introduced and some second-order consequences for political factionalism are derived from the model.

The background for this model is a stylized description of institutional features of the developed West. But the assumptions of the model are consistent with the rereading of developed world cases that I began in this section. As in this section, I emphasize the relevance of risk neutrality and risk aversion in transitions to independence, but these assumptions are now played out in a different institutional context. These background conditions include the rule of law and democratic institutions, state monopolies in the use of force, and advanced capitalist economies.

This argument turns the empirical implication of these three propositions on its head, for I am suggesting that the barriers to exit, in fact, are higher in the developed Western nations than in developing nations. If individuals support secession despite the costs, and do so because to do otherwise would violate their ethnic identity, the developed West should be the relevant class of cases because it fulfills the central condition underlying these propositions: the presence of significant costs. If identity is required when the barriers are comparatively high, then it should be movements in the developed West that most "need" identity to scale these barriers.

A model of mobilization

Enabling condition: Counterhegemony

Several scholars have argued that nationalist mobilization is facilitated to the extent that leaders can fashion interpretations of the situation of the group that build on structures of meaning embodied in collective identities (Anderson, 1983; Horowitz, 1985; Mayo, 1974). Preference formation and identity are closely tied together in theories of counterhegemony. To overcome hegemony, activists may have to resocialize others. This educational activity forms identities and helps individuals to recognize their "real" interests (Adamson, 1980). Counterhegemony also has an institutional dimension. Counterhegemony, at this level, involves the development of a countersociety and a set of institutions that exist as an alternative to those of the central state, thus contributing to the political self-sufficiency of the group.

This institutional capacity of a group has been argued to vary with patterns of political incorporation and the group infrastructure retained (Laitin, 1988; Orridge, 1982). Scotland, for example, retained a distinctive infrastructure when politically incorporated (Levack, 1987). Independence movements thus have different historical baselines, depending on the carrying capacity of the institutions of the group. Federalism also is an important source of institutional capacity because it provides a set of political levers and access to resources that make group mobilization more likely. While often put in place as a means of accommodation and cooption, federal institutions can be quickly turned to new agendas when a coopted leadership is replaced or changes its preferences. Roeder (1991) has made a case for the latter in his interpretation of contemporary nationalist mobilization in the USSR. Another case, Quebec, combines replacement and change associated with the Quiet Revolution.

Organized religion also often becomes the institutional carrier of nationalist mobilization because it supplies means of information transmission, meeting places, and a leadership. Nonconformist chapels provided an organizational framework for Welsh nationalism in the early twentieth century (Morgan, 1981), the Lithuanian Catholic church became a channel of expression for Lithuanian nationalism after annexation and during glasnost (Vardys, 1978). The role of organized religion in transitions from authoritarian rule (Szajkowski, 1985) thus has its nationalist analogues. Conversely, where organized religion is deeply embedded in local life but its leaders hostile to or divided on the national issue, mobilization is weakened (Meadwell, 1991a, 1990). However, institution building cannot directly solve the problem of the costs of the transition to independence, and the problem of viability, once independent.

Counterhegemony is a strategy of political activists. The goal of this strategy is to "push back" the constraint on mobilization produced by the problem of viability. The tactics of this strategy are identity formation and organizational encapsulation. It is designed, therefore, to form preferences, and to direct and monitor behavior. Identity and organization are analytically separate dimensions of counterhegemony and have a reciprocal relationship. Identity formation is easier to the extent that encapsulation is present because individuals are then less exposed to cross pressures and alternative identities. Identity formation legitimates and justifies group-specific organization. Encapsulation and identity formation together create "communities of fate" that shape the perception of grievances, and facilitate collective action.

These two moments of counterhegemony are not exclusively determined by these mutual effects. The success of identity formation will vary with preexisting patterns of political alignments and identities and exogenous changes in these patterns. Organizational encapsulation will vary with the institutional infrastructure of the group and the territorial distribution of power.

Constraining condition: Economic viability and the transition to independence

If we distinguish short- and long-term effects on opinion formation the problem of viability has long-term, stable negative effects on support for independence because it sets outer limits on the level of support. This does not mean, however, that the problem of viability is insurmountable, unchanging or the same across cases. The problem of free-riding, on the other hand, affects the ability to mobilize support within the constraints set by viability.[5]

There is an important justification for this distinction between the problems of viability and free-riding. The goal of independence is inextricably linked to a unique mobilization dilemma. Other forms of nationalist politics, which are organized around the goal of cultural preservation (language revivals, for instance) or decentralization, will not be constrained by the problems of viability or transition. This difference means that theories of collective action that do not explicitly take this dilemma into account must be modified when applied in cases in which independence is a goal of the nationalist movement. These problems are independent of each other and, as a consequence, the usual theories of collective action, which predict cooperation under specifiable conditions (iterated Prisoner's Dilemma, contingent consent, threshold models of collective action, for example) will be incomplete when applied to independence movements.

The effects of the problem of viability ultimately rest on individual assessments of individual position in the status quo and in projected future states of affairs under varying degrees of decentralization, including political independence. I assume, however, that these assessments are affected by the interdependence of the local economy. Consider, for example, an economy with an agri-

---

[5] The problem of viability is independent of the free-riding problem in much the same way as the "Przeworski problem" is independent of free-riding in working-class collective action. See Cohen (1988: 79, n. 34). The work of Przeworski (1985) has been useful in developing the model presented later in the chapter.

cultural sector that depends on a market that would be lost under independence. All else equal, independence will present direct costs to farmers, and indirect costs to others, depending on the backward and forward linkages and interdependencies in the economy. Local manufacturers of farm machinery, suppliers of fertilizers, bankers who have provided agricultural credit, and agricultural wholesalers will assess the consequences of the loss of the market for their activities, and the possibilities of diversification and substitution in their portfolios of activities under independence. Moreover, local manufacturers dependent on local markets will consider the extent and consequences of changes in disposable income among consumers. They may consider that this change outweighs any gain in advantage vis-à-vis foreign competition that may follow from independence.

Interdependent relationships in the economy mean that nationalist activists do not face an atomized, potential mass public. There can be individuals and strata whose support has a multiplier effect. In other words, there may be a subset of the group composed of persons who are more likely to support independence, if others join before them. However, this relationship depends not only on *levels* of support. Who has joined is as important as how many have joined. Economic interdependence in the group thus means that mobilization may be characterized by sequencing effects. Mobilization is then not additive over individuals, but interactive over interdependent relationships.

These consequences are quite specifically the result of economic interdependence. They therefore are different from, although still related to, other forms of nonlinear effects in mobilization processes. Multiplier effects, for example, can follow from social interdependence when opinion leaders cue others, or when authority figures can bring along their informal clienteles or associational memberships. Sequencing effects can occur under different circumstances: when the production function for a public good is discontinuous, or where potential bandwagons are present. I have emphasized the relevance of economic interdependence in the group because of the importance of the problem of viability (and transitions to independence) for nationalist politics.

The problem of viability is made more salient when political independence threatens trading relations between the ethnic group and the previous "national" territory. When political separation is accompanied by economic separation, the transition can mean a period of economic adjustment with negative consequences for individual livelihood. However, there are circumstances that can contribute to a solution to the problem of future economic viability, thus defined. Individuals in the group may prefer independence to the status quo when the group can "trade for independence." By this, I mean an ethnic group might be able to substitute through trade for resources, skills or markets supplied by the national territory (Meadwell, 1989b).

The strategy of independence through international trade is attractive, for just this reason, in periods of relatively stable or institutionalized openness in the international or a regional economy. The emergence of a North American free-trade area, for example, has been used by the Parti Québécois to mobilize support for independence. They argue that the North American Free-Trade Agreement lowers the risks of independence (Parizeau, 1987). In Scotland, the European Economic Community currently is seen as an institutional counter-weight to the English state and as an alternative to the British market (Levy, 1990). In Spain, support for regional parties varies with attitudes toward the EEC (Lancaster and Lewis-Beck, 1989). There was also support in Catalonia for Community membership because nationalists saw the Community as a way of weakening the central state (Clavera, 1988: 101–2) and industrialists saw it as a means of access to a larger market (Tsoukalis, 1981).

Self-sufficiency thus has become a less necessary nationalist strategy as economic interdependence has become stabilized in the postwar period. Small regional economies can now base economic viability on participation in an open regional or international economy. Individuals should be less risk averse under these conditions because the probability of market diversification is higher and risks therefore lower. Survey evidence in several cases supports this argument. In Quebec, support for sovereignty association (which provides for a continued economic relationship with Canada) is higher than for independence, and support for sovereignty declines when the economic association is in doubt. This holds even in the post–Meech Lake period (Meadwell, 1993). In Scotland, there is more support for an independent Scotland when the country is projected to be a member of the European Community (McCrone, 1990). There are other kinds of supporting evidence, notably the importance of expanded access to markets in decisions by regional elites in earlier periods to accept the incorporation of regional economies into larger imperial units or free-trade areas (Levack, 1987: 138–68; Spechler, 1989). The rhetorical maneuvering around the meaning of independence in parties such as the Parti Québécois (Meadwell, 1993) and the Scottish National Party (Levy, 1990) is also supportive because this behavior is based on a recognition of the political consequences of the risks associated with independence.

At this point, we can summarize the discussion in two simple models. The model of mobilization implicit in identity theory is

$$Y = sX, \tag{3}$$

where Y is the level of support, X is the number of self-identified collectivists in the group, and s is the efficiency of mobilization. According to these theories, s should be extremely high, approaching unity. Levels of support can be increased essentially through processes of socialization which increase the size of X. Identity theorists have great faith in the likelihood of preference and motivational change in the processes of social interaction and identity formation that together constitute the socialization process in organizational networks.

This is a robust interpretation of the consequences of collective identity. However, it may need to be qualified. Even those individuals whose primary identity is tied to the ethnic group may not support independence because of the problems of transition and economic viability.

One way to incorporate the constraining effects of risk aversion is to divide X from Equation (3) into two subsets. In the first subset, the relationship between identity and support for independence is assumed to hold. The size of this subset, however, depends on the extent of risk aversion in the group. In the second subset, the relationship between identity and support does not hold because of the effects of the extent of risk aversion in the group.

There are real limits to identity formation as a means of increasing support for independence. In other words, I am not as optimistic as identity theorists are about the likelihood of personal transformation, which they assume comes with interaction and dialogue. Indeed, the relationship between identity and risk propensity may be quite different. Collective identity may be associated with support for independence only as the risks of independence decline. This is to say that supporters of independence might be recruited among those whose primary identity is as a member of the group (Québécois, Breton, etc.) only when the political-economic situation of the group makes independence an improvement on the status quo, the transition to independence is short, and involves only a minor deterioration of the status quo conditions of individuals in the group. The identity theorists assume that individuals in the group can be brought along through identity formation. I am skeptical, and think that preference change in the mass public of the group is more likely when the political-economic situation of the group changes. Without this kind of change, nationalist leaders may have to modify their program if they want to increase support.

For identity theorists, the preferences of the mass public are at no point fixed and nationalist leaders should be less likely to modify their programs to increase support, simply because this is not necessary. Our differences are best expressed as differences about the size of the subset of the group over which their arguments about identity hold.

One representation of this constraint on mobilization is

$$Y^* = qX, \tag{4}$$

where q measures the average level of risk aversion on the unit interval $[0, 1]$ and Y^* represents the size of the second subset defined by risk aversion. Where q = 0, there is no risk aversion and Y^* is empty. When $q = 1$, individuals are absolutely risk averse. There is no support for independence. Where $0 < q < 1$, the form of Equation (3) is

$$Y = s(X - qX) \tag{5}$$

According to the propositions introduced in the first section, Y^* is always empty. Secession is always on the agenda, and there is really no problem of mobilization, as long as leaders build or tap into the appropriate symbolic system. But when Y^* is not empty, this constraint has effects that must be taken into account. In the next section, I consider some of the consequences of this constraint on mobilization for some of the strategic choices of organizational leaders.

Factional conflict in nationalist organizations

Equation (4) shows when the problem of viability establishes an upper limit to support for independence. Then the only way for a nationalist organization to increase its support in the cultural group is by taking into account the effects of risk aversion. In seeking to mobilize support among individuals who are risk averse, however, the organization may lose support among collectivists who are not risk averse. Thus there is a trade-off between the gains made and the loss incurred in the two subsets when the organization moves from independence to decentralization as its political goal.

Regionalism is explained by a modified form of this model when organizations that support independence can increase their popular support by modifying their programs. The extent of regional preferences in the group, first of all, will vary with the seriousness of the problem of viability. For regionalists, the balance of expected benefits under independence is too unfavorable to warrant support for statehood. Regionalists want to improve their position within existing institutional arrangements between center and periphery without losing completely those components of center–periphery relationships that they value. The policy profile of a nationalist organization, second, will vary with the type of activist who controls the organization. Finally, the ability to mobilize broader support will depend on the combination of these two features: the strategic choices of activists and the distribution of preferences in the broader group.

Consider the case when X is divided into two subsets: those who support independence and those who do not. By construction, those who are supporters accept the risks of independence. By hypothesis, the reason for this is that to do otherwise would violate their identity. Those who do not support independence do not accept the risks of independence. Suppose, further, that the actual level of support is lower than the support preferred by an *indépendantiste* leadership. For my purposes, the reasons for the gap between actual and preferred levels of support are less important than the gap itself. When there is a gap, however, leaders can recruit support in the second subset. In other words, the organization has a core base of support and may build on this base by recruiting outside this core constituency. Therefore its level of support, in these circumstances, can be represented as

$$\bar{Y} = \hat{Y} + aY^*, \tag{6}$$

where a is the relative efficiency of mobilization in Y^*, $\bar{Y}$ is simply the level of combined support from the two subsets, and $\hat{Y}$ is the level of support in Y after recruitment in Y^*.

Two features of the model and of Equation (6) remain to be demonstrated. The first is the effect of recruitment in Y^* on the level of support in Y. The second is the extent of recruitment in Y^*. Both come down to specifying linear equations for $\hat{Y}$ and Y^* that are consistent with (6).

Support in Y^* under a program of independence is impossible because individuals in Y^* are averse to the risks of independence. The organization must modify its program in order to recruit in Y^*. As it modifies its program, however, the organization may lose support among the individuals in Y. Therefore, any gains in Y^* must be discounted by a parameter d.

$$\hat{Y} = sY - dY^*. \tag{7}$$

The decision to recruit in Y^* will depend on the strategies of organizational leaders. Leaders are sensitive to levels and composition of support. I assume they prefer their chosen level of support to be composed of some proportion of individuals from Y and Y^*. Purists prefer not to recruit outside of Y. Pragmatists are willing to recruit in Y^*. A purist strategy of mobilization will forgo increased support in order to maintain a political program. A pragmatic strategy of mobilization will change the program in order to increase support.

According to equation (7), the only costs to a strategy of recruitment in Y^* are the supporters lost in Y. As it stands, however, this model represents recruitment when support is all of one kind – whether, say, votes, membership, turnout for street demonstrations or financial contributions. It must be modified for organizations such as a political party that can be constrained by their internal structure in ways that are not picked up in Equation (7). In some circumstances, leaders will pay a price if they seek to increase their support in this way. When activists prefer some constraint on mobilization in Y^*, the result of office seeking in the electoral arena is intraorganizational conflict that weakens the activist base and mobilizational capacity of the party.

When leaders do not enjoy autonomy from party activists and they have different preferences over recruitment in Y^*, external (electoral) and internal (organizational) strategies are interdependent. Leaders may not pursue their opportunity in Y^* because of the costs this move imposes on them within the party (Tsebelis, 1990). A parameter, k, takes this set of issues into account, when we consider the mobilization of support in Y^*, and represents how deep into Y^* the leadership is able to go.[6] When $k = Y^*/Y$, leaders are relatively unconstrained in their move to Y^* when $k \geq 1$. As k approaches zero, leaders are increasingly constrained. It follows from the definition of this parameter that the level of support in Y^* is

$$Y^* = kY \tag{8}$$

---

[6] I would argue that the model can hold at different levels of difference between actual and preferred levels of support. The recruitment history of an organization and the history of the stability of political preferences in the group are more important than the size of the difference. Even when the gap between Y and a preferred level of support is large, purists may resist ideological change (and carry the day within an organization) when the history of the group is punctuated by periods of preference volatility and dealignment. When the gap is small, even purists may tolerate some recruitment based on the modification of the political programme, when the organization has had a relatively constant level of support for some time and the group has demonstrated relatively stable political preferences.

Actual support in Y^* varies also with the efficiency of mobilization, so

$$Y^* = a(kY) \tag{9}$$

Equations (7) and (9) can be used to determine the levels of support[7] in Y and Y^*.

This model specifies aggregate levels of support. The most basic parameter is q, which picks up the effects of the problem of viability and identity formation. The parameters, d and k, measure the second-order consequences of constraints associated with the problem of viability. The parameter, a, measures the effects of free-riding in one subset, Y^*.

The effects of these parameters, alone and in some combinations, are illustrated in diagram form (Figures 7.2A–D). Two groups with the same ratio of X to N (total size of group), but with different values of q, will have core constituencies of different sizes. These constituencies are measured as Y_1 and Y_2 and $Y_2 - Y_1 = (q_1 - q_2)X$. When the leaders of a nationalist organization decide to move outside their core constituency, the support that they will maintain in their core constituency ($\hat{Y}$) is a consequence of the degree to which they move outside Y and the discount parameter d. The depth of their recruitment in Y^* is measured by Equation (9). When the discount parameters of two groups, d_1 and d_2, are equal (and all else is equal, notably k in (9)), the groups will have different levels of support in Y when the core constituencies are of different sizes. This is illustrated in Figure 7.2B. When discount parameters are different and core constituencies are the same size, levels of support in Y are different, as illustrated in Figure 7.2C. The value of Y^* in (9) is a function of k (I disregard a here) and the relative size of the core constituency. This is illustrated in Figure 7.2D. The proportion of Y to Y^* is the same in the two groups, but $Y_2^* > Y_1^*$ because $Y_2 > Y_1$ and $k = Y^*/Y$.[8]

This model of macro-outcomes, however, needs some further development at the microlevel. Most important, we should consider the position and dilemma of organizational leaders, specifically leaders of nationalist parties. When we do this, we can simultaneously consider the electoral and organizational consequences of programmatic change. The linear equations for $\bar{Y}$, $\hat{Y}$, and Y^* do not indicate the conditions under which it is rational for leaders to modify the position of the party. However, when we consider the strategic structure of the position of leader, we can specify those conditions, and that specification, in turn, combines electoral and organizational consequences.

Suppose leaders have the choice between maintaining a status quo position and moderating their position by moving toward the median voter, and activists have the choice of supporting their leadership or withdrawing their support (perhaps

---

[7] This result assumes no protest vote for the party in Y^*. This could be taken into account with no loss in generality.

[8] There is also another relevant feature of these parameter values to which attention can be drawn. The relationship between Y and Y^* is linear. This means that the structure of a group can be normalized. The dimensions of the normal form vary with q.

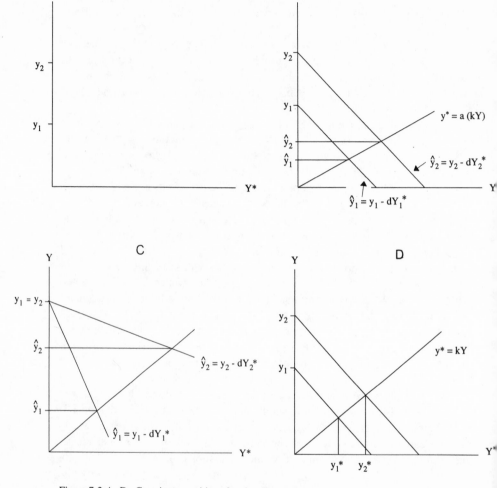

Figure 7.2 A–D. Carrying capacities of nationalist parties.

even leaving the party). The Table 7.1 matrix shows the distribution of activists under these assumptions.[9] In the matrix the number of activists in the organization is normalized to equal 1, and h represents the proportion of activists who do not support the maintenance of the status quo, but who support the moderation of the position of the party. If leaders prefer that the number of supportive activists be as large as possible and the number of nonsupportive activists be as small as

---

[9] More exactly, the matrix shows the expectations held by leaders, should they remain steadfast or become more moderate. The argument could be made in terms of degrees of confidence over different expected distributions, but nothing is lost with this simpler version.

Table 7.1

		Activists	
		Supportive	Nonsupportive
Leaders	Maintain status quo	$1 - h$	h
	Moderate position	h	$1 - h$

possible, then they will choose the status quo whenever $1 - h > h$. So if $1 - h > h$, it is irrational in this organizational context for leaders to moderate by moving toward the median voter.

However, moderation is rational whenever the net electoral benefits (b) are greater than the costs associated with the withdrawal of activist support. When the leadership moderates its position, it still retains h activists; hence moderation is rational when $b > 1 - h$. Although b and h are measured in different units, the costs of the withdrawal of activist support can be translated into the units of electoral benefit by considering the consequences of a weaker activist base for the efficiency of electoral mobilization. If e_s and e_m measure the efficiency of mobilization under the status quo and moderation, and are a linear function of q, then moderation is rational when $e_m(b_m) > e_s(b_s)$ or $h(b_m) > (1 - h)(b_s)$. If $1 - h > h$ and $h(b_m) < (1 - h)(b_s)$, the net electoral benefits are less than the costs associated with the withdrawal of activist support. The party remains steadfast, and loyal to its core constituency.

Moderation, however, need not imply movement towards the median voter. Organizational leaders can face a similar dilemma when movement toward the median implies, not moderation, but a more radical party program. It is the gap between the positions of the party and the rank and file of the group that produces the incentive for programmatic change. Therefore the inequality that should hold for movement toward the median to be rational is

$$e_{med} (B_{med}) > e_s(b_s) \tag{10}$$

or

$$h_{med} (b_{med}) > (1 - h_{med})(b_s). \tag{11}$$

This inequality specifies the relationship among leaders, activists and mass publics of the ethnic group. When the substantive political positions of these actors are identified, the inequality can account for two different types of ethnic mobilization.

The first type of mobilization develops when the position of the nationalist organization is more extreme than that of the median individual. This relationship creates incentives for moderation. Indeed, this is the classic model of political mobilization in the developed West and the pressure for moderation has been identified in many other social movements and political parties in the

West, including working-class (DeNardo, 1985; Przeworski, 1985), ecological (Kitschelt, 1990) and peace movements (Rochon, 1988). This pattern of ethnic mobilization is typical of Scotland (Levy, 1990); Wales (Morgan, 1981); Brittany (Meadwell, 1992) and Quebec (with some qualifications due to very recent changes [Meadwell, 1993]).

There can be recurrent conflicts within nationalist parties, consistent with this model, over the kinds of concessions to be made in exchange for electoral success. Factional conflicts also should worsen after perceived popular defeats on significant issues. In the case of the Parti Québécois, for example, the referendum failure in 1980 and electoral defeat in 1985 lowered morale and increased mutual blame among hard- and soft-liners, pushed the leadership to table sovereignty association for a program of "national affirmation," and thus alienated more fundamentalist activists and leaders. Sovereignty association itself was devised in the early 1970s in anticipation of the electoral dilemma of a pure *indépendantiste* party (Meadwell, 1993). In the SNP, factionalism also worsened after a referendum in 1979. Byelection defeats in the 1930s produced conflicts between purists and pragmatists in the *Parti Autonomiste Breton* (Meadwell, 1992). Significantly, factionalism occurred despite very different levels of popular support for independence in these three cases.

But the inequality in (11) can also account for a second type of mobilization, which develops when the position of the median individual is more extreme than the program of the organization. Moderation then can be costly because it sacrifices support for the sake of the maintenance of a programmatic position. The pressure for extremist outcomes in Northern Ireland can be understood in these terms. The problem of achieving an accommodation has been made more difficult because elites have had little reason to engage in conflict regulation. Each group has a set of competing, rival activists and activists generally do not enjoy autonomy from their followers. Together, elite competition and the absence of autonomy contribute to extremism (O'Leary, 1989). Intergroup agreements around moderate positions therefore are difficult to make and enforce because of the incentives for leaders within groups to defect toward extremism. Other cases, which have been subject to vicious cycles of competitive outbidding such as the Sikhs, or the Basques (Shabad, 1992), are also instances of this type of mobilization.

Conclusion

I wanted to accomplish two tasks in this chapter. The first was to show that these three propositions are not as straightforward as they may appear. The second was to construct a model of mobilization that linked the problem of viability and organizational factionalism. While I have no doubt that these propositions tell part of the story, it is very unlikely that they can do all of the explanatory work demanded of them.

References

Adamson, Walter L. (1980). *Hegemony and Revolution*. Berkeley and Los Angeles: University of California Press.

Anderson, Benedict. (1983). *Imagined Communities*. London: Verso Books.

Bacho, Peter. (1987–8). "The Muslim Secessionist Movement." *Journal of International Affairs* 41: 153–64.

Badal, R. K. (1976). "The Rise and Fall of Separatism in Southern Sudan." *African Affairs* 75: 463–74.

Beer, William R. (1980). *The Unexpected Rebellion. Ethnic Activism in Contemporary France*. New York and London: New York University Press.

Calhoun, Craig. (1991). "The Problem of Identity in Collective Action." In Joan Huber (Ed.), *Macro-Micro Linkages in Sociology*. Beverly Hills, Calif.: Sage Publications.

Clarke, Harold D. (1983). "The Parti Québécois and Sources of Partisan Realignment in Québec." *Journal of Politics* 45: 64–85.

Clavera, Joan. (1988). "Reflexions sobre determinants aspects de l'économia catalana." In Gaetan Tremblay and Manuel Parés i Maicas (Eds.), *Catalunya-Québec*. Barcelona: Generalitat de Catalunya.

Cohen, G. A. (1988). "Historical Inevitability and Revolutionary Agency." In G. A. Cohen, *History, Labour and Freedom*. Oxford: Clarendon Press.

Connor, Walker. (1987). "Ethnonationalism." In Myron Weiner and Samuel P. Huntington (Eds.), *Understanding Political Development*. Boston: Little Brown.

DeNardo, James. (1985). *Power in Numbers: The Political Strategy of Protest and Rebellion*. Princeton, N.J.: Princeton University Press.

Gopinath, Aruna. (1991). "International Aspects of the Thai Muslim and Philippine Moro Issues: A Comparative Study." In K. M. de Silva and R. J. May (Eds.), *Internationalization of Ethnic Conflict*. London: Pinter.

Gunther, Richard, Giacomo Sani, and Goldie Shabad. (1986). *Spain after Franco*. Berkeley and Los Angeles: University of California Press.

Horowitz, Donald L. (1991). "Irredentas and secessions: adjacent phenomena, neglected connections." In Naomi Chazan (Ed.), *Irredentism and International Politics*. London and Boulder: Lynne Rienner.

(1985). *Ethnic Groups in Conflict*. Berkeley and Los Angeles: University of California Press.

(1981). "Patterns of Ethnic Separatism." *Comparative Studies in Society and History* 23: 165–95.

Kitschelt, Herbert. (1990). *The Logics of Party Formation*. Ithaca, N.Y.: Cornell University Press.

Koohi-Kamali, Fereshteh. (1992). "The Development of Nationalism in Iranian Kurdistan." In Philip G. Kreyenbriek and Stefan Sperl (Eds.), *The Kurds*. London and New York: Routledge.

Laitin, David H. (1988). "Language Games." *Comparative Politics* 20: 289–302.

Lancaster, Thomas D. (1987). "Comparative Nationalism: the Basques in Spain and France." *European Journal of Political Research* 15: 561–90.

Lancaster, Thomas D., and Michael Lewis-Beck. (1989). "Regional Vote Support: the Spanish Case." *International Studies Quarterly* 33: 29–44.

Lemarchand, René. (1962). "The Limits of Self-Determination: The Case of the Katanga Secession." *American Political Science Review* 56: 404–16.

Levack, Brian. (1987). *The Formation of the British State*. Oxford: Clarendon Press.

Levy, Roger. (1990). *Scottish Nationalism at the Crossroads*. Edinburgh: Scottish Academic Press.

Luis de la Granja, José. (1991). "El nacionalismo vasco entre la autonomia y la independencia." In Justo Beramendio and Ramón Máiz (Eds.), *Los nacionalismos en la España de la II República*. Madrid: Siglo Veintiuno.

McCrone, David. (1990). "Opinion Polls in Scotland: August, 1988 –July, 1989." In *The Scottish Government Yearbook, 1990*. Edinburgh: Unit for the Study of Government in Scotland.

Machina, Mark J. (1990). "Choice under Uncertainty: Problems Solved and Unsolved." In Karen S. Cook and Margaret Levi (Eds.), *The Limits of Rationality*. Chicago: University of Chicago Press.

McVey, Ruth. (1984). "Separatism and the Paradoxes of the Nation-State in Perspective." In L. Joo-Jock and S. Vani (Eds.), *Armed Separatism in Southeast Asia*. Pasir Panjang: Institute of Southeast Asian Studies.

Mayo, Patricia. (1974). *The Roots of Identity: Three National Movements in Contemporary European Politics*. London: Allen Lane.

Meadwell, Hudson. (1993). "The Politics of Nationalism in Quebec." *World Politics* 45: 203–42.

(1992). *Nationalism and Rationality*, manuscript, McGill University.

(1991a). "The Catholic Church and the Breton Language in the Third Republic." *French History* 5: 325–44.

(1991b). "A Rational Choice Approach to Political Regionalism." *Comparative Politics* 23: 401–23.

(1990). "The Politics of Language: Republican Values and Breton Identity." *European Journal of Sociology* 31: 263–83.

(1989a). "Cultural and Instrumental Approaches to Ethnic Nationalism." *Ethnic and Racial Studies* 12: 309–28.

(1989b). "Ethnic Nationalism and Collective Choice Theory." *Comparative Political Studies* 22: 139–54.

Morgan, Kenneth O. (1981). *Rebirth of a Nation: Wales 1880–1980*. Oxford: Oxford University Press.

Nafziger, E. Wayne, and William L. Richter. (1976). "Biafra and Bangladesh: The Political Economy of Secessionist Conflict." *Journal of Peace Research* 33: 91–109.

Nixon, Charles R. (1972). "Self-determination: The Nigeria/Biafra Case," *World Politics* 24: 473–97.

O'Leary, Brendan. (1989). "The Limits to Coercive Consociationalism in Northern Ireland," *Political Studies* 37: 562–88.

Orridge, Andrew W. (1982). "Separatist and Autonomist Nationalisms: The Structure of Regional Loyalties in the Modern State." In Colin H. Williams (Ed.), *National Separatism*. Vancouver: University of British Columbia Press.

Parizeau, Jacques. (1987). "Interview." In Alvin R. Riggs and Tom Velk (Eds.), *Canadian–American Free Trade: Historical, Political and Economic Dimensions*. Montreal: Institute for Research on Public Policy.

Pinard, Maurice, and Richard Hamilton. (1986). "Motivational Dimensions in the Québec Independence Movement: A Test of a New Model." In *Research in Social Movements, Conflicts and Change*. Greenwich, Conn: JAI.

Przeworski, Adam. (1985). *Capitalism and Social Democracy.* Cambridge: Cambridge University Press.

Raghavan, Nandini. (1990). "The Southern Sudanese Secessionist Movement." In Ralph R. Premdas, S. W. R. de A. Samarasinghe and Alan Anderson (Eds.), *Secessionist Movements in Comparative Perspective.* London: Pinter Publishers.

Rashid, Harun-or-. (1990). "Bangladesh: The First Successful Secessionist Movement in the Third World." In Ralph R. Premdas, S. W. R. de A. Samarasinghe, and Alan B. Anderson (Eds.), *Secessionist Movements in Comparative Perspective.* London: Pinter.

Rochon, Thomas R. (1988). *Mobilizing for Peace: The Antinuclear Movements in Western Europe.* Princeton, N.J.: Princeton University Press.

Roeder, Philip G. (1991). "Soviet Federalism and Ethnic Mobilization." *World Politics* 43: 196–232.

Shabad, Goldie. (1992). *Still the Exception? Democratization and Ethnic Nationalism in the Basque Country of Spain.* Delivered at the Eighth International Conference of Europeanists, Palmer House, Chicago, March 27–29, 1992.

Smith, Anthony D. (1987). *The Ethnic Origins of Nations.* Cambridge: Basil Blackwell.

Spechler, Martin. (1989). "The Economic Advantages of Being Peripheral: Subordinate Nations in Multinational Empires." *East European Politics and Society* 3: 448–64.

Szajdowski, Bogdan. (1985). "The Catholic Church in Defense of Civil Society in Poland." In Bronislaw Misztal (Ed.), *Poland after Solidarity.* New Brunswick, N.J.: Transaction Books.

Tsebelis, George. (1990). *Nested Games.* Berkeley and Los Angeles: University of California Press.

Tsoukalis, Loukas. (1981). *The European Community and Its Mediterranean Enlargement.* London and Boston: Allen and Unwin.

Vardys, Stanley V. (1978). *The Catholic Church, Dissent and Nationality in Soviet Lithuania.* New York: Columbia University Press.

PART III

International politics

8. Economic nationalism and economic progress

Mancur Olson

Even though the issue has been debated for more than two centuries, there is still a great deal of disagreement about protectionism and other forms of economic nationalism. Among the general public, it is widely believed that developing nations need at least a period of protection of manufacturing industry in order to industrialize and that they should curtail the entry of multinational firms. Economic nationalism is probably less popular in the developed democracies than in the less developed countries, but even the electorates in the developed nations tolerate a fair amount of protectionism. Many commentators believe most of these countries now need more protection of their manufacturing industries against imports from Japan and other nations of the Pacific Rim, and perhaps also against imports from countries with unusually low wages. There is also often support for special restrictions on foreign companies even in many developed countries.

Among my fellow economists, there has been by contrast an intense skepticism about protectionism and most other forms of economic nationalism. Nonetheless, when it comes to the different question of how *important* free trade is for the progress and prosperity of economies, many economists have estimated or concluded that the degree of protectionism is *not* of overwhelming importance for the level of development or the rate of growth of a country. Arnold Harberger (1984) did some well-known work on the losses from monopoly in manufacturing in the United States, and found them to be less than 1 percent of the U.S.

This is the text of the sixth Harry G. Johnson Memorial Lecture delivered at the Institut Universitaire de Haute Études Internationales, University of Geneva, on March 12, 1987. Some tributes to Harry Johnson in that lecture are not included in this version of the paper. The lecture argued that Harry Johnson was an extraordinarily productive and insightful economist with a profound understanding of the gains from international trade as well as other subfields of economics.

The author is thankful to the National Science Foundation, Resources for the Future, and the Thyssen Stiftung for support of his research, and to Bela Balassa and Christopher Clague for helpful suggestions.

gross national product. So famous did this work (quite rightly) become, that many economists are in the habit of saying that "all Harberger triangles are small." Though protection is a different thing from monopoly, an approach somewhat similar to Harberger's has on several occasions been applied to measure the losses from tariffs or the gains from freer trade, and the results normally suggest that the degree of protection is of only minor importance to the level of per capita income. For example, skilled estimates by Mordechai Kreinen (1974) and by Edwin Truman (1969) find that, though the Common Market mainly created rather than diverted trade, it added 2 percent or less to EEC manufacturing consumption. Bela Balassa (1967), in another skilled study, concluded that, even after taking economies of scale into account, the creation of the European Community led to only a three tenths of 1 percent increase in the ratio of the annual increment of trade to that of the GNP.

Many economists also regard changes in the degree of protection as relatively unimportant in comparison with the size of the welfare state, or the quality of monetary and fiscal policy, in explaining economic performance. In Europe and the United States today, the growth of government and growth of the welfare state appear to generate more concern and debate than does the level of protection or barriers to international mobility of the factors of production. It is often recognized that the level of protection in the developed countries was incomparably higher in the years between World War I and World War II than it was before World War I, or than it came to be in the 1960s, yet this is not usually considered a factor of any significance in explaining the dramatic deterioration in economic performance in the interwar period or in the great depression of the thirties. In recent years a number of economists who focus on the developing nations have begun to argue that the degree of openness may be a crucial variable in determining how fast poor nations develop, but on the whole most economists have not regarded the degree of openness of an economy as the decisive determinant of the progress or prosperity of a country.

Many men of genius have contributed to the debate over the last two centuries on the virtues and shortcomings of free trade. The literature on this subject in the last few decades has benefited from some of the finest and most energetic minds in the economics profession. The calculations suggesting that the gains from freer trade are of modest size are undoubtedly honest and skillful and it appears that all of them reveal broadly similar results. How then will it be possible for another economist, who is not even a specialist on international trade, to offer anything that is both novel and valid?

On an issue like this one that is important to the welfare of literally billions of people, there is nonetheless something to be said for considering new perspectives, and the one that I shall offer here is greatly different from those that other economists have offered. I specify the degree of protection in a way that, though very simple, is not conventional. The effects of protectionism and other forms of economic nationalism that I emphasize are effects that are normally not explained in at least the formal and abstract statements of the theory of international trade, and they are also effects that escape measurement in the comparative-static calculations of the gains and losses from the creation of common markets and other changes in the degree of protection. My perspective includes some phenomena that most economists of an earlier generation would have considered outside the boundaries of economics. Thus I ask indulgence for raising yet again one of the oldest questions in all of economics.

I shall begin by summarizing one especially pertinent part of the argument in my book on *The Rise and Decline of Nations* (1982), for this will be necessary to make the present analysis comprehensible to those who have not read the book. Then I shall go on to present some arguments that are not in that book. These further arguments focus on trade in manufactures in small and medium-sized countries. In the course of this argument I shall present some statistics. Some of these statistics have appeared in a prior article and some have been calculated mainly for this study. I believe these statistics, taken together, are somewhat startling. At the least, they are pertinent to the question of whether poor countries that wish to develop a competitive and profitable manufacturing industry should or should not have high levels of protection of manufactured products.

Trade barrier mileage more important than height

It seems to me that previous examinations of the issue of protection have given relatively too much attention to the height of tariffs and other forms of protection and relatively too little attention to the length or mileage of tariffs. That is to say, too little attention has been given to the size of the jurisdiction around which there are tariffs and other forms of protection. The importance of the size of jurisdiction for the significance of protection can best be seen by using a thought experiment. Suppose that we were to imagine a country so large that it was all the world except for Luxembourg. Suppose that this colossal country had prohibitive tariffs on trade with the rest of the world, namely Luxembourg. It is obvious that this hypothetical country could not be affected that much by its tariffs against Luxembourg, because even if this gigantic country had had no tariffs, most of what it purchased would in any event have been purchased internally. The protection, in other words, would have affected only a relatively small number of markets to a minor degree and thus could not have had a great quantitative effect. So I conclude that in looking at the effects of protection, it is essential to look at the size of the jurisdiction that has the protection and to note that the biggest economies, like the United States and Japan, are not affected nearly as much by protection as are small and medium-sized countries.

This emphasis on the mileage rather than the height of tariff barriers leads to the question of whether the great periods of freeing of trade in history have been due to the reductions in the mileage of tariffs and other forms of protection rather than in their height. I argue that that is indeed the case; that the most significant periods of the freeing up of trade have come from national unification and other developments that have created larger jurisdictions within which there was free trade, even though these jurisdictions usually had tariffs against the outside world. A reduction in the mileage of tariff barriers was brought about by the creation of the Common Market in Europe through the Treaty of Rome in 1957. What happened when the Common Market was created has happened many times in history, usually through national unification.

In Germany, for example, there was in the 1830s the creation of a Zollverein, or customs union, that was gradually extended and deepened, and culminated in the German Reich, completed by 1871. It is interesting that most of the German-speaking areas of Europe were relatively poor in the period before the Zollverein and the German Reich were created. In the eighteenth and early nineteenth centuries, Germany was far poorer than Britain, poorer than Holland, and probably also had a distinctly lower income than France. Nonetheless, we know that in the second half of the nineteenth century and the years up to World War I, the German economy grew at an extraordinary rate, so that by World War I Germany was undoubtedly one of the greatest industrial powers of the world.

In *The Rise and Decline of Nations,* I called phenomena such as the creation of the Common Market and German unification examples of "jurisdictional integration." Such integration occurs whenever a much bigger jurisdiction is created that has *internal* free trade.

Japan offers another example of jurisdictional integration and it occurred at approximately the same time as German unification. Before the Meiji Restoration of 1867–8, Japan was divided into nearly three hundred separate feudal domains, each under its own feudal lord, or *daimyo*. Normally each of these domains had high levels of protection, limiting trade from that jurisdiction to other parts of Japan. To the extent the Shogunate had some control over the whole of Japan, it used that control in part to make Japan as a whole virtually autarchic with the rest of the world, limiting trade and factor mobility with the outside world to a negligible level; even travel abroad was punishable by death.

The Meiji Restoration or revolution of 1867–8 created a free trade area within Japan. It eliminated the separate feudal jurisdictions and thus also the trade restrictions that went with them. At about the same time, a group of Western powers imposed upon Japan what the Japanese call the "humiliating treaties." The treaties are described as humiliating because the Japanese were too weak to resist their imposition. One of these treaties restricted the Japanese for fifty years to a tariff for revenue only of no more than 5 percent. Because of the jurisdictional integration plus the "humiliating treaties," Japan experienced a fantastic increase in freedom of trade.

Japan was definitely a poor and underdeveloped country before this process occurred. Some Western observers believed that the Japanese would never be able to manage modern economic life. Yet Japan grew rapidly after the Meiji Restoration. One symptom of that growth, besides the evidence from the statistics, is that by 1904–5 Japan was already a sufficient power to defeat Russia in a war.

At the very end of the eighteenth century there was another example of jurisdictional integration – the United States. The U.S. government was not really created at the time of the Declaration of Independence in 1776, but only several years after the success of the American Revolution. Until 1789, when the U.S. Constitution went into effect, the separate states were essentially independent countries. One of the effects of this Constitution was to outlaw tariffs that some states had against imports from other states. New York state had tariffs against imports both from New Jersey and Connecticut and these were abolished by the U.S. Constitution. So the United States then became a substantial market and one in which, internally, there has been free trade to this day. To be sure, through most of the nineteenth century and into the 1930s, the United States was a highly protectionist country. Nonetheless, because of the absence of tariffs by states and the large size of the country, the United States has enjoyed a very large free market internally.

If we go back to the golden age of Holland in the seventeenth century, we again see a similar phenomenon. When the United Provinces rebelled against Spain, they created an area in which generally speaking there was internally free trade. Though not large by modern standards, it was large by the feudal standards of the time, and the special suitability of that country to canals meant that a relatively large area was accessible to water-borne transportation. This was, as we know, also a period when Holland began to lead the world in economic activity.

If we go back still further, to the end of the Middle Ages, we find that the first country in Europe to establish true unification was England, or more precisely, England and Wales. By the sixteenth century, essentially, the parochial feudal system had been largely abolished in England. Some time later Scotland was added as well and all of Great Britain could be considered as essentially one free market. The semiautonomous towns and feudal fiefs with their separate trade restrictions were made part of a unified Britain. Though the textbooks emphasize that this was the mercantilistic period and there were high national tariffs, there was nevertheless a great freeing of trade because of the reduction in the internal trade restrictions. This was also the period when the Commercial Revolution occurred; it was a period of substantial economic progress. After the interruption and disruption of the English Civil Wars of the seventeenth century, and the effective integration of Scotland and Ireland into the United Kingdom, there was also the Industrial Revolution.

Thus there are several periods in history in which protection was dramatically reduced because a big market replaced many small markets with protection. Even though the big markets were sometimes highly protected, there was a great freeing of trade. This great freeing of trade, moreover, seems to have been followed in each case by striking rates of economic development.

An intellectual framework

What could be the reason for this improvement in economic performance at the time of the jurisdictional integrations? In order to answer this question, we need to look not only at the familiar theory of comparative advantage and the case it makes for freer trade, but also at the institutional patterns. These patterns, I will argue, were changed substantially by the freeing up of trade and the establishment of a larger jurisdiction. To see why this is so, we need to go into some more fundamental questions.

Specifically, we must ask, "What determines the level of collective action in society?" Far removed as this might seem to be from the questions of trade and protection, we need to look at the development in societies of organizations that act collectively to lobby government or to collude and cartelize markets to fix prices or wages. Although these matters are usually ignored in analyses of international trade, they are intimately tied up with protection.

The key to the matter, in my opinion, is the great difficulty of collective action, and the fact that many groups can overcome these difficulties if they have enough time. I must begin with my book, *The Logic of Collective Action* (1965), in which I argued that efforts to lobby or to cartelize provide to the recipient group what, analytically speaking, is a collective or public good. The benefits of collective action reach everyone in some market, occupation, or category, whether or not the firm or individual in question has helped support the collective action. If a group of firms obtains a tariff any firm that sells the product protected by the tariff will get the benefit of the higher price whether or not that firm has borne any of the costs of lobbying the government to provide the tariff. That is true of special-interest legislation generally, which will normally affect everyone in some industry, occupation, or other category. Similarly, if we have a combination of sellers in some market to restrict the supply and raise the price or wage, that higher price or wage is again available to everyone in the relevant market, irrespective of whether they shared the sacrifice of restricting output in order to bring about the monopolistic price or wage.

It follows from this free-rider argument developed in *The Logic of Collective Action* that large groups will be able to organize for collective action only if they have what I call selective incentives. That is to say, there must be some incentive separate from the public good provided by the collective action that makes it worthwhile for the individuals and firms in question to support the action that is in their collective interest. There must be some reward or some punishment given out on an individual basis that discriminates between those who do and do not support the collective action, since the collective or public good resulting from the collective action does not so discriminate. I claim to have shown in *The Logic of Collective Action* that, at least in the United States, there have been no large lobbying groups or cartelistic groups that lasted for any length of time without some kind of selective incentive that mainly accounted for their membership. The most conspicuous examples of selective incentives are the union shop, the closed shop, and the coercive picket line. These devices provide an obvious incentive to pay union dues and to respect picket lines, but there is no incentive for the individual to make sacrifices on behalf of the union that arises from the higher wages due to collective bargaining, for these higher wages are available to all workers who remain in the firm or industry affected by the collective action.

Devices such as the union shop and the closed shop are just the tip of an iceberg. All large organizations for collective action that I've been able to find anywhere, if they last any length of time, always will have some kind of selective incentive that mainly accounts for their membership.

Small groups may, however, be able to organize even without selective incentives. Organizations with small numbers of members, like trade associations representing a few large firms in some manufacturing industry, may be able to organize because each of the members gets a significant share of action in the interest of the group. The "externality" to other members of the group from action in the group interest is less. When the group is small, there is also strategic interaction among the members, so they may bargain with each other and agree on a "group optimal" level of provision of the collective good.

Because collective action has to overcome the public goods problem and is therefore very difficult, it will be possible only for those groups that can find selective incentives or are small in number. Some groups will never be able to act collectively. Groups dispersed in the way that consumers, or the poor, or the unemployed, or taxpayers are, will never be able to work out picket lines or anything else that would bring about effective collective action in the form of a consumers' buying cartel, or as a lobby for the poor, the unemployed, or the taxpayer.

Even those groups that are able to act collectively will succeed in doing so only when they have good leadership and lucky circumstances that enable the complex selective incentives or bargains needed for collective action to be worked out. If I might use an example of which I am rather fond, it's that of the late Jimmy Hoffa, once leader of the American teamsters' or truckers' union. When Jimmy Hoffa was a teenager working in a warehouse in Michigan, one hot summer day a large shipment of fresh strawberries and other fresh produce came in that had to be got out quickly to the customers before it spoiled. The young Jimmy Hoffa, cunning and courageous as he was, chose that moment to organize a strike and a union, and the employer gave in rather than lose the fresh produce. My general proposition, then, is that those groups that can organize for collective action will be able to do so only when they have good leadership and good circumstances. That will happen only in fullness of time.

Once organizations for collective action get started, however, they will almost never disband. In a stable society – that is to say a society where such organizations are not destroyed by violence or repression – they are likely, once they are organized and have found selective incentives, to last indefinitely. So this leads to the proposition that stable societies will have accumulated a large number of organizations and collusions for collective action. Because some groups can never organize, even long-stable societies do not obtain a symmetric organization of all groups with common interests. This means that there is no possibility of what a game theorist would call a "core" and efficient allocation of resources, but there will eventually be many groups organized for collective action in their own interest.

The most perverse incentives

The significance of this is evident the moment we look at the incentives organizations for collective action face. Let us focus first on countries like the United Kingdom or the United States, in which none of the organizations for collective action is large in relationship to the whole society. In these countries lobbying or cartelistic organizations may have hundreds of thousands of members, but they will nonetheless represent only a tiny fraction of the income-earning capacity of the country. A trade association, a professional association, a union, or an organization representing farmers producing some commodity will represent, say, only 1 percent or so of the income earning capacity of the country.

Let's assume that the organization represents exactly 1 percent of the society for easy figuring. This immediately tells us something about the structure of incentives facing organizations of the kind I have in mind. If an organization represents 1 percent of the income-earning capacity of a country, then it will be the case that if it uses its resources to make the country in which the members of the organization live and work more prosperous, those members will on average get only 1 percent of the benefit of this use of its resources. So only in the rarest circumstances will it be rational for an organization for collective action in these countries to use its resources to make the country more efficient. It will generally be the case that these organizations can best serve the interests of their members by obtaining a larger share of what the society produces through special-interest legislation or monopoly prices or wages.

As economists we are aware that monopolization of prices and wages, and replacing impartial and general laws with special-interest legislation that favors particular types of income or particular industries or occupations, will generally lead to a less efficient allocation of resources. Though there are "second-best" considerations that could keep particular price and wage distortions from doing any damage, the second best logic almost certainly applies to only a limited number of cases.

Now we have to take into account the fact that the excess burden or social costs due to the lobbying of organizations for collective action will somewhat reduce the income in the country in question, and that the members of the organizations for collective action are part of that country and will bear some of the loss that comes from the excess burden of their own activities. Consider a typical special-interest group (or "distributional coalition" as I prefer to call it) that represents 1 percent of the income-earning capacity of a country. When such an organization gets more for its members through distributional struggle that imposes an excess burden on the economy, it will find that its members are better off up to the point where the national income falls by a hundred or more times as much as the amount that this group wins in distributional struggle! The coalition bears on average only 1 percent of the social costs of its action, but gets all that is redistributed. Thus there is an incentive in special-interest groups to engage in distributional struggle with very little concern for the prosperity and growth of the society.

Note that the structure of incentives facing distributional coalitions is very different from the structure of incentives facing an incumbent political party or a president seeking reelection in a society without distributional coalitions. In general, the incumbent political party or president will have a considerable incentive to run for reelection with a prosperous economy and to tell the electorate that they never had it so good. Contrary to what some economists have claimed, democratic political competition need not entail that the political parties or leading politicians face utterly perverse incentives akin to those that confront distributional coalitions (Olson, 1986; 1982: ch. 3).

Benefits of jurisdictional integration

Let us now consider how the argument I have loosely sketched out here, and stated more precisely in *The Rise and Decline of Nations* (1982: 41–53), relates to the protection of manufactures and jurisdictional integration. If the difficulties of collective action insure that it emerges only slowly, and it is also true that narrowly based distributional coalitions face perverse incentives that work against economic efficiency (and, for reasons there isn't time to go into here, also against innovation and growth), then we can understand what has happened when jurisdictional integration has occurred. The creation of a much bigger market and of a bigger jurisdiction that determines at least some aspects of economic policy will undercut most of the existing distributional coalitions and it will take some time before new ones form, so for a time there can be exceptionally rapid economic growth.

Consider a small protected market like a medieval town with its own walls and economic policies. Suppose that suddenly the protection in the small jurisdiction is eliminated because there is national unification or a common market. Then the organizations for collective action that have had time to develop in the town, and that have profited from the use of their cartelistic powers and lobbying powers, will find that after jurisdictional integration their customers can purchase from other suppliers in other towns or in the suburbs or in the countryside. Suddenly, because of the creation of a wider market, the cartels have lost their monopoly power. Since the jurisdictional integration creates a much larger jurisdiction, it also requires lobbying on a far larger scale, so the organizations that were of a size suitable to lobby the town will usually not be strong enough to influence the new governmental unit.

So the theory leads to the prediction that the extent of damage done by organizations for collective action will be much smaller than usual after there has been a big freeing of trade, whether through national unification, a common market, or unilateral freeing of trade.

Organizations for collective action will eventually emerge again on a scale suitable to lobbying or cartelizing the larger jurisdiction and markets that have been created. But if my argument is right, it takes quite some time to overcome the difficulties of collective action, especially when the groups at issue are large ones. Thus for a considerable period there can be unusually rapid growth.

As the theory predicts, there was unusually rapid growth after the creation of the EEC, after the German Zollverein, after the Meiji Revolution, after the Dutch rebellion against the Spanish, and after the national unifications in England and the United States. Though the timing of the economic growth certainly is consistent with the theory, this correlation is not, of course, necessarily sufficient to establish causation.

Happily, various special features of the pattern of growth after jurisdictional integration offer striking support for the argument. If we look, for example, at England in the early modern period, we find that the main form of manufacturing, textile production, came to be handled under the merchant-employer or "putting-out" system. Manufacturing was not done mainly in the cities where the guilds, the distributional coalitions of the times, held sway, but rather mostly in the scattered cottages of the countryside. Merchants went out to the countryside to leave with cottagers the wool to be spun into yarn, or yarn to be woven into cloth. This system was expensive in terms of both transportation costs and transactions costs, but it was nonetheless cheaper than production under guild rules in the towns. We also find that the growth tended to be concentrated in new towns or in suburbs where guilds did not exist. When the bigger national markets were created, firms could locate wherever they found it most efficient, and locations that were not under the control of guilds were most efficient. Economic growth in England, for example, was concentrated in new towns that had not had much of any population or any guilds before the national unification of England took place (Olson, 1982: 121–3).

Coalition-free scorched earth

Now let us note the parallel between the jurisdictional integration that I have described and what happens in frontier areas and after political upheavals and catastrophes. If my argument is right, frontier areas should grow rapidly not only because they have got the heretofore unexploited natural resources of the frontier, but also because on a frontier there will not have been time for many distributional coalitions to develop. It should also be the case that after upheavals and catastrophes that bring a lot of destruction, there will be, if a free and stable order is then created, unusually rapid growth.

In Germany, Japan, and Italy after World War II, where totalitarianism and defeat in war had destroyed the organizations for collective action, we should expect exceptionally rapid growth. That is exactly what happened with the "economic miracles" after World War II in all three of these countries.

Similarly, we should expect the problems of which I speak to be most serious in long-stable countries like the United Kingdom, for example, and thus I would offer this argument as the single most important explanation for the "British disease" of slow growth. The argument also is consistent with the regional pattern of growth in the United States. Most of the long-settled, always stable states of the United States, and especially those in the older industrial parts of the

Midwest, are in dramatic decline, whereas the more recently settled "frontier" areas in the West and the until lately turbulent and once-defeated South of the United States are doing relatively better. The western and southern regions of the United States have had less time to accumulate organizations for collective action. There are so many states in the United States and such variations across them that statistical tests of the theory could be used. The regressions on the data on the contiguous states of the United States are all clearly consistent with my argument and all have statistical significance (Olson 1982: 94–117).

The foregoing argument summarizes certain parts of *The Rise and Decline of Nations*. Several of the most central arguments of that book (on matters like macroeconomics, technical innovation, political divisiveness, and class, caste, and ethnic discrimination) have not even been mentioned and certain peripheral portions of the argument that most commentators ignore have been emphasized, in order that the application of the theory to international trade could be made most evident. The hope is that what has been said here will make the present essay comprehensible to those who do not know the book.

We must now go on to consider how international trade in primary products, manufactured goods, and services vary in the extent to which they can provide information about the efficiency or inefficiency of the policies and institutions of a country. After that we examine some familiar explanations of why countries succeed or fail in developing profitable industries that export a lot of manufactures. Some of these familiar explanations are drawn from the formal theory of international trade and some from the literature that advocates protection, or at least infant industry protection for manufactures in developing nations. These varying theories or arguments about what makes countries successful in developing manufacturing industry that can earn profits by exporting, and the theory in *The Rise and Decline of Nations*, are then tested against data on the exports of manufactures from the small and medium-sized countries that are most strongly affected by protection.

Trade in manufactures less influenced by natural resources

Where international trade is at issue, manufacturing industry is for certain purposes more instructive for the economist than other types of economic activity. Saudi Arabia and Iran produce and export a lot of oil, but this does not tell us very much about what policies or institutions these countries have nor offer a good basis for judgments about the efficiency of resource allocation in them. The oil production and exports of these countries tell us more about their geology than about their economic and political systems, because oil production is, of course, dependent in large part on where the geological evolution of our planet has left the major basins of crude oil. In the extractive industries generally, and even to a considerable extent in agriculture, the pattern of production and international trade is especially sensitive to the natural resource or climatic endowments of a country.

To be sure, the location of manufacturing, or at least some types of manufacturing, also is influenced by endowments of raw materials. If we look at the emergence of modern manufacturing in the Industrial Revolution in eighteenth-century England, or at the industrialization of continental Europe and North America in the nineteenth century, we see a definite tendency for most manufacturing industry to be in countries and in areas well endowed with iron, coal, and other raw materials useful for manufacturing. A large part of the heavy industry in Europe, for example, has been concentrated in an area extending from the Midlands of England through Belgium and Northern France to the Ruhr, and that is a part of Europe that has been relatively well endowed with coal and iron ore. Heavy industry in the United States also began in places like Pennsylvania with a lot of coal and at sites on the Great Lakes with relatively inexpensive access to deposits of iron ore.

On the other hand, there are many areas and countries, especially in more recent times, that are very successful in manufacturing yet have little or nothing in the way of iron, coal, or other natural resources needed for manufacturing. Consider Hong Kong, Japan, and Singapore, most notably, or diverse other locations that are not well endowed with these natural resources but that are nonetheless major exporters of manufactured goods. Thus, though proximity to the appropriate natural resources is undoubtedly a factor in determining the success of most types of manufactures, manufacturing is usually not tied down by geological factors or by climate to the extent that extractive industry and even agriculture are. The necessary raw materials can be imported, albeit usually at extra cost, so there is at least some opportunity for manufacturing in a vast variety of locations and climates.

The location of service industries is often even less restricted by natural resources than manufacturing, but the statistics and other information on services is much poorer than it is for manufacturing. Since manufacturing is often not dramatically dependent on natural resources and is better recorded in the available statistics than trade in services, the pattern of exports of manufactures can sometimes tell us more about what types of economic arrangements or systems are effective than can trade in raw materials, agricultural commodities, or services.

Conventional explanations of success in manufacturing

Many reasons have been offered for why some countries are major producers and exporters of manufactured goods and others are not. In the formal theory of international trade, the emphasis in explaining comparative advantage is on the relative endowments of the different factors of production, and most notably the relative endowments and relative prices of labor and capital. The Heckscher-Ohlin-Stolper-Samuelson (HOSS) theory suggests that countries with the appropriate mix of labor and capital would have comparative advantage in manufacturing and that free trade would tend to equalize factor price ratios across countries.

The HOSS theory is certainly an interesting and useful part of the theory of international trade, and sophisticated econometric studies by economists such as Edward Leamer have shown it has some explanatory power. Nonetheless, it falls very short of providing an adequate explanation of which countries have comparative advantage in manufacturing.

The Common Market countries and the United States are major exporters of manufactured goods, but so are Hong Kong, Korea, and Taiwan. Does anyone believe that the capital–labor ratio and the wage–rental ratio is the same in the Common Market and the United States as it is in Hong Kong, Korea, and Taiwan? The wage–rental ratio appears to be similar in Australia and West Germany, yet the former country exports very little of its manufactures and the latter a high proportion of its manufacturing production. To be sure, if "manufactures" were disaggregated into product categories we would probably see that the wage–rental ratio had an influence, but the great diversity of the wage–rental ratios in different manufacturing countries, and even in countries that export the same manufactured products, suggests that the HOSS theory is very far indeed from being sufficient to explain comparative advantage in manufacturing.

If we change our assumptions and assume that capital is mobile and labor not, while staying within the framework of established formal trade theory, we get the prediction that capital will move toward the countries with lower wages and that manufacturing will tend to take place in these countries. There are certainly instances where this sort of movement of capital and location of manufacturing activities occurs, but again we do not get even a moderately good explanation of where most manufacturing occurs. Though there are some fairly low-wage countries, like Hong Kong, Korea, and Taiwan, that export a lot of manufactures, the great preponderance of manufacturing exports come from some of the most prosperous and high-wage countries in the world, such as the Common Market countries, Japan, and the United States. The major exporters of manufactures have been high-wage countries ever since the British Industrial Revolution. Thus our conventional formal trade theory, valuable as it is, is by no means sufficient to explain what countries have comparative advantage in manufacturing.

It is sometimes said that a large domestic market is necessary for comparative advantage in manufacturing. This can help, but it is neither necessary nor sufficient for the development of internationally competitive manufacturing. Austria, Hong Kong, Finland, Korea, Norway, Sweden, Switzerland, and Taiwan all sell a large part of their manufactures on competitive international markets, but none of these countries has a large home market. The Soviet Union has a huge home market and allocates much of its resources to manufacturing, but about the only goods it is able to sell on competitive world markets are the outputs of its extractive industries. So a large market cannot be a crucial determinant of comparative advantage in manufacturing.

It is similarly sometimes argued that proximity to the largest markets for manufactures in Western Europe and North America is necessary if a country is to be able to export much manufactures. But the success in exporting manufactures of Hong Kong, Japan, Korea, and Taiwan shows that this is not true. Mexico is right next to the country with the largest market for manufactures, and it devotes a large part of its resources to manufacturing, yet unlike the countries just mentioned, it is able to sell very little of its manufactures in the United States or in any other foreign country. (The buoyant demand of American employers for Mexican workers that have legally or illegally entered the United States, and indeed the preference of some of these employers for these employees over indigenous workers, shows that the explanation for Mexico's failure to develop competitive manufacturing cannot be the characteristics of its labor force.) Egypt, Greece, Turkey, East Germany, and the other countries of Eastern Europe are also well placed to sell manufactures in the huge and Common Market, which (like the United States), has *relative* to other countries, only modest protection of manufactures. So proximity to the large markets of Europe and North America is again neither a necessary nor a sufficient condition for the emergence of comparative advantage in manufacturing.

Does protection of manufactures promote industrialization?

Let us now turn to the common contention that the development of manufacturing in a country depends to a great degree on the extent to which manufactures are protected. Many people suppose that successful manufacturing almost always begins with protection. Even many economists would argue that protection of infant industries may in due course give a country a comparative advantage in manufacturing that it would not otherwise have had, and that the country may profit significantly from taking advantage of the new pattern of comparative advantage that protection has given it. Comparative advantage is certainly not something that is given and static, but something that is made or achieved.

One way to develop a competitive manufacturing industry, it is often said, is to protect this sector so that there will be learning-by-doing, and in due course the industry will be competitive. When opposing the protection of manufactures, economists usually emphasize the point from static analysis that the marginal social product of the resources that flow into the protected manufacturing sectors would be less than it would have been in other sectors had there been no protection, but take it for granted that protection of manufactures would increase the extent of manufactured output in a country.

The conventional wisdom about the need for protection of manufactures in developing countries and the very different argument in *The Rise and Decline of Nations* can each be tested against the facts in a new way by looking at the trade in manufactures of the small and medium-sized countries. We know from our earlier thought-experiment with the hypothetical country including all the world except Luxembourg, that it is only in small and medium-sized countries that protection will have its greatest impact. Thus if we ignore the largest countries and focus on manufacturing in small and medium-sized countries with very different degrees of protection, we stand a chance of getting effects from protec-

Table 8.1. *Comparisons of export percentages for small, medium-sized, and developing countries, 1973*

	Manufactured exports/ manufactured output	Exports of "true" manufactures[b]/ total exports	Exports of manufactures and processed primary products[c]/total exports
Argentina	2.5*	17	66
Australia	7.5[a]	11	57
Austria	32.5	53	97
Brazil	5.0*	16	54
Canada	20.0	36	72
Chile	2.5*	1	86
Colombia	7.5*	12	31
Denmark	42.5	42	90
Finland	27.5	30	97
Greece	12.5	22	71
India	7.5	44	62
Ireland	37.5	36	83
Israel	15.0*	27	47
Korea	40.0*	64	93
Mexico	5.0*	30	64
Netherlands	45.0	33	85
New Zealand	5.0	14	80
Norway	35.0	40	91
Portugal	27.5	48	89
Singapore	42.5	37	76
Spain	16.0	43	85
Sweden	37.5	52	95
Taiwan	50.0*	na	85
Turkey	2.5*	13	34
Yugoslavia	17.5*	47	91

[a]Average of 1972, 1973, and 1974.
[b]Manufactured exports include International Standard Industrial Classification subcategories 32 (textiles), 38 (metal manufactures), and 39 (other manufactures).
[c]Manufactured exports include all processed primary products that are classified as manufactures in UN statistics.
Source: For column 1, United Nations statistics, except for the asterisked figures, which were obtained from Bela Balassa, of Johns Hopkins University, Washington; for column 2, *Yearbook of International Trade Statistics*, United Nations, New York; for 1978 and 1979; and for column 3, the same two UN yearbooks plus *Economic Daily News*, Taipei, and *Economic Yearbook of the Republic of China 1980*, Taipei.

tionist as compared with open trading policies that are large enough to overwhelm the many other variables that are relevant.

The econometric results about the small quantitative importance of freer trade mentioned at the beginning of this essay suggest that we are not likely to get any decisive results even in small and medium-sized countries. On the other hand,

Table 8.2. *Average levels of industrial tariffs*

	No trade weighting:[a] simple average		Own-country import weighting[b]		"World" weights[c]			
					Import weights on BTN aggregates[d]		Import weights on each BTN commodity[e]	
	1976	Final[f]	1976	Final	1976	Final	1976	Final
Australia								
Dutiable[g]	28.8	28.0	29.1	28.1	27.8	26.7	26.4	25.2
Total[h]	16.9	16.5	15.4	15.1	13.3	12.8	13.0	12.6
New Zealand								
Dutiable	31.4	28.3	28.6	25.5	33.0	30.4	30.2	27.5
Total	24.3	21.9	19.7	17.6	20.5	18.7	18.0	16.3
European Community								
Dutiable	8.8	6.0	9.8	7.2	9.5	7.0	9.6	7.1
Total	8.0	5.5	6.3	4.6	7.0	5.2	6.9	5.1
United States								
Dutiable	15.6	9.2	8.3	5.7	9.2	5.5	7.6	4.8
Total	14.8	8.8	6.2	4.3	7.1	4.1	5.6	3.5
Japan[i]								
Dutiable	8.1	6.2	6.9	4.9	8.0	5.7	7.9	5.5
Total	7.3	5.6	3.2	2.3	6.1	4.4	5.8	4.1
Canada								
Dutiable	13.7	7.8	13.1	8.9	12.0	7.3	12.9	8.3
Total	12.0	6.8	10.1	6.8	8.9	5.5	9.4	6.1
Austria								
Dutiable	14.2	9.8	18.8	14.5	15.9	12.0	17.0	13.3
Total	11.6	8.1	14.5	11.2	10.5	7.9	10.9	8.5
Finland								
Dutiable	17.0	14.6	11.6	9.2	11.2	9.0	11.5	9.1
Total	14.3	12.3	8.2	6.5	6.7	5.3	6.7	5.3
Norway								
Dutiable	11.1	8.2	10.5	8.0	10.2	7.4	10.0	7.5
Total	8.5	6.3	6.4	4.9	5.8	4.3	5.8	4.4

(continued)

various arguments in *The Rise and Decline of Nations* claim to show that distributional coalitions can have a colossal quantitative significance and that protection, especially in manufacturing, can greatly facilitate collective action to collude and cartelize. Thus, especially if the tests should be favorable to countries with relatively low protection of manufactures, we should be sensitive to whether the effects are large or small.

Unfortunately, the test of the argument in *The Rise and Decline of Nations* will be complicated by the fact that different countries have been stable for different lengths of time. By my own argument this is another factor that will have to be taken into account in assessing the extent to which the results support or confirm the theory in that book. Nonetheless, I would suggest that a study of the effects of

Table 8.2. (*cont.*)

	No trade weighting,[a] simple average		Own-country import weighting[b]		"World" weights[c]			
					Import weights on BTN aggregates[d]		Import weights on each BTN commodity[e]	
	1976	Final[f]	1976	Final	1976	Final	1976	Final
Sweden								
Dutiable	7.8	6.1	7.7	5.9	7.4	5.3	7.1	5.2
Total	6.2	4.9	6.3	4.8	4.6	3.3	4.5	3.3
Switzerland								
Dutiable	3.7	2.7	4.1	3.3	4.2	3.1	4.0	3.1
Total	3.7	2.7	4.0	3.2	3.3	2.4	3.2	2.4

[a]An average of tariff levels on the assumption that all commodities are of equal significance.
[b]The relative weight attributed to each tariff is given by the imports of that commodity by that country.
[c]The significance of each tariff determined by world imports of the commodity, or aggregate of commodities, to which the tariff applies. World imports are the imports of the countries listed and the European Community.
[d]BTN stands for the Brussels Tariff Nomenclature. The weight attributed to each tariff is given by the world imports of the BTN class of commodities in which it falls.
[e]Each tariff weighted by world imports of that particular commodity – the maximum attainable disaggregation.
[f]"Final" means after the tariff reductions agreed in the Tokyo Round multilateral trade negotiations of 1973–79.
[g]Average tariff levels considering only those commodities on which tariffs are levied.
[h]Average tariff levels of duty-free commodities as well as those to which duties apply.
[i]Some anecdotal evidence, as well as casual impressions of the relatively high costs that Japanese consumers must pay for many imported goods, and the fact that agricultural tariffs are not included raise the question whether these figures may give the impression that the level of protection is lower than it actually is.
Source: Office of the United States Trade Representative, Washington, D.C.

protection that focuses only on small and medium-sized countries will be more instructive than any study that leaves the size of the market out of the account, and that the neglect of the length of time countries have had to form distributional coalitions will not matter for testing the conventional case for protection of manufacturing.

Thanks to the research assistance of Kim Chohan, Alfred Forline, Michael Kendix, and Young Park, I can present calculations of the percentage of the manufacturing output of various small and medium-sized countries that is exported. In other words, for all those small and medium-sized countries on which we found the needed data, I had the gross value of each country's manufacturing exports divided by the gross value of its manufacturing output. I would have liked to divide the value added in manufactured exports by the value added in manufacturing in a country, but we did not find the data needed to do this. So what is presented in Table 8.1 is the gross value of manufacturing exports divided by the gross value of manufacturing output, providing of course the percentage of a country's manufacturing that a country succeeds in exporting.

To ensure that the water is not muddied by countries so large that most of their trade would be internal trade even without any protection, I have excluded Italy and all larger developed industrial countries, and above all Japan and the United States. If countries are undeveloped and thus small in industrial firms, they are included however large their populations might be. I should also mention that the year for which we have the most data is 1973, because Bela Balassa and his associates at the World Bank made the needed estimates and calculations for that year for various developing countries, and for these developing countries we don't always have data in other years. So we have in Table 8.1 a sample of countries that includes almost all of the developed democratic countries that are small or medium-sized and those of developing countries on which there is Balassa data for 1973. Table 8.2 contains the indexes of levels of tariffs on manufactured goods in the developed democracies that I had previously published in *The Rise and Decline of Nations*.

There is a striking pattern: If the countries have high levels of protection on manufacturing, without a single exception, they export very little of their manufactures. Argentina, a country that is unquestionably highly protectionist, exports only about 2.5 percent of its manufactures. (I have rounded all numbers to the nearest 2.5 percent to underline the shortcomings of the data and the approximate character of the calculations.) So it was with other highly protectionist countries in 1973. Chile exported only 2.5 percent of its manufactures; Colombia only 7.5 percent; Greece only 12.5 percent; India only 7.5 percent; Mexico only 5 percent; Turkey only 2.5 percent. Brazil (a questionable inclusion because of its large size) exported only 5 percent of its manufactures. New Zealand, which Table 8.2 shows is the most protectionist of manufacturing of all the developed democracies, also exported only 5 percent of its manufacturing production. Australia is the second most protectionist on manufactures of the developed democracies, and exported only about 7.5 percent of its manufactured output. In many of these countries there is a lot of labor and other resources devoted to manufacturing, but only a small percentage of the manufactured output can advantageously be sold in the competitive world market.

Let us look now at countries of similar industrial size with relatively open policies. Austria, a member of the European Free Trade Association with relatively low tariffs, exports about 33 percent of its manufactures. Denmark, a country singularly lacking in natural resources for manufacturing, nonetheless exports 42.5 percent of its manufactured output. Korea, with relatively open policies on manufacturing, at least by the standards of developing countries, exports 40 percent of its manufacturing output. Similarly, the other countries with relatively little industrial protection export a large part of their manufactures: the Netherlands, 45 percent; Norway, 35 percent; Portugal, 27.5 percent; Singapore, 42.5 percent; Sweden, 37.5 percent; Taiwan, 50 percent. *For the small and medium-sized countries on which I have succeeded in getting data, there is not a single exception to the rule that the countries that protect manufactures least, export manufactures most.*

A general equilibrium qualification

At this point a specialist in international economics, or any economist who remembers his general equilibrium theory, may object that there is an alternative explanation of the results. The country that has high levels of protection for manufactures may export very little of its manufactures, not because the protection promotes an institutional sclerosis that is fatal to the efficiency of its manufacturing industry, but simply because protection that reduces imports will also tend to reduce exports. Over the long run the imports and exports of a country must tend to balance, so countries that do not import much also will not export much.

If protection of all kinds and exports of all kinds were at issue, this objection would have more force. But it is protection of industrial products only that has been considered. Consider countries such as Austria, Switzerland, the Scandinavian countries, and the Common Market nations. All of these countries are exceptionally protectionist where agriculture is concerned, but relatively speaking they are not very protectionist in manufacturing. The high protection of agriculture in these countries raises the value of their currencies and reduces the extent of their exports of manufactures. Yet they nonetheless export a large percentage of their manufactures, and my hypothesis is that this is because the low levels of protection for industry in these countries have kept them from being as sclerotic as they could otherwise be. Similarly, many of the countries, such as Argentina, with extraordinarily high levels of industrial protection do nonetheless export a fair amount of primary products. Again, I hypothesize that the primary product exports of these countries show that the problem is in large part sclerosis in their manufacturing industry, not simply the higher value of their currency due to protection in general.

To test this argument in a general way, I turn now to some new calculations. These calculations are in the two rightmost columns in Table 8.1. These columns provide alternative measures of the *proportion* of a country's *exports* that are manufactured or "processed" products. Though any definition of manufactures is somewhat arbitrary, the middle column is probably the better measure of "true" manufactures. (Fortunately, the results are probably not very sensitive to the definition of manufactures as the two columns are positively correlated.)

These data show that there is a distinct (though not a very strong) tendency for the countries with *high* levels of *protection* of *manufactures* to have a *relatively low percentage* of exports that are *manufactures*. This suggests that the protection of manufactures may well discourage efficiency *disproportionately* in the manufacturing sector, as high levels of collusion in and lobbying for these sectors would be predicted to do.

There is further evidence that the failure of those small and medium-sized countries that lavishly protect manufactures to develop profitable manufacturing export industries is not due only to exchange rate effects. A country that changes from relatively open policies to high protection of manufactures may actually reduce the rate of growth of manufacturing output for domestic as well as international use. After 1930 and especially under the regime of Juan Peron, Argentina dramatically increased its protection of manufactures and systematically exploited its agricultural export industries. As a skillful and apparently balanced study by Carlos Diaz Alejandro puts it, "The most ironic lesson of postwar Argentine experience is that if there had been less discrimination against exports, manufacturing expansion would have been greater. Indeed, the annual growth rate of manufacturing during 1900–29 (5.6 percent) was higher than during 1929–65 (3.7 percent)" (Diaz Alejandro 1970: 138; see also 126, 139–40, 252, 259–60 and 271–2). This Argentine experience also provides a further fragment of evidence that high manufacturing protection generates a generalized sclerosis with quantitatively significant effects.

There is another factor that probably also helps to explain the limited proportion of exports that are manufactures in countries that are very protective of manufacturing. The supply curves of many primary product industries may be relatively inelastic, so *some* of the enterprises in these industries will be able to produce *some* output at modest costs even when the country's institutions are not efficient. Countries with some exceptionally good mines or oil wells may be expected to export some of the yield of their natural resources even if the whole economy is badly organized.[1] The Soviet Union fails to sell much manufactured goods in free foreign markets, and has even lost the large agricultural exports it had in Czarist times; it does nonetheless export relatively large amounts of the production of its mines and wells, and thus may illustrate this point.

Drawing the strands together

Let us recapitulate. It appears that the patterns of trade in manufactured goods provide better insights into the efficiency of the institutions and policies of a country than do patterns of trade in primary products or services. This is because the dependence of manufactures on the endowments of natural resources is not as strong as in the case of primary products and because the data on manufacturing are better than those on services. Many people have argued that nations can often achieve comparative advantage in manufacturing, or at the least greatly increase a country's output of manufactured goods, by protecting manufacturing production, at least in the early stages of manufacturing development. The nurture of infant industries and learning-by-doing can sometimes give a country a compara-

---

[1] I am thankful to Christopher Clague for calling this point to my attention.

tive advantage in manufactures that it would not otherwise have had, and at the least protection of manufactures will induce resources in a country to shift into manufacturing and therefore increase the output of manufactures.

Other factors that are widely supposed to influence the international location of manufacturing industry, such as the size of the domestic market, the distance to the large markets of Europe and North America, the capital–labor ratio in a country, and (at least when capital is mobile) low wage levels, do not in fact explain the successes or failures of nations in manufacturing exports at all well. They are accordingly probably not of decisive quantitative significance, and may even be relatively unimportant.

Previous studies of the impact of protection have focused upon the height of protective barriers, but the mileage of such barriers, which is determined principally by the size of the jurisdictions around which there are barriers to trade, should be of greater quantitative significance. An examination of the major cases of "jurisdictional integration" indicates that the most notable instances of the freeing of trade through reductions in the mileage of protective barriers have been associated with dramatic economic advances. The extent of these advances is inconsistent with the comparative-static calculations of the losses from protection of the kind that were cited earlier in this analysis, which suggest that these losses are relatively modest. This in turn suggests that protection, particularly in long-stable jurisdictions with unchanged boundaries, not only deprives countries of the gains from following their comparative advantage, but also has other adverse effects of probably greater quantitative significance. Theories developed in my other publications indicate that protection hastens the development of an "institutional sclerosis" in stable societies, and the presence or absence of such sclerosis is dramatically correlated with economic performance.

All of the available data, for the small and medium-sized countries that can be affected most by protection, on the proportions of the manufactured output that are sold on competitive international markets fit into a clear pattern. This pattern is exactly what would be expected from the theory and from the history of jurisdictional integration. It is, on the other hand, strikingly inconsistent with the familiar notion that comparative advantage in manufactures is normally attained by using protection to nurture infant industries and promote learning-by-doing. The strong pattern in the data even raises grave questions about whether the conclusion from comparative-static theory, that protection of manufactures, however inefficient, will increase manufacturing output, is always correct for the long run, when the interaction between protection and distributional coalitions will also have an impact. The success of so many countries with relatively low levels of protection in developing competitive manufacturing industries and exports of manufactures, even when they lack most of the raw materials needed for manufacturing, and the failure of the small and medium-sized protectionist countries to attain impressive outputs of manufactured goods, implies that there can be no confidence that protection of manufactures will in the long run increase manufacturing output in a country.

It would be going too far, of course, to conclude that the interaction between protection and distributional coalitions is the entire explanation of the correlation between openness to imports of manufactures and jurisdictional integration, on the one hand, and success in developing competitive manufacturing industry, on the other. Economists have long been aware that protection of manufactures tends to raise the cost of the manufactured inputs needed by the manufacturers in the country with the protection. The protection in many countries of the steel industry, for example, obviously raises the costs of manufacturing many other goods in these countries and thus tends to discourage other types of manufacturing. The tendency for protection of manufacturing to raise the costs of inputs needed by other manufacturing industries has been dramatically evident in Argentina, for example, where after heroic increases in levels of protection the cost of the capital goods needed to expand manufacturing as well as other industries increased substantially and were relatively far higher than in less protectionist countries (Diaz Alejandro, 1970: 310, 319, 330, 346–7).

How could economists possibly have underestimated free trade?

If the theoretical argument and the historical and statistical evidence presented in this chapter are correct, the specialists in international trade were right to be very skeptical about protection, and probably even right in being cautious about protection of infant industries. But some of them were probably wrong in concluding that protection was of only modest quantitative significance. It may seem incredible that economists, with their centuries-old bias in favor of free trade, could possibly have underestimated the losses from protection. How could this be?

There are at least two reasons why modern economists have probably underestimated the gains from freer trade.

The first reason is that the usual method of calculating the gains from freer trade captures only areas under *given* supply and demand curves. But, if the argument here is correct, protection also tends to keep firms from attaining the more efficient production functions and lower costs that they would have attained with freer trade. Thus the traditional method fails to capture the gains to a country from lower cost production of what it produces under both protection and free trade, but produces more cheaply under the latter policy. Since these smaller countries that succeed in developing profitable exports of manufactures appear to be much less protective of manufactures, they are apparently more likely to develop manufacturing export industries that the countries that are highly protective of manufactures fail to develop; the relatively open small economy is a very different economy that even produces different goods and different exports than it would have produced had it been protectionist. But the gains to a country from profitably exporting a good that it would not be able to export, or to produce at all, under protection are obviously not captured in the economists' familiar comparative-static calculations. These calculations can, accordingly, colossally underestimate the gains from freer trade.

The second reason why economists have probably underestimated the gains from adopting the trade policies they prefer is evident only when we remember that traditionally economists looked only at the market, and left "political," "social," and "historical" factors to other disciplines. This traditional conception of economics goes back to the late nineteenth century, though admittedly not all the way back to Adam Smith, or even to Karl Marx and John Stuart Mill. I hypothesize that the narrower definition of economics that was dominant from the late nineteenth century until very recent years has introduced a bias that has worked in the opposite direction from the economists' traditional presumption in favor of free trade: It has until lately kept the economist from looking to the side, at what he thought was the domain of other disciplines. But it is only there that the organizational or coalitional mechanisms through which protection does the most damage can be seen.

References

Balassa, Bela. (1967). "Trade Creation and Trade Diversion in the European Common Market." *Economic Journal* 77: 1–21.

Diaz Alejandro, Carlos. (1970). *Essays on the Economic History of the Argentine Republic*. New Haven, Conn.: Yale University Press.

Harberger, Arnold C. (Ed.). (1984). *World Economic Growth*. San Francisco: ICS Press.

Kreinin, Mordechai. (1974). *Trade Relations of the EEC: An Empirical Investigation*. New York: Praeger.

Olson, Mancur. (1986). "A Theory of the Incentives Facing Political Organizations: Neo-Corporatism and the Hegemonic State." *International Political Science Review* 2: 165–89.

(1982). *The Rise and Decline of Nations: Economic Growth, Stagflation and Social Rigidities*. New Haven, Conn.: Yale University Press.

(1965). *The Logic of Collective Action*. Cambridge, Mass.: Harvard University Press.

Truman, Edwin. (1969). "The European Economic Community: Trade Creation and Trade Diversion." *Yale Economic Essays* 9: 201–51.

9.   Comparative advantage and public security perceptions in Western alliance security policies

Mark A. Boyer

Western alliance nations[1] possess a core of security objectives that one might broadly identify as containment of hostile influences in the world (which, for decades, referred primarily to the Soviet Union), perpetuation of a stable and open international economy, and domestic and international political stability, all of which can be identified to some degree as public goods. Quite naturally, each nation possesses a different hierarchy of preferred policy tools and also has other private objectives aside from the collective's security concerns.[2] But although such differences can at times divide the alliance, they can also be a resource for strengthening alliance security by focusing attention on the positive exploitation of divergent policy preferences (and variations in the intensity with which these preferences are held) rather than to the extent to which these preferences divide the alliance. With this in mind, this chapter examines the common and divergent preferences that exist within the alliance as they pertain to the recurrent debate about sharing the burden of security.

For many years burden-sharing has been an apparent point of controversy among the Western allies. Beginning with Olson and Zeckhauser's "An Economic Theory of Alliances" (1966), many authors[3] have pointed to the persistent

This research has been supported by an award of a Social Science Research Council–MacArthur Foundation Fellowship in International Peace and Security and a Faculty Research Grant from the University of Connecticut Research Foundation. The author wishes to thank Davis Bobrow, Richard Flickinger, Elizabeth Hanson, Pat James, and Jonathan Wilkenfeld for helpful comments and suggestions. This paper originally was prepared for presentation at the annual meetings of American Political Science Association, Atlanta, August 31 to September 3, 1989.

[1] Throughout this chapter the Western alliance is understood to be the series of political, economic, and military relationships that exist among the European countries of the North Atlantic Treaty Organization (NATO), the United States, and Japan.

[2] In reality, no goods produced by an alliance will be purely public. To the contrary, alliance goods will range from nearly pure public goods (e.g., containment of Soviet influence is at least public within the Western "club") to mixed public and private goods (e.g., conventional defense; see Sandler, 1977) to private (e.g., the use of military forces for internal security).

[3] See, for example, Murdoch and Sandler, (1984, 1982); Nelson and Lepgold, 1986; Oneal, 1989; Russett, 1970; Sandler and Forbes, 1980; and Ypersele de Strihou, 1967.

"free-riding" by many allies on the defense efforts of the United States. In addition, members of the U.S. Congress (e.g., Mike Mansfield in the 1960s and 1970s and Sam Nunn in the 1980s) have repeatedly proposed legislation that would pressure the Europeans and Japan to increase their military spending in an effort to move some of the alliance defense burden from American shoulders. Rather surprisingly though, burden-sharing has rarely become a particularly divisive alliance issue, even though some have taken steps to make it one. In fact, the *Report to Congress on Allied Contributions to the Common Defense*, mandated by the Nunn Amendment and published annually by the American Secretary of Defense, is an amazingly upbeat appraisal of the military security efforts undertaken by the allies, even though the actual numbers contained in the report offer a somewhat different picture. This apparent free-riding occurs because a public good, in this case Western defense, is by definition jointly supplied (i.e., consumption by one individual does not diminish the amount available for others) and nonexcludable (i.e., once the good is provided for one, others cannot be excluded from consumption). Allies are, therefore, theoretically expected to free-ride on the defense expenditures of larger alliance nations.

Nonetheless, one is struck by the apparent complacency of the United States regarding the alliance burden-sharing state of affairs. Why has greater emphasis not been placed on promoting defense burden-sharing by American policymakers? The answer to this question becomes clearer when considering the changes that have occurred in the international system over the past thirty years: Examination of the burden-sharing issue only from a military spending perspective neglects the broader security interests and varying policy tools used within the Western alliance system. Events such as the two oil shocks of the 1970s and the collapse of the Bretton Woods international economic system forced a redefinition of national security beyond the narrow military realm. Authors such as Brown (1977), Mathews (1989), and Ullman (1983), also point to the increasing need to broaden concepts of national security to include problems relating to resource supply security, terrorism, demographics, and the environment. Along these lines, the Western nations have shown an increasing tendency to consider nonmilitary problems as part of their security calculations both domestically and within the collective alliance context.[4] Moreover, a recent study found that even in the United States where strong support for military spending continues,[5] nearly 60 percent of the respondents felt "that threats to our national security are changing, and that these new threats require different kinds of national policies than the ones the United States has relied upon in the past" (Marttila, 1989: 266).[6]

---

[4] See Bobrow, 1984, and Defense Agency, 1987, for discussion of Japanese definitions of security. Flynn et al. (1981), Flynn and Rattinger (1985), Schmidt (1978), and Sloan (1985) all present ideas regarding the redefinition of national security by various NATO countries.

[5] See data in tables of this chapter.

[6] The poll data found in the Marttila study show that in 1988 the American public was more concerned about threats to security posed by international drug trafficking, terrorism, and nuclear proliferation in the Third World than it was about the threat of Soviet expansionism (p. 265–7).

So if alliance nations are increasingly defining security in more than military terms, analyses of burden-sharing should not continue to focus only on military spending as the measure of national contributions to alliance security. In more technical terms, if the security utility functions (the curve that illustrates the combination of security goods desired) of individual allies are defined across multiple alliance goods, evaluations of alliance security must also consider the levels of provision of goods other than military defense. Otherwise, the analysis assumes that a nation's security, or utility, is defined only by the results shown by a single policy instrument.

More accurately, burden-sharing analyses must move toward the examination of the many other ways Western nations contribute to alliance security. Quantitatively, one could examine foreign aid expenditures and research and development spending, as each produces goods that serve alliance purposes. One can also examine cooperation among alliance nations in the monetary realm in an effort to understand which nations are bearing the brunt of the monetary adjustment burden of promoting stable and prosperous Western economies. Other alliance contributions, such as efforts to maintain the liberal trading order or efforts to bolster alliance political solidarity, can also be identified and analyzed.

As a result, this chapter moves toward more comprehensive analyses of burden-sharing by examining the divergent security preferences that exist within the Western alliance system. This task serves two purposes. At a theoretical level, such an endeavor is based on the assumptions of Ricardian trade theory[7] that policy constraints produce conditions that can facilitate a division of labor among the allies regarding alliance security. These political comparative advantages can promote alliance contribution specialization and ultimately produce more efficient alliance security provision.[8] This is particularly relevant when considering that past work in burden-sharing and the theory of alliances has focused on the provision of a single public good, alliance military defense, and has neglected the potential gains from trade that occur when alliance nations

---

[7] Ricardian trade theory is based on the idea that nations can obtain increases in welfare by specializing in the production of certain goods that they can produce more efficiently than can other nations. This nation should then send the good or goods it produces to other nations in exchange for the goods it does not produce at home but that are produced more efficiently by the other nations. Through specialization and trade, all nations receive the goods they desire for the lowest possible prices and thus reach the highest welfare levels possible.

[8] Efficiency in this context refers to the Pareto criterion. If an outcome is Pareto optimal, no individual in the collective can be made better off without making someone else worse off. When dealing with private goods, this means that the marginal rate of substitution (the slope of the utility function at a given point) equals the marginal rate of transformation (the slope of the production constraint at a given point). For public goods the *sum* of the marginal rates of substitution for all members of the collective must equal the marginal rate of transformation. Because of the nature of public goods, an efficient production outcome is unlikely in a decentralized decision-making setting. But by introducing intraalliance consultation, comparative advantage, and considerations of multiple alliance goods, one can hypothesize that moves toward Pareto optimality are possible (see Boyer, 1989a,b).

pursue specialization. Such concepts as political comparative advantage and multidimensional burden-sharing necessarily spring from the divergence of national priorities and objectives discussed here.[9] These divergencies can be turned to the advantage of the alliance, if exploited in a productive manner and not taken as evidence of lack of commitment to longer-run collective strategies. Instead of intraalliance differences causing crises in the alliance, as they are often said to do, they can in theory be turned to the advantage of the alliance by promoting more efficient use of alliance political, economic, and military resources.

In and of itself, the concept of political comparative advantage springs from the requisite political responsiveness of national elites in Western political systems. Political responsiveness and the bounded policy-making process it implies in Western nations can be examined through the use of public opinion data on security issues. Although one cannot assert that policymakers will always follow the will of the people, particularly because of its apparent volatility,[10] one should be able to garner a broad outline of the constraints confronting Western national security policymakers and the policy tools that are available to those officials. A number of further clarifications of these concepts are contained in the next section.

From a policy perspective, by examining security preferences, alliance burden-sharing strategies can be devised that focus on the exploitation of political comparative advantages rather than ones that seek to obtain across-the-board spending increases in all expenditure categories. As has been witnessed regarding the NATO 3 percent real growth goal for defense spending (Cheney, 1989:52), some nations have been unwilling or unable to increase one type of spending and should thus be encouraged to devote resources to the areas where they are politically able to do so. In essence, by understanding the policy constraints that exist in each Western alliance nation, one can more finely tune policy initiatives to focus on particular security policy tools that will ultimately yield increased alliance security through contribution specialization.

Some conceptual and methodological concerns

Before moving to the empirical section of this chapter, a number of conceptual and methodological concerns should be addressed. First, a nation's policy constraints and the implications they have for alliance resource allocation are under-

---

[9] It is interesting to note that Olson and Zeckhauser in two pieces (1971, 1967) that followed their seminal article introduced the possibility that comparative advantages could be used to improve the efficiency of defense provision. In these pieces, however, they continued to view security in purely military terms and did not consider the political aspects of comparative advantage in the alliance context.

[10] See Almond (1950) and Converse (1964) for ideas regarding the instability of and lack of solidity in public attitudes toward foreign policy issues. In the public choice literature, Arrow (1951) and numerous others have pointed to the potential for cyclical and unstable outcomes in majority rule settings and the logrolling and vote trading associated with these outcomes.

stood to be functions of political as well as economic factors. The particulars of an ally's domestic political culture create production advantages that differ from the other allies, because no two polities will support identical mixes of policy instruments. In any nation, whether democratic or authoritarian, national security decision-makers face limits to the available range of policy choices by the desires and powers of the constituencies they must serve. In essence, to remain in power decision-makers must maintain a coalition composed of the various constituencies that have supported them in the past or develop new coalitions to remain in power. Either way, decision-makers must satisfy a proportion of the polity large enough to remain in power, but need not satisfy all or even the same constituencies over time.

Thus, if one begins from the assumption that decision-makers will actively work to maintain the required support, then it is logical to assume that policy choices are responsive to constituent interests. In the alliance context this responsiveness might take the form of military spending if the public exhibits support for such spending. In the same country, a leader may be reluctant to adopt domestic economic measures required to correct international economic imbalances, if such policies would have direct negative effects on important constituencies. In countries where opposition to military spending exists, but alliance goals more generally are supported, economic contributions, such as foreign aid or trade concessions, or political contributions, such as accepting military deployments in the face of international pressures, might be the security contributions of choice (or of mandate) for those countries. In this vein, the spring 1989 compromise between Chancellor Kohl and President Bush regarding the elimination of short-range nuclear weapons from German soil and the more active pursuit of arms reduction in Europe can be interpreted as a series of political contributions to the alliance effort made by both sides during the short-lived controversy.

Although the political bases of comparative advantages are the focus of this chapter, it is also instructive to discuss briefly the more purely economic considerations that influence national decisions regarding alliance contributions. The different national endowments of the factors of production, such as land, labor, capital, and technology, naturally affect the shape of national production frontiers. In the case of the production of military goods, substantial economies of scale can be obtained by nations producing large amounts of military goods (see for instance, Hoag, 1967). It is easy to imagine, for example, that it would be cheaper on a per unit basis for a nation to produce 1,000 armored personnel carriers than for a nation to produce only 20 of the same piece of hardware. As for economic security tools, Sloan (1985: 87–9) argues that nations with colonial histories might well be more efficient foreign aid donors than those without colonial histories, because of cultural, historical, and linguistic affinities between donor and recipient nations. Public support (or nonsupport) for research and development and foreign and domestic investment might make certain nations more efficient producers of these types of alliance goods.

A second conceptual point relates to Oppenheimer's (1979) criticism of the application of public goods theory (and its associated "rational actor" viewpoint) to problems of international politics.[11] As he suggests, the assumption that nation-states in aggregate form are the primary decision-making units in the international system may well lead to conceptual errors regarding hypotheses about the ability of nation-states to cooperate effectively with one another (pp. 396–8). In many respects this argument echoes that made by Allison (1971) against the validity of the rational unitary actor model of national decision making. As we all know, policy decisions are often the result of parochial concerns within a governmental system rather than rational evaluations of economic efficiency. Drawing on a wide and varied literature, Oppenheimer enumerates the problems associated with group decisions, such as cyclical outcomes shown in voting theory and the suboptimality theorem of public goods theory.[12] As he suggests, to assume that nations are rational utility maximizers internationally implies that these same collectives have produced a Pareto-optimal result at the national level (1979: 395–6). Theoretical inconsistency as obvious as this requires that one take a much closer look at the assumptions of the public goods theories as applied to international cooperation.

One can respond to Oppenheimer's criticism, as Sandler, Cauley, and Forbes do (1980: 542–4), by stating that the relevant utility maximizers in the international realm are national decision-makers. This idea also suggests that to understand national utility maximization one must investigate the decision making and electoral structures of the nation-states in question. By answering Oppenheimer's criticism of the application of public goods theory to international relations in this way, one can begin to understand the political dimension of comparative advantage and how it affects the ways nations can and do allocate resources to alliance security concerns. For instance, if a particular policy choice would result in loss of office for a decision-maker, that choice will not be found on or within the bounds of a nation's production function. This is analogous to saying in a purely economic context that if a firm has the raw materials to produce only twenty tractors per year, it cannot choose to produce twenty-five tractors per year. Obviously, then, the types of policy decisions discussed in this chapter rule out intentional political suicide. True, the outcomes of policy decisions are often unknown, as evidenced by the myriad political miscalculations that occur in any political system, but in the present context, it is assumed that conscious disregard of the political dimensions of the national production constraint does not occur.

---

[11] As I mentioned previously, public goods theory and its application to alliances by Olson and Zeckhauser (1966) is the intellectual basis of the recurrent free-rider argument in the burden-sharing debate.

[12] The suboptimality theorem of public goods theory as it relates to questions of free-riding and the provision of public goods has been discussed above with reference to the Olson and Zeckhauser alliance article. Cyclical outcomes refer to the existence of the potential for vote trading and logrolling in majority rule decision-making situations, making it difficult for a stable (and lasting) majority decision to be achieved under majority rule.

Several other limitations of the following analysis should also be mentioned. First, the public opinion data discussed in the following pages is data on mass attitudes and not the attitudes of the opinion leaders in Western alliance countries. As a result, this chapter examines the potential constraints on decision-makers rather than the actual preferences of the decision-makers. In addition, the intensity of these opinions is also not examined. Thus, one runs the risk of examining only the views of a "silent majority" and not those of a potentially vociferous and important, even if small, minority (Flynn and Rattinger, 1985: 3–4). Unfortunately, data for opinion leaders is much more difficult to come by and one thus must make conjectures from data once removed from the source of interest. By breaking the data down along educational and age lines, one can also get a more direct reading of opinion leaders' attitudes, but one again is also limited by data availability and faces decreased sample size when categorizing the data in this way.

Second, the following analysis is not so bold as to suggest that definitive answers can be obtained regarding the security preferences of Western alliance countries. Rather, the following is an effort to highlight both the commonalities and the differences that exist within the alliance. The patterns seen throughout the following analysis can and do change over time, but as will be discussed more thoroughly in the concluding section, changing patterns can lead the alliance to adapt to new and different challenges to its security concerns and not necessarily lead to alliance disintegration. This adaptability will likely be tested in the near future in the face of the rapid pace of change in Eastern Europe.

Third, the use of opinion polling in this context implies that respondents will truthfully reveal their preferences regarding security policy choices. As discussed above, one of the principal reasons why public goods are provided at suboptimal levels is that public goods are joint and nonexcludable. As a result, individuals have incentives to lie about their demand for a public good. If the individual reveals his or her true demand, he or she will be expected to pay that share (the marginal rate of substitution) of the cost of public good provision. But if the individual purposely underestimates his or her true demand, he or she is still able to consume the good if it is provided for any individual, thereby free-riding on those showing higher levels of revealed demand. As a result, some skepticism about the absolute validity of public opinion results is warranted, particularly as they relate to questions of provision of public goods. On the other hand, one should note that in contrast to this theoretically identified problem, a variety of experimental studies of the free-rider problem have found that individuals are more inclined in reality to reveal their demand for a public good than they are in theory (Alfano and Marwell, 1981; Marwell and Ames, 1981; 1980; 1979; Scherr and Babb, 1975; Sweeney, 1973; Bohm, 1972).

Public security preferences and national political advantages

Before examining the ways in which allied perceptions of security differ from one another, it is useful to first recognize the degree to which various alliance

Table 9.1A. *Allied commitment to NATO (percentages)*

mo./yr.	NATO is still essential–No longer essential[a]						
	UK	FR	WG	IT	BE	DE	HO
??/67	59–15	34–30	67–17				
10/69	68–15	47–37	76–13	66–23			
07/71	81–12	54–35	84–11				
04/73		42–34	73–13				
07/76	69–15	42–35	85–10	58–30			
03/77	73–08	44–29	79–07	54–24			78–11
03/78	70–10	39–35	84–05	58–22		62–16	71–10
10/80	79–13	44–34	88–08	54–25	56–20		63–26
03/81	70–15		62–20	62–27			62–15
07/82	65–25	34–26	66–18	55–31			67–16
07/83	72–16		86–12	61–26			
05/84	76–12		87–10	63–24	60–20	63–19	58–20
02/87	72–17	49–28	71–11	58–29			
09/87	72–16	48–19	70–15	65–23			
10/87						61–22	
10/88	72–17	58–22	76–13	53–31	66–22	70–23	64–25

[a]"Don't know" answers not listed but can be derived by adding percentages and subtracting from 100.

Note: The following abbreviations apply to all tables in this chapter.

UK = United Kingdom   FR = France   WG = West Germany
US = United States   BE = Belgium   DE = Denmark
IT = Italy   NW = Norway   J = Japan
HO = Netherlands

Sources: Domke, Eichenberg, and Kelleher, 1987: 386; *Public Opinion*, May/June 1989: 21.

nations have been and continue to be committed to the maintenance of their alliance relationships. Tables 9.1A and B show that in each country listed a large degree of support exists regarding the essentiality of NATO, a state of affairs that has not changed much over the past two decades. Not surprisingly, France with its penchant for an independent course shows the most ambivalence regarding the need for NATO, although there appears to be an upswing in support in recent years. Even so, French opinion has always shown at least a plurality supporting NATO. Although asked a somewhat different question, the American public appears to have as strong a commitment to NATO as that of its European partners, a fact demonstrating that throughout the alliance a large degree of solidarity exists with reference to NATO's present and future course. Fitting closely with these findings, Flynn and Rattinger (1985: 375) also found that the NATO publics continue to believe "that NATO is the best way to organize

Table 9.1B. *U.S. commitment to NATO (percentages)*

	Increase or keep commitment	Decrease or end commitment	Don't know
1974	54	20	26
1978	67	13	20
1982	67	15	18
1986	70	16	14

Sources: Domke et al., 1987, p. 387. *Public Opinion,* March/April 1989: 30.

security," even though the publics do not believe that current NATO policies are necessarily the best ways to pursue security. Domke, Eichenberg, and Kelleher (1987) and Capitanchik and Eichenberg (1983) have reached similar conclusions. As Capitanchik and Eichenberg suggest (pp. 80, 86–7), labeling European public sentiments as "neutralism" is too simple an appraisal of European attitudes toward security and defense. The differences that do exist, however, will be seen in what follows.

Table 9.2 highlights some of these differences and provides a good starting point for the analysis of the political comparative advantages possessed by eight Western alliance nations. This table shows wide variation in the menu of issues deemed important in these eight nations. Some of the differences break down along regional lines; others do not. First, one should notice that a high unemployment rate was the most important issue in each nation except Japan. This is not surprising considering the economic slump of the early 1980s and the date the survey was taken. The United States, however, should not be lumped together with the six European countries registering high marks on this issue. As the data show, 61 percent or more of those surveyed in each European country felt unemployment to be an important issue, while only 46 percent felt this way in the United States. Although unemployment was seen as the most important issue for the United States in this survey, it is a much stronger concern for the Europeans. This may have been due to the fact the American economy was somewhat quicker to pull out of the recession than were its European counterparts, making unemployment a more intense concern in Europe (Fitoussi and Phelps, 1986).

Continuing at the macroeconomic level, inflation was accorded lower priority than unemployment in each nation except Japan, where it was a more important issue. Respondents surveyed in France, Italy, and the United States show the greatest concern over this issue of the nations surveyed. Japan was a somewhat distant fourth. Overall, the lower priority results should not be too surprising because of the tendency for lower inflation rates during times of recession.

A number of interesting ideas also emerge in this table regarding military issues. First, respondents in all the countries accorded some concern over the

Table 9.2. *Most important issues (percentages)*

Question: What is the most important issue for you and for your country at the present time?[a]

	FR	WG	UK	IT	HO	NW	US	J
Threat of war	44	28	31	55	37	36	45	42
Energy crisis	14	14	5	22	9	2	23	26
Inflation	46	16	21	41	10	7	38	29
Insufficient defense capability	5	8	7	7	5	6	24	10
High unemployment rate	76	73	61	72	70	66	46	22
Unfairness, inequality in society	26	24	14	30	19	17	24	27
Crime	27	34	37	56	47	16	44	33
Nuclear weapons	26	38	29	35	49	38	37	34
Excessive government deficit	20	25	9	22	17	6	37	21
Poor political leadership	24	15	16	27	19	11	35	22
Other, No answer	1	9	2	4	6	4	3	11

[a]Multiple answers with figures representing percentage of respondents choosing that issue.
Sources: *Asahi Shimbun* (Japan), Atlantic International Issues Research (France), Harris-France, September–November 1983. Taken from Hastings and Hastings, 1986: 718–9.

threat of war, with the highest threat perceived by Italian respondents. In addition, except for high unemployment, the threat of war received the highest values on average across the eight nations.[13] But the response to this issue is only put into perspective when it is examined in tandem with the insufficient defense capability issue. Only in the United States was there a substantial block of respondents (24 percent) finding defense capability an important issue. All other nations showed only small numbers concerned about defense capability, even though in each there were large groups perceiving a threat of war. Tables 9.3A and B provide greater insight into allied support for military spending, as will be seen momentarily.

A number of other patterns should also be identified in Table 9.2. First, nuclear weapons, not surprisingly, were a major concern for respondents in each nation. This result likely reflects the high visibility of nuclear weapons issues in general, but more specifically, the reaction to the beginning of the development

[13] The threat of war results are also supported by survey data obtained in the Group of Five (G-5) countries (United States, United Kingdom, France, Japan, and West Germany). This data showed 54% of Americans answering that war was either very or somewhat likely in the next fifteen years. Thirty-five percent of the Japanese respondents, 29% of the French respondents, 25% of the British respondents, and only 16% of the West German respondents chose either of those two categories. Except for the juxtaposition of Japan and France, the rank ordering of these percentage figures is the same as that in Table 9.2 for the "threat of war" category (Hastings and Hastings, 1987: 592, survey by Gallup International Research Institutes).

Table 9.3A. *Desired level of defense spending (percentages)*

Question: Do you think that *survey country* defense spending should be increased, decreased, or kept at its present level?

	United Kingdom				France		
	10/80	3/81	4/82	?/84	10/80	3/81	4/82
Increase	30	33	44	23	4	15	16
Decrease	10	15	16	20	32	24	24
Keep at present level	47	44	36	52	38	49	55
Don't know	7	8	4	5	25	11	5

	West Germany					Italy			
	10/80	3/81	1/82	4/82	?/84	10/80	3/81	4/82	?/84
Increase	22	15	11	15	7	10	16	16	18
Decrease	19	20	13	26	33	39	43	46	42
Keep at present level	53	50	60	43	58	36	36	34	34
Don't know	17	15	16	16	2	15	6	4	6

Sources: United States Information Agency, 1984, *NATO and Burden-Sharing,* Research Report R-11-84; United States International Communications Agency, 1982, *West European Public Opinion on Key Security Issues 1981–1982,* Research Report, R-10-82; Harris Survey taken from Hastings and Hastings, 1987: 300.

of the Pershing II and ground-launched cruise missiles (GLCMs) in the fall of 1983, coinciding with the time when these surveys were taken. Second, as one would expect, the energy crisis was of greatest importance for Japanese respondents because of the high degree of Japan's dependence on energy imports. The United States and Italy also showed some concern over this issue. Third, excessive governmental deficits were also an important issue for a number of countries, most notably – but not surprisingly – the United States, with 37 percent of the respondents citing it as important.

So from Table 9.2, one can begin to make some general conjectures about the political comparative advantages possessed by various alliance nations. The most striking one pertains to defense capability and threat of war. This concern over defense capability, particularly in the United States, is also reflected in survey data displayed in Tables 9.3A and B regarding support for defense spending. As these tables show, throughout the early 1980s, American support for increases in defense spending was much higher than that in Europe. And even though support for increases tailed off by 1983, strong support for maintenance of the Reagan era defense budgets continued. So although all of the European allies shown here exhibited at least pluralities in favor of current levels of military spending, none, except possibly Great Britain, exhibited the upward pressure shown in the United

Table 9.3B. *Desired level of defense spending (percentages)*

Question: Do you think that *survey country* defense spending should be increased, decreased, or kept at its present level?

	Netherlands		Norway		Denmark	Belgium
	3/81	?/84	3/81	?/84	?/84	?/84
Increase	11	8	21	30	14	7
Decrease	36	29	16	21	22	37
Keep at present level	35	49	52	26	53	46
Don't know	17	14	11	23	11	10

	United States[a]				
	2/80	8/81	3/82	11/83	6/85
Increase	71	58	43	28	14
Decrease	6	16	18	20	32
Keep at present level	21	22	37	47	52
Don't know	2	4	2	5	2

[a]Respondents in the United States were asked, "In general, do you favor increasing or decreasing the present defense budget, or keeping it the same as it is now?"
Sources: United States Information Agency, 1984, *NATO and Burden-Sharing,* Research Report R-11-84; United States International Communications Agency, 1982, *West European Public Opinion on Key Security Issues, 1981–1982,* Research Report R-10-82; Harris Survey taken from Hastings and Hastings, 1987: 300.

States. Next to the United States, Great Britain showed the largest public support for defense increases of any of these allies. This parallels Great Britain's tendency to spend more of its GDP on defense than most other Western allies.[14] If one starts from the more narrow military approach to alliance burden sharing, these findings also tend to support the Olson and Zeckhauser notion that the "small exploit the large" in terms of contributions to alliance military defense. As will be seen shortly, this apparent public tendency is not the same for other policy instruments.

An aversion to increased defense spending similar to that of most Europeans is also shown in Japanese data in Table 9.4, as most favor staying within the limit of 1 percent of gross domestic product or decreasing the military budget. But as will be seen in a moment, such reluctance on the part of the Japanese and the Europeans to increase military spending is not necessarily evidence of reluctance toward taking an active role in alliance and international affairs. As a result, one

[14] In 1987, for instance, among alliance members only the United States and Greece spent more on defense as a percentage of GDP than did Great Britain (Cheney, 1989: 96).

Table 9.4. *Japanese opinions on defense spending (percentages)*

Question: The government has had a policy of maintaining defense spending at less than 1% of GNP (gross national product). However, under the Defense Reorganization Five-Year Program adopted by the Nakasone cabinet, the total defense expenditure is expected to exceed slightly 1% of GNP. What do you think of this plan?

Oppose because it ignores the 1% limit	21
Approve because the excess is slight	29
Defense expenditure should be increased regardless of past limits	6
Defense expenditures should be decreased	31
Other/No answer	13

Question: If the defense budget continues to increase, it may exceed the 1% of the GNP in spite of the government's policy. What do you think about this?

Should keep it within 1%	43
Exceeding 1% may be inevitable	16
Should increase beyond 1%	3
Defense budget should be greatly decreased	23
Don't know/No answer	15

Sources: First question–*Asahi Shimbun*, October 1985; taken from Hastings and Hastings, 1987: 300. Second question–Nippon Hoso Kyoka (Japan Broadcasting Association), February 1984; taken from Hastings and Hastings, 1986: 326.

can then assert that much of the defense buildup decided upon by the alliance in the late 1970s was supported by the American public and largely carried out by American spending levels,[15] fitting closely with the issue concerns shown in Table 9.2. In this sense, the United States put its political comparative advantage to good use in terms of devoting resources to strongly supported spending categories serving alliance security interests at the same time that the allies were politically unable to make the same allocation decisions.

A number of other ideas about allied security perceptions and requirements can be gleaned from public attitudes toward foreign aid. As I mentioned previously, development assistance spending should be viewed as a security policy tool as it promotes a positive alliance image in the world. It also serves the economic interests of the alliance by contributing to economic prosperity and

[15] In 1978 NATO decided that each alliance nation should increase defense spending by an average of 3% above inflation over a five-year period (Sloan, 1987: 80), but few nations have met this goal. The non-U.S. NATO average (ranging from 0.2% to 3.0% during the 1981–86 period) only hit this mark in 1981. The United States, however, exceeded the goal throughout (ranging from 4.6% to 7.9% during the 1981–86 period) (Carlucci, 1988: 53).

Table 9.5A. *Opinions toward development assistance efforts (percentages)*

Question: Now I would like to ask if you think that our aid to the developing countries should be increased, remain the same, or decreased?

1980	BE	CA	DE	FR	UK	IT[a]	LU	HO	WG
Increased	14	25	15	31	13	58	36	16	16
Same	40	40	42	43	36	24	47	61	54
Decreased	34	28	33	18	45	7	13	28	20

[a]Asked the following variation: "Now I would like to ask if you think that aid to the developing countries should be increased, remain the same, or decreased?"
Source: Gallup Political Index, 1980, Report No. 238, June.

Table 9.5B. *Opinions toward development assistance efforts (percentages)*

Question: Do you feel that [country name] should or should not increase aid to underdeveloped countries to assist them to become self-sufficient in the future?

1981	CA	US	WG	UK
Should increase	51	32	35	35
Should not	37	60	64	58
Don't know	12	8	1	8

Source: Gallup Political Index, 1981, Report No. 250, June.

Table 9.5C. *Opinions toward development assistance efforts (percentages)*

Question: If you were told that in order to give more help to Third World countries it would be necessary to hold back 1% from your salary, would you agree to this idea or not?

1983	BE	DE	WG	FR	IT	LU	HO	UK	GR
Agree	39	59	34	48	69	67	63	46	72
Do not agree	46	27	42	45	24	24	27	44	24
No reply	15	14	24	7	7	9	10	10	4

Source: European Economic Community, September–November 1983. Taken from Hastings and Hastings, 1986: 667.

stability in out-of-area regions. The data contained in Tables 9.5A–C, 9.6, and 9.7 demonstrate that just as support for defense spending varies greatly among alliance nations, foreign aid shows varying degrees of public support. Looking over the three questions asked in Tables 9.5A–C, a number of interesting points emerge. First, in the two questions containing Italian data, public support for

Table 9.6. *American attitudes toward foreign aid and defense spending* *(percentages)*

Question: We are faced with many problems in this country, none of which can be solved easily or inexpensively. I'm going to name some of these problems, and for each one I'd like you to tell me whether you think we're spending too much money on it, too little money, or about the right amount. First . . . are we spending too much, too little, or about the right amount on . . .[a]

	Too little	About right	Too much	Don't know
		Foreign aid		
1973	4	20	70	5
1974	3	17	76	4
1975	5	17	73	5
1976	3	18	75	4
1977	3	24	66	7
1978	4	24	67	6
1980	5	20	70	5
1982	5	18	72	5
1983	4	17	74	5
1984	4	21	70	5
1985	7	24	65	4
1986	6	19	71	4
1987	7	20	69	4
1988	5	22	68	5
		The Military, armaments and defense		
1973	11	45	38	6
1974	17	45	31	7
1975	17	46	31	7
1976	24	42	27	7
1977	24	45	23	8
1978	27	44	22	8
1980	50	26	11	6
1982	29	36	30	5
1983	24	38	32	6
1984	17	41	38	3
1985	14	42	40	3
1986	16	38	40	5
1987	15	41	41	4
1988	16	40	38	6

[a]Sampling of national adults done February–April of each year. In 1984 and 1987 this question was asked of approximately one third of total sample. In 1985, 1986, and 1988 this question was asked of approximately half of total sample.
Source: National Opinion Research Center, 1989, *General Social Survey*, Chicago: NOPR.

Table 9.7. *Japanese opinions on security and sea-lane defense (percentages)*

Question: One of the United States' requests for Japan's increased defense capability is that Japan should cover a 1,000-mile sea lane outside of Japan. Have you heard of this request?

Have heard	37
Have not heard	58
No answer	5

(If "have heard":) Which of the following opinions on sea lane defense do you agree with? (Choose one)

It is necessary for Japan's security and continued access to natural resources.	33
It is currently impossible because the defense plan requires a large increase in Japan's defense capability	14
Security should be maintained by diplomacy and economic cooperation, rather than military measures. Therefore, I am against the defense plan.	46
Other	1
No answer	6

Source: *Yomiuri Shimbun*, October 1984. Taken from Hastings and Hastings, 1986: 328.

foreign aid in Italy appears quite high. This is particularly striking in the 1980 question, as Italy registers by far the highest support for increased foreign aid of any country surveyed. Second, support for foreign aid is also rather strong in Luxembourg, Denmark, the Netherlands, Canada, and Greece. French opinion also tends toward the supportive side. The United Kingdom, Belgium, and West Germany exhibit somewhat lower support for foreign aid than the other Europeans. Initially, one might be inclined to attribute these differences in attitudes toward foreign aid to ideological differences among the various countries. Noting the degree to which the welfare state is an entrenched part of the political system, one should not be too surprised at the high support found for Luxembourg, Denmark, and the Netherlands, but is left with questions regarding the low degree of support found in Belgium and West Germany. In addition, it would also be instructive to obtain data on attitudes toward bilateral foreign aid donations (more purely private goods) and donations to multilateral aid-giving organizations (more purely public goods). In any case, more refined opinion measures are needed to evaluate European attitudes thoroughly in this policy area.

The verdict for the United States becomes clearer when one combines the results of the 1981 question in Table 9.5B with those of Table 9.6, which compare public support for foreign aid with that of military spending. It is clear from Table 9.6 that the American opposition to foreign aid increases indicated in Table 9.5B is not an isolated occurrence. Table 9.6 shows that while the defense budget is generally supported during the 1973–88 period, foreign aid spending is widely opposed by the American public.[16] This opposition is reflected in the relatively low percentage of GDP that the United States has traditionally devoted to foreign aid donations and also fits with the substantial military buildups (under Truman, Kennedy, Carter, and Reagan) that have occurred during the post-war era.

Moving to another ally, Table 9.7 presents a number of ideas relating to Japanese security preferences. Specifically, with regard to the 1,000-mile sea-lane defense question, a substantial plurality (46 percent) of the respondents who have heard of the sea-lane defense issue prefer that security be maintained through diplomacy and economic cooperation rather than military means.[17] Accordingly, one can conjecture that Japan possesses a potential political advantage in alliance burden-sharing in the economic realm. This follows logically from policy statements and analyses of the Japanese policy of comprehensive security as discussed by Bobrow (1984), Chapman, Drifte, and Gow (1982), Satoh (1982) and others. Moreover, one also has reason to believe that the Japanese government has the political capital to devote to increase foreign aid donations because of its recent governmental pledges to do so and past Japanese success in meeting the targets of other aid increase pledges (Bobrow and Boyer, 1983: 1–2).[18]

Putting all these ideas together then, one gets the impression that Italy, Japan, Denmark, the Netherlands, Luxembourg, Canada, and Greece are better equipped at least politically to bear relatively large alliance foreign aid burdens. Moreover, considering that these nations, with the exception of Greece, have shown a general reluctance or inability to increase military spending, foreign aid appears as an alternative, and yet still potent way, for these nations to contribute to alliance affairs. Alliance decision-makers should then encourage these countries to capitalize on these apparent political advantages and specialize at least partly in the foreign aid realm. In the case of Greece, because it obtains large amounts of private benefits from high levels of military spending (e.g., maintenance of internal order and defense against Turkey), it possesses yet another security utility function than exhibited by the other nations mentioned. The

---

[16] It is also worth noting that of the fifteen budget categories mentioned by the National Opinion Research Center in the survey used for Table 9.6, foreign aid ranked by far the lowest priority for government spending. The categories mentioned were as follows: space exploration, improving and protecting the environment, improving and protecting the nation's health, solving the problems of the big cities, halting the rising crime rate, dealing with drug addiction, improving the nation's education system, improving the conditions of blacks, welfare, highways and bridges, social security, mass transportation, parks and recreation, the military (armaments and defense), and foreign aid.

[17] "Economic cooperation" is the term commonly used by Japanese officials for foreign aid.

[18] It might be interesting to investigate whether the larger alliance nations are the ones providing the "purer" public goods for the alliance, while the smaller nations provide the more "impure" public goods. The central problem with attempting to do this is that it is extremely difficult to rank order alliance goods by degrees of "publicness," since there is no way to derive the percentage of private to public benefits from a particular good. Moreover, one must also recognize that the degree to which a good is *perceived* to be public or private may vary across alliance nations, thus making any rank ordering limited in applicability.

Table 9.8. *Attitudes toward trade liberalization (percentages)*

Question: What do you think of the opinion that, although liberalization of trade may result in great benefit, importing goods should be limited in order to prevent worsening of the unemployment situation?

	FR	WG	UK	IT	HO	NW	US	J
AGREE: In the short run, unemployment is the most serious for my nation.	48	39	53	53	29	45	63	35
DISAGREE: It will worsen the unemployment situation in the long run because other nations are going to limit imports in revenge.	40	27	36	21	47	47	31	33
DIFFERENCE: Agree minus disagree.	8	12	17	32	−18	−2	32	2
Don't know/No answer.	12	34	11	26	24	8	6	32

Source: *Asahi Shimbun* (Japan), Atlantic International Issues Research (France), Harris-France, September–November 1983. Taken from Hastings and Hastings, 1986: 719.

Table 9.9. *Importance of coordination (percentages)*

Question: How important do you think it is for the economic health of (survey country) to closely coordinate our policies with the United States?

	Very/fairly important to closely coordinate our policies with the United States
France	63
Italy	66
Britain	58
Germany	56
Canada	79
Japan	84

Source: Smith and Wertman, 1989: 42.

Greek case illustrates that the particular mix of security goods desired and available for use will vary from ally to ally, although some commonalities will also be evident.

Continuing at an economic level, contributions to the maintenance of a liberal international economic order should also be examined when looking at the burden-sharing question, as the maintenance of the liberal economic order established after World War II is directly related to the future prosperity and security of alliance nations. Tables 9.8 and 9.9 give some indication of public support of cooperative economic measures in various alliance countries. Table 9.8 displays survey results for eight alliance countries regarding trade liberalization and un-employment. As Smith and Wertman (1989) state and as is generally supported by the data in Table 9.8, although free trade is widely supported in principle, this support breaks down when the issue or question is related to unemployment or protection of domestic industries (pp. 42–3). This tendency has occurred throughout the 1980s:

In a March-April 1983 survey, for example, majorities in Britain, Italy, and the United States and pluralities in France, Japan, and West Germany wanted to "progressively reduce trade restrictions and encourage free international trade" as a means to deal with economic difficulties; in the same battery of questions, however, majorities or pluralities in each of these countries wanted to "protect national producers by increased import restrictions." (43).[19]

Similar anomalies were found in April 1983 and March 1984 surveys (43).

Nonetheless, Table 9.8 does point to wide variation in the intensity of allied feelings about protectionism and free trade as indicated by the "Difference" line in the table. This line represents a somewhat better measure of the degree of political power protectionist sentiment carries and was obtained by subtracting the "disagree" percentages from the "agree" percentages. At a political level, a positive result indicates strong protectionist orientation, while a negative result shows support for liberalization. Results approaching zero can be interpreted as either a "nonissue" or a controversy. The results from this subtraction suggest that the United States and Italy have the strongest protectionist support of the eight countries shown, with Great Britain, West Germany, and France having somewhat less. The Netherlands shows the strongest support for liberalization and Japan and Norway are on the threshold between the two tendencies. At a policy level, this survey suggests that the Netherlands can make contributions to alliance security in the form of support for liberalization efforts. Considering the export dependence of this small nation, such an outcome is not surprising, but its domestic political advantage may well be constrained by its participation in the EEC. Depending upon whether trade is controversial or not in Japan and Norway, these nations could also contribute in this way. Since Japan is often labeled a free-rider in the military realm and because it relies heavily on its export reve-nues, it might well be able to contribute to alliance security by further opening its markets and supporting strong liberalization efforts. Japanese efforts in this area might yield high rewards in terms of intraalliance reactions, because of persistent accusations about the closed nature of Japanese markets. Elites in nations with strong protectionist sentiments may not be as able politically to support (or at least not be the leaders of) liberalization efforts. So at least in the short term these nations possess some bargaining power in alliance trade relations because of these political constraints. It is also interesting to note the strong protectionist

[19] The surveys cited by Smith and Wertman (1989: 43) were sponsored by the Atlantic Institute and coordinated by Louis Harris France.

feelings within the United States, especially when recognizing the historic American role as supporter and promoter of a liberal international order.[20] In all instances, issues of reciprocity are most likely crucial to public perceptions on trade liberalization. Where reciprocity is perceived, free trade and the policy choices is entails will likely garner the support necessary in particular constituencies. As Axelrod and Keohane (1986: 249) suggest, cooperation in international relations is "attained best not by providing benefits unilaterally to others, but by conditional cooperation," based on both positive and negative reciprocity. In the case discussed here, this means supporting liberal trade policies when others do and effectively being able to punish overly protectionist nations when the situation warrants.

As for the need for economic policy coordination among the alliance nations, Table 9.9 provides a good indication of the importance given this concept by respondents in six alliance nations. Majorities in each of these six countries feel that it is very or fairly important to closely coordinate policies with the United States. Considering the rise of cooperation in the form of the Group of Seven (G-7)[21] negotiations on monetary policy since 1985, this finding is not too surprising. This may also bode well for the future of cooperation in the trade realm in the face of the changes brought by the 1992 unification of the EEC. It is somewhat surprising, though, that of the six countries surveyed, Britain and Germany showed the smallest majorities in favor of coordination, as these two are often seen as the most steadfast of the European allies. The two non-EEC countries, Japan and Canada, placed the highest value on policy coordination with the United States. Despite these tendencies toward somewhat lower support for policy coordination in the EEC countries surveyed, these results taken with those of Tables 9.1A and B indicate that the ties that bind the alliance together in all policy realms remain quite strong, even though "crises" recur within the alliance and spur debate regarding the future of this set of Western relationships. As Flynn (1981) puts it, "disharmony is not necessarily rooted in the objectives, but in the means to accomplish them" (p. 230).

These policy coordination poll results can also be taken as evidence of the degree to which the allies feel that they possess a "shared destiny." This interconnectedness, while at times the source of contention among the allies, also bodes well for the future of the alliance in that efforts toward policy coordination today

[20] Some would even argue that the American role was one of enforcer of free trade, even if a benevolent enforcer. Much has been written in recent years regarding the role of the United States in the building and maintenance of the liberal trading system and what its relative decline means for the future of this system. One can turn to Gowa (1989), Keohane (1984), Lake (1983), and Snidal (1985) for critiques and reviews of the hegemonic stability literature.

[21] The Group of Seven comprises the United States, Japan, (West) Germany, France, the United Kingdom, Italy, and Canada. The monetary discussions began in 1985 as the Group of Five, but was later expanded to include Italy and Canada. Depending on how one views the role played by these nations in Western security affairs, one might identify this group as an intermediate or privileged group, to use Olson's terms, formed to provide public goods for the larger Western alliance group.

lead to increased interdependence among the allies and an increased need for future cooperation. As a result, the cooperative efforts of alliance nations in economic, military, and political realms ultimately lead to a more integrated alliance system in the long run. Taken with tendencies to specialize in different sorts of alliance security policies, the incentives for continued alliance participation by individual countries remain large. Specialization and division of labor among allies, then, is a positive force working for alliance duration.[22]

In summation, although the data presented in Tables 9.1 through 9.9 are rather superficial appraisals of allied security perceptions, one does obtain an idea of the political constraints confronted by national security decision-makers and the political comparative advantages these nations possess. One should not assert that the political advantages revealed by public opinion will necessarily reflect the policy choices of an individual government, but in liberal democracies at least some responsiveness to public wants and needs must be assumed. As a result, it is not unrealistic to derive some hypotheses about the present and future pattern of alliance burden-sharing from these data and to discuss alliance policy options in the face of such constraints. A more complete picture of these advantages and the policy choices they entail can only be made through examination of data on the actual resources allocated to particular policy tools. In this way, one is then able to discuss which constraints discussed above had the greatest impact on the policy choices made by national security decision-makers.

Two other points of clarification are necessary regarding the nature of the political advantages revealed above. First, one must keep in mind that Ricardian trade theory, and the hypotheses it suggests regarding comparative advantage and specialization, does not require that nations possess an absolute advantage in the production of a particular good, but rather only a comparative advantage as measured by the opportunity costs of production in that nation. In other words, in a world with only two goods, although one nation may be able to produce more of both goods than another nation, if the opportunity costs of producing one of those goods is higher in the first country than it is in the second, then each nation should specialize in the production of the good for which they possess lower opportunity costs and trade with the other nation for the good with higher opportunity costs. By extension to the political advantage argument, in a two-good world, one only needs to establish that a nation does not have a political advantage in the production of a particular alliance good to identify which good it should produce. For example, taking the American political advantage in military spending discussed above, one can conclude that the other nations should specialize in the production of other types of alliance security goods such as foreign aid or contributions to monetary stabilization. In essence, every nation will possess some sort of political comparative advantage, no matter what its size or particular capabilities and can thus make worthwhile contributions to the alliance effort.

---

[22] The actual security policy specialization exhibited by the various allies has been examined in Boyer (1989a,b, 1988).

With this in mind, it would also be interesting to investigate the correlation of national political imperatives with economic comparative advantages to understand the interplay of these two components of the production constraint. This would have implications for evaluations of the future economic health and political stability of a particular alliance nation. If a nation is economically advantaged in a certain good's production, but politically advantaged in another, given the political responsiveness of decision-makers, one can envision economically shortsighted decisions being made for politically foresighted reasons. When political and economic comparative advantages correspond in a particular alliance nation, one can hypothesize that that nation is well situated for economic growth and political stability over the long term.

Second, as the pieces of time series public opinion data shown above illustrate, political advantages are not static in nature. Each table displaying several points in time showed that shifts in public sentiment do occur. For instance, American opinions on defense expenditures as depicted in Tables 9.3B and 9.6 show the fluctuations in public support on this issue. Although somewhat less striking, the military spending data for the Europeans in Table 9.3A and B provide another illustration of the shifting public tide. As a result of this, one should not assume that a political advantage possessed by a nation at any one point in time is permanent. In reality, these advantages and preferences will change over time, thus changing the exact specialization tendencies of the various allies and prompting periodic reevaluations of the patterns of alliance security burdens in all contribution areas. But considering the degree to which basic foreign policy objectives remain reasonably stable over time in Western nations as evidenced by the data in Tables 9.1A and B, changes in contribution levels and types should most often be only a matter of adjustment and incremental change rather than a fundamental reorganization of the patterns of alliance burden-sharing. Fundamental changes may occur, but will likely not be the norm. In and of itself, the forces for change in alliance policies can be used to help the alliance adapt to new challenges and need not necessarily be the roots of intraalliance conflict or alliance disintegration.

Conclusions

The burden-sharing debate within NATO has persistently focused on the military efforts made by the various alliance nations. But as has been seen in this chapter, continuation of this narrow appraisal of the security efforts made by alliance nations ignores the increasing tendency of alliance nations to define security in nonmilitary ways and also does not examine the policy choices made outside the military sector that serve security purposes. As a result, analyses of military burden-sharing alone only capture a small segment of the alliance security equation.

This chapter has sought to illustrate the commonalities and differences that exist among the Western allies in an effort to move the analysis of Western security cooperation beyond the previous one-dimensional military analyses. By demonstrating that commitments to the alliance remain as strong as ever, one is able to understand that the differences that exist within NATO are not the roots of conflict and disintegration, but rather can be the source of increased intraalliance reliance through security policy specialization. Moreover, by recognizing that low military spending is not necessarily synonymous with either free-riding or lack of commitment to the alliance, alliance burden-sharing initiatives can be focused on the exploitation of political comparative advantages.

The maintenance of a healthy awareness of the political and economic constraints that exist within and among alliance members regarding the various security policy tools available allows alliance leaders to make positive use of the differences that exist within the alliance rather than letting these differences degenerate into "fingerpointing" and accusations of free-riding. Initiatives, such as the Nunn Amendment, that seek to force allies to implement across-the-board spending increases in particular policy categories are counterproductive for the alliance. These types of initiatives push many allies in unacceptable political directions and only emphasize the negative aspects of allied security contributions. This is not to say that all allies are doing everything they can in pursuit of the alliance security effort, but rather that alliance policy initiatives should promote specialization and a division of labor within the alliance and press for spending increases and policy decisions that capitalize on the advantages possessed by alliance members. Multiple policy initiatives such as this will ultimately strengthen the alliance by promoting greater coordination and international reliance through security policy specialization.

References

Alfano, G., and Gerald Marwell. (1981). "Experiments on the Provision of Public Goods III: Non-divisibility and Free Riding in 'Real' Groups." *Social Psychology Quarterly* 43: 300–9.

Allison, Graham T. (1971). *Essence of Decision: Explaining The Cuban Missile Crisis*. Boston: Little Brown.

Arrow, Kenneth J. (1951). *Social Choice and Individual Values*. New York: John Wiley and Sons. (rev. ed. 1963).

Almond, Gabriel A. (1950). *The American People and Foreign Policy*. New York: Harcourt, Brace.

Axelrod, Robert, and Robert O. Keohane. (1986). "Achieving Cooperation under Anarchy: Strategies and Institutions." In Kenneth A. Oye (Ed.), *Cooperation under Anarchy*. Princeton, N.J.: Princeton University Press.

Bobrow, Davis B. (1984). "Playing for Safety: Japan's Security Practices." *Japan Quarterly* 31(1): 33–43.

Bobrow, Davis B., and Mark A. Boyer. (1985). "Priming the Pump: Japan's Use of the Foreign Aid Instrument." Presented at the annual meeting of the International Studies Association, Anaheim, Calif.

Bohm, P. (1972). "Estimating Demand for Public Goods: An Experiment." *European Economic Review* 3: 111–30.

Boyer, Mark A. (1989a). "Trading Public Goods in the Western Alliance System." *Journal of Conflict Resolution*, 33: 700–27.

(1989b). "A Simple and Untraditional Analysis of Western Alliance Burden-Sharing." Unpublished paper.

(1988). "Burdens and Specialized Contributions in the Western Alliance System: Toward a New Economic Theory of International Cooperation." Unpublished Ph.D. diss., University of Maryland, College Park.

Brown, Lester. (1977). "Redefining National Security." *Worldwatch Paper 14.* Washington, D.C.: Worldwatch Institute.

Capitanchik, David, and Richard C. Eichenberg. (1983). *Defense and Public Opinion.* Chatham House Papers, No. 20. London: Routledge and Kegan Paul.

Carlucci, Frank. (1988). *Report on Allied Contributions to the Common Defense.* Washington, D.C.: Department of Defense.

Chapman, J. W. M., R. Drifte, and I. T. M. Gow. (1982). *Japan's Quest for Comprehensive Security: Defense – Diplomacy – Security.* New York: St. Martin's Press.

Cheney, Richard. (1989). *Report on Allied Contributions to the Common Defense.* Washington, D.C.: Department of Defense.

Converse, Philip E. (1964). "The Nature of Belief Systems in Mass Publics." In David E. Apter (Ed.), *Ideology and Discontent.* New York: Free Press.

Defense Agency. (1987). *Defense of Japan, 1987.* Tokyo.

Domke, William K., Richard C. Eichenberg, and Catherine M. Kelleher. (1987). "Consensus Lost? Domestic Politics and the 'Crisis' in NATO," *World Politics* 39, 3: 382–407.

Fitoussi, J.-P., and E. S. Phelps. (1986). "Causes of the 1980s Slump in Europe." *Brookings Papers on Economic Activity,* No. 2.

Flynn, Gregory. (1981). "Western Security in the 1980s: A Familiar European Context in a Changing World." In Gregory Flynn et al. (Eds.), *The Internal Fabric of Western Security.* London: Allanheld, Osmun.

Flynn, Gregory, and Hans Rattinger (Eds.). (1985). *The Public and Atlantic Defense.* London: Rowman and Allanheld.

Gallup Political Index. (1981). Report No. 250, June.

(1980). Report No. 238, June.

Gowa, Joanne. (1989). "Rational Hegemons, Excludable Public Goods, and Small Groups: An Epitaph for Hegemonic Stability Theory?" *World Politics* 41, no. 3: 307–24.

Hastings, Elizabeth Hann, and Philip K. Hastings. (1986 and 1987). *Index to International Public Opinion, 1984–1985 (1985–1986).* New York: Greenwood Press.

Hoag, Malcolm W. (1967). "Increasing Returns in Military Production Functions." In Roland N. McKean (Ed.), *Issues in Defense Economics.* New York: Columbia University Press.

Keohane, Robert O. (1984). *After Hegemony: Cooperation and Discord in the World Political Economy.* Princeton, N.J.: Princeton University Press.

Lake, David A. (1983). "International Economic Structures and American Foreign Economic Policy, 1887–1934." *World Politics,* 36: 517–43.

Marttila, John. (1989). "American Public Opinion: Evolving Definitions of National Security." In Edward K. Hamilton (Ed.), *America's Global Interests: A New Agenda.* New York: W. W. Norton.

Marwell, Gerald, and Ruth E. Ames. (1981). "Economists Free Ride, Does Anyone Else?: Experiments on the Provision of Public Goods IV." *Journal of Public Economics* 15: 311–36.

(1980). "Experiments on the Provision of Public Goods II: Provision Points, Stakes,

Experience, and the Free Rider Problem." *American Journal of Sociology* 85: 926–37.

——— (1979). "Experiments on the Provision of Public Goods I: Resources, Interest, Group Size, and the Free Rider Problem." *American Journal of Sociology* 84: 1335–60.

Mathews, Jessica Tuchman. (1989). "Redefining Security." *Foreign Affairs* 68, no. 2: 162–77.

Murdoch, James C., and Todd Sandler. (1984). "Complementarity, Free Riding, and the Military Expenditures of NATO Allies." *Journal of Public Economics* 25: 83–101.

——— (1982). "A Theoretical and Empirical Analysis of NATO," *Journal of Conflict Resolution* 26: 237–63.

National Opinion Research Center. (1989). *General Social Survey.* Chicago.

Nelson, Daniel N., and Joseph Lepgold. (1986). "Alliances and Burden-Sharing: A NATO-Warsaw Pact Comparison." *Defense Analysis* 2: 205–24.

Olson, Mancur. (1965). *The Logic of Collective Action: Public Goods and the Theory of Groups.* Cambridge, Mass.: Harvard University Press.

Olson, Mancur, and Richard Zeckhauser. (1970). "The Efficient Production of External Economies." *American Economic Review* 60, no. 3: 512–17.

——— (1967). "Collective Goods, Comparative Advantage, and Alliance Efficiency." In Roland N. McKean (Ed.), *Issues in Defense Economics.* New York: National Bureau of Economic Research.

——— (1966). "An Economic Theory of Alliances." *Review of Economics and Statistics* 48: 266–79.

Oneal, John R. (1989). "Testing the Theory of Collective Action: NATO Defense Burdens, 1950–1984." Presented at the annual meeting of the International Studies Association, London.

Public Opinion. (1989). "Opinion Roundup," March/April, 21–33, and May–June, p. 21–9.

Oppenheimer, Joe. (1979). "Collective Goods and Alliances: A Reassessment." *Journal of Conflict Resolution* 23, 3: 387–407.

Russett, Bruce. (1970). *What Price Vigilance?: The Burdens of National Defense.* New Haven, Conn.: Yale University Press.

Sandler, Todd. (1977). "Impurity of Defense: An Application to the Economics of Alliances." *Kyklos* 30: 443–60.

Sandler, Todd, and John F. Forbes. (1980). "Burden Sharing, Strategy, and the Design of NATO." *Economic Inquiry* 18: 425–44.

Sandler, Todd, Jon Cauley, and John F. Forbes. (1980). "In Defense of a Collective Goods Theory of Alliances." *Journal of Conflict Resolution* 24: 537–47.

Satoh, Yukio. (1982). "The Evolution of Japanese Security Policy." Adelphi Paper No. 178, International Institute of Strategic Studies, London.

Scherr, B., and E. Babb. (1975). "Pricing Public Goods: An Experiment with Two Proposed Pricing Systems." *Public Choice* 23: 35–48.

Schmidt, Helmut. (1978). "The 1977 Alastair Buchan Memorial Lecture." *Survival,* January–February.

Sloan, Stanley R. (1985). *NATO's Future: Toward a New Transatlantic Bargain.* Washington, D.C.: National Defense University Press.

——— (1987). "The Political Dynamics of Defense Burden Sharing in NATO." In Catherine M. Kelleher and Gale A. Mattox (Eds.), *Evolving European Defense Policies.* Lexington, Mass.: Lexington Books.

Smith, Steven K., and Douglas A. Wertman. (1989). "Summing Up before the Economic Summit," *Public Opinion,* March/April: 41–5.

Snidal, Duncan. (1985). "The Limits of Hegemonic Stability Theory." *International Organization* 39: 579–614.

Sweeney, J. (1973). "An Experimental Investigation of the Free Rider Problem." *Social Science Research* 2: 277–92.

Ullman, Richard. (1983). "Redefining Security." *International Security* 8, no. 1: 129–53.

United States Information Agency. (1984). *NATO and Burden-Sharing.* Research Report R-11-84, Washington, D.C.

United States International Communication Agency. (1982). *West European Public Opinion on Key Security Issues, 1981–1982,* Research Report R-10-82, Washington, D.C.

Ypersele de Strihou, Jacques van. (1967). "Sharing the Defense Burden among Western Allies." *Review of Economics and Statistics* 49: 527–36.

10. Mediators, allies, and opportunists: Third parties in international crises

T. Clifton Morgan

Virtually every international crisis is characterized by the involvement, or attempted involvement, of parties other than the original disputants. Other states, international organizations, and private individuals often intrude in the hopes of aiding an ally, preserving the peace, or achieving their own aims on the issues at stake. The frequency of third-party involvement is suggested by a cursory examination of recent U.S. history, which shows at least some level of American involvement, as a third party, in disputes all over the world – such as the Middle East conflict, Afghanistan, Southern Africa, the Greco-Turkish disputes, and the Falklands/Malvinas dispute, among others. This is sufficient to indicate that third-party involvement in international disputes is a pervasive phenomenon and the U.S. experience represents only a fraction of relevant cases. While the frequency with which third parties attempt to affect crisis outcomes does not guarantee that such behavior is consequential, it is safe to assume that crisis outcomes are often affected greatly by the behavior of additional actors. Clearly, any theory designed to explain behavior and outcomes in international crises cannot be complete without accounting for the behavior of third parties. It is necessary to explain why additional actors become involved, what form their involvement takes, and what effect, if any, their involvement has.

The importance of third parties has been frequently overlooked by scholars developing formal theories of crisis bargaining.[1] Snyder and Diesing (1977), for example, based their well-known study on 2×2 game theory, which makes it virtually impossible for them to evaluate adequately the impact of third parties. If we accept that third-party involvement can often affect crisis outcomes, this is a serious restriction on this type of research. In recent papers I have presented a model to be used in the study of international crisis (Morgan, 1986, 1984) and have utilized this model to derive a number of hypotheses relating characteristics

I would like to thank Patrick James, Jack Levy, Michael McGinnis, and Richard Stoll for their comments and suggestions on earlier drafts of this chapter.
[1] Exceptions can be found in Morrow (1986) and Sebenius (1983).

of the parties involved and the bargaining agenda to crisis outcomes (Morgan, 1990, 1989). A basic premise of this project is that crises can result either in a bargained agreement, or in war, and that an understanding of crisis behavior will greatly increase our knowledge of why wars occur. I have thus far focused on developing such an understanding through the use of a formal model (to be discussed more fully in the following pages) which represents a synthesis between traditional utility based bargaining theory and the spatial theory of voting. In the previous studies I too have restricted the analysis to two-party disputes. The model is extremely fertile, however, in that it can be extended to incorporate additional explanatory variables, and the spatial representation of conflict can handle any number of actors (see, e.g., Morrow, 1986). The purpose of this chapter is to extend the spatial model to examine the role of third parties in international crises.

There does exist a fairly substantial nonformal literature concerning third parties in conflicts and, although I will not attempt a thorough review of it, I will draw heavily from this literature in the discussion that follows. The majority of this work falls into one of two categories: (1) There is a substantial amount of scholarship devoted to the examination of third parties as mediators or arbitrators. This track is aimed at determining what characteristics of mediators and what tactics used by them best facilitate the resolution of conflict by the principal actors (see, e.g., Carnevale and Wittmer, 1987; Lall, 1966: ch. 7; Pruitt, 1981: ch. 7; Raymond and Kegley, 1987; Rubin, 1981; Rubin and Brown, 1975; Touval and Zartman, 1985; Young, 1972, 1967; Zartman and Touval, 1985). (2) Many have approached the analysis of multiple-party conflicts through the use of n-person game theory that, in general, conceptualizes the problem as a coalition game (see, e.g., Luce and Raiffa, 1957; Morrow, 1986; Riker, 1962).

The distinction between these two traditions is somewhat artificial in that coalition analyses can allow for more than two coalitions (with one interested in a compromise between the others) and, as Touval (1975) has argued, we can view a mediator as a potential coalition partner for the initial disputants. Each tradition has some difficulty in dealing with some questions regarding additional parties in international crises, however. Much of coalition analysis centers on the free-for-all competition for membership in a decisive coalition. Such a conceptualization is limited for the study of crises primarily because possible coalitions are largely preestablished. This is because many potential third parties will be closely tied to one of the original disputants and because feasible coalitions will be restricted, at least to a degree, in that it is hard to imagine the original actors coalescing against a mediator. Any straightforward use of coalition analysis that recognized these constraints would somewhat trivialize the problem by tending to reduce the situation to a two party dispute. Viewing third parties strictly as mediators, on the other hand, forces one to ignore other roles that the additional actors might play. Even if we consider biased mediators, we are still implying a level of impartiality that may not exist in many situations.

My goal in this chapter is to extend the spatial model of crisis bargaining in such a way as to provide, *in the context of international crises,* an analysis of third-party involvement that is a generalization of both of these traditions. The model will permit the analysis of both coalition games and the effects of mediation and will thus allow us to compare the impact on crises outcomes of the different types of third-party involvement. Many of the conclusions to be drawn can undoubtedly be found elsewhere in the literature. The goal here is to incorporate these into the context of a well-integrated theory of crisis bargaining as well as to use the model to provide additional insights. In the next section I briefly present the basic model that will be used. For the sake of brevity I will not elaborate on many of the assumptions, features, and derivations that have been presented elsewhere. Interested readers can consult my previous publications (Morgan, 1990, 1989, 1986, 1984).

The basic model

The model draws heavily from traditional utility-based bargaining theory (see, e.g., Nash, 1950; Pen, 1952; Zeuthen, 1968) and the spatial theory of voting (see especially, Davis and Hinich, 1972; Enelow and Hinich, 1984; and Hinich and Pollard, 1981). A crisis is seen as occurring in an m-dimensional space where each axis represents one of the issues involved in the dispute. These issues will usually be the "values" under contention in the crisis (e.g., how many Soviet missiles remain in Cuba). However, they may also represent intangible issues, such as the prestige of the bargainers, or other values affected by the crisis itself, such as the stability of a region or alliance. Each point along a particular axis will represent a possible outcome on the relevant issue. Figure 10.1 provides a two-issue example of the bargaining space. For illustrative purposes, this will represent a simplified version of the Greco-Turkish dispute over Cyprus. Issue 1 will be the fate of Cyprus. Given any two points in the issue space, the one farther to the right will represent an outcome of greater Greek influence in Cyprus, the point to the left will represent greater Turkish influence. The vertical axis captures the issue of the cohesiveness of the NATO alliance. Higher points on the axis represent greater alliance cohesiveness than do lower points.

Each actor is located in the issue space by a point, the coordinates of which represent that participant's initial bargaining position, or most preferred outcome. Any number of participants can be located in the issue space; in Figure 10.1 there are three: Turkey, Greece, and the United States.[2] As can be seen, the initial Greek position calls for a greater amount of Greek influence in Cyprus than does the Turkish position. The American position is between these points on the dominance over Cyprus issue and calls for a greater amount of cohesiveness in NATO than the other actors prefer. Within this context, bargaining is viewed

---

[2] In this research I view each actor as a unitary nation-state. Using this model it would be possible to treat actors as subnational units or even individuals, but this would complicate matters considerably and it is not clear that, when dealing with crises, the payoff would be great.

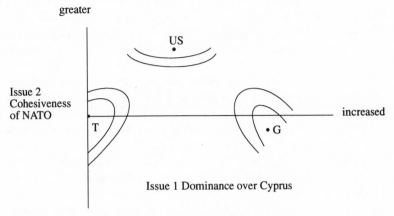

Figure 10.1. A spatial representation of the Cyprus dispute.

as attempts by every side to induce the others to accept an outcome closer to its own ideal point. Negotiating concessions occur when a party moves toward another by proposing an outcome closer to the other's ideal point. Bargaining continues until all participants agree on an outcome or until a war is begun.

Each actor's decisions regarding whether to accept a proposal, offer a counter-proposal, or initiate a war will be made on the basis of how much benefit can be expected from each option. This is affected by the actor's preferences over possible outcomes. Note the association between distance in the issue space and the actors' preference orderings: The closer a proposal is to an actor's ideal point, the more preferred it is. We assume that actor i prefers proposal π to proposal π' if and only if $\|\pi - O_i\|_{A_i} < \|\pi' - O_i\|_{A_i}$ where $\|\pi - O_i\|$ refers to the simple Euclidian distance between the proposal and the actor's ideal point and A_i refers to an $m \times m$ matrix specifying the parameters by which we can represent the issues as having different saliences for the actor (Enelow and Hinich, 1984: 16–18; Hinich and Pollard, 1981: 331). For example, in a two-issue case where

$$\pi = (x,y), \quad \pi' = (x',y'), \quad A_i = \begin{bmatrix} a_{11} & a_{12} \\ a_{12} & a_{22} \end{bmatrix}$$

and, by setting i's ideal point at the origin, $O_i = (0,0)$[3] the weighted Euclidian distance preference rule says that i prefers to π to π' if and only if

$$[a_{i11} (0 - x)^2 + 2a_{i12} (0 - x) (0 - y) + a_{i22} (0 - y)^2]^{1/2}$$
$$< [a_{i11} (0 - x')^2 + 2a_{ai12} (0 - x') (0 - y') + a_{i22} (0 - y')^2]^{1/2}.$$

In general, the farther away from a player's ideal point in the issue space a proposal is, the less preferred it is; however, since all issues may not be equally

---

[3] Note that in the salience matrix A_i, $a_{12} = a_{21}$. For simplicity of notation, I use only a_{12}.

important to each player, those issues that are more important to a player are given more weight. Thus, if i is more concerned with issue 1 than with issue 2, that can be reflected by setting $a_{i11} > a_{i22}$. In the Cyprus dispute it was probably the case that the Greeks and Turks were more concerned with who would control Cyprus than with the effect their dispute would have on NATO while the United States became an important actor because of its concern for the alliance. This is reflected in the indifference contours in Figure 10.1. These indicate that Greece and Turkey would be willing to trade a relatively large amount of alliance cohesiveness for a small increase in their influence over Cyprus while the United States is willing to move fairly far from its ideal position on Cyprus for relatively small increases in alliance cohesiveness. Also note that the example is drawn so that the axes of the ellipses representing the Greek and Turkish indifference contours are not parallel with the issue axes, while those for the United States are. This suggests that for the United States the issues in dispute are separable; that is, the United States would argue that the threat to the alliance comes from the possibility that the protagonists could resort to war to settle their dispute, not from any possible outcome on the issue per se. This is reflected in the mathematical formulation by setting $a_{US12} = 0$, indicating no interaction between the issues. The Greeks or Turks, on the other hand, would probably see a grossly unfavorable outcome on Cyprus as an indication that they would be better off outside the alliance. The outcome on the Cyprus issue is thus linked to these actors' preferences on the alliance issue and this is reflected by setting a_{t12} and a_{g12} as unequal to zero.

Much, though not all, of the analysis performed with this model requires that we make additional assumptions regarding how the actors react in specific situations. In particular, it is important to specify how the actors should behave given the power relationship of the protagonists and their resolve. Once these decision rules are specified we can derive hypotheses relating crisis situations to crisis outcomes. Since the justifications of the assumptions and the derivations of the hypotheses that I have made are somewhat lengthy I will not discuss them at this time. Many of the points to be made in this chapter can be made on the basis of what has been presented thus far and a discussion of the additional assumptions and hypotheses can be found in the earlier papers cited before. For the analyses requiring reference to previous work, I will briefly mention the pertinent material and refer to the relevant piece.

Third parties in international crises

The first question we must address is why additional parties become involved in international crises. The answer to this question is important not only for its own sake but also because it may provide some indication as to the impact of third-party involvement. The general answer to this question has been provided by Young (1972) and Touval (1975), among others, who have argued that third parties become involved when they perceive it is in their interest to do so; that is, they become involved when they are concerned with the outcome of the issues in dispute or with the issues that are created by the conflict. We can see at least three ways in which the issues can draw third parties into a crisis and that each of these will have ramifications for the nature of the involvement.

First, a third party may be concerned with one or more of the issues over which the crisis began. This does not suggest that the third party brings no additional issues into the conflict, only that it views these as secondary concerns. In cases such as this, the nature of the third party's involvement will depend on its issue positions relative to that of the other actors. If the third party's preferences are nearly identical to those of one of the original participants, we would expect these actors to align. If the third party's ideal point falls roughly between the original participants' ideal points, it is likely to behave much like a mediator; but, rather than attempt to facilitate a "fair" or "acceptable" (to the original parties) outcome, it would attempt to persuade the others to accept a "split-the-difference" solution. Finally, if the additional actor is neither near one party nor between the parties (i.e., the actors' ideal points form a triangle in the issue space) we would expect a three-way bargaining game. Each would attempt to achieve an outcome close to its own ideal point, but much of the competition would be carried out by the parties attempting to form coalitions. This would be particularly interesting when the actors have different relative saliences for the issues at stake that would open the possibility of "logrolls" (i.e., an agreement by two, or more, actors, each of whom considers a different issue to be most important, by which each receives its most preferred outcome on the issue with which it is most concerned).[4]

An example of each of these types of third-party involvement can be seen in Figure 10.2. This is constructed with two issues, generically labeled Issue 1 and Issue 2 and there are two original participants, i and j. For simplicity, suppose that all indifference contours are circular. Because their issue positions are so similar, we would expect i and an actor at point k to align against j. An actor at l would attempt to persuade i and j to accept an intermediate outcome, which would be close to l's ideal point, but we might also expect l to align with one of the primary actors in certain situations. For example, l may support i if i is a superpower and l and j are minor powers, because i may be able to achieve its aims even against j and l together; but, to achieve its victory at lower cost, i may grant some concessions to l if l will support it. Finally, with an actor at m, we have a third party who is in agreement with each of the original participants on one issue. This would result in a classical coalition game in which each of the disputants would attempt to lure m into an alliance against the other. Such a game could also be affected by the shape of the actors' indifference contours. Where

---

[4] This situation clearly can be seen as a generalization of all others though I am treating it as a "residual" category. Any analysis conducted at the general level (such as Morrow, 1986) is worthwhile in that it provides insight into all such situations. I find it more useful to categorize the cases more finely. In this way, our understanding can incorporate more than the general conclusions.

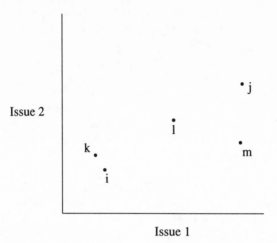

Figure 10.2. Third parties concerned with original issues. (Indifference contours are circular.)

the issues are not seen as equally salient by all actors, the possibility of logrolls exists. Actor *m* could achieve most of its aims on the issue of greater importance by cutting a deal with the actor for whom this issue is less important. All this, of course, assumes the parties are relatively equal in power. If one is over-whelmingly superior to the others combined, it could take what it wants. The illustration also shows that the analysis could become more interesting and complicated if there is more than one potential third party. With actors at *l* and *m*, for example, we might see a coalition of third parties attempting to force an intermediate outcome that represents a compromise between the third-party positions.

Third parties can also become involved when the crisis generates additional issues with which they are primarily concerned. The third party may have prefer-ences on the original issues, but these issues are much less salient to the actor than are the created issues. Furthermore, the original issues are most salient for the original parties – after all, these were the issues over which they became involved in a crisis. At this point, we can draw a further distinction between types of third-party involvement on the basis of whether the third party views these additional issues as being separable from the original issues.

In many cases, the third party enters the bargaining out of concern with additional issues which are seen (by the third party) as separable from the original issues. This would be the case when the motivation for involvement is concern for the effect the crisis is having on, for example, the cohesiveness of an alliance or the stability of a region. Here, the third party is worried more about *how* the conflict is resolved than about what form the solution takes and we would expect the third party to assume the role of mediator. This is what we have seen in cases such as the Cyprus conflict depicted in Figure 10.1 or the Falklands dispute. In both cases the United States sought to mediate because it was more concerned with maintaining peace and preserving its relationship with allies than with the outcome on the original issue. If the third party is unable to achieve its aims on the issue it deems important, however, it may take sides either to preserve the more important relationship (as in the Falklands case) or to achieve its preferences on other issues.

Finally, a third party may become involved when a crisis creates, for it, other substantive issues that are not separable from one or more of the original issues. That is, while the third party is relatively unconcerned about the original issues per se, it does perceive them as creating an important additional issue and it believes that the outcome on the former issues will affect what is desired on the latter. In these cases, the created issue will usually pit the third party against one of the original protagonists, causing an alliance between the third party and the other original actor. This will not result in a "coalition game," however, because the "allies" are, in a sense, forced together by their common enemy. Each is concerned with an issue about which the other cares little and has little control, and (most important) actions taken by their opponent affect each ally's interests in a similar way. Each ally may desire similar behavior from the opponent, but for different reasons,[5] thus, such situations will appear very much like separate, parallel crises except that the "allies" have similar goals (in terms of the behavior of the enemy) and should be expected to attempt to coordinate their actions to a degree.

A classic case of such a crisis was the 1911 Agadir crisis, depicted in Figure 10.3. The French and the Germans were in conflict over the degree of French dominance in Morocco and the amount of compensation to be paid to Germany for this dominance. In an attempt to force the French hand the Germans sent a warship to the port of Agadir, which created in the British the fear that Germany would attempt to establish a fortified port in Agadir. The British participation was aimed at protecting their interests on this additional issue. The British preferences on the original issues were actually somewhat closer to those of the Germans than to those of the French, but these issues were much less salient than the created issue. Even though the Germans had little intention of establishing a fortified port at Agadir, their actions created in the British the perception that this issue was closely linked to the degree of French control in Morocco (they believed that low French control would mean a strong German presence), which had the effect of shifting the British ideal point on this issue toward the French. Thus, the British and French were aligned in seeking a German withdrawal from Agadir.

In Figure 10.3, we can see that the Germans and French were not too far apart

---

[5] Note that these situations are very similar to what Lebow (1981) has termed "spinoff crises." The difference, of course, is that spinoff crises are those that result from the behavior of a party already involved in a war.

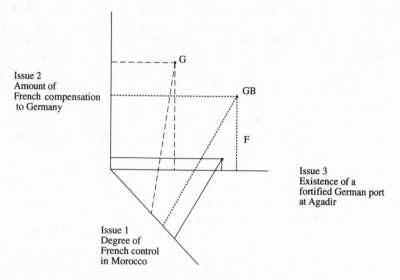

Figure 10.3. A spatial representation of the Agadir crisis.

on the issue of French control in Morocco – the question mainly concerned the form of guarantees to German economic interests – but were far apart on the amount of compensation to be paid Germany. Britain was between the two principals on these issues, but was somewhat closer to Germany. The three were actually fairly close on the issue of the fortified German port, in that Germany had little intention of seeking one though she was willing to use the prospect of such an action to gain bargaining leverage. The major differences were in the shapes of the indifference surfaces (which I have not attempted to draw). For Germany and France, the most salient issue was the amount of compensation; the issue of the German port was, in their mind, so unimportant as to be almost nonexistent, and the issues were separable. For the British, the original issues paled in importance to the issue of the port and this issue was not separable from the issue of French control. This, in effect, shifted the British ideal point on Issue 1 to a place very near the French.[6]

In this case, our expectations about the third-party behavior are largely borne out. The British did, to a great extent, behave as if they were in a separate crisis

---

[6] These differences are reflected in the salience matrices which determine the shape of the indifference surfaces. There are an infinite number of such matrices consistent with the construction of this example at the present level of generality, but for purposes of illustration the relative saliences of the issues and their degree of nonseparability can be represented with the following matrices:

$$A_F = \begin{bmatrix} 1 & 0 & 0 \\ 0 & 3 & 0 \\ 0 & 0 & .1 \end{bmatrix} \quad A_G = \begin{bmatrix} 1 & 0 & 0 \\ 0 & 4 & 0 \\ 0 & 0 & .2 \end{bmatrix} \quad A_{GB} = \begin{bmatrix} 1 & 0 & .5 \\ 0 & .1 & 0 \\ .5 & 0 & 4 \end{bmatrix}$$

with the Germans. Though they did confer with the French, they bargained with the Germans more or less independently and the crisis was resolved for the British long before it was for the French. It is also interesting to note that the British came much closer to going to war than did the French. We would expect this to occur only in a situation such as this in which the third party is, for the most part, involved in its own crisis.

Third parties and crisis outcomes

We can speculate from the preceding discussion that the effect third parties have on crisis outcomes depends, in part, on what form the third-party involvement takes. In this section, I will discuss the effect third parties have on crisis outcomes, primarily with regard to their impact on the probability of war. Within each type of involvement, I will show, to a degree, how different characteristics of the crisis situation and participants affect the likely outcome.

Consider first situations in which the third party acts not as a mediator, but as a potential ally for at least one of the disputants. If the third party has issue positions so close to one of the original parties that an alliance is dictated, the analysis of its impact on outcomes is a straightforward extension of the results I presented in Morgan, 1989. Since the allies can be expected to behave as one, the third party serves to augment the military capabilities of its ally and its impact can be determined by the results relating the power relationship to outcomes. If the additional state adds insignificant capabilities to the alliance, the likely outcome will change none at all. On the other hand, if the third party adds to the alliance's capabilities vis-à-vis the opponent, the alliance can expect a negotiated settlement to be more favorable. The derivations of the model suggest that crises are more likely to end in war when the parties are disparate in power (Morgan, 1989); thus, if the enhanced capabilities create a situation of power parity, war is less likely, whereas if they create a situation of power disparity, war is more likely.

If the third party is located such that a three-way conflict results (as would be an actor at point m in Figure 10.2), the effect is more complicated and more interesting. This situation is one for which traditional n-person game theory provides a great deal of insight. The analyses by Morrow (1986) are especially relevant for international relations scholars in this regard. Essentially, Morrow has shown that the game is one in which the actors compete for coalition partners and in so doing, must decide whether the support of an ally is worth the concessions one must make to that ally. For example, if j and m in Figure 10.2 were to align, the alliance position would presumably lie somewhere between their ideal points. Each must decide if it is preferable to advocate a less desirable solution in exchange for the increased capabilities an alliance provides. When such a coalition forms, the likely negotiated settlement, should one occur, will be altered. This is because the conflict line (which is analogous to a contract curve, or Pareto set) has as its end points the ideal points of the protagonists. When the initial position of one side is shifted by coalition formation, the set of likely outcomes will also shift. As to the probability of war, it is affected in the same way that the situations described were by the changes in the capability relationship. It is also affected in another way. Since the coalition members are defending a position somewhat removed from their ideal points, each may be less willing to go to war to achieve the coalition demands than it would have been to achieve its own ideal point. If this is the case, we would expect a coalition to be less likely to push a crisis to war than would be a single state, all else being equal (i.e., the reduced willingness to fight from this factor may not be sufficient to overcome any increased willingness from an increase in capabilities).

Finally, if the alliance is formed because the crisis created a nonseparable additional issue for the third party, we would expect the probability of war to be increased by the third-party involvement. Since the coalition members are adopting nearly an identical issue stance, the mitigating effect of defending a less than perfect solution would not exist. Furthermore, since the situation resembles, to an extent, two separate crises with the alliance partners acting somewhat independently, there is a greater chance of at least one choosing to go to war (e.g., if the probability of war between i and j is .25 and the probability of war between k and j is .2, the probability that at least one of i and k would go to war with j is .4). Naturally, this would be lessened somewhat to the extent the enemy is inhibited from fighting by the possibility of a costlier war against two foes.[7]

Turning to third parties who act as mediators, we can again see that the reasons for adopting this role affect the impact the third party has on the outcome. If the mediator assumes this role because of issue preferences that lie between those of the protagonists, we can again usefully approach the problem from the perspective of n-person game theory. This will probably be a coalition game in which the original actors shift their positions toward one another (and the mediator) in hopes of attracting the third party to their side. While the general effect of the third party will be similar to that discussed above, there should also be an additional lessening of the probability of war since the actions of the parties competing for the mediators' favor would tend to lessen the degree of conflict between them. This is clearly consistent with the conventional view of mediation advanced by Morrow (1986), Touval (1975), and others.

Mediators can also serve a number of functions that reduce the probability of war. These have been well documented elsewhere (e.g., Rubin, 1981; Touval, 1975; Young, 1967) and some of the major points are that mediators can serve to

---

[7] It is also interesting to note that in this type of case the enemy of the coalition has an additional conflict strategy available. Since the basis for the coalition is the perception by the third party that the issue it deems important is nonseparable from another issue, the enemy can try to change this perception and convince the third party that it need not be involved. In the Agadir crisis, Germany handled this very poorly, with almost disastrous consequences. The French, on the other hand, were able to capitalize on the situation by manipulating the British perception of a linkage between the issues. This case also illustrates the danger in such a strategy, since the British almost caused the war the French hoped to avoid.

improve the communications between the disputants and that mediators make concessions more likely since they result in less loss of face if made to a third party. We might expect mediators trying to achieve their aims on the issues at stake to serve less well in this capacity than those who work toward a peaceful resolution of the conflict out of concern for issues threatened by the crisis, but their conflict easing function should still be important.

A mediator can also reduce the likelihood of war by bringing additional issues into the bargaining. We know that, when additional issues are included, the probability of a settlement can be increased if the issues provide an opportunity for logrolls (Morgan, 1990). A mediator may be exceptionally able to bring in such issues, especially if they are in the form of guarantees or side payments. An example of this is the Camp David agreement, in which the United States, acting as mediator, was able to bring Egypt and Israel to an agreement, largely by using its economic resources to make the agreement acceptable to the parties. This point also illustrates that the ability of a mediator to reduce the probability of war will partially depend on its capabilities. The more resources a mediator has relative to the disputants, the more likely it will be to "pull" them toward a compromise.

The ability of a mediator to reduce the probability of war should not be exaggerated, however. If there are outcomes that the disputants prefer to war, a mediator can increase the chances of achieving one, but if none exist, the mediation attempt will fail. Even if the "bargaining zone" is not empty, a mediator can still fail for a number of reasons. We can consider the mediator's task essentially one of bargaining with two disputants over the issue of whether they should engage in conflict. If the mediator is in a weak bargaining position, it may fail. One such source of weakness would be a lack of resolve. If the disputants are highly resolved to achieve their aims, even if it means a high risk of war, and the mediator is not resolved to achieve its aims, the mediation is not likely to affect the crisis outcome.

This model can also contribute to the debate regarding whether mediators must be unbiased. The conventional wisdom that mediators could not be biased and be effective has recently been challenged on empirical and theoretical grounds (Carnevale and Wittmer, 1987; Rubin, 1981; Touval, 1975). It has been shown that many mediators have had preferences for one side's position and have still been effective. The general argument as to how this can be the case is essentially that it requires the party against whom the mediator is biased to prefer the likely outcome with the mediator to that without. It may also be the case that a biased mediator can exert greater influence on its "ally" and persuade it to make concessions. The spatial construction shows that there is a more basic reason why a biased mediator can function effectively. Figure 10.4 illustrates a situation in which i and j are in dispute over the division of territory x. We have two potential mediators, k and l, who are concerned with a separable second issue, the stability of the region. Actor k prefers an outcome on Issue 1 in between the ideal points of i and j while l prefers an outcome closer to i's ideal point. The important point

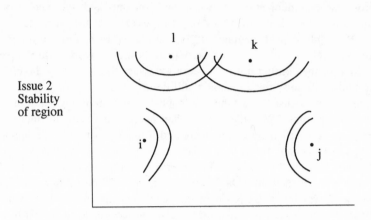

Issue 2
Stability
of region

Issue 1 Ownership of territory X

Figure 10.4. Biased and unbiased mediators.

to note is the shape of the indifference contours. Both k and l see the second issue as much more salient than the first and would move a great distance from their preferred points on Issue 1 to achieve relatively little additional stability. Thus, even though l appears more biased than k on the initial issue in dispute, in the context of the entire situation, their positions are virtually indistinguishable because l's bias is overwhelmed by the salience of the second issue. If there are characteristics of l that would make it an effective mediator (such as a great resource endowment, or a history of close relations with both i and j) it could be a preferable mediator to k, even though it is biased.

Conclusion

The purpose of this chapter has been to develop further the spatial model of bargaining in international crises by evaluating the impact of third parties on crisis outcomes. A number of familiar arguments have been placed in the context of an integrated theory of crisis behavior and a few additional insights have been provided. The main point has been that a third party will not have a straightforward impact on the outcome of a crisis. The impact will depend on the role the third party takes – whether mediator or ally – and the motivations for adopting this role. Though the impact will depend on each of the variables incorporated into the model, at least two general propositions can be stated: (1) When the third party becomes involved as a potential ally for one, or both, of the disputants, the probability of war will increase if the third party is acting out of concern for an issue created by the crisis that is nonseparable from one of the other issues or when the coalition creates a situation of power disparity. If the coalition creates a situation of power parity, or if the process of coalition formation leads to a significant softening of the actors' positions, then the result will be a decrease in the probability of war. (2) When the third party is involved as a mediator, the probability of war will generally decrease, especially when the mediator is motivated by an issue created by the crisis.

I have also argued that the reasons for the third-party involvement will have an impact on the nature of the bargaining that occurs. If the third party is a potential coalition partner, much of the bargaining will be aimed at enticing the third party to join one of the coalitions. If the third party is an ally to one side because of an additional, nonseparable issue, much of the effort will be aimed at its perception that the issues are nonseparable. If the third party is a mediator, much of the bargaining will originate with the third party and will be aimed at cajoling the disputants to accept a compromise outcome, and the third party may use side payments to achieve this end. In addition, I have presented another theoretical argument showing that mediators need not be impartial to be effective.

Clearly this does not represent the final word on third parties in international crisis. Many more questions could be asked, and more precise predictions of third-party impacts and behaviors could be made. Finally, the propositions must be tested empirically. While they appear to be supported by the examples I have cited here, much more work is required before they can be accepted with confidence.

References

Carnevale, Peter, and Jerry M. Wittmer. (1987). "Biased Mediators in International Mediation." Presented at the 1987 annual meeting of the International Studies Association, Washington, D.C.

Davis, Otto A., and Melvin J. Hinich. (1972). "Spatial Competition under Constrained Choice." in Richard G. Niemi and Herbert F. Weisberg (Eds.), *Probability Models of Collective Decision Making*. Columbus: Charles E. Merrill.

Enelow, James M., and Melvin J. Hinich. (1984). *The Spatial Theory of Voting*. Cambridge: Cambridge University Press.

Hinich, Melvin J., and Walker Pollard. (1981). "A New Approach to the Spatial Theory of Electoral Competition." *American Journal of Political Science* 25 (May): 323–41.

Lall, Arthur. (1966). *Modern International Negotiation: Principles and Practice*. New York: Columbia University Press.

Lebow, Richard N. (1981). *Between Peace and War*. Baltimore: Johns Hopkins University Press.

Luce, R. Duncan, and Howard Raiffa. (1957). *Games and Decisions*. New York: John Wiley and Sons.

Morgan, T. Clifton. (1990). "Issue Linkages in International Crisis Bargaining." *American Journal of Political Science* 34: 311–33.

——— (1989). "Power, Resolve, and Bargaining in International Crises: A Spatial Theory." *International Interactions* 15: 279–302.

——— (1986). *Bargaining in International Crises: A Spatial Model*. Ph.D. diss., University of Texas at Austin.

——— (1984). "A Spatial Model of Crisis Bargaining." *International Studies Quarterly* 28: 407–26.

Morrow, James D. (1986). "A Spatial Model of International Conflict." *American Political Science Review* 80: 1131–50.

Nash, John. (1950). "The Bargaining Problem." *Econometrica* 18: 155–62.

Pen, Jan. (1952). "A General Theory of Bargaining." *The American Economic Review* 27: 24–42.

Pruitt, Dean G. (1981). *Negotiation Behavior.* New York: Academic Press.

Raymond, Gregory A., and Charles W. Kegley, Jr. (1987). "Third Party Mediation and International Norms: A Test of Two Models." *Conflict Management and Peace Science* 10: 33–49.

Riker, William H. (1962). *The Theory of Political Coalitions.* New Haven, Conn.: Yale University Press.

Rubin, Jeffrey Z. (Ed.). (1981). *Dynamics of Third Party Intervention.* New York: Praeger.

Rubin, Jeffrey Z., and Bert R. Brown. (1975). *The Social Psychology of Bargaining and Negotiation.* New York: Academic Press.

Sebenius, James K. (1983). "Negotiation Arithmetic: Adding and Subtracting Issues and Parties." *International Organization* 37: 281–316.

Snyder, Glenn H., and Paul Diesing. (1977). *Conflict among Nations: Bargaining, Decision Making, and System Structure in International Crises.* Princeton, N.J.: Princeton University Press.

Touval, Saadia. (1975). "Biased Intermediaries: Theoretical and Historical Considerations." *Jerusalem Journal of International Relations* 1: 51–69.

Touval, Saadia and I. William Zartman (Eds.). (1985). *International Mediation in Theory and Practice.* Boulder, Colo.: Westview Press.

Young, Oran R. (1972). "Intermediaries: Additional Thoughts on Third Parties." *Journal of Conflict Resolution* 16: 51–65.

(1967). *The Intermediaries: Third Parties in International Crises.* Princeton, N.J.: Princeton University Press.

Zartman, I. William, and Saadia Touval. (1985). "International Mediation: Conflict Resolution and Power Politics." *Journal of Social Issues* 41: 27–46.

Zeuthen, Frederick. (1968). *Problems of Monopoly and Economic Warfare.* New York: Augustus M. Kelly.

11. Rational choice in the crisis domain: An appraisal of superpower interactions, 1948–1979

Patrick James

> In times of passion and confusion, there can be no scientific prediction or justified certainty in advance of the outcome. But in order for it to be rational to desist from a course of action, it is not necessary that it should be certain to have a catastrophic result: it is sufficient that catastrophe should be a consequence that is more or less likely. (Kenny, 1985: 43–4)

> Why does conflict management so often fail? (Frei, 1985: 586)

Although each emphasizes a different aspect, these assertions combine to describe the dilemma of modern deterrence. On the one hand, Mutually Assured Destruction (MAD) is credited with stabilizing superpower crises, because the risk of catastrophe outweighs the potential gain from challenging well-established commitments. On the other, international conflict is sustained, with some crises reaching a very high level of intensity. Since every conflict holds some risk of escalation – perhaps even resulting in superpower confrontation at the nuclear level – it is worthwhile to explore more effective means of crisis management.[1]

This is precisely the objective of a recent series of game-theoretic studies by Brams and Kilgour (1987a,b, 1988). Using a modified version of "Chicken," referred to as the Threat Game, they have developed a theoretical model of rational retaliation in superpower crises. Brams and Kilgour derive explicit thresholds for sufficient retaliation against provocations to deter them in the first place. In other words, for any given level of noncooperation by an adversary, the appropriate degree of coercion is specified for the response, in order to deter that level of noncooperation. When the retaliatory move meets or is more coercive than the threshold, it is rational for the adversaries to prefer to desist from

---

[1] Crisis prevention and early warning are important goals also. However, these more ambitious objectives are beyond the scope of this investigation, which focuses upon the management of crises in progress.

conflict, whereas a response that is too cooperative will not provide the same incentive. Brams and Kilgour also have produced a decision calculus for optimal threats, a model of threat escalation and crisis stability, and a more specialized model of crisis deescalation.[2]

While all of these contributions are noteworthy, only the first – the model of rational retaliation – will be dealt with in the analysis to follow. The overall objective of this study is to use data on superpower crises to test a modified version of the model of rational retaliation developed by Brams and Kilgour. A description of their model, culminating in some revisions, is the first stage of the investigation. Selection of cases and operationalization of the model comprise the second phase and testing is the third. The final stage concerns the implications of the findings for the further study of crisis management.

The Threat game and rational retaliation

According to Brams (1985), the game of Chicken is well suited as a model of nuclear deterrence between the superpowers. Table 11.1 represents the basic form of the game. Two drivers, Row and Column, approach each other on a road. The objective of the game is to force the adversary to swerve out of the way. The payoffs in a given cell in the matrix correspond to those of Row and Column, respectively (where $r_4 > r_3 > \cdots$ and $c_4 > c_3 > \cdots$). If each swerves, both receive the second-best payoff (r_3, c_3). If Row/Column swerves and Column/Row does not, Column/Row obtains the best payoff and Row/Column the third-best, corresponding to (c_4, r_2) and (r_4, c_2), respectively. When neither swerves, both receive the worst payoff (r_1, c_1).

With two modifications, as Brams and Kilgour (1987a,b) have demonstrated, Chicken can be transformed into a superior model of bargaining at the superpower level:

(i) The players can make quantitative choices of levels of cooperation (C) or noncooperation (C'), not just qualitative choices of C or C'.

(ii) Once these initial choices, which can be interpreted as levels of non-preemption (versus preemption) are made, the less preemptive player (i.e., who chose the lower level of preemption initially, if there was one) can retaliate by choosing a different – and presumably higher – level of noncooperation subsequently (Brams and Kilgour, 1987a).

This version of Chicken is known as the Threat game. The two changes effectively respond to some of the most telling criticisms of game matrices.

Specifically, the players are no longer assumed to have just two options. There is a continuum of cooperation and conflict, unlike the pure form of Chicken. Simultaneous choices that conclude play also are not entailed by the Threat

---

[2] The deescalation model, which appears in Brams and Kilgour (1987c), is not based on the Threat game. It therefore will not be discussed in further detail.

Table 11.1. *The game of Chicken*

		Column	
		Swerve	Do not swerve
Row	Swerve	r_3,c_3	r_2,c_4
	Do not swerve	r_4,c_2	r_1,c_1

game, because the second modification allows for further play following the first move, including altered tactics for at least one of the antagonists.[3] This also appears to be more consistent with the reality of superpower bargaining in crises.

There are two ways in which the game can terminate. If the initial levels of C or C' are the same, play is terminated; when they are not equivalent, the game ends after the more cooperative player has retaliated. This is intended to replicate the process of escalation in a bilateral crisis: "If escalation were unilateral, and one player simply became more and more aggressive without provoking retaliation from the other, then the process would not be two-sided escalation but rather one-sided aggression" (Brams and Kilgour, 1987a: 835).

Brams and Kilgour "telescope" escalation into a "single retaliatory counter-move" by the less preemptive player (1987a: 835). Further rounds of escalation could be included, but "the present simple sequence captures well both the process that might trigger further escalation and the core meaning of deterrence: averting conflict through the threat of retaliation, which, if carried out, could be costly to both players" (Brams and Kilgour, 1987b).

Figure 11.1 displays the Threat game, which is played on the unit square.[4] The players, Row and Column, select preemption levels s and t, respectively. These choices range from 0 (maximum) to 1 (minimum) preemption. This simultaneous selection by the players results in (t, s), referred to as the initial position. The preplay position is $(1, 1)$, prior to noncooperation by the players.

Movement from the preplay to the initial position means noncooperation at certain levels, resulting in (t, s) as the initial position, with t and s measured along the horizontal and vertical axes, respectively. If $s > t$, Row is the more cooperative player and retaliates according to the retaliation function $q(t)$, making the final position of the game $(t, q(t))$. If $s < t$, then Column retaliates with

---

[3] For an interesting critique of game-theoretic and other models of crisis bargaining, consult Morgan (1984: 408–14); a specific argument in favor of the Prisoner's Dilemma (PD) game as a superior model of deterrence appears in Zagare (1985). However, the equilibrium of the latter game, in which both players defect, is not consistent with the record of MAD. Furthermore, the outcome of mutual noncooperation does not produce the worst payoff for each player in a PD game: A nuclear exchange, as opposed to experiencing unilateral coercion in crisis bargaining, should result in the lowest utility level for a target state.

[4] The following description of the Threat Game is based on Brams and Kilgour (1987a,b).

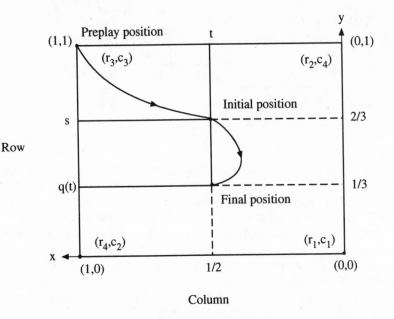

Key:
(r_i, c_j) = (payoff to row, payoff to column);
(r_4, c_4) = best; r_3, c_3 = next best; r_2, c_2 = next worst; r_1, c_1= worst;
s,t = initial strategy choices of row and column, respectively;
q(t) = subsequent strategy choice of row (more cooperative player initially).

Figure 11.1. The Threat game. (*Source:* Brams and Kilgour, 1987a: 836.)

$p(s)$, resulting in ($p(s)$, s) as the final position. The retaliation function in each case depends upon the level of noncooperation selected by the adversary, and the relative magnitudes of s and t determine which player will retaliate.

Each payoff on a corner of the unit square corresponds to one of the "pure" states of Chicken (Brams and Kilgour, 1987a: 836).

(a) Both players cooperate (CC) – next best outcome for both players: (r_3, c_3) at upper-left corner in Figure 11.1.

(b) One player cooperates and the other does not (CC') and $(C'C)$ – best outcome for the player who does not cooperate and next-worst for the player who does: (r_2, c_4) and (r_4, c_2): at upper-right and lower-left corners, respectively.

(c) Both players do not cooperate $(C'C')$ – worst outcome for both players: (r_1, c_1) at lower-right corner.

The points along the axes combine to cover all possible payoff combinations to the players.

Payoffs at the final position are weighted averages of the payoffs at the corners of the game board. The payoff functions are bilinear, meaning linear in each coordinate. For example, the final position of the game would correspond to $x = t$, $y = q(t)$ or $x = p(s)$, $y = s$, with Row and Column, respectively, as the initially more cooperative player. In calculating payoffs for Row and Column at any point (x, y), referred to as $P_R(x, y)$ and $P_C(x, y)$, respectively, the payoffs at each corner are "weighted by the product of the distances, parallel to the axes, from (x, y) to the opposite corner." Payoffs to Row ($P_R(x, y)$) and Column ($P_C(x, y)$) therefore are calculated as follows (Brams and Kilgour, 1987a: 837):

$$P_R(x, y) = xyr_3 + x(1 - y)r_4 + (1 - x)yr_2 + (1 - x)(1 - y)r_1. \tag{1}$$
$$P_C(x, y) = xyc_3 + y(1 - x)c_4 + (1 - y)xc_2 + (1 - x)(1 - y)c_1. \tag{2}$$

One equilibrium that results from the Threat game is the deterrence equilibrium (DE). The initial strategies and retaliation functions that produce payoffs (r_3, c_3) are as follows:

$$s = 1, \quad q(t) \le q_1(t), \tag{3}$$
$$t = 1, \quad p(s) \le p_1(s), \tag{4}$$

where

$$q_1(t) = \frac{c_3 - tc_2}{1 - t(1 - c_3 + c_2)}, \quad 0 \le t < 1, \tag{5}$$

and

$$p_1(s) = \frac{r_3 - sr_2}{1 - s(1 - r_3 + r_2)}, \quad 0 \le s < 1. \tag{6}$$

At DE (or $s = t = 1$) neither player preempts. Equations (3) and (4) create a Nash equilibrium because

> any level of preemption by each player's opponent will be at least as costly (after retaliation) as no preemption. Hence, the players do at least as well, and generally better (if the inequalities are strict, by choosing no preemption initially ($[s_0=t_0]=1$).

Equations (5) and (6) give the minimal levels of threatened retaliation needed to render (1, 1) stable, yielding payoffs of $P_R(1, 1) = r_3$ and $P_C(1, 1) = c_3$. If the superpowers seek to restore the nonpreemption position at (1, 1), then the retaliation function $q_1(t)$ and $p_1(s)$ determine the threshold for rational response by the less coercive player.[5] Although a different weighting system would alter the

---

[5] Brams and Kilgour also have identified points of crisis stabilization at (x_0, y_0), with $x_0 = t$ and $y_0 = s$ as the initial position, with and without threat escalation. "It may be preferable," as they have observed, "for the players to try first to stabilize the status quo (x_0, y_0), postponing further ameliorative measures for restoring the nonpreemption position at (1, 1) until the crisis atmosphere is cleared." Assuming that the players view (x_0, y_0) in such terms, the reduced deterrence equilibrium (RDE) is defined by the following equations:

$$s = y_0, \quad q(t) \le q_{x_0,y_0}(t),$$

proportions of the resulting payoffs, as Brams and Kilgour observed, it would not alter the "basic nature" of the Nash equilibria within the game.[6]

Numerous questions about crisis decision making and outcomes emerge from the preceding analysis of the Threat game. Brams and Kilgour have not derived and tested propositions dealing with foreign policy decisions and attainment of objectives, although they do discuss the impact of varying the corner payoffs on the process of escalation. To take the analysis one step further, three hypotheses focusing on rational choice and the outcomes of crises will be formulated and

Note 5 (cont'd.)

$$t = x_0, \quad p(x) \le p_{x_0,y_0}(s),$$

where

$$p_{x_0,y_0}(s) = \frac{P_R(x_0,y_0) - sr_2}{1 - s(1 - r_3 + r_2)}, \quad 0 \le s < y_0,$$

and

$$q_{x_0,y_0}(t) = \frac{P_C(x_0,y_0) - tr_2}{1 - t(1 - c_3 + c_2)}, \quad 0 \le t < x_0.$$

Depending on the relative magnitudes of the corner payoffs, (x_0, y_0) may be stabilized with or without escalating threats. Brams and Kilgour have demonstrated mathematically that threat escalation is unnecessary if and only if

$$\frac{1 - c_3}{c_3 - c_2} > \frac{r_3 - r_2}{1 - r_3}.$$

When the inequality is reversed, an escalating threat will be required to stabilize (x_0, y_0). This result is derived formally in the appendix to Brams and Kilgour (1987a).

[6] A salient alternative would be the use of Euclidean distances to weight the payoffs, calculated as follows:

$$P_R(x,y) = \frac{r_1}{(x^2 + y^2)^{0.5}} + \frac{r_2}{(x^2 + (1 - y)^2)^{0.5}}$$

$$+ \frac{r_3}{((1 - x)^2 + (1 - y)^2)^{0.5}} + \frac{r_4}{((1 - x)^2 + y^2)^{0.5}} \tag{1'}$$

$$P_C(x,y) = \frac{c_1}{(x^2 + y^2)^{0.5}} + \frac{c_2}{((1 - x)^2 + y^2)^{0.5}}$$

$$+ \frac{c_3}{((1 - x)^2 + (1 - y)^2)^{0.5}} + \frac{c_4}{(x^2 + (1 - y)^2)^{0.5}} \tag{2'}$$

To derive a DE, assume that Row is more cooperative initially, making the final position $(t, q(t))$. Following the procedure of Brams and Kilgour (1987a), with $c_1 = 0$ and $c_4 = 1$, $q_1(t)$, c_2 and c_3 are related in the following manner:

$$\frac{c_2}{((1 - t)^2 + q_1(t)^2)^{0.5}} + \frac{c_3}{((1 - t)^2 + (1 - q_1(t))^2)^{0.5}}$$

$$+ \frac{1}{(t^2 + (1 - q_1(t))^2)^{0.5}} - c_3 = 0 \tag{3'}$$

This expression reveals the basic problem entailed by use of simple Euclidean distances. When $t = 1$, $q_1(t)$ cannot also be 1, because (3') becomes undefined.

tested. Although it would be possible to test further auxiliary propositions, those included cover the basic components of the model of deterrence and retaliation. With no loss of generality, each hypothesis will be presented with Column as the initiator (or more preemptive player) and Row as the defender (or more cooperative player), that is, $s > t$.

One proposition deals with rational choice in a fundamental sense:

Proposition 1. *If the players desire a return to the preplay position* $(1, 1)$, *then* $q(t) \le q_1(t)$ *should be fulfilled.*

This threshold must be matched or passed in order to create an incentive toward deescalation or stabilization.

Two propositions deal with the impact of the defender's choice on goal achievement specifically and, in more general terms, satisfaction with the outcome of the crisis:

Proposition 2. *If* $q(t) \le q_1(t)$, *it is more likely that the defender will achieve at least some of its specific goals in a crisis.*

Proposition 3. *If* $q(t) \le q_1(t)$, *it is more likely that the defender will be satisfied with the outcome of the crisis.*

Specific policy objectives and overall satisfaction for the defender depend upon the selection of a sufficiently coercive response. The value for $q_1(t)$ sets the standard because $(1, 1)$ is the eventual target for the defender. The latter also seeks to preserve (and even advance) its own interests, not necessarily achieved at $(1, 1)$ a possibly Pareto-inferior point. Consequently, $q_1(t)$ is the relevant criterion in the appraisal of superpower response. By contrast, if $q(t) > q_1(t)$, there is no incentive for Column to return to the preplay position. Thus achievement of immediate goals and overall satisfaction for the defender are less probable when $(t, q(t))$, where $q(t) > q_1(t)$, rather than $(1, 1)$ is more appealing to the initiator.

Certain aspects of the Threat game require further discussion, because revisions are needed in order to test the preceding hypotheses. These alterations and extensions will affect operationalization and the approach toward testing.

One area of difficulty is that the path of crisis bargaining is not incorporated in the original model. Brams and Kilgour (1987a: 848–9) explicitly acknowledge that the "route by which the final position is attained from the preplay and initial positions may be relevant but will not be modeled here." The fundamental problem with that approach is that $s < 1$ and $t < 1$ may not emerge at about the same time in actual crises. In other words, what if the initial preemptive move of the more cooperative player always approximates full cooperation? If so, that would entail movement along the horizontal axis from $(1, 1)$ to $(t, 1)$, as opposed to a position (t, s) on the interior of the unit square. Figure 11.2 displays a modified version of the Threat game that incorporates this process. The initial

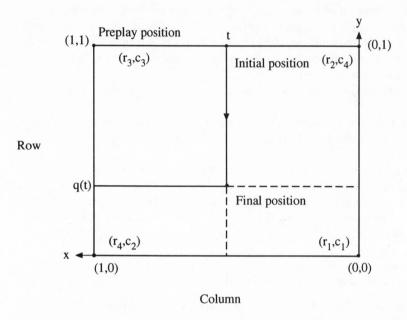

Figure 11.2. The modified Threat game.

Key:
(r_i, c_j) = (payoff to row, payoff to column);
(r_4, c_4) = best; r_3, c_3 = next best; r_2, c_2 = next worst; r_1, c_1 = worst;
s,t = initial strategy choices of row and column, respectively;
q(t) = subsequent strategy choice of row (more cooperative player initially).

position $(t, 1)$ is reached by movement along the upper horizontal axis. When Row retaliates, the final position $(t, q(t))$ is reached. This process, according to Brams and Kilgour, constitutes a special case of the model.

Symmetry is implicit in the Threat game formulated by Brams and Kilgour. However, it is not clear that the superpowers, which played the game in reality, attached equal values to the four pure outcomes. In other words, symmetric ordering of the alternatives would be preserved, as Brams and Kilgour require, but cardinal symmetry might not hold true. The most salient potential difference concerns the preplay position (r_3, c_3). Perhaps the leader and challenger, to use the terminology of Organski and Kugler (1980), would view that situation differently. Compared to the USSR, the United States might have been expected to see a smaller difference between c_3 and c_4 and a greater gap from c_3 to c_2 because it found the status quo relatively more appealing. In other words, it would seek to preserve the status quo and avert losses. By contrast, as challenger for global leadership, the USSR would not have been inclined toward a risk-averse outlook regarding the pure states of the game. Thus the eventual measurement of payoffs should allow for both identical and symmetric but unequal values.

Even if the game is assumed to have cardinal symmetry, the identity of the defender could affect the predictive performance of the model. It is possible that one superpower would be more inclined than the other to conform to expectations generated by the retaliation function. Different roles could affect response patterns; the leading state might be more inclined to react vigorously to any threat from the challenger. Regardless of the theoretical rationale, it would be of some practical value to discover which (if either) of the contenders has followed the dictates of the model more consistently.

The meaning of threat is a further question arising about the sequence of play. A "threat," in the narrow sense, is not an action but an assertion of intent to commit some act contingent upon the adversary's subsequent behavior. Crisis bargaining, however, frequently entails tangible acts as well as statements regarding intentions. To deal with this variation, a scale of coercion must grant more credibility, all other things being equal, to an action rather than a threat. Specifically, violence should be accorded more weight than nonviolent military actions, which in turn would stand above threatening statements. In sum, "actions speak louder than words."

Credibility is a further question that arises regarding the initial model of crisis stability. Although Brams and Kilgour did not distinguish between direct and extended deterrence, past evidence regarding deterrence and crisis bargaining suggests that these situations differ significantly. The logic of Brams and Kilgour may be more relevant to cases of direct deterrence, because there is virtually no ambiguity about the defender's degree of commitment.

Finally, it is possible that a more comprehensive model of crisis management could be derived from a supergame analysis.[7] In other words, individual crises might be regarded as iterations in an extended conflict. Such an approach might alter the basic structure of the game on the unit square, with the introduction of discount parameters and the like. However, a model of retaliation in serial crises lies beyond the scope of the present investigation.

Several measurements must be derived prior to testing the present model. An operational definition of crisis is required, in order to permit selection of relevant cases. The payoffs and levels of preemption that are central to the Threat game require explicit measurement. Finally, the outcome variables must be rendered operational.

Selection of cases and operationalization of the model

Superpower crises comprise the subset of conflicts in world politics to which the Threat game is directly relevant. In generic terms – leaving aside the status of participants – an international crisis has been defined by Brecher, Wilkenfeld, and Moser (1988: 3) as

a situational change characterized by two necessary and sufficient conditions: (1) distortion in the type and an increase in the intensity of *disruptive interactions* between two or

---

[7] For example, a supergame analysis of Chicken by Ward (1987) suggests that a reputation for toughness will have different implications depending on the complexity of the game.

more adversaries, with an accompanying high probability of *military hostilities,* or, during a war, an *adverse change* in the military *balance;* and (2) a *challenge* to the existing *structure* of an international system – global, dominant or subsystem – posed by the higher-than-normal conflictual interactions.

This definition is based upon objective criteria dealing with the structure and process of the international system. It has been used as the foundation for a large-scale inquiry into military-security crises by the International Crisis Behavior (ICB) Project, which identified 278 international crises from 1929 to 1979.[8] Within each of these macrolevel cases is a set of microlevel crises, some of which pertain to the superpowers. As will become apparent, the microlevel or foreign policy crises defined by Brecher et al. (1988: 3) is the appropriate unit of analysis for this investigation:[9]

A foreign policy crisis, that is, a crisis viewed from the perspective of an individual state, is a situation with three necessary and sufficient conditions deriving from a change in a state's external or internal environment. All three are perceptions held by the highest level decision-makers of the actor concerned: a *threat to basic values,* along with the awareness of *finite time for response* to the external value threat, and a *high probability of involvement in military hostilities.*

The trigger of a foreign policy crisis, which creates these perceptions, corresponds to some level of noncooperation by one of the players in the Threat game. It constitutes the opening move of the game, that is, a departure from the preplay position $(1, 1)$.

Without loss of generality, Column will be designated arbitrarily as the first player to commit a noncooperative act, thus triggering a foreign policy crisis for Row. The trigger moves the players from $(1, 1)$ to $(t, 1)$, the initial position.

This description of the first move following the preplay position constitutes a special case of the theoretical treatment of crisis initiation and retaliation presented by Brams and Kilgour. They asserted that the initial strategy choices of Row and Column, s and t respectively, are "simultaneous and determine a point on the unit square" (Brams and Kilgour, 1987a: 835). However, in practical terms, the trigger and response moves cannot be treated as simultaneous choices. It is not uncommon in foreign policy crises for the principal response of a target state to occur several days – and sometimes much later than that – after a noncooperative act.[10] Therefore, $s = 1$ by definition, with the "initial position" being $(t, 1)$.

---

[8] The ICB Project has compiled data for each international crisis as a whole on twenty-eight variables that are grouped into seven clusters of crisis dimensions: setting, breakpoint-exitpoint (or trigger-termination), crisis management techniques, great power/superpower activity, international organization involvement, outcome, and severity. Two coders gathered the data for each case independently, under the supervision of a senior ICB scholar, and showed an overall reliability of 0.85.

[9] This definition, which forms the basis of a 627-case data set from 1929 to 1979, is derived from Brecher (1977: 43–4).

[10] While there are cases in which the trigger and major response occur in close proximity, for those which appear in Table 11.2, the average time lag is over one month.

Since Row, the actor experiencing a foreign policy crisis, is the more cooperative player initially, Row then can retaliate at some level $q(t)$. This action corresponds to the major response variable in the ICB data set. The major response by the crisis actor is the most salient form of reply to the threat. Thus the final position of the game is $(t, q(t))$, as in the case of the Brams and Kilgour model, although the path toward it is via $(t, 1)$, as opposed to movement through (t, s), with $s < 1$ and $t < 1$.

Since the focus of this investigation is on the reaction of a specific actor to a threat, foreign policy crises provide the appropriate data. A provocation (t) is issued to a given state, which replies in some salient manner $(q(t))$. An international crisis, by contrast, encompasses the behavior of all actors involved in the disruption of process and challenge to structure. In order to test the complete model of superpower crisis behavior specified by Brams and Kilgour – including optimal deterrent threats, action and reaction, and deescalation – data on international crises would be required. As noted earlier, however, the other components of the model lie beyond the consideration of the present study.

Table 11.2 displays the twenty-seven foreign policy crises that are regarded as appropriate for testing the game-theoretic model of superpower deterrence and crisis stabilization proposed by Brams and Kilgour. There are several reasons behind the selection of these cases from the 627 available in the ICB data set of foreign policy crises from 1929 to 1979 (Wilkenfeld, Brecher, and Moser, 1988).

First, it is appropriate to include only cases of deterrence that involve the (former) Soviet Union and the United States as adversaries. In order to test the analysis of Brams and Kilgour, one superpower must be threatened directly (or indirectly) by the other. This criterion eliminates intrabloc crises such as Hungary in 1956, where one superpower threatens its own client state, not the more immediate interests of the rival.

Second, cases in which the client state of one superpower threatens the client state of another also are excluded. In these crises it can be virtually impossible to attribute responsibility. For example, Israel experienced a crisis in its relations with Egypt on April 10, 1973, when intelligence reports suggested that an Egyptian attack would occur on May 15 (Brecher et al. 1988: 333–4). At that time Egypt and Israel could be regarded as clients of the Soviet Union and the United States, respectively. Yet the Israeli leadership could not have known whether the potential attack had been prompted by Moscow, despite the latter's close connection to Cairo. Furthermore, had the anticipated attack occurred, Israel – and the United States – still could not be certain that the attack had – or had not been – encouraged or dictated by Moscow. Such crises, in short, make it difficult to apply the framework of Brams and Kilgour because the responsibility for initiating hostilities cannot be attributed clearly to one of the superpowers.

Third, it is essential to focus on the period in which the superpowers had some nonnegligible chance of reaching (r_1, c_1), the worst outcome on the unit square. This result, viewed in practical terms, would amount to a nuclear exchange. The United States achieved nuclear status before the end of World War II, while the Soviet Union demonstrated its nuclear capacity in 1949 by testing a weapon

Table 11.2. *Superpower interactions in foreign policy crises, 1948–1979*

Case	Initiator	Target	Protector	Trigger date	Termination date	t	$q(t)$	$T1$	$T2$
Berlin Blockade	U.S.	USSR	USSR	07/06/48	12/05/49	0.88	0.56	0.86	0.92
Berlin Blockade	USSR	U.S.	U.S.	24/06/48	12/05/49	0.56	0.56	0.77	0.77
Korean War I	U.S.	PRC	USSR	26/06/50	–/07/50	0.56	0.56	0.77	0.85
Korean War II	U.S.	USSR	USSR	07/10/50	26/12/50	0.14	0.56	0.68	0.77
Korean War III	U.S.	PRC	USSR	22/05/53	27/07/53	0.88	0.80	0.91	0.95
Taiwan Straits I	U.S.	PRC	USSR	–/08/54	–/11/54	0.80	0.39	0.86	0.92
Taiwan Straits I	U.S.	PRC	USSR	02/12/54	23/04/55	0.80	0.39	0.86	0.92
Suez–Sinai Campaign	USSR	U.S.	U.S.	05/11/56	08/11/56	0.88	0.88	0.91	0.95
Syria–Turkey border	U.S.	Syria	USSR	07/09/57	29/10/57	0.80	0.61	0.91	0.95
Berlin deadline	U.S.	USSR	USSR	15/12/57	15/09/59	0.56	0.80	0.77	0.85
Taiwan Straits II	U.S.	PRC	USSR	27/08/58	30/09/58	0.88	0.88	0.91	0.95
Berlin deadline	U.S.	U.S.	USSR	27/11/58	30/03/59	0.88	0.88	0.91	0.91
Bay of Pigs	U.S.	Cuba	USSR	15/04/61	24/04/61	0.21	0.88	0.69	0.78
Berlin Wall	USSR	U.S.	U.S.	13/08/61	07/10/61	0.66	0.56	0.80	0.87
Cuban missiles	USSR	U.S.	U.S.	16/10/62	20/11/62	0.56	1.00	0.77	0.85
Cuban missiles	U.S.	USSR	USSR	22/10/62	20/11/62	0.56	0.56	0.77	0.77
Gulf of Tonkin	U.S.	N. Vietnam	USSR	04/08/64	07/08/64	0.27	0.80	0.70	0.79
Congo II	U.S.	USSR	USSR	24/11/64	17/12/64	0.21	0.88	0.69	0.78
Pleiku	U.S.	N. Vietnam	USSR	02/02/65	02/03/65	0.07	0.21	0.68	0.76
Six Day War	USSR	U.S.	U.S.	06/06/67	11/06/67	0.88	0.56	0.91	0.91
War of Attrition II	USSR	Israel	U.S.	19/03/70	07/08/70	0.66	0.07	0.80	0.80
Cienfuegos Base	USSR	U.S.	U.S.	16/09/70	23/10/70	0.71	0.88	0.82	0.82
Invasion of Laos II	U.S.	N. Vietnam	USSR	08/02/71	23/03/71	0.07	0.07	0.68	0.76
Vietnam-ports mining	U.S.	N. Vietnam	USSR	08/05/72	19/07/72	0.07	0.88	0.68	0.76
Christmas bombing	U.S.	N. Vietnam	USSR	17/12/72	27/01/73	0.07	1.00	0.68	0.76
October–Yom Kippur War	USSR	U.S.	U.S.	12/10/73	31/05/74	0.80	0.61	0.86	0.86
Soviet threat to Pakistan	USSR	Pakistan	U.S.	01/06/79	03/07/79	0.88	0.88	0.91	0.91

Key: Case = foreign policy crisis; Initiator = actor responsible for triggering crisis, directly or indirectly; Target = actor experiencing crisis; Protector = actor supporting target; Trigger Date = start of crisis; Termination Date = end of crisis; PRC = Peoples Republic of China.

successfully. Foreign policy crises in progress at the outset of 1949 will be included in the analysis because, at that time, the USSR had reached the threshold of nuclear status. While any choice for a transition point would be arbitrary, the inclusion of crises in motion by 1949 means that all cases in which (r_1, c_1) could occur will appear in the analysis.[11] At the same time, foreign policy crises that terminated prior to the nuclear threshold year of 1949 are excluded. The twenty-seven cases listed in Table 11.2 include crises initiated as late as 1979, the current terminal point of the ICB data set.

Fourth, and finally, there are a few cases to consider in which one superpower simultaneously threatens both the other superpower and a client state. For example, the United States announced a blockade of all "offensive military equipment en route to Cuba" on October 22, 1962, triggering a crisis for the USSR and Cuba (Brecher et al., 1988: 290–1). In such cases it is appropriate to treat the incident as one crisis, directly involving the superpowers. The response by the threatened superpower is assumed to cover its client state as well.

The cases appropriate for testing having been selected, payoffs within the Threat game require operationalization.

Measurement of superpower utilities before the onset of a crisis might suggest the use of data such as that introduced by Bueno de Mesquita (1981). However, the practical value of that approach is questionable, considering the standard method of generating interstate utility scores. The conventional approach, developed by Bueno de Mesquita, focuses on the degree of overlap in alliance commitments. The more alike two states are along this dimension, the higher the utility that one is deemed to have for the policies of the other. Over the last four decades, the relevant figures for the USSR–U.S. dyad have been quite stable. Thus building in these numbers from one case to the next would greatly complicate the model with only a marginal impact on the results.

Two tentative measurement schemes will be presented. Each entails different assumptions about the decline in payoffs from r_4 to r_1. To simplify matters, only Column's payoffs $(c_j, j=1, \ldots, 4)$ will be presented, because the values for Row are identical in this game.

One approach is to treat the decline as equal for both actors, with $c_4 = 1$, $c_3 = \frac{2}{3}$, $c_2 = \frac{1}{3}$, and $c_1 = 0$, regardless of the identity of the initiator. In a given crisis, c_4 would refer to unilateral concessions made by the adversary, with c_2 being the reverse. It should be pointed out that neither victory nor defeat would entail a nuclear strike. Instead, the utility values correspond to gains or losses over the issues at hand, military, economic, or others. The status quo, c_3, is an intermediate value reflecting the situation at the outset of the crisis. Of course, c_1 represents nuclear destruction.

---

[11] Obviously (r_1, c_1) has different connotations in more recent years, with the superpowers possessing far greater destructive capacity with the passage of time. However, the impact of even one crude nuclear weapon would be viewed as a catastrophe by a target state, much more damaging than, for example, defeat in a battle involving conventional forces. Nuclear weapons, in other words, few or many in number, are essential to the superpower Threat game presented by Brams and Kilgour.

Every national leader, it could be argued, attaches a very high value to the status quo, c_3, perhaps close to 1.0. However, crises that involve the super-powers are not that uncommon, indicating that the Soviet Union and the United States sometimes had been willing to risk war in order to obtain concessions. The most straightforward approach therefore is to use linear increments as a first approximation to the true values.

Another measurement option is to assume that the payoff intervals decline in magnitude differently for the United States and the Soviet Union. In other words, for the United States, as indicated earlier, the relative value of the preplay payoff (r_3 or c_3) would be greater. A straightforward way of representing this difference would be to expand the gap between c_3 and c_2, thus achieving the intended impact on Equation (5), with the United States as the Column player. Appropriate values are $c_4' = 1$, $c_3' = 0.750$, $c_2' = 0.250$, and $c_1' = 0$. The difference between the intermediate payoffs for the two sets of values is 0.333 and 0.500, respectively. Each of the two measurement schemes will play a role at the stage of testing.

These measurement options for the decline in Row and Column's payoffs can be compared easily using the equations for the DE developed by Brams and Kilgour. Consider two threats facing the Row player, $t = 0.3$ and $t = 0.6$. With the first set of values for the corners of the unit square, the retaliation function (conveyed by Equation [5]) generates the following values, assuming the desire to return to (1,1):

$$q_{1w}(0.3) = \frac{0.667 - 0.3(0.333)}{1 - 0.3(1 - 0.667 + 0.333)} \tag{5'}$$

$$= 0.709$$

$$q_{1w}(0.6) = \frac{0.667 - 0.6(0.333)}{1 - 0.6(1 - 0.667 + 0.333)} \tag{5''}$$

$$= 0.778$$

The other set of payoffs produces the following results:

$$q_{1a}(0.3) = \frac{0.750 - 0.3(0.250)}{1 - 0.3(1 - 0.750 + 0.250)}$$

$$= 0.794$$

$$q_{1a}(0.6) = \frac{0.750 - 0.6(0.250)}{1 - 0.6(1 - 0.750 + 0.250)}$$

$$= 0.857$$

The subscripts w and a refer to the original and modified payoffs, respectively. The retaliation function with the original payoffs is more intense. Regardless of

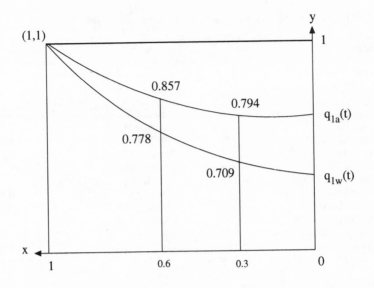

Key: $q_{1w}(t)$ = threat line resulting from first set of payoffs.

$q_{1a}(t)$ = threat line resulting from second set of payoffs.

Figure 11.3. Threat lines for the two sets of payoffs.

the magnitude of t, $q_{1w}(t)$ is lower than $q_{1a}(t)$, therefore requiring a more noncooperative response to the threat. The respective threat lines are displayed by Figure 11.3. Each curve shows the level of retaliation from Row required to deter Column. For example, with the original set of payoffs, the utility to Column from (0.3, 1.0) is 0.9. This is better than c_3, which has the value 0.667. However, when Row responds with $q_{1w}(0.3) \leq 0.709$, the new point on the interior surface is (0.3, 0.709). Column's utility at this point is 0.667, meaning that the status quo – (r_3, c_3) or (1.0, 1.0) – is just as valuable.

This logic also holds for the point (0.6, 1.0); the retaliatory level $q_{1w}(0.6) \leq 0.778$ entails a payoff of no more than the status quo for Column. At the final position, (0.6, 0.778), Column obtains a payoff of 0.667. In sum, the curve $q_{1w}(t)$ is continuous, with a minimum retaliation level specified for any level of noncooperation by Column.

At this point it is appropriate to develop the measurements for t, the act of noncooperation that initiates the foreign policy crisis, and s and $q(t)$, the actions taken by the superpower on the defensive. The relevant variables from the ICB data set are the crisis *trigger* and *major response*. The trigger of a foreign policy crisis creates, for the decisional elite of the target state, a perception of threat to basic values, finite time for response, and the likelihood of involvement in

Table 11.3. *Intensity of superpower bargaining techniques*

Technique	Intensity	Technique	Intensity
Nuclear strike	0.000	Multiple, including non-violent military	0.611
Full-scale conventional war	0.072	External change, political and military	0.661
Indirect full-scale conventional war	0.141	External change, nonviolent military	0.709
Serious clashes	0.208	Economic act	0.755
Indirect serious clashes	0.272	Political act	0.800
Minor clashes	0.334	Internal verbal challenge to regime	0.843
Indirect minor clashes	0.393	Verbal act	0.884
Multiple, including violent military	0.451	Other	0.924
Internal physical challenge to regime	0.506	No action	0.963
Nonviolent military	0.560	Cooperation	1.000

military hostilities. Put differently, the trigger constitutes a precise measurement of the initial noncooperative act, t. The major response is the act that best represents the thrust of a target actor's reaction to its new situation. In the previous example dealing with the perceived invasion threat from Egypt, Israel responded with mobilization in April 1973. Thus the major response of a crisis actor corresponds to $q(t)$, its retaliatory move in the Threat game.

Table 11.3 displays a continuum of coercive acts, ranging from a nuclear strike through full cooperation with the adversary.[12] The points on the scale correspond to the theoretically possible triggers and major responses in a given superpower crisis. The scale points that appear are based on the ICB coding for major response and trigger, although there has been some adjustment of the categories for present purposes.[13]

Some explanation of the scale values is in order. The polar points of nuclear strike = 0.000 and cooperation = 1.000 are self-explanatory. (These are the only scale values explicitly designated by Brams and Kilgour.) The increments between 0 and 1 are not evenly spaced. Each difference between scale points is considered to be lower in magnitude than the one preceding. In other words, the difference between a nuclear strike and full-scale conventional war outweighs the gap between the latter and indirect full-scale conventional war, and so on. The rationale is that more cooperative behavior leads to diminishing returns at

---

[12] With respect to triggering acts, it is obvious that neither cooperation nor a lack of action (the final two scale points) can trigger a crisis. However, the Threat game is assumed to be in progress at all times. Thus each of these nonthreatening forms of behavior may be regarded as a choice available to the players at any given moment.

[13] The ICB categories and coding procedures are explained in detail by Brecher, Wilkenfeld, and Moser (1988).

the interstate level. Put differently, the decline across the categories from cooperation to nuclear war occurs at an accelerating pace.

Several functions could be used to generate scale values with the property noted. A straightforward approach is to transform the intervals between the twenty scale points in the following manner:

$$s'_k = 2 - e^{0.693(s_k)} \tag{7}$$

where s'_k = transformed scale point ($k = 1, \ldots, 20$); s_k = linear scale point. Each s_k would have the value $(k - 1)/19$, so $s_1 = 0$, $s_2 = 1/19$, $\ldots$, $s_{20} = 1$. The transformed s'_k then would have the desired exponential rate of decline.

From the perspective of the crisis actor, the results of a crisis are the relevant evidence upon which to evaluate its major response. Thus the dependent variables in the quantitative analysis to follow are goal achievement and overall satisfaction for the defender. The first variable is trichotomous, with the categories being (1) full achievement of the specific goals of the crisis actor, namely victory, (2) stalemate or compromise, and (3) failure to achieve goals (i.e., defeat). Satisfaction with the outcome, the second variable, refers to the overall reaction of the actor to the situation resulting from the crisis. It incorporates goal achievement and the general strategic and tactical position of the actor. This variable is dichotomous, with the categories being (1) satisfied and (2) dissatisfied. Each of the twenty-seven crisis actors in the data set can be assigned scores for these dependent variables.[14]

Given the relatively abstract nature of the preceding discussion of measurement, it may be instructive to outline the coding of a sample case. The crisis over the Congo experienced by the Soviet Union in 1964 will be used to illustrate the measurement procedures.

Congo II, the international crisis that encompasses the foreign policy crisis experienced by the Soviet Union, started on August 4, 1964.[15] On that date a Revolutionary Council was formed in Stanleyville, after rebel forces had occupied the city. The Congo responded with an appeal to the United States and Belgium for direct military aid. Premier Tshombe of the Congo also presented his case against the rebels to the Organization for African Unity, which agreed to set up a committee to assess the conflict and to act as a mediator among rival African countries supporting the rebellion.

Given the presence of 1,500 foreign civilians as hostages in Stanleyville, and rebel threats of physical harm, the United States and Belgium dispatched paratroops to a British base in the Congo to prepare for a rescue attempt. These paratroops occupied Stanleyville on November 24 and released the hostages within hours. The rescue mission triggered a crisis for the Soviet Union on

---

[14] The contingency coefficient for the component variables – specific goal achievement and overall satisfaction – is 0.58. This positive, moderate value is appropriate because the two variables should be linked, but not to the extent that one is merely redundant.

[15] The following case history is based upon Brecher et al. 1988: 303.

November 24. The Soviet Union supported the rebel movement and viewed the U.S.-led intervention as a threat to its influence in the region. The Soviet Union responded on November 26, accusing the United States, Belgium, and Britain of "aggressive intervention." The Soviet crisis terminated on December 17 with the closing of its embassy in Kinshasa.

This crisis for the USSR over the Congo started with the rescue mission, a nonviolent military trigger, hence $t = 0.560$. The major response, an accusation directed primarily against the United States, fits the description of a verbal act, so $q(t) = 0.884$. The retaliation function for the Soviet Union is calculated as follows, using each set of payoffs in turn:

$$q_{1w}(0.560) = \frac{0.667 - 0.560(0.333)}{1 - 0.560(1 - 0.667 + 0.333)}$$

$$= 0.766$$

$$q_{1a}(0.560) = \frac{0.750 - 0.560(0.250)}{1 - 0.560(1 - 0.750 + 0.250)}$$

$$= 0.847$$

Each measurement renders the same verdict: The Soviet Union failed to react with sufficient intensity to the threat, thus contradicting Proposition 1. (Note that payoffs for the *United States* are properly used in this equation assessing Soviet choice.) The USSR did not achieve its specific goals and it emerged dissatisfied with the outcome, consistent with Propositions 2 and 3.

Analysis of data

Each of the Propositions 1–3 will be tested twice. The first set of results is generated under the assumption of cardinal symmetry in the payoffs. In other words, $c_1 = 0$, $c_2 = \frac{1}{3}$, $c_3 = \frac{2}{3}$, and $c_4 = 1$ for the United States and the Soviet Union alike. The second set of results is derived by another scheme of payoffs. The Soviet Union still is assumed to have the values noted previously. However, the United States is judged to favor the status quo more and has the payoff values $c'_1 = 0$, $c'_2 = \frac{1}{4}$, $c'_3 = \frac{3}{4}$, and $c'_4 = 1$. The thresholds generated by each scheme of payoffs appear in Table 11.2 as T1 and T2 respectively.

Proposition 1 is supported by the results generated by both sets of payoffs. In the former instance, 19 of 27 (70.4%) of the defenders responded below or at the threshold value $q_{1w}(t)$. Put differently, in most cases the defender's response gave the initiator an incentive to prefer a return to the status quo. The difference in mean level of response $(q(t))$ compared to the threshold value $(q_{1w}(t))$ also is noteworthy. Assuming $q(t) = 0.657$ as a hypothetical population mean, with $N = 27$, the 95 percent confidence interval is from 0.558 to 0.756. The observed mean, $q_{1w}(t) = 0.796$, therefore lies beyond the boundaries of that confidence interval, suggesting that the mean response level is lower than the mean threshold value. In other words, defenders generally retaliated with sufficient force to induce rational pursuit of de-escalation by the initiator.

With respect to the results generated by the second set of payoffs, 20 of 27 (74.1%) of the defenders responded at or below the threshold value. The combined average value for $q_{1a}(t)$ and $q_{1w}(t)$, corresponding to Soviet and U.S. cases, respectively, also falls beyond the 95 percent confidence interval. This result indicates that the mean response and threshold values are significantly different.

The seven crises in which the defender failed to respond adequately share an interesting trait: Each of these cases occurred from 1961 onward. This result suggests that the relative emphasis on crisis stabilization at (t, s) – as opposed to efforts toward an immediate return to the preplay position – has increased over the years. These milder responses could reflect increasing awareness of the dangers of confrontation. Rather than seeking a direct return to the preplay position, the defender in a given crisis might favor stabilization of the initial position and, under certain conditions, a response above the threshold would be consistent with such an objective.

For each of the seven anomalies, an initial position $(t, q(t))$ can be identified from the data displayed by Table 11.3. For example, that is $(0.21, 0.88)$ in the Bay of Pigs crisis. If the objective of the Soviet Union – the defender in that case – is assumed to be stabilization of $(0.21, 0.88)$, as opposed to a return to $(1, 1)$, the threshold of retaliation is calculated as follows: $q_{0.21, 0.88} (0.21) = 0.88$. This result means, not surprisingly, that the Soviet Union would have to escalate its response in order to make $(0.21, 0.88)$ stable for the United States. The Bay of Pigs and the other anomalies could be studied in greater depth, in order to see whether subsequent actions by the defender suggested pursuit of crisis stability.

Even if all of the seven cases had that property, it still would be essential to explain why defenders in other crises of the 1960s and 1970s appeared to prefer an immediate return to the status quo. Further research will be required to account for this variation from 1961 onward.

Contingency tables will be used to test Propositions 2 and 3, with goal achievement and overall satisfaction as the dependent variables. Inferences about these tables are based upon the tau b statistic, a standard measure of association between nominal variables.[16]

Table 11.4 is based on the first set of payoffs and links goal achievement to response level. The connection is nonnegligible ($\tau b = 0.20$).[17] Table 11.5,

---

[16] The $\tau\ b$ statistic measures the percentage reduction in error in predicting categories of the dependent variable. For example, $\tau\ b = 0.25$ would mean that use of the independent variable in question leads to a 25% reduction in error when predicting the outcome variable. Put differently, the 0.25 score indicates that the independent variable does 25% better than chance in anticipating values of the dependent variable. Statisticians regard a value such as 0.25 for $\tau\ b$ as moderately strong. For a more extensive explanation of the $\tau\ b$ statistic, see Blalock (1979).

[17] This series of coefficients also is reported in James (1991).

Table 11.4. *Response level and goal achievement with first payoff function*

	Goal achievement							
	Success		Stalemate or compromise		Failure		Total	
Response level	No.	(%)	No.	(%)	No.	(%)	No.	(%)
Below or equal to threshold	10	(52.6)	8	(42.1)	1	(5.3)	19	(70.4)
Above threshold	3	(37.5)	3	(37.5)	2	(25.0)	8	(29.6)
Total	13	(48.1)	11	(40.7)	3	(11.1)	27	(100.0)

Note: There are two points of explanation concerning the format of Tables 11.4–11.7. (1) Regarding the entries in the first three columns of numbers (i.e., those listed under "Success," "Stalemate or compromise," and "Failure"), the figures in parentheses correspond to the percentage of cases in the row represented by the cell frequency. For example, 2 of 8 (or 25.0%) cases above the threshold resulted in failure. Similarly, 13 of 27 (or 48.1%) cases in the table had success as the outcome. (2) In the fourth and final column ("Total"), the figures in parentheses correspond to the percentage of cases in the column represented by the cell frequency. For example, the defender responded at a level above the threshold value in 8 of 27 (or 29.6%) of the cases in the table. The parenthetical figures in the final column will be the percentage of cases in that column represented by the cell frequency, while the parenthetical figures in the other columns will be the percentage of cases in the row represented by the cell frequency.

Table 11.5. *Response level and goal achievement with second payoff function*

	Goal achievement							
	Success		Stalemate or compromise		Failure		Total	
Response level	No.	(%)	No.	(%)	No.	(%)	No.	(%)
Below or equal to threshold	11	(55.0)	8	(40.0)	1	(5.0)	20	(74.1)
Above threshold	2	(15.4)	3	(27.3)	2	(66.7)	7	(25.9)
Total	13	(48.1)	11	(40.7)	3	(11.1)	27	(100.0)

generated by the second payoff scheme, is stronger ($\tau b = 0.29$). Each of these tables points to a linkage between achievement of the coercion threshold and immediate goal achievement.

Table 11.6, generated by the first payoff function, offers solid support to Proposition 3 ($\tau b = 0.36$). This proposition is more strongly confirmed by Table 11.7, which is based on the second set of payoffs ($\tau b = 0.42$). Although cases with the defender's response above the threshold are divided about evenly in the tables, at least 16 of 20 (80.0%) of the crises in which $q(t)$ matched or fell below the threshold resulted in satisfaction for the actor.

Table 11.6. *Response level and actor satisfaction with first payoff function*

	Actor satisfaction					
	Satisfied		Dissatisfied		Total	
Response level	No.	(%)	No.	(%)	No.	(%)
Below or equal to threshold	16	(80.0)	4	(20.0)	20	(74.1)
Above threshold	3	(42.9)	4	(57.1)	7	(25.9)
Total	19	(70.4)	8	(29.6)	27	(100.0)

Table 11.7. *Response level and actor satisfaction with second payoff function*

	Actor satisfaction					
	Satisfied		Dissatisfied		Total	
Response level	No.	(%)	No.	(%)	No.	(%)
Below or equal to threshold	17	(85.0)	3	(15.0)	20	(74.1)
Above threshold	3	(42.9)	4	(57.1)	7	(25.9)
Total	20	(74.1)	7	(25.9)	27	(100.0)

Three other observations can be made about the results, collectively speaking. The first concerns relative performance by the two sets of payoffs. A second point pertains to the impact of the defender's identity on the predictions of the model, while the third focuses on direct versus extended deterrence.

With respect to the initial issue, the second set of payoffs consistently produced better results than the first. Although the difference should not be exaggerated, when cardinal symmetry is replaced with the assumption that the United States values the status quo more than does the Soviet Union, the model appears to be more valid.

A second aspect of the results as a whole concerns the identity of the defender. It had been suggested that the behavior of one superpower might be more consistent with the model than that of the other. But consider, for example, the anomalies from the second phase of testing for Proposition 1. The United States plays the role of protector or defender in 2 of these 7 cases, while for the data set as a whole it is the protector in 10 of 27 crises. The respective proportions, 28.6 percent and 37.0 percent, are not dramatically different. Analogous figures for other stages of testing are similar, in that neither superpower appears to follow the dictates of the model more consistently.

A third point focuses on cases of direct versus extended deterrence. The possibility had been raised that cases in which the target and protector had the same identity (e.g., United States as a crisis actor in the Berlin Blockade) would follow a different pattern from those in which a superpower protected a client (e.g., the Soviet Union, with North Vietnam as a crisis actor in Gulf of Tonkin). Once again referring to the second phase of testing from Proposition 1, very little difference emerges between these two types of cases. There are three crises among the anomalies in which the identity is the same (42.9%); the proportion overall is 13 of 27 (48.1%). The figures elsewhere in the analysis are quite similar.

Conclusion

Theoretical revision, measurement, and testing have combined to produce encouraging results. The $q_1(t)$ threshold appears to have predictive power with respect to superpower retaliation in crises. The threshold also is able to distinguish the goal achievement and overall satisfaction levels of defending states. These results are stronger when the United States, commonly cast in the role of hegemonic power, is assumed to place a higher value upon preserving the status quo.

Some defenders failed to meet the $q_1(t)$ threshold, raising questions about why these choices were made. With respect to the outcome variables, each of the tables contains deviant cases in need of further explanation. More long-term objectives include the operationalization and testing of other stages in the Threat game, referring to optimal threats, crisis stability, and threat escalation (James and Harvey, 1989, 1992; Harvey and James, 1992). At this point, it is fair to say that the model of retaliation has received tentative support, thus confirming the view that crises can be understood as rational interactions.

References

Blalock, Hubert M., Jr. (1979). *Social Statistics*. Rev. 2d ed. New York: McGraw-Hill.

Brams, Steven J. (1985). *Superpower Games: Applying Game Theory to Superpower Conflict*. New Haven, Conn.: Yale University Press.

Brams, Steven J. and D. Marc Kilgour. (1987a). "Threat Escalation and Crisis Stability: A Game-Theoreti Analysis." *American Political Science Review* 81: 833–50.

(1987b). "Optimal Threats." *Operations Research* 35: 524–36.

(1987c). "Winding Down If Preemption or Escalation Occurs: A Game-Theoretic Analysis." *Journal of Conflict Resolution* 31: 547–72.

(1988). *Game Theory and National Security*. Oxford and New York: Basil Blackwell.

Brams, Steven J., and Donald Wittman. (1981). "Nonmyopic Equilibria in 2 × 2 games," *Conflict Management and Peace Science* 6: 39–62.

Brecher, Michael. (1977). "Toward a Theory of International Crisis Behavior: A Preliminary Report." *International Studies Quarterly* 21: 39–74.

Brecher, Michael, Jonathan Wilkenfeld, and Sheila Moser. (1988). *Crises in the Twentieth Century, Vol. I: Handbook of International Crises*. Oxford and New York: Pergamon Press.

Bueno de Mesquita, Bruce. (1981). *The War Trap*. New Haven, Conn.: Yale University Press.

Frei, Daniel. (1985). "Empathy in Conflict Management." *International Journal* 40: 586–98.

Harvey, Frank, and Patrick James. (1992). "Nuclear Deterrence Theory: The Record of Aggregate Testing and an Alternative Research Agenda." *Conflict Management and Peace Science* 12: 17–45.

James, Patrick. (1991). "Rational Retaliation: Superpower Response to Crisis, 1948–1979." *Public Choice* 68: 117–35.

James, Patrick, and Frank Harvey. (1989). "Threat Escalation and Crisis Stability: Superpower Cases, 1948–1979." *Canadian Journal of Political Science* 22: 523–45.

(1992). "The Most Dangerous Game: Superpower Rivalry in International Crises, 1948–1985." *Journal of Politics* 54: 25–53.

Kenny, Anthony. (1985). *The Logic of Deterrence*. Chicago: University of Chicago Press.

Morgan, T. Clifton. (1984). "A Spatial Model of Crisis Bargaining." *International Studies Quarterly* 28: 407–26.

Organski, A. F. K., and Jacek Kugler. (1980). *The War Ledger*. Chicago: University of Chicago Press.

Ward, Hugh. (1987). "The Risks of a Reputation for Toughness: Strategy in Public Goods Provision Problems Modelled by Chicken Supergames," *British Journal of Political Science* 17: 23–52.

Wilkenfeld, Jonathan, Michael Brecher, and Sheila Moser. (1988). *Crises in the Twentieth Century, Vol. II: Handbook of Foreign Policy Crises*. Oxford and New York: Pergamon Press.

Zagare, Frank. (1985). "Toward a Reformulation of the Theory of Mutual Deterrence." *International Studies Quarterly* 29: 155–69.

Index